GARDENING
INDOORS
With Soil &
HYDROPONICS

by George F. Van Patten

Gardening Indoors

I would like to express my sincere thanks to all of the wonderful gardeners who helped to make this book a reality. Many individuals, garden-center and hydroponic garden-center employees and owners contributed information, photos, and drawings. Thank you all for your assistance in making *Gardening Indoors with Soil & Hydroponics* the best book possible.

Special thanks to: Tom Alexander and *Growing Edge Magazine,* everybody from The Garden Spout in Willits, CA, and Ross from Hydroponic Garden Center in New York!

Published by Van Patten Publishing
Written by George F. Van Patten

Editors: Linda Meyer, Estella Cervantes
Book Design: Chris Thompson
Artwork: Christopher Valdes, Chris Thompson
Photographs: George F. Van Patten, Christopher Valdes, Chris Thompson, Patti Thompson, Skip Stone
Cover Photograph: istockphotos.com/thepalmer
Back Cover Illustrations: Christopher Valdes
Copyright 2008, George F. Van Patten
First Printing
9 8 7 6 5 4 3 2 1
ISBN-10:1-878823-32-9
ISBN-13: 978-1-878823-32-8

Ordering Information
Individual Copies: www.amazon.com
www.amazon.ca   www.amazon.co.uk
www.amazon.fr   www.amazon.jp
www.amazon.de

Wholesale Orders:
Green Air Products (GAP): 1-800-669-2113
Bloomington Wholesale Garden Supply (BWGS): 1-800-316-1306
Hydrofarm: 1-800-634-9990
National Garden Wholesale (NGW):1-888-478-6544

A History of Hydroponics

From the earliest writings of man, we find many references to the plants used for food and the cultivation techniques they employed as civilization advanced. Cultivating one's own crops was essential to survival.

It is not know when a plant was first grown in a container. But the Bible tells us of King Nebuchadnezzar, who built the fabulous hanging gardens of Babylon.

In the first century A.D., the Romans used panes of mica as glass to construct some of the earliest greenhouses. Emperors demanded the freshest green vegetables and salads year round. Their slaves grew cucumbers year round in cloches, using early attempts at fertilization treatments.

Early "horticulturists" commonly believed that a plant needed nothing but water to grow, and that the soil merely held the plant upright! This led to early experiments, such as the willow tree that grew to a weight of 169 pounds in a tub filled with 200 pounds of soil. When the tree was removed, all but two ounces of soil was still there.

This led to experiments growing plants in nothing but water, or various solutions. Sir Francis Bacon described growing plants this way in the 1620s.

By the 1900s, scientists and others were experimenting with plants grown in sand, charcoal, and other support materials, with solutions soaking the roots.

In the United States, the rapidly growing population demanded lots of food, and the farmers around urban areas were having difficulty supplying all the mouths. Greenhouses started sprouting around the major cities, and farmers were looking for alternatives to manure, which was the major form of fertilizer available at the time.

W. F. Gericke, from the University of California, coined the name "hydroponics" (from the Greek hydros, water, and ponos, labor) in 1936, when he published a paper describing how to grow tomatoes this way. In 1940 he wrote a book called *Complete Guide to Soilless Gardening*.

In 1937 gravel cultures were introduced, and modern hydroponics was on the way to feeding the nation. Many huge commercial growers installed some type or another of a soilless garden bed with irrigation into vast greenhouses. Many were also embracing the new "science" of hydroponics, as it answered a need for increased production, in less area, at a lower cost.

There was a huge jump in interest for hydroponics during World War II, when the Air Force ordered a hydroponics setup to feed some remotely stationed pilots. This was so successful that many units in remote areas grew their own produce hydroponically during the war. The public also rallied to hydroponics during World War II, and gardening in general, as they were urged to grow much of their own food at home.

After the war, interest boomed , as hydroponics answered a need—for food. From island nations in the Caribbean to the Indian subcontinent, the race was on to build and experiment with hydroponics. Huge successes were reported worldwide from New Zealand and Australia to the Netherlands and Europe as growers exploited the technology to grow everything from ornamental flowers to the food we put on our tables.

To promote this, the International Working Group on Soilless Culture held a series of meetings worldwide during the late 1960s and the 1970s. More than 100 nations participated, and the use of hydroponics expanded worldwide as a result.

In 1982, Walt Disney opened the Land Pavilion at Epcot Center in Florida, and it features a huge hydroponics display.

Today, research continues into hydroponics, and the liquid nutrients plants need to grow this way. As our climate continues to change, it is becoming ever more apparent that we need to shift from a dependence on burning fossil fuels, and to rethink our present methods of food production. You can free yourself from potentially unsafe foods contaminated with pesticides or worse, by growing your own clean healthy food indoors—either in soil or hydroponically.

~ Chris Thompson

Table of Contents

Chapter 10 - Hydroponic Gardening 211

Chapter 11 - Air 245

The Internet

FREE Gardening and horticulture information!

Information and the velocity at which it travels is the most important innovation in gardening and horticulture during the last five years.

The Internet allows millions of indoor and outdoor gardening enthusiasts all over the world to share information. Gardeners can ask and answer questions online and download information about nurturing vegetables and flowers indoors and out. Here are some of my favorite websites:

www.maximumyield.com

www.growingedge.com

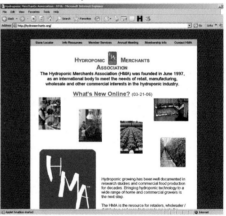

www.hydromerchants.com

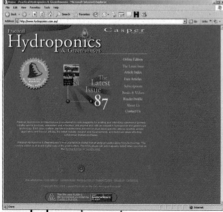

www.hydroponics.com/au

www.carbon.org

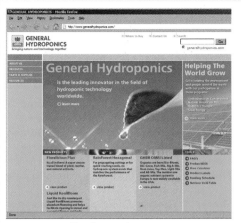

www.generalhydroponics.com

www.hydrofarm.com

www.everybodysgardencenter.com

www.hydroasis.com

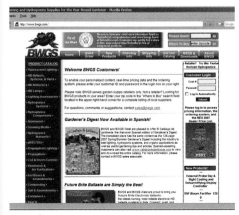

www.bwgs.com

www.greenair.com

Gardening Indoors

www.sunlightsupply.com

www.wikipedia.com

Trade Shows and Expos

Another source of information for gardeners are the many trade shows, fairs, and expositions that are held around the country and around the world. Here is a short list of some of the more interesting shows to attend.

(In alphabetical order)

Augusta Home & Garden Show – Augusta Civic Center

Austin Home & Garden Show(s) – Austin Convention Center (Spring & Fall)

Bahrain Garden Show – Manama, Bahrain

BC Home & Garden Show – BC Place Stadium, Vancouver, BC

Bloom 'n Garden Expo – Nashville, TN

Boise Garden & Flower Show – Boise, ID

Canada Blooms – Ottowa, Canada

Chelsea Flower Show – London, UK

Chicago Flower & Garden Show – Chicago, IL

Cincinatti Flower Show – Lake Como, OH

Epcot's International Flower & Garden Festival – Walt Disney World, FL

Floriade Australia – Canberra, Australia

Floriade Holland – (every ten years, next date 2012 in Venlo, NL)

Flower & Garden Show of New Jersey – Edison, NJ

Melbourne International Flower & Garden Show – Melbourne, Australia

Northwest Flower & Garden Show – Seattle's Washington State Convention Center

Philadelphia Flower Show – Pennsylvania Convention Center

Portland Home & Garden Show – Portland, OR, Expo Center

San Francisco Flower & Garden Show – San Francisco's Cow Palace

Southeastern Flower Show – Georgia World Congress Center

Southern California Home & Garden Show – Anaheim Convention Center

US Botanical Gardens – Washington, DC (year-round displays)

Virginia Flower & Garden Show – Virginia Beach, VA

Wichita Garden Show – Wichita, KS

The Internet is a vast resource of information about Garden Shows and Expositions being held worldwide. Go to your favorite search engine and look for shows nearby that you can attend.

Worldwide, there are thousands of these shows where you can see the equipment and supplies you will need. Often you can buy these products at the show itself, and take them home with you that day. The other main advantage of attending these shows is the ability to talk to the experts about your specific gardening needs or problems.

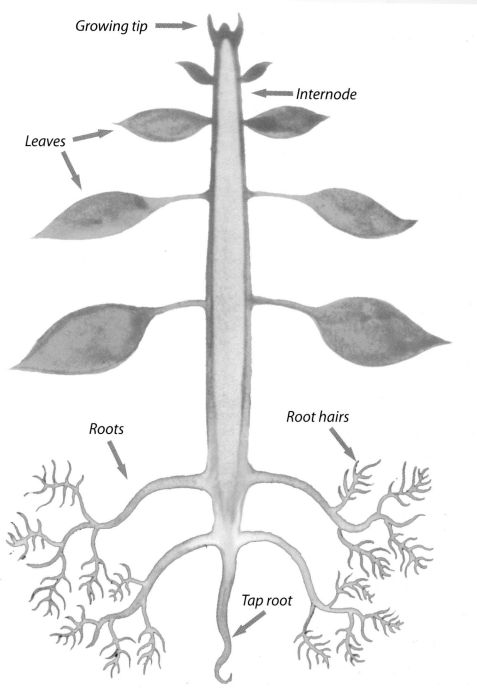

Growing tip

Internode

Leaves

Root hairs

Roots

Tap root

The parts of a plant are clearly labeled in this drawing.

Gardening Indoors

Introduction

The key to successful indoor gardening is to understand how warm-season annuals produce food and grow. Plants, vegetables, and flowers, whether cultivated indoors or out, have the same requirements for growth. Plants need light, air, water, nutrients, a growing medium, and heat to manufacture food and to grow. Without any one of these essentials, growth stops and death soon results. Indoors, the light must be of the proper spectrum and intensity; air must be warm, arid, and rich in carbon dioxide; water must be abundant but not excessive; and the growing medium must contain the proper levels of nutrients for vigorous growth. When all these needs are met consistently at optimum levels, optimum growth is the result.

Annual vegetables and flowers normally complete their life cycle within one year. A seed planted in the spring will grow strong throughout the summer and will flower in the fall, producing more seeds. The annual cycle starts all over again when the new seeds sprout the following year. In nature, plants go through distinct growth stages. This chapter delineates each stage of growth.

Life Cycle of Annual Vegetables and Flowers

After three to seven days of germination, plants enter the seedling growth stage, which lasts about a month. During the first growth stage, the seed germinates or sprouts, establishes a root system, and grows a stem and a few leaves.

Germination

During germination, moisture, heat, and air activate hormones (cytokinins, gibberellins, and auxins) within the durable outer coating of the seed. Cytokinins signal more cells to form and gibberellins to increase cell size. The embryo expands, nourished by a supply of stored food within the seed. Soon, the seed's coating splits, a rootlet grows downward, and a sprout with seed leaves pushes upward in search of light.

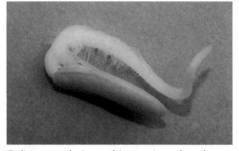

Delicate root hairs on this germinated seed must not be disturbed.

Strong, healthy seedling emerges from a Jiffy™ cube. The sprouted seed was carefully inserted into a hole with the taproot pointing down.

Seedling Growth

The single root from the seed grows down and branches out, similar to the way the stem branches up and out above ground. Tiny rootlets draw in water and nutrients (chemical substances needed for life). Roots also serve to anchor a plant in the growing medium. Seedling should receive 16–18 hours of light to maintain strong, healthy growth.

Strong, healthy roots are vibrant white.

This tomato seedling was recently transplanted into a bigger pot.

Vegetative Growth

Vegetative growth is maintained in most plants by giving them 16–24 hours of light every day. As the plants mature, the roots take on specialized functions. The center and old, mature portions contain a water transport system and may store food. The tips of the roots produce elongating cells that continue to push farther into the soil in search of more water and food. The single-celled root hairs are the parts of the root that actually absorb water and nutrients. Without water, frail root hairs will dry up and die. They are very delicate and easily damaged by light, air, and klutzy hands if moved or exposed. Extreme care must be exercised during transplanting.

You can see a small growth tip emerging between the branch and stem in this delicate tomato seedling.

Gardening Indoors

Basil seedlings grow exceptionally fast once they develop true leaves.

Cucumber seedlings also grow exceptionally fast. You will have to give this vining plant a trellis for best production.

Colorful leaves make this peperomia a big hit in the garden.

Like the roots, the stem grows through elongation, also producing new buds along the stem. The central, or terminal, bud carries growth upward; side, or lateral, buds turn into branches or leaves. The stem functions by transmitting water and nutrients from the delicate root hairs to the growing buds, leaves, and flowers. Sugars and starches manufactured in the leaves are distributed throughout the plant via the stem. This fluid flow takes place near the surface of the stem. If the stem is bound too tightly by string or other tie-downs, it will cut the flow of life-giving fluids, thereby strangling and killing the plant. The stem also supports the plant with stiff cellulose located within the inner walls. Outdoors, rain and wind push a plant around, causing much stiff cellulose production to keep the plant supported upright. Indoors, with no natural wind or rain present, stiff cellulose production is minimal, so plants develop weak stems and may need to be staked up, especially during flowering.

Once the leaves expand, they start to manufacture food (carbohydrates). Chlorophyll (the substance that gives plants their green color) converts carbon dioxide (CO_2) from the air, water, and light energy into carbohydrates and oxygen.

This process is called photosynthesis. It requires water drawn up from the roots, through the stem, into the leaves where it encounters carbon dioxide. Tiny breathing pores called stomata are located on the underside of the leaf and funnel CO_2 into contact with the water. In order for photosynthesis to occur, the leaf's interior tissue must be kept moist. The stomata open and close to regulate the flow of moisture, preventing dehydration. Plant leaves are also protected from drying out by an outer skin. The stomata also permit the outflow of water vapor and waste oxygen. The stomata are very important to the plant's well-being and must be kept clean to promote vigorous growth. Dirty, clogged stomata would breathe about as well as you would with a sack over your head!

Green tomato leaves are packed with chlorophyll. They convert CO_2, water, and light energy into food—carbohydrates and oxygen.

Mother Plants

Gardeners select strong, healthy mother plants. Mothers are given 18–24 hours of light daily so they stay in the vegetative growth stage. Gardeners cut branch tips from the mother plants and root them. The cut tips are called "cuttings." Cultivating several strong, healthy mother plants is the key to having a consistent supply of cuttings.

You can take cuttings from geraniums even when they are flowering.

Taking cuttings

Branch tips are cut and rooted to form cuttings. Cuttings take 10–20 days to grow a strong, healthy root system. Cuttings are given 18–24 hours of light so they stay in the vegetative growth stage. Once the root system is established, cuttings are transplanted into larger containers. Now they are ready to grow for one to four weeks in the vegetative growth stage before being induced to flower.

Flowering

Many annuals flower outdoors in the fall when days become shorter and plants are signaled that the annual life cycle is coming to an end. At flowering, plant functions change. Leafy growth slows, and flowers start to form. Flowering is triggered in most commercial varieties by 12 hours of darkness and 12 hours of light every 24 hours. Plants that developed in tropical regions often start flowering under more

Gardening Indoors

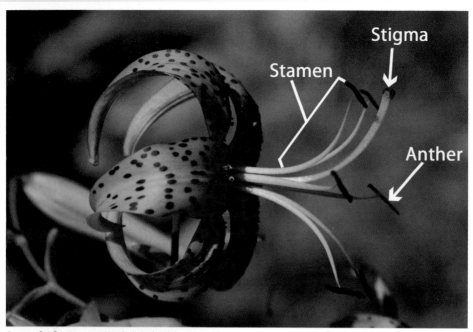

Parts of a flower are clearly labeled above.

Imagine being able to grow this much color in the middle of winter!

Orchids are one of the favorite indoor plants grown year-round worldwide.

light and less darkness. Flowers form during the last stage of growth.

Most plants have male and female plant parts within the same flower. When both male and female flowers are in bloom, pollen from the male flower lands on the female flower, thereby fertilizing it. The male dies after producing and shedding all his pollen. Seeds form and grow within the female flowers. As the seeds are maturing, the female plant slowly dies. The mature seeds then fall to the ground and germinate naturally or are collected for planting next spring.

Dried organic whole Red Limo chile with seeds.

Dried organic Panca chile with seeds.

Dried organic Amarillo chile with seeds.

Tied with a string, and left to dry last fall, these dried chiles are full of seeds ready to be planted.

These sweeter chiles dried perfectly during the winter and are now crushed and used for flavor until the next crop comes in.

Gardening Indoors

This chile has tiny black seeds; use a tweezers to separate them from fragments of dried chile.

Slice one of your home-grown squashes open and collect the seeds for next year.

A closeup of some very hot chile pepper seeds ready to be used for another crop.

Above: Using a fork, it is easy to separate seeds from the slimy strings that connect the seeds inside the squash.

Some chile pepper seeds are quite large, and easily separate from their pods.

Right: After separating the seeds dry them in a cool, dark, dry place. When completely dry, they can be stored in glass jars for next year.

A closeup of the chile pepper seeds above.

Healthy seedlings at just three weeks old, these chili peppers, basil, and spearmint sprouted from seed in Jiffy Pots.

Introduction

A seed contains all the genetic characteristics of a plant. Seeds are the result of sexual propagation and contain genes from each parent, male and female. Some plants, known as hermaphrodites, bear both male and female flowers on the same plant. The genes within a seed dictate a plant's size; disease and pest resistance; root, stem, leaf, and flower production; and many other traits. The genetic makeup of a seed is the single most important factor dictating how well a plant will grow under artificial light or natural sunlight and the quality of its flowers or produce.

Seeds

Careful seed selection can make the difference between a successful garden and complete failure. Certain seed varieties are better adapted to grow under certain conditions than others. For example, the early-maturing, cold-tolerant 'Oregon Spring' tomato grows in cool weather, setting flowers and fruit well before the larger Beefsteak varieties. If you live in a cool region with a short growing season, selecting 'Oregon Spring' rather than a late-maturing Beefsteak variety such as 'Brandywine' will make a fruitful harvest almost certain. If you love broccoli but live in a warm climate, planting heat-tolerant 'Premium Crop' rather than 'Green Valiant' will prolong the harvest.

Many vegetable seed varieties available today are developed for agriculture. They are bred for qualities such as long shelf life, uniformity, disease resistance, and the ability to withstand mechanical harvesting with little damage. Taste is usually the last quality considered. Eating carefully selected varieties with superior taste, rather than tough vegetables that were developed for mechanized handling, is one of the rewards of indoor gardening.

Open-pollinated seeds, also referred to as heirloom seed varieties, are the products of parents selected at random by nature. You can produce these seeds yourself and save them to sow the following year. They will produce plants very similar to their parents. Some open-pollinated seeds are very popular today, such as the 'Kentucky Wonder' pole bean. But since the advent of hybrids, many varieties have become difficult to find, even extinct. Several groups have been organized to preserve

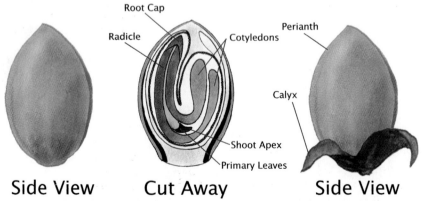

The cutaway drawing in the center shows how the seed will develop into different plant parts.

the heirloom varieties. The Seed Savers Exchange is the largest.

The introduction of hybrid or F[1] hybrid seed has revolutionized modern agriculture and gardening. Hybrid seed is the product of crossing true-breeding parents that have desirable characteristics. The resulting seed is known as an F[1] hybrid. The F[1] hybrid has *hybrid vigor*, the ability to grow stronger and faster than its parents. The greater the vigor, the more obstacles, such as pests and diseases, it can overcome to produce a better plant. Hybrids are usually uniform in shape and size and become ripe at the same time. Even though the seeds are often more expensive, they are an excellent value. Carefully selecting hybrid seed for such qualities as taste, disease and pest resistance, cold and heat tolerance, and conditions that prevail both indoors and outdoors in your climate will help make your garden a success.

Today, modern seed production has largely replaced the older method of open field pollination. But this technology also has disadvantages. The growing of one variety on a very large scale can be dangerous. With no genetic diversification, it can be wiped out if attacked by pests or diseases. Diversify. Grow more than one variety, and it will help overcome unchecked diseases and pests.

When selecting seed, you may notice that some carry the label "All-American Selection" or "AAS Winner." Seed varieties that were chosen as AAS winners have demonstrated superior growth characteristics in a wide variety of climates across America. Such AAS winners are easy to spot on seed racks and are a good choice for indoor gardens.

Timeline for germinating seeds

At 55–72 hours
Water is absorbed
Root tip (radicle) is visible

At 10–14 days
First roots become visible

At 21–30 days
At least half of seeds are rooted by day 21. Seeds not rooted by day 30 will probably grow slowly

Once seeds are rooted, cell growth accelerates; stem, foliage, and roots develop quickly. Seedlings develop into full vegetative growth within four to six weeks of germination.

Some seed is treated with a fungicide to prevent such diseases as damping-off, which causes seedlings to rot at the soil line. Typically, the fungicide is color-coded, and some seed companies state in their catalogs or on their seed packets that it is treated. Some seed is available with a coating of fungicide. The most common fungicide in use is Captan (Carbaryl), known to be carcinogenic. At least one major seed producer is using naturally occurring diatomaceous earth to protect seed.

Typically, a gardener buys seeds from a reputable company. Once germinated, the seeds are carefully planted and grown to adults. For example, if 100 seeds are planted, some will be weak and grow poorly; others may fall victim to insect or fungal attacks, and a percentage will grow into strong adults.

Strong, healthy parents and proper care yield strong seeds that germinate well.

Strong seeds produce healthy plants and heavy harvests. Seeds stored too long will germinate slowly and have a high rate of failure. Vigorous seeds initiate growth within seven days. Seeds that take longer than a month to germinate could always be slow and produce less. However, some seeds take longer to germinate even under the best conditions.

The cask, or outer protective shell, on some seeds never properly seals, which allows moisture and air to penetrate. It also causes hormone concentrations to dissipate, making seeds less viable. Permeable seeds signal diseases and pests to move in. Such seeds are immature, white, fragile, and crush easily with slight pressure between finger and thumb. These are weak seeds and do not have enough strength to grow well.

mottled and have the highest germination rate. Soft, pale, or green seeds are usually immature and should be avoided. Immature seeds germinate poorly and often produce sickly plants. Fresh, dry, mature seeds less than a year old sprout quickly and grow robust plants.

The seed above is shown before germination. The seed on the right has a brand new delicate taproot and is ready to be planted.

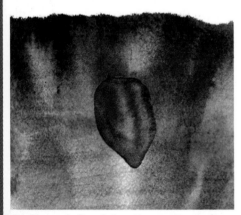

Sowing seeds directly in moist growing medium will signal the outer shell to open.

A simple picture of a seed reveals an embryo containing the genes and a supply of food wrapped in a protective outer coating. Mature seeds are generally hard, beige to dark brown, and spotted or

Germination

Seeds need only water, heat, and air to germinate. They do not need extra hormones to germinate. Seeds sprout without light in a wide range of temperatures. Properly nurtured seeds germinate in two to seven days, in temperatures from 70–80°F (21–27°C). Temperatures above 90°F (32°C) impair germination. At germination, the outside protective shell of the seed splits, and a tiny, white sprout (radicle) pops out. This sprout is the root or taproot. Cotyledons, or seed leaves, emerge from within the shell as they push upward in search of light.

To scarify seeds, place a small piece of sandpaper inside a container along with seeds.

Close the container with the seeds and sandpaper inside.

Shake the box for about 30 seconds to rough up and scuff the seeds, so water can penetrate the outer shell.

Seeds are prompted to germinate by:
Water
Temperature
Air (oxygen)

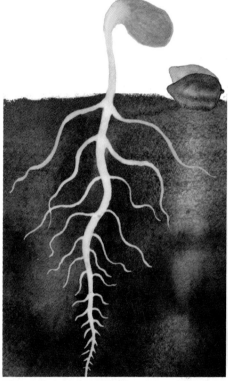

The cotyledon or seedling leaves are the first to appear after the seed sprouts.

Water

Soaking seeds in water allows moisture to penetrate the protective seed shell within minutes. Once inside, moisture continues to wick in to activate the dormant hormones. In a few days, hormones activate and send enough hormone signals to produce a radicle. The radicle emerges upward to bring a new plant into the world. Once a seed receives moisture, there must be a constant stream of moisture to transport nutrients, hormones, and water in order to carry on life processes. Letting germinated seeds suffer moisture stress will stunt seedling growth.

New seedlings are delicate and must be treated with care. Keep water, temperature, light, and air at proper levels.

Temperature

Most seeds grow best at 78°F (25°C).

Low temperatures delay germination.

High temperatures upset seed chemistry causing poor germination.

Seeds germinate best under the native conditions where they were grown.

Once germinated, move seedlings to a slightly cooler growing area and increase light levels. Avoid high temperatures and low light levels, which cause lanky growth.

Air (oxygen)

Seeds need air to germinate. Moist, soggy growing mediums will cut off oxygen supplies, and the seed will literally drown.

Start feeding two to four weeks after seedlings have sprouted. Some growers wait until leaves yellow to begin feeding. Use a mild quarter-strength solution. If yellowing persists, give seedlings a little more fertilizer.

Some seeds have a very hard outer shell, or testa, and must be scarified to allow water to penetrate. To scarify, line a small box with a piece of fine-grain sandpaper or emery board. Put the seeds in the box and shake for about 30 seconds. Remove the seeds, and make sure they have been scuffed a bit. Just a little scuffing will allow water to enter and set germination in motion.

Two Popular Germination Techniques

One: Pre-soaking in water

Soak seeds overnight in a glass of water. Make sure seeds get good and wet so growth is activated. Do not let seeds soak more than 24 hours, or they might get too wet, suffer oxygen deprivation, and rot. Once soaked, seeds are ready to be placed between moist paper towels to sprout or to be planted in a root cube or fine, light soilless mix.

In a warm location (70–90°F, [21–32°C]), place seeds in a moist paper towel or cheesecloth, making sure they are in

To germinate, place seeds between folds of a paper towel on a plate.

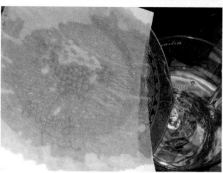

Tip plate to drain excess moisture.

Add water to moisten the paper towel.

Jiffy pellets expand when water is added. They make excellent pop-up pots to grow seedlings. They are also very easy to transplant.

darkness. Set the moist cloth or paper towel on a grate (for drainage) on a dinner plate.

Water the cloth daily, and keep it moist. Let excess water drain away freely. The cloth will retain enough moisture to germinate the seed in a few days. The seed contains an adequate food supply for germination. Prevent fungal attacks by watering with a mild two-percent bleach or fungicide solution. Once seeds have sprouted and the white radicle is visible, carefully pick up the fragile sprouts (with tweezers) and plant them. Take care not to expose the tender rootlet to prolonged intense light or air. Cover the germinated seed with 0.25–0.5-inch (1–2 cm) of fine planting medium with the white root tip pointing downward.

Two: Direct seed

One of the problems with rockwool can be that the seeds heave out before germinating. That is why it is best to germinate seeds before putting them into the rockwool substrate.

When seeds sprout, the white radicle will be visible; use tweezers to gently pick up the fragile sprouts and plant them in a pre-drilled hole in the rockwool with the white root tip pointing down. Be very careful and do not expose the tender rootlet to extended periods of light or air. Cover the seed with 0.25–0.5-inch (1–2 cm) of moist rockwool.

Keep the rockwool evenly moist. Once the taproot sprouts, small, fuzzy feeder roots will grow in 12–14 days.

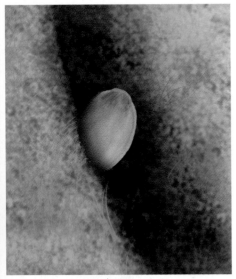

Seeds set inside rockwool blocks often heave up and out. Germinate seeds before planting to avoid this common problem.

Water penetrates the outer protective shell, continues to wick in, and activates dormant hormones that induce germination. Once a seed receives moisture, there must be a constant stream of moisture to transport nutrients, hormones, and water to carry on life processes. Letting germinated seed suffer moisture stress now will stunt or stop seedling growth. The telltale sign of a moisture-stressed germinated seed is a dry root tip.

Soggy growing mediums cut oxygen supplies and cause seeds to drown. Planting seeds too deeply causes poor germination. Seedlings do not have enough stored energy to force through too much soil before sprouting. Plant seeds twice as deep as the width of the seed. For example, plant an eighth-inch seed one-quarter inch deep.

Seeds do not need any extra hormones to germinate. Household water contains enough dissolved solids, food, to nourish seeds through their first few weeks of life. Supplemental nutrients will disrupt internal chemistry. Some gardeners prefer to germinate seeds with distilled water, which contains virtually no dissolved solids.

Sow (direct seed) or move the sprout into a shallow planter, small seed pot, peat pellet, or rooting cube. Keep the planting medium evenly moist. Use a spoon to contain the root ball when transplanting from a shallow planter. Peat pellets or root cubes may be transplanted in two to three weeks or when the roots show through the sides. Feed with a dilute, quarter-strength fertilizer solution.

This outdoor grower made a seedbed from fine potting soil. He has started hundreds of seeds in this seedbed.

The seeds on this page are examples of very easy-to-grow herbs, vegetables, and foods. These seeds are easily available in most groceries, garden centers, department stores, or on the Internet. Growing your own vegetables at home is quite therapeutic and good for the planet, while rewarding you with tasty food!

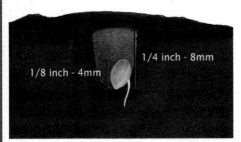

Plant seeds twice as deep as the seed is wide.

Construct a moisture tent over the seedling container to help retain even grow-medium moisture. To build, place a baggie or piece of cellophane over the seeded soil. The cover will keep the humidity and temperature elevated. Seeds usually need only one initial watering when under a humidity tent. Remove the cover as soon as the first sprout appears above ground. Leaving the tent on after seeds sprout through soil will lead to damping-off and other problems.

Place planted seeds under an HID lamp to add dry heat while germinating. The heat dries soil, which requires more frequent watering. Place a heat pad or soil heating cables below growing medium to expedite germination. Most seeds germinate and sprout quickest when the soil temperature is 78–80°F (24–27.5°C) and the air temperature is 72–74°F (22–23°C). But stems of many plants will stretch between internodes if temperatures exceed 85°F (29°C) for long.

Overwatering and underwatering are the biggest obstacles most gardeners face when germinating seeds and growing seedlings. Do not let the growing medium surface dry for long. Keep it evenly moist, not waterlogged. Setting root cubes or planting flats up on a grate allows good drainage. A shallow flat or planter with a heat pad underneath may require daily watering, while a deep, one-gallon pot will need watering every three days or more. A properly watered flat of rockwool cubes needs water every three to five days when sprouting seeds. When the surface is dry (0.25-inch [7 mm] deep), it is time to water. Remember, there are few roots to absorb the water early in life, and they are very delicate.

This germinated seedling at right was allowed to dry out for a little more than an hour. Notice how the tip of the root has shriveled. This seemingly small oversight caused the resulting plant to have a very slow start in life.

Ordering Seeds

Ordering seeds via a magazine ad or the Internet is commonplace. Many reputable companies advertise. You are most secure to order from a company you can contact by telephone. Speak to a qualified representative who will provide good answers to your questions. Companies with an e-mail address and web site are usually okay to order from, but make sure they answer your e-mails promptly. Do not be afraid to call several companies and ask them specific questions about the varieties they sell.

Storing Seeds

Store seeds in a cool, dark, dry place. Make sure to label containers! Some seeds will remain viable for five years or longer when stored properly. When 50 percent of the stored seeds do not germinate, the average storage life is over. But seeds a year old or older often take longer to sprout and have a lower rate of germination.

Seeds store for a long time when humidity is less than 5 percent and temperature is 35–40°F (2–5°C).

Seed hormones—ABA, cytokinins, and gibberellins—are primed to respond to moisture, which is the first signal to germinate. Prevent moisture from signaling seeds to germinate by keeping them dry. Small amounts of moisture in the form of condensation can give seeds a false start on germination and cause them to expend all their stored energy. Avoid moisture levels above five percent to ensure viable seeds. Moisture levels above five percent will cause germination levels to decrease rapidly. Seal seeds in an airtight container, and place silicon crystal packages in the container to absorb excess moisture.

Seeds need enough moisture to initiate this process within 48 hours.

Dry seeds are temperature-sensitive; they can be disinfected with a short application of heat. Low temperatures slow internal seed activity so are best for preserving seeds. You can use super-cold liquid nitrogen and cryogenics to store seeds for a long time.

Air, once it enters the outer seed shell, signals seeds to germinate. Viable seeds are preserved longer when vacuum-packed to remove all oxygen.

Seeds with a thin, outer protective shell never truly go dormant, because moisture and air are always present within. Moisture and air cause hormone levels to slowly dissipate. Such seeds do not store well for a long time.

Seed Pests

Seed pests become active when there is more than ten percent moisture content. When the growing medium contains more than fifteen percent moisture, fungi become active. Excess fertilizer slows seedling growth and promotes fungus attacks.

Temperatures from 68–85°F (20–30°C) promote *Pythium* (damping-off) and *Rhixoctonia* fungi. Warm-season annual seeds grow best at 78°F (25°C). Most fungi reproduce fastest in a temperature range of 68–86°F (20–30°C).

Keep a wary eye on problems. Nutrient overdose burns leaf tips and fringes, which can look like damping-off to the untrained eye. Do not fertilize. Applying a fungicide now will make the problem worse.

Seedlings

When a seed sprouts, the white taproot emerges. Soon afterward, the cotyledon, also known as seed or seedling leaf, appears. The seed leaves spread out as the stem elongates. Within a few days, the first true leaves appear, and the little plant is now officially a seedling. This growth stage lasts for three to six weeks. During seedling growth, a root system grows rapidly while green, aboveground growth

The outer shell from this tomato seedling will fall as soon as the leaves expand. The outer shell protects the seedling within as long as possible.

Bursting with life, these seeds are being sprouted under optimum conditions, 74°F (22°C) and 100% humidity.

This tomato seedling broke through the soil yesterday and will continue to grow upward toward the light.

Little spearmint seedlings were planted very close together. They must be transplanted while roots are still small to minimize transplanting stress.

is slow. Water and heat are critical at this point of development. The new, fragile root system is very small and requires a small but constant supply of water and warmth. Too much water will drown roots, often leading to root rot and damping-off. Lack of water will cause the infant root system to dry up. As the seedlings mature, some will grow faster, stronger, and appear healthier in general. A little heat now will help nurture small seedlings to a strong start. Other seeds will sprout slowly, and seedlings will be weak and leggy. Cull sickly, weak plants, and focus attention on the remaining strong survivors. Seedlings should be big enough to thin out by the third to fifth week of growth. Thinning out seedlings is very difficult for gardeners who have nurtured seeds.

Seedlings need at least 16 hours of light daily. They require less intense light now and grow well under fluorescent tubes for the first two to three weeks. Compact fluorescent and HID light can also be used. The compact fluorescent should be 12–18 inches (30–45 cm) and the HID 3–4 feet (90–120 cm) above seedlings for best growth.

The seedling stage is over when rapid foliage growth starts. Rapid growth above ground is the beginning of the vegetative

Delicate root hairs are visible on this seedling. Moisture and nutrients are absorbed via the fragile root hairs. Disturbing the roots will break many root hairs, causing them to stop taking in water and nutrients.

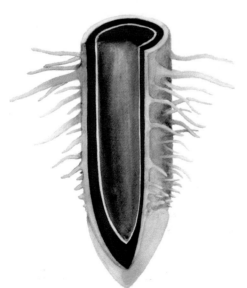

The tip of the root is where the growth takes place. White root hairs draw in water and nutrients.

Seedlings are packed with energy! This seemingly delicate seedling is sprouting through the growing medium in search of sunlight.

growth stage. Plants will need more room to grow; transplanting into a larger container hastens development.

Buying Seedlings

Purchasing flower and vegetable starts at a tip-top retail nursery takes little skill. Purchasing from some discount outlets can be a bit risky if the staff is not familiar with the proper care of seedlings.

Buy seedlings that are kept in good growing conditions. Do not buy seedlings that are housed in a sunny location. The small amount of soil around the roots in small plastic pots/packs can heat up, effectively cooking the roots. The temperature is more constant in a shade house, which also protects the tender plants from other climate extremes. The root system is the most important part of the seedling.

Select plants that have good color and are of uniform size. The best seedlings to transplant have a root system that holds the soil together and has just begun to reach the outside of the soil in the small container.

If only rootbound plants are available, soak the soil with water before planting. Remove any matted roots, then gently separate the remaining roots just before planting so they will penetrate the soil better and not be inclined to bunch up.

You may prefer to buy seedlings with root systems that are not fully developed and hold them in a partially shady location for a week or two before transplanting. This way you can watch their progress as they gradually get used to their new environment.

Pull plants apart gently when transplanting from flats. Take care not to squeeze roots and crush tender root hairs.

Seedlings emerging from peat pots develop seed (cotyledon) leaves before growing their first set of "true leaves." (Above and below)

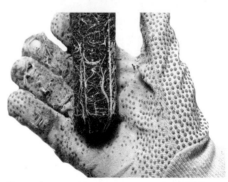

Deep plugs grow a deeper root system. This seedling was transplanted outdoors and grew very well.

Basil is very profitable and in high demand year-round from Asian markets and other outlets. Easily grown indoors under lights, this hydroponics setup has an air-cooled lighting system and good overall ventilation.

These seedlings are in the early stage of vegetative growth.

Introduction

The seedling growth stage lasts for about two to three weeks after seeds have germinated. Once a strong root system is established and foliage growth increases rapidly, seedlings enter the vegetative growth stage. When chlorophyll production is full speed ahead, a vegetative plant will produce as much green, leafy foliage as it is genetically possible to manufacture as long as light, CO_2, nutrients, and water are not limited. Properly maintained, some plants will grow from one-half to two inches per day. A plant stunted now could take weeks to resume normal growth. A strong, unrestricted root system is essential to supply much-needed water and nutrients. Unrestricted vegetative growth is the key to a healthy harvest. A plant's nutrient and water intake changes during vegetative growth. Transpiration is carried on at a more rapid rate, requiring more water. High levels of nitrogen are needed; potassium, phosphorus, calcium, magnesium, sulfur, and trace elements are used at much faster rates. The larger a plant gets and the bigger the root system, the faster the soil will dry out. The key to strong vegetative growth and a heavy harvest is supplying roots and plants with the perfect environment.

Vegetative growth is maintained with 16 or more hours of light. I used to believe a point of diminishing returns was reached after 18 hours of light, but further research shows that vegetative plants grow faster under 24 hours of light. Many plants will continue vegetative growth a year or longer (theoretically forever), as long as an 18-hour photoperiod is maintained.

These cuttings share all genetic characteristics. They will all grow up to look like their mothers.

Most warm-season annuals are photoperiodic-reactive; flowering can be controlled with the light and dark cycle. This allows indoor horticulturists to control vegetative and flowering growth.

Taking cuttings, transplanting, pruning, and bending are all initiated when plants are in the vegetative growth stage.

Cuttings and Taking Cuttings

Plants can be reproduced (propagated) sexually or asexually. Seeds are the product of sexual propagation; cuttings are the result of asexual or vegetative propagation. In its simplest form, taking a cutting involves cutting a growing branch tip and rooting it. Technically, taking cuttings is taking one cell of a plant and promoting its growth into a plant. Gardeners and horticulturists commonly refer to a *cutting* as meaning a branch of a plant that has been cut off and rooted.

Growth Stage	Time	Number of plants
Clone	3 weeks	30
Vegetative	2 weeks	10
Flower	8 weeks	30
Total		**70**

Taking cuttings reduces the time it takes for a crop such as basil or tarragon to mature. Productive gardeners have two rooms, a vegetative/taking cuttings room, about a quarter the size of a second room used for flowering. Smaller vegetative plants take up less space than older flowering plants. For example, a 250- or 400-watt metal halide could easily illuminate vegetative plants and cuttings that would fill a flowering room lit by three 600-watt HP sodiums. If the halide is turned off, fluorescent and compact fluorescent lamps are more economical and work well to root cuttings.

Combine eight-week flowering/harvest cycles with the continuous taking of cuttings to form a perpetual harvest. One easy-to-implement scenario is to take two cuttings every four days, and harvest a plant or cut it back every other day. Every time a plant is harvested, one or two rooted cuttings are moved from the vegetative room into the flowering room.

Short crops of cuttings in small containers are much easier to move and maintain than big plants in big containers. Short cuttings are also easy and efficient to grow in greenhouses and outdoors.

Well-illuminated, strong cuttings grow fast and have less chance of being affected

Annuals and herbaceous perennials that propagate easily by cloning:

African violets
Aloes
Alyssum (Goldentuft)
Anthuriums
Anemones (Poppy Anemone)
Begonias (certain types only)
Bird of Paradise
Cactuses
Chrysanthemums
Crassula argentia *(jade plant)*
Dahlias
Carnations
Ficuses
Geraniums
Heliconias
Hyacinths
Irises
Lavender
Lobelia
Orchids
Phlox
Primroses
Sage
Sansevieria (snake plant)
Strawberry geraniums
Scheffleras
Succulents (including agave, aloe, crassula, echevaria, hoya, kalanchoe, portulacaria, yuccas)
Thyme
Tulips
Vincas

Source: Plant Propagation Principles and Practices, Hartmann and Kester, 4th Edition, Prentice-Hall, Inc., publisher.

Cuttings from lower branches root the easiest because they contain more of the proper hormones.

Negative points

Cuttings grow slower than F^1 hybrid plants grown from seed. An F^1 hybrid is the heterozygous first filial generation—pollen and ovule. F^1 hybrids have "hybrid vigor" which means that this cross will grow about 25 percent bigger and stronger than cuttings. Hybrid vigor also makes plants less susceptible to pest and disease problems.

Always start with the best mothers you can find. A mother plant yields cuttings in her image. If the mother plant lacks vigor, harvest weight, or is not pest and disease resistant, the cutting shares her drawbacks. These weaknesses are compounded when growing only one variety. An unchecked pest or disease infestation could wipe out the entire crop.

Some gardeners have a difficult time learning to take cuttings. If this is the case, continue to work through the little problems one step at a time, and you will learn. Some people have a little longer learning curve when the taking of cuttings is involved. Take five to ten practice cuttings before taking a serious number of cuttings. You can also work with varieties that are easy to propagate via cutting.

by pests and diseases. Fast-growing cuttings develop more quickly than spider mites can reproduce. By the time a spider mite infestation is noticed and sprayed, the plants are a few weeks from harvest. Cuttings are also easy to submerge in a miticide when small.

Experiments with cuttings are consistent and easy to control. Genetically identical cuttings respond the same to different stimuli, such as fertilizer, light, bending, etc. After experimenting on several crops of cuttings from the same mother, a gardener has a very good idea what it takes to make them grow well.

Mother Plants

Any plant can have cuttings taken, regardless of age or growth stage. Take cuttings from mother plants that are at least two months old. Plants having cuttings taken before they are two months old may develop unevenly and grow slowly. Cuttings taken from flowering plants root quickly but require a month or longer to revert to vegetative growth.

Such rejuvenated cuttings occasionally flower prematurely, and are more prone to pest and disease attacks.

Mother plants must stay very healthy to be able to produce many cuttings. The roots on this mother are very healthy!

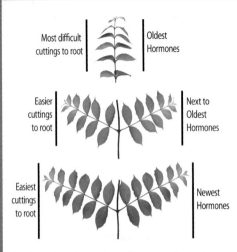

Most difficult cuttings to root — Oldest Hormones

Easier cuttings to root — Next to Oldest Hormones

Easiest cuttings to root — Newest Hormones

Cuttings from lower branches root the easiest because they contain more of the proper hormones.

Many plants can become a parent or mother. For example, a tomato can be grown from seed or be a cutting of a cutting. I interviewed several gardeners who made cuttings of cuttings more than 20 times! That is, cuttings (C-1) were taken from the original plant grown from seed. These cuttings were grown in the vegetative stage, and cuttings (C-2) were taken from the first cuttings (C-1). Blooming was induced in (C-1) two weeks later and (C-2) was grown in the vegetative stage. Then, cuttings (C-3) were taken from the second cuttings (C-2). This same growing technique is still going on with cuttings of cuttings well past (C-20) and there has been no apparent breakdown in the vigor of the cutting. However, if mothers suffer stress, they produce weak cuttings. Mothers that are forced to flower and revert to vegetative growth not only yield less, they are stressed and confused. Cuttings that grow poorly are generally the result of poor, unsanitary cutting practices.

A cutting is an exact genetic replica of the mother plant. Each mother's cell carries a DNA blueprint of itself. Radiation, chemicals, and poor cultural practices can damage this DNA. Unless damaged, the DNA remains intact.

When grown in the exact same environment, cuttings from the same mother look alike. But the same cuttings subjected to distinct environments in different indoor gardens will often look different.

A six-month old plant produces more growth hormones than a one-month old plant. By taking cuttings, a horticulturist is planting a hormonally advanced plant that will continue to grow at a very rapid rate.

Keep several mother plants in the vegetative stage for a consistent source of cutting stock. Start new mothers from seed every year. Give mother plants 18-24 hours of light per day to maintain fast growth. For best results, give mothers about ten percent less nitrogen, because less nitrogen promotes rooting in cuttings.

Gardeners and sick plants cause most rooting problems for cuttings. Weak plants that lack vigor provide slow-rooting, weak cuttings. Poor growing conditions also affect cutting strength.

Transplant into the same type or similar growing medium; otherwise, a water pressure differential could develop between the different mediums, which slows water movement and causes slow root growth. Starting seeds and cuttings in root cubes or peat pots makes them easy to transplant. Set the cube or peat pot in a hole in the growing medium, and make sure growing medium is in firm contact. Remember to keep root cubes and substrates evenly moist after transplanting.

Transplanting is the second most traumatic experience after the taking of cuttings. It requires special attention and manual dexterity. Tiny root hairs are very delicate and may easily be destroyed by light, air, or clumsy hands. Roots grow in darkness, in a rigid, secure environment. When roots are taken out of contact with the soil for long, they dry up and die.

Transplanting should involve as little disturbance to the root system as possible. Water helps the soil pack around roots and keeps them from drying out. Roots need to be in constant contact with moist soil in order to supply water and food to the plant.

After transplanting, photosynthesis and chlorophyll production are slowed, as are water and nutrient absorption via roots. Transplant late in the day so transplanted plants will have all night to recover. Transplants need subdued light, so foliage can grow at the rate roots are able to supply water and nutrients. Give new transplants filtered, less-intense light for a couple of days. If there is a fluorescent lamp handy, move transplants under it for a couple of days before moving them back under the HID or outdoors to harden-off.

Ideally, plants should be as healthy as possible before being traumatized by transplanting. But, transplanting a sick, rootbound plant to a bigger container has cured more than one ailing plant. Once transplanted, plants require low levels of nitrogen and potassium and increased quantities of phosphorus. Any product containing *Trichoderma* bacteria or Vitamin B_1 will help ease transplant shock. Plants need a few days to settle in and re-establish a solid flow of fluids from the roots throughout the plant. When transplanted carefully and disturbed little, there will be no sign of transplant shock or wilt.

Double potting is a simple transplanting technique that disturbs roots very little. To double pot a plant, cut the bottom out of a rootbound pot, and set on top of another bigger pot of soil. Roots grow down into second pot.

Getting Ready

Having cuttings taken is the most traumatic incident plants can experience. Cuttings go through an incredible transformation when they change from a severed growing tip to a rooted plant. Their entire chemistry changes. The stem that once grew leaves must now grow roots in order to survive. Cuttings are at their most tender point in life now.

Cuttings quickly develop a dense system of roots when stems have a high carbohydrate and low nitrogen

	Cut from Young	Cut from Old
Cell division starts	Day 4	Day 6
First root nubs form	Day 6	Day 10
Roots start to grow	Day 7	Day 20
Enough roots to transplant	Day 14	Day 28

This chart shows average times for roots to grow from the cambium. Note clones taken from younger growth root about twice as fast as those taken from older growth.

concentration. Build carbohydrate levels by leaching the growing medium with copious quantities of water to flush out nutrients. The growing medium must drain very well to withstand heavy leaching without becoming waterlogged. Reverse foliar feeding will leach nutrients from leaves, especially nitrogen. To reverse foliar feed, fill a sprayer with clean water and mist mother heavily every morning for three or four days. Older leaves may turn light green; growth slows as nitrogen is used and carbohydrates build. Carbohydrate and hormonal content is highest in lower, older, more mature branches. A rigid branch that folds over quickly when bent is a good sign of high carbohydrate content.

Integrity in parents:

Maintain 18–24-hour-day photoperiod
Keep plants healthy
Grow for 6–9 months
Repot
Grow hydroponically

Hormone content is different in different parts of a plant. Root growth hormones are concentrated near the base of the plant close to the main stem. This is the oldest portion of the plant and is where most root hormones are located. The top of the plant contains older hormones; cuttings taken from this part root slowly.

While rooting, cuttings require a minimum of nitrogen and increased levels of phosphorus to promote root growth. Sprays should be avoided during rooting as they compound cuttings' stress. Given good instruction and a little experience, most gardeners achieve a consistent, 100 percent cutting survival rate.

Large cuttings with large stems packed with starch grow roots slower than small cuttings with small stems. The excess starch in moist substrate also attracts diseases. Thin-stemmed cuttings have fewer reserves (accumulated starch), but they only need enough reserve energy to initiate root growth.

Small cuttings with few leaves root faster than big cuttings with many leaves. At first leaves contain moisture, but after a few days, the stem is no longer able to supply enough moisture to the leaves, and the cutting suffers stress. A small amount of leaf space is all that is necessary for photosynthesis to supply enough energy for root growth.

Precautions

An embolism is a bubble of air that is trapped in the hole in the stem. Embolisms occur when you take big cuttings and lay them on the counter before placing in water or a growing medium. When an embolism happens, fluid flow stops and cuttings die. After taking cuttings, immediately dip them in water or a growing medium to prevent air from becoming trapped in the hollow stems. Eliminate the threat of an embolism by taking cuttings under water.

Cuttings root well within a pH range of five to six. Aeroponic cutting gardens normally do best with a pH of five to five and a half. Most diseases grow poorly below these pH levels. Always make sure there is plenty of air in the rooting medium; this will stimulate root growth.

Do not use fertilizers on cuttings or seedlings.

Rooting Hormone	Contents	Notes
Algimin® Maxicrop	Dry kelp product Liquid seaweed	NO IBA or NAA. Soak cuttings overnight in a solution of two ounces Algimin® to one gallon of water. After planting, continue watering with this solution.
Clonex®	First cloning gel	Blend of seven vitamins, eleven minerals, two anti-microbial agents, 3000 ppm rooting hormones. Gel seals cutting tissues, reducing chance of infection and embolisms.
Dip-N-Grow® Earth Juice Catalyst®	IBA, NAA, antibacterial	Cost is one penny per 100 cuttings. Organic, derived from oat bran, kelp, molasses, vitamin B complexes, amino acids, hormones, and low levels of nutrients.
Hormex	IBA based powder	Available in six different strengths ranging from 1000 ppm to 45,000 ppm.
Hormodin®	IBA	Powder available in three strengths: 1000, 3000, and 8000 ppm.
Nitrozyme®	Natural product	Seaweed extract, contains cytokinins, auxins, enzymes, gibberellins, and ethylenes. Spray Nitrozyme on mothers two weeks before taking cuttings.
Olivia's Cloning Solution® Olivia's Cloning Gel	IBA, antifungal agents, nutrients	Very high success rate.
Rhizopon AA® (Rhizopon B.V.)	IBA	World's largest company devoted to research and manufacture of rooting products. Powder and water-soluble tablets in strengths from 500 to 20,000 ppm.
Rootex	IBA vitamins, hormones	From Tecknaflora, is one of the favorite products in North America.
Vita Grow	IBA NAA.	Customers say "you could root a popsicle stick"

Warning!
Some products are not recommended for use with edible plants.
Read the label carefully before deciding to use a product.

Avoid problems:

Keep the work area clean. Wash work surfaces and tools before starting.

Have grow medium ready.

Prepare mother plant (scion).

Take cuttings.

Store unused cuttings.

Insert (stick) cutting in growing medium or aeroponics system.

Place cuttings under humidity tent.

Look for root growth.

Transplant when roots emerge from root cube or medium.

Harden-off by gradually exposing to new environment.

Do not kill cuttings with kindness and fertilizer. At best, an excess dose of fertilizer will delay rooting. In fact, a good dose of ammonium nitrate, a common fertilizer, will stop root hairs from growing.

If an infestation occurs, apply aerosol pyrethrum. Remember, all pesticides, natural or not, are phytotoxic. Spraying cuttings is a bad idea in general. If you must use sprays, use natural organic sprays, apply them when it is cool, and keep their use to a minimum.

Use antidesiccant sprays sparingly, if at all, and only if a humidity dome is unavailable. Antidesiccant sprays clog stomata and can impair root growth in cuttings.

Do not overwater cuttings. Keep the medium evenly moist, and do not let it get soggy.

Any kind of stress disrupts hormones and slows rapid growth.

Keep the cutting area clean. Do not take cuttings where fungus spores and diseases are hiding! *Pythium* is the worst! *Pythium* flourishes in high temperatures and excessive moisture. Mites, whiteflies, thrips, etc., love weak, tender cuttings. Remove infested cuttings from the room. Cooler conditions, 65–78°F (18–25°C), slow mite and fungal spore reproduction and allow you to avert an infestation.

Rooting Hormones

Root-inducing hormones speed plant processes. When the stem of a cutting develops roots, it must transform from producing green stem cells to manufacturing undifferentiated cells and, finally, to fabricating root cells. Rooting hormones hasten growth of undifferentiated cells. Once

Sterilize all tools before cutting clones.

undifferentiated, cells quickly transform into root cells. Three substances that stimulate undifferentiated growth include napthalenaecetic acid (NAA), indolebutyric acid (IBA), and 2, 4-dichlorophenoxyacetic acid (2, 4 DPA). Commercial rooting hormones contain one, two, or all of the above synthetic ingredients and often include a fungicide to help prevent damping-off.

Rooting hormones are available in liquid, gel, or powder form. Liquid and gel types penetrate stems evenly and are the most versatile and consistent. Powdered rooting hormones adhere inconsistently to stems, penetrate poorly, spur uneven root growth, and yield a lower survival rate.

Liquid rooting hormones can be mixed in different concentrations. Always mix the most dilute concentration for softwood cuttings. Apply any rooting hormone containing IBA only once. If exceeded in concentration or duration, IBA applications impair root formation. As soon as cuttings are taken, rooting hormones are dispatched to the wound. They arrive in full force in about a week. The artificial rooting hormone fills the need until natural hormones take over.

Give cuttings a 5–15-second dip in concentrated solutions of IBA and NAA, 500–20,000 ppm. With a quick dip, stems evenly absorb the concentrated hormone.

Relatively new to the market, gels have caught on everywhere. They are easy to use and practical, but are not water soluble. Once applied, gels hold and stay with the stem longer than liquids or powders.

Grow More Roots

Split the stems of cuttings to expose more of the cambium layer just under the "skin" of the stem. It is the only place that generates new roots.

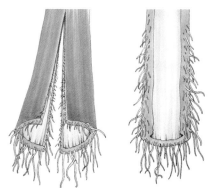

Exposing the cambium layer causes many roots to grow there. Lightly scraping away the outer layer of the stem to expose only the cambium allows hormones to concentrate where roots start. Splitting the cuttings' stem exposes more surface area to grow roots. Both practices increase the number of healthy roots, but rooting time is a few days longer.

After the cutting has been trimmed and scraped, dip the bare stem into a rooting hormone. Now it is ready to "stick" into the substrate.

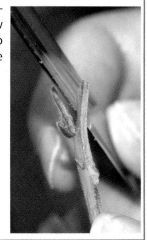

Split the stem to initiate more surface area for roots to grow.

Rooting powders are a mixture of talc and IBA and/or NAA and are less expensive than liquids or gels. To use, roll the moistened end of your cutting in the powder. Apply a thick, even coat. To avoid contamination, pour a small amount into a separate container, and throw away any excess. Tap or scrape excess powder off the cutting; excess hormones can hinder root growth. Make a hole bigger than the stem in the rooting medium. If the hole is too small, the rooting powder is scraped off upon insertion.

You can also spray cuttings with a single foliar spray of dilute IBA (50–90 ppm). Be careful to spray just enough to cover leaves. Spray should not drip off leaves. An IBA overdose slows growth, makes leaves dwarf, and could even kill the cutting.

Some gardeners soak their cuttings in a dilute solution (20–200 ppm IBA and/or NAA) for 24 hours. But I have seen few gardeners use this time-consuming technique.

To determine the rooting hormone concentration in parts per million, multiply the percentage listed by the manufacturer by 10,000. For example, a product with 0.9% IBA contains 9000 ppm IBA.

An all-natural, root-inducing substance is willow (tree) water. The substance in all willow trees that promotes rooting is unknown, but repeated experiments have proven willow water promotes about 20 percent more roots than plain water. This willow water is mixed with commercial rooting hormones for phenomenal results.

To make willow water rooting compound, find any willow tree and remove some of this year's branches that are about one and one-half inches in diameter. Remove the leaves, and cut the branches into one-inch lengths. Place one-inch willow sticks on end, so a lot of them fit in a water glass or quart jar. Fill the jar with water, and let sticks soak for 24 hours. After soaking, pour off the willow water, and use it for rooting hormone. Soak the cuttings in the willow water for 24 hours, then plant in rooting medium. If using a commercial liquid rooting hormone, substitute the willow water in place of regular water in the mix.

Some commercial products contain *Trichoderma* bacteria. The bacterium causes roots to grow and absorb nutrients better.

Before Taking Cuttings

Taking cuttings is the most efficient and productive means of plant propagation for small gardeners, both indoors and out. Once you have chosen the parent plant, you are ready to practice the simple, productive art and science of taking cuttings.

Disinfect all tools and working surfaces to kill bacteria, fungi, viruses, and other diseases already present. Use sharp scissor or razor blade dipped in alcohol, vinegar, or bleach (five to ten percent solution). Wash your hands thoroughly beforehand.

Make sure to have all cutting supplies within arm's reach—rooting cubes, hormone, razor or scissor, humidity dome, etc.—before you start to take cuttings.

Taking Cuttings: Step-by-Step

Step One: Choose a mother plant that is at least two months old. Some varieties give great cuttings even when pumped up with hydroponics and fertilizer. If a variety is difficult to take cuttings from, leach the soil with two gallons of water for each gallon of soil every morning for a week

Get all cutting supplies ready before starting.

Make a 45-degree cut across the stem to take the cutting.

Trim off one or two sets of leaves.

LEFT: Hold cuttings in a glass of water until you are ready to dip in hormone and plant.

Dip trimmed stem into the rooting gel or liquid hormone. Make sure stem is covered with the proper amount of rooting hormone.

Place the stem covered with rooting hormone into the root cube.

Pinch the top of the root cube so growing medium is in full contact with the stem.

before taking cuttings; drainage must be good. Or, mist leaves heavily with plain water every morning. Both practices help wash out nitrogen. Do not add fertilizer.

Cloning gels are very popular because they keep root-inducing hormones evenly distributed along the subterranean stem.

Step Two: With a sharp blade, make a 45-degree cut across firm, healthy 0.125–0.25-inch-wide (3–6 mm) branches, two to four inches (3–5 cm) in length. Take care not to smash the end of the stem when making the cut. Trim off two or three sets of leaves and growth nodes so the stem can fit into the soil. There should be at least two sets of leaves above the soil line and one or two sets of trimmed nodes below ground. When cutting, make the slice halfway between the sets of nodes. Immediately place the cut end in water. Store cuttings in water while taking more.

Step Three: Rockwool and Oasis™ root cubes are convenient and easy to maintain and transplant. Fill small containers or nursery flats with coarse washed sand, fine vermiculite, soilless mix, or, if nothing else is available, fine potting soil. Saturate the substrate with water. Use an unsharpened pencil, chop stick, nail, etc., to make a hole in the rooting medium, a little larger than the stem. The hole should stop about one-half inch from the bottom of the container to allow for root growth.

Place a tray containing rooting cubes or

plugs into a standard nursery rooting flat. If none exists, make holes through three-fourths of the cube for cutting stems.

Fill rockwool tray with water, pH 5–6. Always use strong plastic trays.

Grow cuttings until they are well-rooted. Always remember to label cuttings when planting.

An aeroponics fogger system ensures humidity stays above 95 percent at the root zone, providing optimum conditions for root growth.

The fogger system fills an enclosed airspace with high humidity where the cuttings' roots dangle.

Step Four: Use a rooting hormone, and mix (if necessary) just before using. For liquids, use the dilution ratio for softwood cuttings. Swirl each cutting in the hormone solution for 5–15 seconds. Place the cutting in the hole in the rooting medium. Pack rooting medium gently around the stem. Gel and powder root hormones require no mixing. Dip stems in gels as per instructions or roll the stem in the powder. When planting, take special care to keep a solid layer of hormone gel or powder around the stem when gently packing soil into place.

Step Five: Lightly water until the surface is evenly moist. Keep cuttings moist at all times. Cuttings have no roots to bring water to leaves. Water arrives from leaves and the cut stem until roots can supply it. Water as needed to keep growing medium evenly moist. Do not let it get soggy.

Step Six: Cuttings root fastest with 18–24 hours of fluorescent light. If cuttings must be placed under an HID, set them on the perimeter of the garden so they receive less intense light; or shade them with a cloth or screen. A fluorescent tube

six inches above cuttings or a 400-watt metal halide lamp four to six feet away supplies the perfect amount of light for cuttings to root. Cool white fluorescents (or a combination of warm and cool white) are excellent for rooting.

Step Seven: Cuttings root fastest when humidity levels are 95–100 percent the first two days and gradually reduced to 80–85 percent during the following week. A humidity tent will help keep humidity high. Construct the tent out of plastic bags, rigid plastic, or glass. Remember to leave openings for air to flow in and out so little cuttings can breathe. If practical, mist cuttings several times a day as an alternative to the humidity tent. Remove any sick, rotting, or dead foliage.

Cut leaves in half to lower transpiration surface and to keep them from overlapping. Moisture that could foster fungus is often trapped between overlapping leaves. Keep the grow medium evenly moist so there is enough moisture to prevent cut leaves from bleeding out plant sugars that attract diseases.

95-100%

Best humidity range for taking cuttings is from 95 to 100%.

Roots/Air

	Roots		Air
80°			27°
75°			24°
65°			18°

The best temperature ranges for growing mediums are shown at right.

Above - Aeroponic systems grow cuttings with a profuse root system extremely fast.

Below - Growing cuttings and seedlings on shelves under fluorescent lamps is convenient and saves space.

Step Eight: Cuttings root faster when the growing medium is a few degrees warmer than the ambient air temperature. A warmer substrate increases underground chemical activity, and lower air temperature slows transpiration. For best results, keep the rooting medium at 75-80°F (24-27°C). Growing medium temperatures above 85°F (29°C) will cause damage. Keep the air temperature 5-10°F (3-5.5°C) cooler than the substrate. A warmer growing medium coupled with cooler ambient temperature slows diseases and conserves moisture. Misting cuttings with water also cools foliage and slows transpiration to help traumatized cuttings retain moisture unavailable from nonexistent roots.

Put cuttings in a warm place to adjust air temperature and use a heat pad, heating cables, or an incandescent light bulb below rooting cuttings.

Step Nine: Some cuttings may wilt but regain rigidity in a few days. Cuttings should look close to normal by the end of the week. Cuttings that are still wilted after seven days may root so slowly that they never catch up with others. Cull them, or put them back into the cutting chamber to grow more roots.

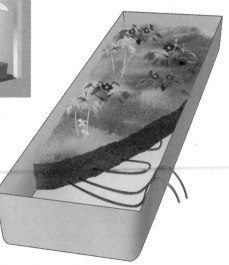

The cutting bed in a tray above is maintained with a subsoil drip system.

Step Ten: In one to three weeks, cuttings should be rooted. Signals they have rooted include yellow leaf tips, roots growing out drain holes, and vertical growth. To check for root growth in flats or pots, carefully remove the root ball and cutting to see if it has good root development. For best results, do not transplant cuttings until a dense root system is growing out the sides and bottom of rooting cubes.

To lower transpiration, snip cuttings' leaves in half before sticking.

An incandescent light bulb attached to a rheostat provides exacting control of bottom heat.

Strong cutting in an aeroponic cutting garden has a mass of roots and is ready to plant.

Cuttings are always strong and healthy-looking after you take them. After five or six days, leaves may start to change color. Leaves stay small and often turn a deeper shade of green. After about a week, lower leaves may start to yellow if their nutrient levels dissipate.

A week after being taken, cuttings' stems will develop stubby callused roots called primordia. The primordia are semi-transparent to white and should look healthy. Cuttings produce very little green growth during this process. Once the root and vascular transport system is in place and working properly, cuttings are able to experience explosive growth with the proper care.

These cuttings have been rooting for a week. The expert grower makes sure the climate is perfect.

Gardening Indoors

Rooting cuttings can handle increasingly more light as roots grow. Move the fluorescent lamps 2-4 inches (6-12 cm) above plants when roots form. Fertilize with a mild fertilizer solution when all cuttings have started vegetative growth.

Any sign of slime, pests, or disease means there are problems, and cuttings should be removed from the garden.

This mass of roots is from a cutting with a split stem; the outer layer of the stem was scraped away to expose the cambium.

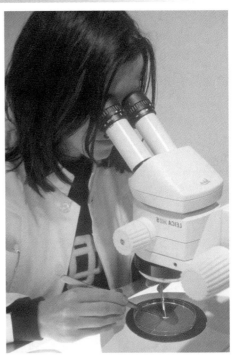

Making cuttings can also get very scientific. Here a scientist is removing the meristem of a "parent" plant to propagate it in an agar solution. Such cuttings are easy to maintain for long periods.

Plenty of roots are growing from this cutting rooted in a Jiffy cube. It is ready to transplant.

Transplant only the strongest, well-rooted cuttings (See "Transplanting"). Slow-rooting cuttings should be kept in the cutting chamber or culled out. Do not move cuttings below bright light until they have fully developed root systems. Once transplanted, cuttings are ready to harden-off (see "Transplanting").

Set up a vegetative pre-growing area that is lit with an HID or bright compact fluorescent lamp for the rooted cuttings. Place them in this area to let them grow for the first week or two of vegetation. This area needs to be just big enough to accommodate plants from the time they are a few inches tall until they are about

Sequence of cloning for sex

Make two cuttings.

Label each cutting.

12 hours

Give 12 hours of light while rooting.

Cuttings will determin sex within 2-3 weeks.

a foot tall and ready to be moved into the flowering room.

Gardeners with only one room root cuttings in a nursery flat and cover it with a light-tight cardboard box for 12 hours every night. To increase air circulation and ventilation, remove the cardboard box after the lights go out.

Cuttings from a Flowering Plant

You can take cuttings from a favorite flowering plant, but it is difficult. Cuttings will take longer to root, and results are not always the best. Powerful flowering hormones must be reversed, and rooting hormone signals must be sent. Now is the time to give plants 24 hours of light to signal them to grow.

Take cuttings from the lower green branch tips. Cut a one to two-inch-long (3–5 cm) stem. Trim off flowers and lower leaves. Keep two or three green leaves. If leaves have yellowed, survival chances diminish exponentially.

The earlier in the flowering stage cuttings are taken, the more rapid the rooting and the re-vegetation rate. Once a plant reaches the senescence point, growth hormones have dissipated, leaving not enough to initiate roots.

You can take cuttings from flowering plants and revert them to vegetative growth once rooted.

Storing Cuttings

To store cuttings for later use, wrap recently cut and trimmed stems in a damp cloth or paper towel. Put the wrapped cuttings into a plastic bag, and store in the refrigerator. On a daily basis, remove the water that condenses inside the bag in the cool refrigerator. Keep the temperature above 40°F (5°C). Temperatures below this level may cause plant cells to rupture. Cuttings should last in the refrigerator for about three weeks.

Clonex Root Matrix, a Growth Technology product, is a gel that allows cuttings to root and be held until they are needed.

To remove large plants from containers, use a knife or blade to separate roots from the inside of the container. Move the blade up and down all the way around the inside of the container to break roots away.

Transplanting

When plants are too big for their containers, they must be transplanted to continue rapid growth. Inhibited, cramped root systems grow sickly, stunted plants. Signs of rootbound plants include slow, sickly growth and branches that develop with more distance between limbs. Severely rootbound plants tend to grow straight up with few branches that stretch beyond the sides of the pot. To check for rootbound symptoms, remove a plant from its pot to see if roots are deeply matted on the bottom or surrounding the sides of the pot.

When growing short plants that reach full maturity in 90 days, there is little need for containers larger than three gallons (11 L). Large plants will need a large pot if they are kept for more than a few months.

Transplanting: Step-by-Step

Step One: Water cutting with half-strength *Trichoderma* bacteria Vitamin B$_1$, two days before transplanting.

Step Two: Fill the three-gallon (11 L) container with rich potting soil or soilless mix to within two inches (5 cm) of the top.

Step Three: Water growing medium with a mild, quarter-strength hydroponic fertilizer solution until saturated and solution drains freely out the bottom.

Step Four: Carefully remove the root ball from the container. Place your hand over top of container with the stem between your fingers; turn it upside down, and let root ball slip out of the pot into your hand. Take special care at this point to keep the root ball in one integral piece.

Step Five: Carefully place the root ball in the prepared hole in the three-gallon (11 L) container. Make sure all roots are growing down.

Step Six: Backfill around the root ball. Gently, but firmly, place soil into contact with the root ball.

Transplanting Seedlings

Mix the cutting dip, and use a rag to cover and contain soil when dipping.

Remove the cutting and shake off excess dip before transplanting.

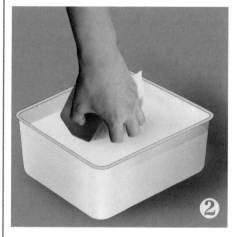

Submerge the entire cutting in the dip to ensure miticide covers all foliage.

Dip rooted cuttings into a miticidal/fungicidal solution before transplanting and before moving into the flowering room.

Mix a miticidal/fungicidal dip (I like Einstein Oil) to disinfect cuttings before sticking them in the growing medium. Fill a container with low pH water (5–6) and add a natural fungicide such as hydrogen peroxide in a two percent solution. Or include a ten percent mix of chlorine or vinegar. Do not mix vinegar and chlorine! The resulting gas is hazardous.

Step Seven: Water with half-strength fertilizer containing *Trichoderma* bacteria or Vitamin B$_1$. Soil should be saturated—not waterlogged—and drain freely. If rooting cube and new substrate are not identical, pay special attention to moisture levels. Let rockwool dry out enough that roots penetrate new growing medium in search of moisture.

Step Eight: Place new transplants on the perimeter of the HID garden or under a screen to subdue sunlight for a couple of days. Once transplants look strong, move them under full light.

Step Nine: Fertilize soilless mixes after transplanting with a complete hydroponic fertilizer that contains soluble chelated nutrients. New potting soil usually supplies enough nutrients for a couple of weeks before supplemental fertilization is necessary.

Step Ten: Seedlings and cuttings can also be transplanted directly into a three-to five-gallon (11–19 L) pot, a system which requires fewer containers and involves less work and less possible plant stress. The larger volume of soil holds water and nutrients longer and requires less frequent watering. When cuttings and seedlings are transplanted directly into a five-gallon (19 L) container, the roots grow down, out, and around the container walls and bottom. In fact, the majority of roots grow out of the soil and form a layer behind the container wall.

To encourage roots to develop a dense, compact system, transplant just before they have outgrown their container. Transplanting a well-rooted cutting in a root cube into a four-inch (10 cm) pot and transplanting the four-inch (10 cm) pot

Minimum Container Size	
Plant age	**Container size**
1–3 weeks	root cube
2–6 weeks	4-inch (10 cm) pot
6–8 weeks	2-gallon (7.5 L) pot
2–3 months	3-gallon (11 L) pot
3–8 months	5-gallon (19 L) pot
6–18 months	10-gallon (38 L) pot

into a three-gallon (11 L) pot or grow bag causes roots to develop a more extensive system in a small ball of growing medium. Successful transplanting causes minimal stress. Most warm-season annuals are in the ground for such a short time that bungled transplanting costs valuable recuperation time and loss in production.

Directly transplant cuttings and seedlings into raised beds and large planter boxes from four-inch (10 cm) pots. As many as 20 plants can be transplanted

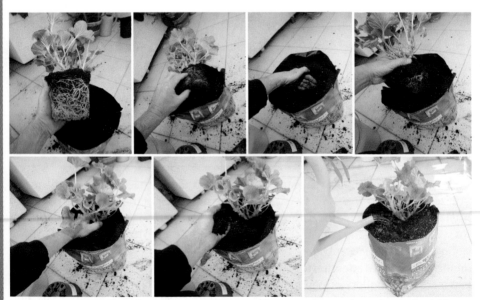

Carefully remove seedlings from containers. These seedlings were kept moist and moved quickly to minimize exposure to air and light. Growers used Vitamin B_1 solution to ease transplant shock.

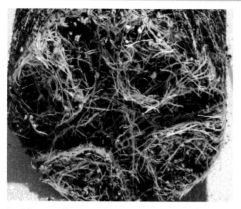

In this container, roots are growing mainly around the sides and along the bottom. This plant is ready to be transplanted.

Transplanting this cutting grown in rockwool into soil or soilless mix is simple and easy. Remove the rockwool's plastic covering before setting the cutting in a pre-made hole in substrate.

Hardening-off

Hardening-off is the process of toughening-up cuttings and seedlings. During the rooting process, leaves supplied much of the moisture for the cutting. Now, healthy white new roots are supplying moisture to the cutting. Check for root damage. Brown roots are rotting and lack oxygen. Thin hair-like dark roots are dried out. Once damaged, roots remain damaged. New roots must grow to replace damaged roots. Cull out any cuttings with damaged roots, because they will grow slowly. The protective wax coating must also grow back on leaves. It is best to acclimate rooted cuttings to the indoor garden over the course of a week. Gradually hardening-off cuttings will assure they suffer a minimum of stress and continue to grow rapidly.

These beautiful little seedlings were started indoors under a fluorescent lamp. The grower moves them outdoors for a few hours every day to harden-off and acclimate to the outdoor environment.

Harden off the strong ones, and introduce them to the real world—the indoor garden where they will see photosynthetically active response (PAR) at full value and nutrients that make their cells quiver. Now is the time to pre-grow cuttings before placing them into the flowering room.

Foliage loses its protective wax coating when it is pampered during the taking of cuttings, so it is very tender now. New roots must start to transport water via the stems to the leaves. The roots and moisture-transport system start to work on strong, healthy cuttings first. Cuttings that lag behind now should be tossed out, because they will always be slow. You can let them root longer and not transplant them until adequate roots develop.

Water cutting with half-strength Trichoderma bacteria Vitamin B$_1$, two days before transplanting.

Fill the container with rich potting soil or soilless mix to within two inches (5 cm) of the top.

Carefully remove the root ball from the container.

Transplanting Larger Plants

Carefully place the root ball in the prepared hole in the new pot.

Backfill around the root ball. Gently, but firmly, place soil into contact with root ball.

into a 24 × 24 × 12-inch (61 × 61 × 30 cm) planter, but six to twelve plants will yield about the same. Once plants start crowding and shading one another, bend stems outward and tie them to a trellis attached to the planter. Large planters require less maintenance. The larger mass of soil retains water and nutrients much longer and more evenly. One downside is that all plants must receive the same water and diet.

Gently remove a portion of the soil from the root ball. I like to remove the part in the center of the root ball where few roots reside.

This photo of a foot-long fibrous mass of roots was taken after the gardener shook off much of the semi-dry soil.

Once 30-40% of the soil has been removed, lay a base of fresh soil in the bottom of the container and fit remaining root ball on top of it. Fill the container with fresh potting soil and gently pack in place. After transplanting, water heavily with a Vitamin B1 solution.

Three-gallon (11 L) containers are the ideal size for two- to three-foot-tall (60–90 cm) plants. Larger pots are usually unnecessary because plants grow no longer than a week or two in the vegetative stage and six to ten weeks flowering. Smaller three-gallon (11 L) pots are easy to move and handle. Roots also grow less during flowering. By the time a plant is potbound, it is ready to harvest. I used to recommend up to a five-gallon (19 L) container for plants that are harvested after 90 total days of life. I now believe this is a waste. While the smaller containers require daily watering, they produce harvests comparable to those of five-gallon (19 L) containers.

Some plants are much larger, grow longer, and can require containers up to

30 gallons (115 L) in size. However, larger plants grow quite well in five or ten-gallon (19–38 L) hydroponic containers for a year or longer. If you plan to keep a mother plant for more than a few months, grow it hydroponically in its own container for best results.

Pruning and Bending

Pruning and bending a plant redirects growth hormones. Pruning affects the plant more drastically than bending. Selective pruning and bending allow us to manipulate auxin hormone levels in branch and flower tips. Removing or bending a branch or branch tip causes hormonal balances to shift. Cutting the plant's meristem (top growth tip) will diffuse auxins and cause greater concentrations in lower branch tips. Bending a growing tip changes hormone concentrations less than pruning.

Pruning

Always use clean instruments when pruning. A straight razor, single-edge razor blade, a sharp pair of pruners, or a pair of scissors all work well. Between cuts, sanitize clippers and blades by dipping in rubbing alcohol. Use indoor pruners only in the indoor garden. Pruners used outdoors have everything from spider mites to fungus spores on them. If outdoor clippers must be used, dip in rubbing alcohol to sterilize before making cuts.

After pruning, the open wound invites diseases and pests. Wash your hands and tools before and after pruning. Make cuts at a 45-degree angle to discourage moisture from sitting on wounds.

Avoid pruning up to a month before inducing flowering. Since pruning diffuses floral hormones, flowering is retarded. If

There are a few basic techniques to pruning warm-season annuals, including:

Prune off the top of the plant below the first set or two of branches to drive hormones to lower branches. Pruning off more of the main stem will increase the effect.

Prune off the tip of plants to diffuse hormones and make lower branches grow more.

Prune the tips of all branches except the main tip to make plants tall.

Remove lower branches that do not receive light. Plants will direct energy into growing tips.

heavily pruned shortly before flowering, peak maturation is delayed for a week or longer. It takes a month or longer for hormones to build up to pre-pruning concentrations.

Pruned plants often seal themselves, but problems can still arise when there is an appealing opening for pests.

Pruning off all lower branches makes inspecting irrigation fittings easy and diminishes problems associated with weak growth.

Remove spindly branches and growth that is not collecting light energy, including dead and dying leaves. Pruning lower branches concentrates auxins in upper branches which forces growth upward. Cut lower branches off cleanly at the stem so no stub is left to rot and attract pests and diseases.

Pruning out spindly branches and growth inside plants opens up the interior and provides more and better air circulation. It also allows light to reach deeper inside plants.

Not pruning has several advantages. Floral hormones are allowed to concentrate in tips of branches causing flowers to grow stronger and bigger. Unpruned plants are crammed into a small area. Crowded plants have less space to bush out laterally and tend to grow more upright. Cuttings are set into the flowering room after 1–30 days in the vegetative room. All the little cuttings are packed tightly together in three-gallon pots. Each one of the plants is taking up the minimum amount of space for the minimum amount of time to produce the maximum harvest of vegetables or flowers.

Most successful gardeners do not prune at all, especially if growing a short cutting crop that is only two to three feet (61–91 cm) tall. Short cutting crops require no pruning to increase light to bottom leaves or to alter their profile. "No pruning" is the easiest and most productive method when growing short crops.

Pinching back or pruning branch tips causes the two growing shoots just below the cut to grow stronger and bigger. This increases the number of main branches. Pruning branch tips also diffuses floral hormones. These hormones (auxins) prevent the lateral buds from growing very fast. All lower branches develop more rapidly when the terminal bud is removed. The further a branch is from hormones at the plant tip, the less effect the auxins have.

To pinch back a branch tip, simply snip it off below the last set or two of leaves. Pinching off tender growth with your fingers helps seal the wound and is often less damaging to plants than cutting. When the main stem is pinched back, side and lower growth is stimulated. When all the branch tips are pinched back, lower growth is encouraged. Continually pinching back, as when taking cuttings from a mother, causes many more little branches to form below the pruned tips. Eventually, the plant is transformed into a hedge-like shape.

Floral hormones are concentrated in four main branches.

Pruning all the branches or removing more than 20 percent of the foliage in a short time frame stresses plants too much and diminishes harvest. But if taking cuttings, some gardeners effectively prune a mother down to stubby branches and let her recuperate for a month or longer.

Pruning too much over time may alter hormonal concentrations, causing spindly growth. This is often the case with mother plants that provide too many cuttings. The mother must rest and gain girth, because small, spindly branches root poorly.

Tomatoes benefit from removing all but the four main branches. The meristem (central stem) is removed just above the four lowest (main) branches. Removing the central leader concentrates the floral hormones in the four remaining branches. Fewer branches are stronger and bear a larger quantity of dense, heavy flowers and fruit. Remove the stem above the four main branches; do not remove leaves on the main branches. Select plants with three sets of branch nodes about six weeks old and pinch or prune out the last set of nodes so that two sets of branches remain. Move plants into the flowering room when they are about 12 inches (30 cm) tall.

Bending

Bending is similar to pruning, in that it alters the flow of hormones. Bending efficiently neutralizes the effect of the growth-inhibiting hormone. Bending is much easier on plants than pruning. To bend, lean a branch in the desired direction and tie it in place. Branches can take a lot of bending before they fold over or break. If a branch folds, tie it in place; if necessary, use a wooden splint. The stem will heal itself. Young, supple branches take bending much better than old, stiff ones. Bending branches horizontally encourages small branches to grow vertically toward the light. A wooden planter box with a lattice trellis alongside makes a great anchor to tie bent plants to.

Wire ties, the kind used to close bread sacks, can be purchased at a nursery. Wire ties are either precut or cut to length by the gardener. Plastic-coated electronic and telephone cable wires also work well. They are fastened with a simple twist and stay rigid, leaving the stem breathing room. But if applied too tightly around a stem, the liquids cannot flow, and death could result.

This plant is growing healthily upward, thanks to its supporting trellis.

Be gentle when bending, even though some plants can take much abuse. Sometimes a crotch will separate or a branch will fold over, cutting off fluid flow. These mishaps are easily fixed with a small wooden splint snugly secured with wire ties or duct tape to support the split and broken stem.

Gardeners also combine bending and pruning. It is easy to prune too much, but it is hard to over bend.

Bending plants will give them a low, inconspicuous profile.

Air Pruning Roots

When roots grow to the end of the container and are exposed to air, they stop growing. The air naturally prunes roots. They cannot grow out the end of the pot, because the climate with little moisture and lots of air is too inhospitable.

Root Pruning

Root pruning could be necessary to give new life to potbound plants outdoors or in greenhouses. Removing roots will not make plants grow faster; in fact, it will slow growth for about two weeks. Once new roots start to grow, growth rebounds. About midsummer, root-prune plants that must stay in the same size container. Root pruning will keep plants manageable and much easier to maintain.

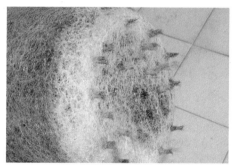

Roots on these cuttings grew through the drainage holes. Once they hit the air, growth stops. Roots are "air pruned." The roots in this potbound plant form a mass around the interior and bottom of the container. Roots that grow out drainage holes are "pruned" when they come into contact with air. This plant needs repotting.

Chemical Root Pruning

Chemical root pruning is an excellent way to control root growth inside containers. Commercial nursery people have been using chemical root pruning for many years with outstanding results. A product called Griffin's Spin-Out consists of copper hydroxide suspended in a carrier. To use, simply spray-paint the inside of the containers with two coats of Griffin's Spin-Out. Roots grow to within a fraction of an inch of the copper hydroxide, then stop and turn! Roots will not touch the unpleasant compound. The result is similar to what happens aboveground when new, lower growth is stimulated as branch tips are pruned. When pruned with copper hydroxide paint, more roots develop overall, and they grow in the entire root ball, especially in the center. Plants with a dense root system dispersed evenly throughout the root ball are easier to maintain, and they grow bigger in smaller containers.

Above left: This close-up of a root ball shows a spot scraped away with roots behind. This demonstrates that the roots will not grow into the copper hydroxide coating.
Above right: The insides of these pots have been painted with Griffin's Spin-Out containing copper hydroxide to prune roots.

Stress

Plants grow best and produce heaviest when given a stable environment. Stressed plants produce less than unstressed plants. Stress-induced traumas include withholding water, photoperiod fluctuation, low light intensity, ultraviolet light, nutrient toxicities and deficiencies, cold and hot soil, ambient temperatures, and mutilation. In addition, any overt applications of growth hormones such as B_9 hormone, gibberellins, cytokinins, abscisic acid, ethylene, etc., cause stress.

Removing large green shade leaves allows more light to shine on smaller leaves, but it also causes growth to slow and harvest to diminish. Remove only leaves that are more than half damaged by pests or diseases. Often, partially yellow leaves green up once stress is eliminated. Removing spindly, dimly lit lower branches stresses plants much less than removing leaves to speed growth of upper foliage.

Mutilating plants by breaking the trunk, driving a stake through the trunk, torturing or slapping them around might increase production, but most often the stress retards growth and causes other problems. Withholding water may also impair growth and diminish leaf, stem, and flower production. Water stress slows or stops cuttings from rooting. If cuttings have too many leaves and are too busy transpiring, root growth is very slow. Conversely, waterlogged rooting mediums harbor no air, and rooting is slowed to a crawl.

Stressed plants with wounded stems and vegetation grow slower and invite pests and diseases.

This beautiful orchid was on display at one of the many flower & garden shows held every year.

Poinsettias are easy to force into flowering with a 12/12 day/night light schedule.

Impress your friends by inducing Christmas cactuses to flower in the middle of summer with a 12-hour photoperiod.

Carnations grow well in containers and are a good example of long-day plants.

Introduction

In order for a plant to complete its annual lifecycle successfully, it must first flower. Dioecious plants are either male (pollen producing) or female (ovule producing). Hermaphrodite plants are bisexual, with both male and female flowers on the same plant. Most plants fall into the latter category. When dioecious plants turn hermaphrodite, any resulting seeds are usually female.

When a plant is fertilized, one of the many tiny grains of pollen from the male (staminate) flower pod lands on a pistil of the female (pistillate) flower. Each calyx harbors an ovule and a set of pistils. Actual fertilization takes place when the grain of male pollen slides down the pistil and unites with the female ovule, deep within the calyx. Once fertilization takes place, a seed will form within the calyx or seed bract. Seeds are the result of this sexual propagation and contain genetic characteristics of both parents.

Long-day plants

In nature, annual plants' lifecycle ends in the fall, after the long, hot days of summer. The long nights and short days of autumn signal long-day plants to start the flowering stage. Growth patterns and chemistry change. Stems elongate and flower formation is rapid at first then slows. All this causes new nutrient needs. Attention is now focused on flower and fruit production, rather than on leafy vegetative growth. Production of chlorophyll, requiring much nitrogen, slows. Phosphorus uptake increases to promote floral formation. Light needs change as well. During autumn, in most climates, the sun takes on a slightly reddish appearance, emitting a light that

Grow poppies indoors or under cover to protect the delicate flowers from harsh wind and rain.

Stigma

Style

Anther

Filament

The filament and anther are part of the male stamen. The stigma and style are part of the female flower parts.

Fuchsias bloom year-round indoors under lights.

Watch your flowers open all year round!

Succulent Mesembryanthemum *flower!*

Tropical anthurium flowers last forever when grown indoors.

Create a perfect tropical environment indoors for Lady's Slipper (Paphiopedilum) *orchids.*

Lavender-color geraniums are beautiful and sensual.

Growing orchids is easy when you can control all the factors that influence growth.

Hydrangeas can be moved outdoors when they get too big for the indoor garden.

is a more red than white. The harvest sun phenomenon is not fully understood. However, experiments have proved that by increasing the amount of red light during flowering, floral hormones are stimulated and flower yield increases substantially. Indoor gardeners switch from halide to HP sodium lamps to simulate the color spectrum of the harvest sun.

During summer, sunlight moves through only one or two atmospheres of air. Blue sky (sky color) is dominant. In the fall, the sun is low on the horizon and light goes through four to five atmospheres of air, blocking out much of the blue light. This is also why sunrises and sunsets are red.

Indoors, flowering may be induced in short-day plants just as it is in nature, by shortening the photoperiod from 18 to 12 hours. Once the days are changed to 12 hours, flowers should be clearly visible within one to three weeks. In fact, some gardeners have two garden rooms: a vegetative garden room with one metal halide that supplies 18 hours of light. The other room for growing short-day plants has both a halide and an HP sodium that is on for 12 hours a day.

Using this combination of rooms and lamps, the electricity bill remains relatively low, and the horticulturist has the luxury of having both summer and fall every day of the year!

The harvest sun is simulated one of three ways: (1) Adding an HP sodium lamp to a garden room already containing a metal halide. This more than doubles the available light, especially in the red end of the spectrum. The halide maintains blues in the spectrum necessary for continued chlorophyll production. (2) Replacing the halide with an HP sodium. This increases the reds, but cuts the blues. A result of this practice has been more yellowing of vegetative leaves due to lack of chlorophyll production and more stem elongation than if the halide were present. (3) Adding or changing to a phosphor-coated halide. Not only are these halides easier on the eyes, their coating makes them produce a little bit more red in their spectrum, thus promoting flowering.

Spray-N-Grow causes plants to produce more blossoms and set more fruit.

Water needs of a flowering plant are somewhat less than in the vegetative stage. Adequate water during flowering is important to carry on the plant's chemistry. Withholding water to stress a plant will actually stunt growth and diminish the yield.

Hermaphrodites

A hermaphrodite is a plant that has both male and female flowers on the same plant. The majority of plants fall into this category.

The outdoor environment is manufactured indoors, and the normal life cycle of any plant can be altered. Creating summer in December, taking cuttings, prolonging the life cycle, and leaching the soil—all the wonderful things we are able to do indoors—slightly confuses even the strongest plant. When this stress is coupled with weak seeds, the outcome is uncertain. High humidity, over-pruning, and old age seem to promote hermaphrodites more than other environmental factors. In short, if a plant starts to go sour and you do not know why, it could be because it was stressed too much.

Seed Crops

Seed crops are harvested when the seeds are mature. Often, seeds may actually split open their containing calyx or seedpod. The flower grows many ready, receptive calyxes until pollination occurs. Seeds are normally mature within six to eight weeks. Watch out for fungus that might attack the weakening flower and cache of ripe seeds.

When seeds are mature, remove them from the pods and store them in a cool, dry place. The seeds are viable and ready for planting as soon as they are harvested, but they may grow sickly plants. Let the seeds dry out a few months before planting. Dry seeds will produce much healthier plants and the germination rate will be higher.

Life Cycle

Warm-season annuals must flower and produce seeds to complete their annual life cycle successfully.

In nature, long-day plants flower in the fall, after the long, hot days of summer. The long nights and short days of autumn signal plants to start flowering. Growth patterns and chemistry change during flowering: stems elongate; leaves grow progressively fewer blades; and flower formation is rapid at first then slows. Nutrient needs change as growth stages change. Plants focus on flower production rather than

White frilly poppies are one of the author's favorites!

vegetative growth. Green chlorophyll production, requiring much nitrogen, slows. Phosphorus and potassium uptake increase to promote floral formation. Shortly before the flowering stage, gardeners change to a "super bloom" fertilizer formula with less nitrogen and more potassium and phosphorus.

Induce flowering in greenhouses, outdoors, and indoors by giving long-day plants more hours of total darkness and fewer hours of light. Give them 12 hours of uninterrupted darkness and 12 hours of light to induce visible signs of flowering in two weeks or less. This program is effective in all but the latest blooming. Gardeners with a vegetative room illuminated 18–24 hours a day and a flowering room with 12-hour days and 12-hour nights, create environments that mimic the photoperiod in summer and fall. With this simple combination, gardeners crank out crops of outstanding vegetables and flowers every six to ten weeks all year long.

Grains of pollen are miniscule. This close-up of a grain of male pollen is magnified 4000 times. It was captured on a scanning electron microscope.

Water intake of flowering plants is usually somewhat less than in the vegetative stage. Adequate water during flowering is important for plants to carry on internal chemistry and production. Withholding water to "stress" a plant will actually stunt growth and diminish yield.

Removing large fan leaves to allow more intense light to reach small buds or to stress plants is crazy! Large leaves are necessary to keep plants healthy. Indoors and in greenhouses where the hours of darkness are controlled, some plants flower for six to ten weeks or longer. This is a very short time. Hacking off branch tips to initiate more budding sites diffuses floral hormones and retards growth. Remove only leaves that are more than 50 percent damaged by diseases, pests, and cultural practices.

Upon pollination, one of the many, tiny grains of pollen from the male (staminate) flower pod, lands on a pistil of the female (pistillate) flower. Actual fertilization takes place when the grain of male pollen slides down the pistil and unites with the female ovule deep within the female calyx. Once fertilization takes place, pistils turn brown and a seed forms within the seed bract. Seeds are the result of this sexual propagation and contain genetic characteristics of both parents. In nature, there is a 50/50 chance for a seed to produce a male or female plant. Once fertilized with male pollen, female plants put the bulk of their energy into producing strong, viable seeds. When flowers are full of ripe, mature seeds, the female will die, having successfully completed her life cycle. The male completes his life cycle and dies after producing and dispersing all of his pollen into the wind, in search of receptive female pistils.

Lilies come in many colors and are very easy to grow.

Grow tropical bougainvilleas indoors during the cool months and move them outdoors when weather permits.

Cyclamens bloom best when the temperature is about 55°F (13°C). Grow them in a cool greenhouse and move them outdoors in the spring.

Edible tuberous begonia flowers have a mild citrus flavor. They bloom profusely under lights!

A bountiful crop of Roma Tomatoes is easily grown indoors with lights.

Introduction

The payoff for all the research, work, expense, and the long, patient wait is a bountiful harvest. Strong, healthy, well-grown cuttings and seedlings yield the heaviest harvests. A well-organized pre-harvest and harvest are essential to preserve produce quality and decrease the workload.

Harvest when plants or fruits are at peak ripeness. Harvest timing is critical. The peak harvest window is open for about five to seven days.

Avoid the taste of organic or chemical fertilizers in harvested vegetables and herbs by flushing with plain water or a clearing solution to remove any residuals and chemicals that have built up in soil or plant foliage. Ten to fourteen days before harvesting, flush the garden with distilled water or water treated with reverse osmosis. Use a clearing solution such as Final Flush® if you have to use plain tap water that contains dissolved solids. Some gardeners fertilize until three to four days before harvest and use a clearing solution to remove fertilizer residues. Apply this water just as you would apply nutrient solution. Always let at least ten percent, preferably more, drain out the bottom of containers. If using a recirculating hydroponic system, change the water after the first four to six days of application. Continue to top off the reservoir with "clean" water.

If growing herbs that will be dried, do not water for one or two days before harvest. The soil should be fairly dry, but not dry enough that plants wilt. This will speed drying time by a day or more and not affect the quality of the end product.

Harvest

Growth stops at harvest. Avoid prolonged periods of light, temperatures above 80°F (27°C), friction from fondling hands, and damp, humid conditions.

This crop of Hungarian Wax Peppers is just starting to bear fruit.

Fresh squash is very easy to grow indoors and yields prolifically.

Harvest long thin-skin cucumbers and sweet eggplant all year round.

Hydroponically grown grapes from Chile.

"Pimientos del Padrón" recently harvested from a hydroponic garden.

Enjoy crops of big green peppers all year round with a hydroponic garden.

Produce from Floriade in the Netherlands, a showcase of high technology for growers.

Spain produces vast quantities of hydroponic lettuces and other foods.

Imagine growing fresh thick-wall red peppers like this in your hydroponic garden.

Gardening Indoors

Bountiful food crops will soon be yours when you start gardening indoors. Just imagine the tasty food you can create at home, instead of paying for it in the grocery.

Easy to grow herbs, chiles, and other exotics are good cash crops from your indoor garden. Grow food and flowers for fun and profit!

This water-cooled lamp is radiating virtually no heat into the indoor garden above. A small electric pump is submerged in a reservoir, and pumps water through a glass enclosure around the bulb, carrying away the heat. You can touch the glass and feel that it is barely warm.

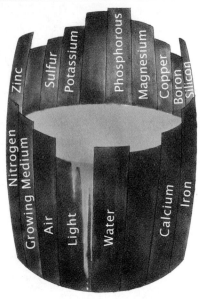

This barrel full of water shows that plants will grow only as fast as their most limiting factor. Light is most often the factor that limits growth indoors.

Air	20%
Temperature	
Humidity	
CO_2 and O_2 content	
Light	20%
Spectrum (color)	
Intensity	
Photoperiod (hours of light per day)	
Water	20%
Temperature	
pH	
EC	
Oxygen content	
Nutrients	20%
Composition	
Purity	
Growing Medium	20%
Air content	
Moisture content	

Introduction

The best location for an indoor garden is in an obscure corner of a basement, where the temperature is easy to keep constant year round. Basements are well insulated by concrete walls and soil. A basement room can be enclosed and out of the way.

Outbuildings, garages, and barns not attached to homes can be some of the worst places for indoor gardens.

Although less common, there are even indoor gardens on wheels! Some innovative gardeners have remodeled trailer houses and buses into indoor gardens.

The indoor garden's size determines the size and the number of lamps. High intensity discharge (HID) lamps that work well to grow warm-season annuals are available in wattages of 150, 175, 250, 400, 600, 1000, and 1100. Smaller wattages from 150–400 work well in closets or spaces with 9–21 square feet (0.8–2 m²) of floor space. Use 600-watt and larger bulbs for larger areas.

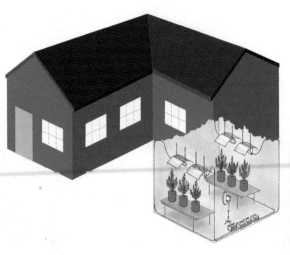

This cutaway basement garden shows a real scenario. Plants on tables stay warmer and are easy to maintain.

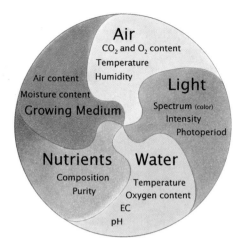

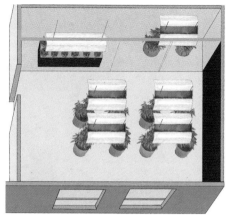

This indoor setup has a big flowering room, a vegetative room, and a cutting chamber.

The drawings show several indoor garden floor plans. As the floor plans demonstrate, there are several basic approaches to indoor garden design and production. Most gardeners start out with a crop grown in a single room. After they harvest the crop, they introduce a new batch of cuttings, switch the photoperiod back to 18 hours, and the cycle continues.

The most productive setups utilize two rooms. The first room is for vegetative growth, and rooting cuttings. This room should be about one-quarter the size of the flowering room. When the flowering room crop is harvested, plants from the vegetative room are moved into the flowering room.

Super productivity is achieved with a perpetual crop. Several cuttings are taken every day or every week. Every day a few plants are harvested. For every plant harvested, a new cutting takes its place.

The productive indoor garden shown below is located in a closed-off corner of the basement.

Gardening Indoors

Take a little time to set up your indoor garden so all the space is used efficiently.

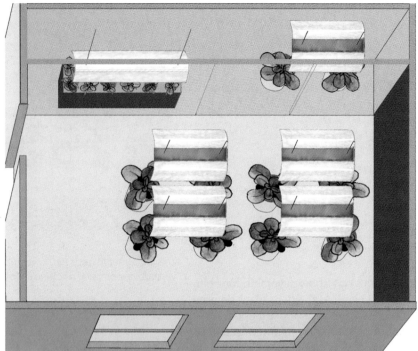

This closet garden has everything necessary to grow a crop—lights, fans, and plants! A 400-watt HID lights the 3 × 4- foot (90 × 120 cm) flowering room above, and two 55-watt CFLs in one reflector illuminate cuttings in this perpetual harvest setup.

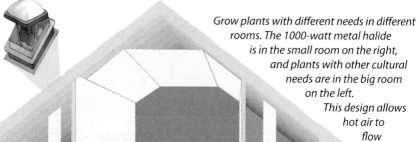

Grow plants with different needs in different rooms. The 1000-watt metal halide is in the small room on the right, and plants with other cultural needs are in the big room on the left. This design allows hot air to flow upward before being evacuated via roof fans. The attic is used as a heat buffer in hot climates.

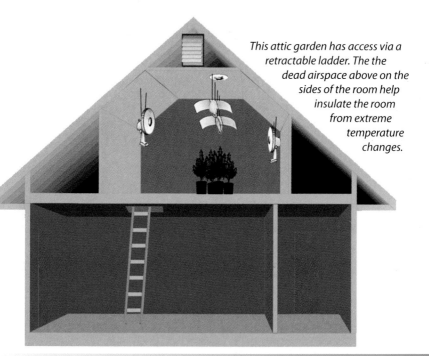

This attic garden has access via a retractable ladder. The the dead airspace above on the sides of the room help insulate the room from extreme temperature changes.

Weekly Checklist

Check the following to see if they function properly:

Air ventilation

Air circulation

Humidity: 40–50 percent

Temperature: day 70–75°F (21–24°C); night 55–60°F (13–16°C)

Soil moisture (dry pockets) water as needed

Cultivate soil surface

Check pH

Rotate (turn) plants

Check for spider mites under leaves

Check for fungi

Check for nutrient deficiencies

Regular fertilization schedule

Check HID system for excessive heat at plug-in, timer, ballast, and near ceiling

Cleanup!

Cleanup!

Cleanup!

Check walls and ceiling for mold

Move lamp up, 12–36 inches above plants

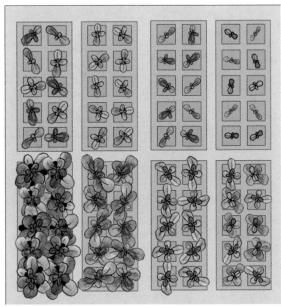

In this simple layout, there are ten plants in each tray (80 total plants) illuminated by a single 1000-watt HID. Each week one tray of ten plants is harvested, and ten new plants are started.

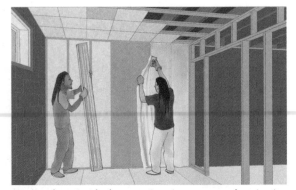

Keeping heat inside the room is as important as keeping it out! Insulation will keep heat out, and the heat generated inside the room will be easy to control.

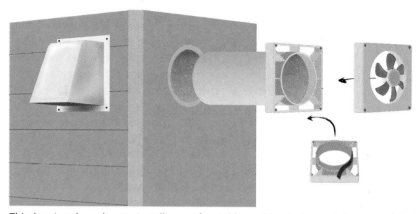

This drawing shows how to install a vent fan. Adding rubber feet or padding around the fan will dampen noise.

Setting Up the Indoor Garden – Step-by-Step

Set up the indoor garden before introducing plants. Construction requires space and planning. An indoor garden under construction offers a terrible environment for plants. Once the garden is set up and operational, it will be ready for plants.

Step One: Choose an out-of-the-way space with little or no traffic. A corner of the basement or a spare bedroom is perfect. A 1000-watt HID, properly set up, will efficiently illuminate up to a 6 × 6-foot (1.8 × 1.8 m) room. The ceiling should be at least five feet (1.5 m) high. Keep in mind that plants in containers are set up at least one foot (30 cm) off the ground, and the lamp needs about a foot (30 cm) of space to hang from the ceiling. This leaves only three feet (90 cm) of space for plants to grow. If forced to grow in an attic or basement with a low four-foot (120 cm) ceiling, much can be done to compensate for the loss of height, including taking cuttings, bending, pruning, and using smaller wattage lamps.

Step Two: Enclose the room, if not already enclosed. Remove everything that does not pertain to the garden. Furniture, drapes, and curtains may harbor fungi. An enclosed room allows easy, precise control of everything and everyone that enters or exits, as well as what goes on inside. For most gardeners, enclosing the indoor garden is simply a matter of tacking up some plywood or fabricating plastic walls in the basement or attic and painting the room flat white.

Step Three: Cover walls, ceiling, floor—everything—with a highly reflective material like flat white paint or Mylar. The more reflection, the more light energy available to plants. Good reflective light will allow effective coverage of an HID lamp to increase from 10 to 20 percent, just by putting a few dollars worth of paint on the walls. Reflective white Visqueen® plastic is inexpensive and protects walls and floors.

Step Four: See "Setting Up the Vent Fan" in Chapter Eleven. Constant air circulation and a supply of fresh air are essential but often inadequate. There should be at least one fresh-air vent in every indoor garden. Vents can be an open door, window, or duct vented to the outside. An exhaust fan vented outdoors or pulling new air through an open door usually creates an adequate flow of air. An oscillating fan works well to circulate air. When installing such a fan, make sure it is not set in a fixed position and blowing too hard on tender plants. It could cause windburn and dry out plants, especially seedlings and cuttings. If the room contains a heat vent, it may be opened to supply extra heat or air circulation.

Step Five: The larger your garden becomes, the more water it will need. A 10 × 10-foot (3 × 3 m) garden could use more than 50 gallons (190 L) per week. Carrying water is hard, regular work. One gallon (3.8 L) of water weighs eight pounds (3.6 kg); 50 × 8 = 400 pounds (180 kg) of water a week! It is much easier to run in a hose with an on/off valve or install a hose bib in the room than to schlep water. A three-foot (90 cm) watering wand attached to the hose on/off valve makes watering easier and saves branches from being broken when watering in dense foliage. Hook up the hose to a hot- and cold-water source so the temperature is easy to regulate.

Step Six: Ideally, the floor should be concrete or a smooth surface that can be swept and washed down. A floor drain is very handy. In indoor gardens with carpet or wood floors, a large, white painter's drop cloth or thick, white Visqueen plastic will protect floors from moisture. Trays placed beneath each container add protection and convenience.

Step Seven: Mount a hook strong enough to support 30 pounds (14 kg) for each lamp. Attach an adjustable chain or cord and pulley between the ceiling hook and the lamp fixture. The adjustable connection makes it easy to keep the lamp at the proper distance from plants and up out of the way during maintenance.

Step Eight: There are some tools an indoor gardener must have and a few extra tools that make indoor horticulture more precise and cost effective. The extra tools help make the garden so efficient that they pay for themselves in a few weeks. Procure all the tools before bringing plants into the room. If the tools are there when needed, chances are they will be put to use. A hygrometer is a good example. If plants show signs of slow, sickly growth due to high humidity, most gardeners will not identify the exact cause right away. They will wait and guess, wait and guess, and maybe figure it out before a fungus attacks and the plant dies. When a hygrometer is installed before plants are brought into the indoor garden, the horticulturist will know from the start when the humidity is too high and causing sickly growth.

Step Nine: Read and complete: "Setting Up the HID Lamp" at the end of Chapter Seven.

Step Ten: Move seedlings and rooted cuttings into the room. Huddle them closely together under the lamp. Make sure the HID is not so close to small plants that it burns their leaves. Position 400-watt lamps 18 inches (45 cm) above seedlings and cuttings. Place a 600-watt lamp 24 inches (60 cm) away and a 1000-watt lamp 30 inches (75 cm) away. Check the distance daily. Hang a precut string from the hood to measure distance.

Indoor Garden Checklist

A checklist helps gardeners know what to do and when to prepare to do it, adding necessary routine to the indoor gardening process. The weekly checklist consists of a few things that must be done every week to ensure a successful crop.

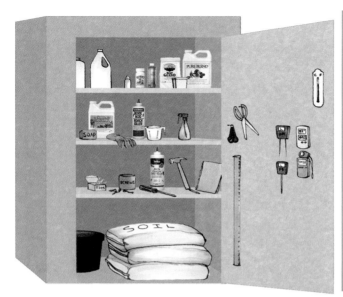

Necessary Tools:

Thermometer

Spray bottle

pH tester

Liquid biodegradable soap

Hygrometer

Pruners or scissors

Wire ties

Sheetrock screws

Screwdriver

Measuring cup and spoons

Pencil and notebook

Moisture meter

Light meter

Yardstick to measure growth!

Savvy gardeners read and consider each and every point on the checklist weekly. They mark each point with a check when finished with it.

Indoor gardeners should spend at least ten minutes per day, per lamp, to have a productive garden. This is enough time to complete all the stuff on the weekly checklist. Much of gardening is simply watching and paying attention, but it takes time to have a decent, productive garden. If using CO_2 enrichment or hydroponics, allow 20 minutes per day for maintenance.

Large chunks of time will be spent setting up the indoor garden and harvesting. These are not included in the 10–20 minute daily schedule.

Greenhouses and Cold Frames

This simple overview of greenhouses and cold frames will give you a feeling of what to look for and how to plan your project and reap a heavy harvest.

Greenhouses, cold frames, and hot frames are all useful in extending the growing season and/or protecting new plants and seedlings. Which type of structure you select depends on the size and location of your growing area, how much money you have to spend, and how much time you have to grow. Simple cold frames and hot frames can be assembled from common materials like old, framed windowpanes and hay bales. Greenhouses are generally larger and more complex. They can be expensive to build and maintain but offer more flexibility for growing time and building use.

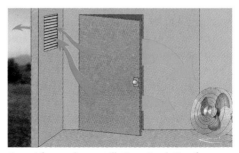

A vent fan and an oscillating circulation fan are essential to maintain a healthy environment.

A watering can works well in small gardens and to apply small amounts of fertilizer.

It is easy to rig a submersible pump in your water reservoir, and then run a hose from it to water your plants as needed.

When deciding on a growing structure, first carefully analyze the project on paper. Consider how much space you have for the footprint and how many plants you can grow safely. Cold frames are small and can be as simple as a glass or plastic frame set on the ground with no artificial heat source. Their basic function is to protect young plants and seedlings from wind and cold in the early spring, but they can also be blacked out to induce early flowering and harvest. Hot frames are similar in size and structure but provide heat through manure, electricity, steam, or a hot-water pipe (radiant heat). You may use a hot frame to raise early seedlings and cuttings, after which the structure can be converted into a cold frame. Both frames share the advantages of economy, simplicity, small size, and portability.

Both large and small greenhouses cost more money, time, and space. With the exception of the lightweight "hoop" house or miniature greenhouse, they are also more permanent. The type of greenhouse selected will be determined by its location and the planned use of the space. A lean-to or attached greenhouse will probably be smaller and less expensive to build than a freestanding structure.

Total area of the greenhouse is determined by the number of plants you intend to grow. Allow one square yard (90 cm^2) per mature plant. Do not forget to allow about six inches (15 cm) space for air circulation between benches and sidewalls. Add space for walkways—standing room only or room for a wheelbarrow—and possibly a center bench. Glass, plastic panels, and sheeting all come in standard widths, and it is easier to build in a size compatible with these units rather than have to cut the panels down. For example, an eight-foot (2.4 m) house can be made with two 48-inch (120 cm) wide fiberglass panels. Center height depends on the level of the eaves. Low growing plants can take an eave of five feet (1.5 m); tall plants need six or seven feet (1.8 or 2.1 m). After determining eave height, a simple formula will give you the center height: Center height = eave + 0.25 width. A twelve-foot wide (3.6 m) house with a five-foot (1.5 m) eave will have a center height of eight feet (2.4 m).

Budget and building skills will weigh heavily in the decision-making process. The

Common backyard greenhouses

least expensive structure per square foot (m^2) is an even-span 16-foot (4.8 m) wide that will house two side-beds or benches, two walks, and a wide center-bed or bench. An eight to twelve foot (2.4 to 3.6 m) wide lean-to with wide beds or benches and a central walk is the least expensive option overall. Whichever option you choose, building it yourself will be cheaper than hiring a contractor. You can purchase many of the plumbing and electricity installations in kits or pre-assembled. Here is an excellent web site for the do-it-yourselfer: http://www.charleysgreenhouse.com. Or, consider a kit: http://www.greenhousekit. com/frame.htm.

Climate will play a role in choosing your greenhouse. For example, a cold frame in the mild Pacific Northwest can give you a six-week jump on the growing season. This would not work in a colder region like the upper Midwest. Likewise, a hot or tropical area will require more shade and water. While the large cold frame is the most economical of structures, it will not function as a cold-climate garden. Location and exposure will depend on climate, but in general, you will want the greenhouse to be sheltered from strong winds and to be away from any areas where falling limbs or other debris might be a problem. There are a number of external design options. Cold frames can be as simple as a window sash laid over a rectangle of straw bales or a piece of plastic stretched over a metal or PVC pipe frame and held in place with clamps. Duct tape also works wonders to keep plastic in place. The advantage to plastic sheeting is that it can be removed during the day to take advantage of fresh air and the sun's warmth and then be replaced at night to protect plants from cold air. The cold frame can be easily converted to a hot frame by installing electric heat and a watering/misting system.

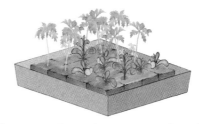

These vegetative cuttings were transplanted a week earlier and grown out under 24 hours of light before being moved into the flowering room.

Greenhouses can be attached (lean-to, window-mount, even-span) or freestanding. A lean-to uses an existing structure for one or more sides and is limited to single or double-row plant benches with a total width of seven to twelve feet (2.1-3.6 m) and length up to that of the building. The advantages of the lean-to are its proximity to electricity, water, and heat, but on the downside are its limited size, light, ventilation, and temperature control.

This cutaway shows the Styrofoam lining to retain heat. The Styrofoam insulates small containers from cold ground. The top is hinged to give complete access and when raised, it acts as an efficient vent.

A window-mount replaces an existing window, providing a relatively low-cost way to grow short plants, small seedlings, or cuttings. It can be installed fairly simply with common household tools. The disadvantage is its small size.

Low-profile greenhouses are perfect for crops of short plants. It is easy to set up a low-profile hoop house or a greenhouse alongside a building that gets full sun. The short greenhouse or cold frame is simple to darken during full summer and lets you reap the benefits of the harvest early!

Small greenhouses and cold frames also work well on patios, balconies, and rooftops. They protect plants from wind.

An even-span can be an attractive op-

This small greenhouse is covered with corrugated fiberglass. A vent on the top is all the ventilation necessary. Enough light penetrates the fiberglass to foster plant growth and keep plants out of public view.

tion. Like the window-mount or lean-to, the even-span is attached to the house and bears similar limitations of size, light, ventilation, and temperature. Unlike the lean-to

Hoop houses are very easy to construct from plastic or metal pipe. Some growers use rebar. Arches can be made with PVC plastic pipe up to 8 feet (2.4 m) tall. You can also make tunnels hug the ground with a height of less than 3 feet (90 cm).

or window-mount, the even-span can be larger and can open into the house—providing heat and humidity—or even function as a conservatory, an attractive place to relax. It is, however, more expensive to heat and maintain. Such greenhouses are most popular.

The freestanding greenhouse offers the most flexibility in size and location. It can be built to take full advantage of the sun, but it does not retain heat well and can be expensive to keep warm. Many frame types and coverings are available in kits or raw materials. There are also a number of good web sites such as http://www.wvu.edu/~agexten/hortcult/greenhou/building.htm to help you choose the plan that works best for you.

Framing can be in wood or metal. You may select a panel frame which is more expensive to build (panels are individual units) but has the advantage of quick installation and breakdown for storage. If portability is an issue, there are miniature greenhouses and hoop houses that can be purchased as a kit for under $300. These structures, because they can be picked up and moved, are usually considered tem-porary by municipalities and often do not require permits. For more information on types and prices, visit web sites such as www.hoophouse.com.

Coverings

Options for coverings are more extensive than those for framing. The traditional greenhouse is glass. Glass is heavy, expensive, and easily broken. Plastics and fiberglass can provide safe, economical alternatives.

Plastic is much cheaper than glass (one-sixth to one-tenth of the cost), can be heated as effectively as glass, and is equal to glass in producing quality plants. Polyethylene (PE) is low cost, lightweight, provides ample light, and can withstand fall, winter, and spring weather. It does not tolerate summer UV levels, however, and must be replaced annually. Ultraviolet-inhibited PE lasts longer, but both types lose heat more quickly than glass. During the day, this can help keep plants cooler, but at night the heat loss requires the use of an artificial heat source. Poly Weave™ is a plastic fabric made of 8-mil polyethylene reinforced with nylon mesh. It transmits up to 90% sunlight, can be sewn or taped, and has a lifespan of up to five years.

Polyvinyl chloride (PVC) is two to five times more expensive than PE but can last five years or longer. Polyvinyl chloride is pliable, transparent or translucent, and comes in four- to six-foot (1.2–1.8 m) widths which can be sealed together to provide a superwide piece. Ultraviolet-inhibited corrugated plastic panels provide another option. The panels can be used in cold frames, propagation houses, and greenhouses to provide excellent wind and snow protection and optimal solar heat collection. Ultraviolet-inhibited corrugated plastic also has insulating properties (2.5 R insulation/3.5 mm panels, 3.0 R/5.0 mm panels).

Corrugated fiberglass is lightweight, strong, and comes in eight- to twelve-foot (2.4–3.6 m) panels. Poor grades will discolor, reducing light penetration, but a good grade of clear fiberglass can cost as much or more than glass. Its lower weight is an advantage, and it is more difficult to see through!

Lexan™ (http://www.geplastics.com/gelexan/) is a thermoplastic that lasts for years and transmits almost as much light as glass while retaining heat. Clear panels like those in glass or Lexan™ may require shading during the heat of the day. Again, there are a number of options. You may select a roll-up shade of wood or aluminum, or a shading compound that is painted onto the outside of the glass. Vinyl plastic is a flexible film that installs easily against wet glass inside the structure and is reusable.

Framework and covering are only the beginning. Growing plants in a greenhouse is often more demanding than growing plants indoors. Air temperature, humidity, light, and air quality must be controlled in relation to a constantly changing greenhouse climate.

Climate Control

Even the best greenhouses will lose heat through radiation; conduction; convection through glass, walls, and floor (or soil); and through vents, doors, and cracks. To counteract external variables, the internal structure of the greenhouse is, in some ways, more complex than the selection of framing and covering materials.

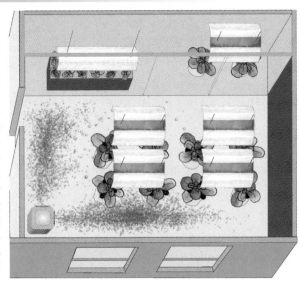

On cold nights, keep your indoor garden warm, making sure the heat circulates through the whole room.

All greenhouses need ventilation, and most need fans. Look for an extraction fan with the capacity to change the air once every minute. Capacity refers to the amount of power needed to circulate the air volume of your structure.

Calculate the volume by multiplying the square footage of your greenhouse by the height. Multiply the volume by sixty air changes per hour to get the cubic feet per minute (cfm) capacity of the greenhouse.

For example, a greenhouse with the following:

$8 \times 12 \times 7$ feet ($2.4 \times 3.6 \times 2.1$ m) greenhouse requires a fan with a cfm of 40,320

$8 \times 12 \times 7$ feet $\times$ 60 minutes = 40,320

Here is a similar metric example:

$2.5 \times 3.5 \times 2 = 17.5$ m^2 $\times$ 60 minutes = 1050 m^3

The combination of louvers and fan will force the hottest, most humid air out while protecting the plants from draft. See Chap-

Darken your greenhouse to force early flowering by pulling a curtain over the whole structure. You can do this by hand, or rig an electric motor to do the work.

ter Eleven, "Air," for more information.

Vents control temperatures in all seasons and improve growing conditions. Hand-operated roof vents will require frequent checks, or you may install automatic vents with an electric motor and thermostat that will respond to conditions around the clock. Venting is important with a cold frame, too. The high-end models have wax-filled vents that operate automatically, opening when the heat rises in the frame and contracting as the temperature cools. You can find the paraffin-filled "Optivent" and many other greenhouse supplies at www.charleysgreenhouse.com.

Heating systems are important to keep plants healthy during cold nights. Most warm-season annuals grow well with night temperatures of 60–65°F (16–18°C), but colder nights will require an additional heat source for sustained growth.

You can turn a cold frame into a hot frame by insulating it with manure or heating it with steam, hot water pipes, or electricity. To make the most efficient use of electricity, purchase soil-heating tape or cable, with a thermostat that will automatically control the temperature. Lay the cable on the soil at the bottom of the bed or on a bed of sand or vermiculite and cover with about two inches (5 cm) of sand. You will need to provide 10–15 watts of electric heat for every square foot (30 cm²) of growing area. Heat cables are also useful in greenhouses for warming seedlings, cuttings, or flowering plants without the cost of heating the entire structure.

Small greenhouses can be heated relatively economically with an electric space heater, or more effectively with thermostatically controlled, forced air using ducts or plastic tubing to distribute the heat. Larger units may be heated with forced air or by a coal or natural hot-water or steam system. Steam can also be used to sterilize growing beds and potting soils. Then there is the low-tech method of greenhouse warming: compost. A gardener in Portland, Oregon, stacks organic matter on the sides of the greenhouse to a height of about five feet (1.5 m) inside and out. As the compost decomposes, it gives off heat keeping the structure warm at a very low cost.

Evaporative cooling eliminates excess heat and adds humidity, reducing water needs. Moist air circulates through the structure while warm air is expelled through roof vents or exhaust fans. Properly installed, a cooler can reduce the interior temperature as much as 30–40°F (15–23°C) in hot, dry climates, less in wetter areas. As with fans, the size of the cooler is determined by the size of the greenhouse. A general guideline is to find a cooler equal to the total cubic space of the structure plus fifty percent. To provide both cooling and humidifying effects, the cooler must be installed on the outside of the greenhouse; otherwise, it simply humidifies without dropping the temperature. Turner Greenhouses has a handy site (http://www.turnergreenhouses.com) with some quick tips on selecting a cooling system for your greenhouse. Other great greenhouse sites include: http://www.igcusa.com/ for some helpful graphics and http://www.cpjungle.com/ for a detailed explanation of cooling needs and resources.

Misting and watering are also important components of greenhouse gardening. Extended periods of growing and higher sustained temperatures make adequate water essential. Again, there are methods to suit every temperament from low-tech to automatic.

Most companies offer watering and misting systems by components, which can be mixed and matched to suit the gardener's needs. Automatic systems will have a timer that triggers the mist or water at preset intervals. You may want a toggle switch that allows you to rotate between manual and automatic watering. For more information on specific uses and types of watering systems, go to a web site such as www.cloud-tops.com, which covers a variety of topics pertaining to the internal greenhouse environment.

A lower-tech method of mist and watering control consists of a series of screens that tilt downward with the weight of the water shutting off the flow then raising to restart the cycle as the screens dry. It is fully automated by the weight of the water or lack thereof. Of course, there is also hand-watering which is very effective and requires no mechanical intervention. Automatic systems, both high- and low-tech, are alternatives to hand-watering that can be most helpful during a gardener's absence.

Heating and watering devices depend on how much time the gardener has to spend tending plants. You can keep equipment costs to a minimum if you plan to spend a lot of time in the greenhouse. For gardeners who are away from the structure for long periods, automatic systems are a good investment.

In addition to shelter, heat, water, and ventilation, plants need light. This section will offer a brief treatment of lighting, since it is covered in greater depth in Chapter Seven. Fluorescent light offers higher efficiency with low heat and is the most widely used. Incandescent light—60 to 500 watts—may be used to extend daylength. High-intensity discharge (HID) offers long life, and the sodium HID lamps emit the best light to be combined with natural sunlight. Regardless of light source selected, you may want to purchase a light meter ($30–$50). It will be very useful in setting the light level in your greenhouse for maximum efficiency.

Carbon Dioxide (CO_2) is another important aspect of the greenhouse environment that will be only touched upon in this section. Closed greenhouses often have too little CO_2 during the day for plants to be able to use light effectively. Enhancing the levels of CO_2 will accelerate plant growth; methods for doing so range from expensive CO_2 equipment with infrared sensors to block dry ice kept in a pressure bottle until needed. More detailed information on CO_2 can be found in Chapter Eleven, "Air."

Planting in the earthen floor of the greenhouse allows you to use organic methods. The plants cannot be moved easily, but they grow bigger and require less maintenance than container-grown plants. Without containers, plants also retain a lower profile. Growing in Mother Earth is always better than planting in pots! Many of the principles that apply to indoor growing apply to growing in a greenhouse, too. Check out Chapter Check out Chapter Eight, "Soil" and "Containers" for more information.

Greenhouses can be darkened to induce flowering during mid-summer. This practice will allow you to harvest up to three crops a year! Warm-season annuals flower when nights are long (12 hours) and days are short (12 hours). When the greenhouse is darkened daily so plants receive 12 hours of darkness to induce flowering, a crop of cuttings planted May 1 can be harvested by the middle of July.

Automatic darkening machinery is available for large commercial greenhouses. Smaller greenhouses are normally covered with black plastic to "black out" the interior for 12 hours.

When combined with natural sunlight, artificial light is optimally used during

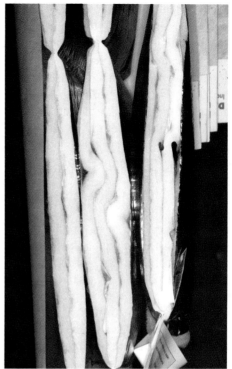

Insulated greenhouse mobile blankets also make great indoor garden partitions.

non-daylight hours. Greenhouse gardeners turn the HID lights on when sunlight diminishes (30 minutes before sunset) and off when sunlight strengthens (30 minutes after sunrise). Turn on the HID when the daylight intensity is less than two times the intensity of the HID. Measure this point with a light meter. Turn off the HID when the daylight intensity is greater than two times the intensity of the HID. A simple photocell that measures light intensity can be used to turn the lights on and off automatically.

Supplementary lighting has greatest effect when applied to the youngest plants. It is least expensive to light plants when they are small.

Gardening Indoors

Many different types of coverings are available for greenhouses and cold frames. The best greenhouse films are UV (ultraviolet)-resistant and still transmit plenty of light. Lexan is rigid and full of thermo-storing channels. It is one of the best greenhouse plastics available. Lexan lasts for years and transmits almost as much light as glass while retaining greenhouse heat. The only problem with Lexan is that it is clear!

Regulating heat in a greenhouse is much more difficult than in an enclosed garden room. Greenhouses heat up quickly on sunny days and cool equally fast when the sun ducks behind a cloud or drops below the horizon. This heat fluctuation is difficult and expensive to control. Hot and cold dips also affect the ratio of nutrient to water plants need and use, which makes growing in a greenhouse more demanding than growing indoors.

Adding a complete greenhouse chapter here is beyond the scope of this book. A

This stunning indoor garden brings joy to the whole family year-round.

couple of my favorite books on greenhouse growing include *Gardening Under Cover*, by William Head, Sasquatch Books, $16.95, and *Gardening in Your Greenhouse*, by Mark Freeman, Stackpole Books, $18.95.

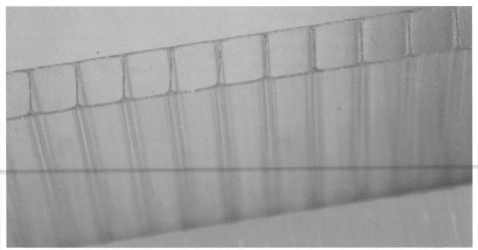

Insulated Lexan plastic panels are revolutionizing greenhouse design and manufacturing. The lightweight super-strong material offers insulation properties not found in glass. It is also shatter-resistant.

These pepper plants are thriving indoors under artificial light and are growing hydroponically in expanded hydroclay.

Gardening Indoors

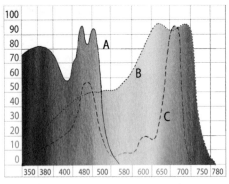

This graph shows the exact level at which A. Phototropic response, B. Photosynthetic response, and C. Chlorophyll synthesis take place.

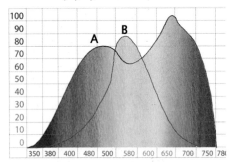

The single-humped line in the center of the graph represents the visible light spectrum humans see. The dual-humped line represents the spectrum plants need to grow.

Kelvin Scale

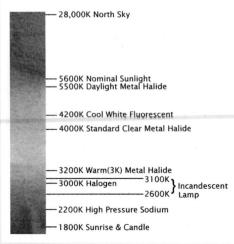

- 28,000K North Sky
- 5600K Nominal Sunlight
- 5500K Daylight Metal Halide
- 4200K Cool White Fluorescent
- 4000K Standard Clear Metal Halide
- 3200K Warm(3K) Metal Halide
- 3000K Halogen
- 3100K } Incandescent
- 2600K } Lamp
- 2200K High Pressure Sodium
- 1800K Sunrise & Candle

Introduction

Until the 1980s, light was the limiting factor for indoor growing of plants requiring medium or high light levels. Until that time, only a few dedicated gardeners grew indoors, mainly African violet and orchid enthusiasts who used fluorescent lamps. Over the last twenty-five years, indoor gardening and horticulture have been revolutionized by advances in lighting technology. By understanding how plants use light, indoor gardeners can use High Intensity Discharge (HID) lamps to grow spectacular flowers, nutritious vegetables, and ornamental plants indoors.

Light, Spectrum, and Photoperiod

Plants need light to grow. The light must have the proper spectrum and intensity to ensure rapid growth. Light is comprised of separate bands of colors. Each color in the spectrum sends the plant a separate signal. Each color in the spectrum promotes a different type of growth.

PAR and Light Spectrum

Plants need and use only certain portions of the light spectrum. The most important colors in the spectrum for maximum chlo-

Bulb Rating	CCT Rating in degrees Kelvin
Warm	3000
Neutral	4000
Cool	6000

Bulb	Kelvin Temp	CRI
Cool White	4150 K	62
Lite White	4150 K	62
Warm White	300 K	52
Deluxe Daylight	8500 K	84
Vitalight	5500 K	96
Noon Sunlight	5300 K	100

rophyll production and photosynthetic response are in the blue and red range. The main portion of light used by plants is between 400 and 700 nanometers (nm).* This region is called the Photosynthetically Active Radiation (PAR) zone.**

"PAR watts" is the measure of the actual amount of specific photons a plant needs to grow. Photons are a measure of light energy. Light energy is radiated and assimilated in photons. Photosynthesis is necessary for plants to grow and is activated by the assimilation of photons. Blue photons are worth more PAR watts than red photons, but scientists have difficulty measuring the exact difference.

Each color of light activates different plant functions. Positive tropism, the plant's ability to orient leaves toward light, is controlled by spectrum. Lightbulbs deliver only a part of the necessary light plants need to grow. However, they deliver enough! Most plants' light needs can be met by artificial means.

*One nanometer (nm) = one billionth (10_{-9}) of a meter. Light is measured in wavelengths; the wavelengths are measured in nanometers.

**Some scientists still disagree as to the exact PAR zone and make their calculations based on 350 to 750 nanometers. PAR watts measured with this scale will be a little higher.

Measuring Light

Virtually all light is measured in foot-candles, lux, or lumens. Foot-candles and lux measure light visible to the human eye. The human eye sees much less of the light spectrum than plants "see." The eye is most sensitive to light between 525 and 625 nanometers. The importance of the blue and red portions in the spectrum is diminished greatly when light is measured in foot-candles, lux, or lumens. A foot-candle is a unit of illumination equal to the intensity of one candle at a distance of one foot. The lux scale is similar to that of the foot-candle; one foot-candle is equal to 10.76 lux.

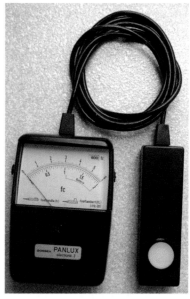

Although this simple light meter measures light in foot-candles rather than PAR, it still gives an accurate idea of light distribution.

Humans see light differently than plants do. Compare the graphs above to see how the light you see differs from the light a plant uses to grow. Plants use the photosynthetically active response (PAR) portion of the spectrum. Humans use the central portion of the spectrum, while plants are able to use large portions of the spectrum not measured by light meters that record foot-candles, lux, and lumens.

Light is also measured in spectrum with kelvin temperature which expresses the exact color a bulb emits. Bulbs with a kelvin temperature from 3000 to 6500 are best for growing plants indoors. The PAR section above explains that plants use specific portions of the spectrum—a complete range from blues to reds. Lamps with a spectrum similar to PAR-rated bulbs can use kelvin temperature of a bulb to ascertain the approximate PAR rating of the lamp. Color spectrum results from a specific mix of different colors. High intensity discharge bulbs are very similar in spectrum. Making these safe assumptions, a rough PAR rating could be extrapolated from a kelvin temperature rating.

The Color Corrected Temperature (CCT) of a bulb is the peak kelvin temperature at which the colors in a bulb are stable. We can classify bulbs by their CCT rating which tells us the overall color of the light emitted. It does not tell us the concentration of the combination of colors emitted. Companies use a Color Rendering Index (CRI). The higher the CRI, the better the bulb is for growing.

Light Meters

Most commercial light meters measure light in foot-candles or lux. Both scales measure light to which the human eye reacts to "see." They do not measure photosynthetic response to light in PAR watts.

Light measurements in this book are made in foot-candles and lux. This information is still valuable, because it records the amount of light spread over a specific surface. The information is then coupled with the PAR rating of different bulbs. Regardless of the lamp, the amount of light emitted is constant. It only makes sense to use the proper reflective hood with a high PAR-rated bulb to grow the best garden.

After all the talk about PAR watts, industry officials are unable to agree on a common scale of measurement. For this reason, we have decided to rely on kelvin color temperature to measure lamp spectrum.

Turn on a green light bulb to work in the indoor garden at night. Green light will not affect the photoperiod of flowering plants.

Photoperiod

The photoperiod is the relationship between the duration of the light period and dark period. Many plants will stay in the vegetative growth stage as long as an 18- to 24-hour light and a six- to zero-hour dark photoperiod are maintained. However, there are exceptions. Eighteen hours of light per day will give plants all the light they need to sustain vegetative growth.

In short-day plants, flowering is most efficiently induced with 12 hours of uninterrupted darkness in a 24-hour photoperiod. When plants are at least two months old—after they have developed sexual characteristics—altering the photoperiod to an even 12 hours, day and night, will induce visible signs of flowering in one to three weeks. Older plants tend to show signs of flowering sooner. Varieties originating in the tropics generally mature later. The 12-hour photoperiod represents the classic equinox and is the optimum daylight-to-dark relationship for flowering in short-day plants.

A relationship exists between photoperiod response and genetics. We can make generalizations about this relationship, because little scientific evidence documents the extent to which specific plants are affected by photoperiod. For example, plants that originated in the tropics respond to long days better than plants that originated elsewhere. On the equator, days and nights are almost the same length year-round. Plants tend to bloom when they are chronologically ready, after completing the vegetative growth stage. However, most gardeners are familiar with ornamental plants or flowers which flower slowly for three months or longer, even when given a 12-hour photoperiod. You can start such plants on a 12/12 day/night schedule, but they still must go through the seedling and vegetative stages before spending three months or longer flowering. Plants grow more slowly in 12-hour days than when given 18 hours of light, and inducing flowering takes longer.

The photoperiod signals short-day plants to start flowering; it can also signal them to remain in (or revert to) vegetative growth. Short-day plants must have 12 hours of uninterrupted, total darkness to flower properly. Dim light during the dark period in the flowering stage prevents short-day plants from blooming. When the 12-hour dark period is interrupted by light, plants get confused. The light signals plants, "It's daytime; start vegetative growth." Given this signal of light, plants start vegetative growth, and flowering is retarded or stopped.

Inverse Square Law Chart

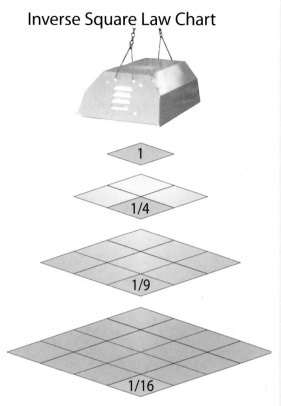

This chart shows that light diminishes to the square of the distance.

Plants will not stop flowering if the lights are turned on for a few minutes once or twice during the flowering cycle. If a light is turned on for a few minutes—long enough to disrupt the dark period—on two or three consecutive nights, plants will start to revert to vegetative growth. Less than one-half of one foot-candle of light will prevent plants from flowering. That is a little more light than reflected by a full moon on a clear night. Some well-bred varieties will revert within three days, and others take four to five days to revert to vegetative growth. Once they start to re-vegetate, it takes four to six additional weeks to induce flowering!

Gardening Indoors

When light shines on a green object, green pigment in the object absorbs all spectrum colors but green, and the green light is reflected. This is why we see the color green. The smart way to visit an indoor garden during the dark period is to illuminate it with a green lightbulb. Plants do not respond to the green portion of the light spectrum, thus a green bulb is usable in the indoor garden at night with no ill effects.

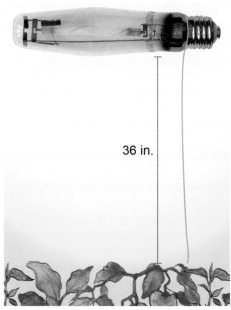

36 in.

Tie a string 12 to 36 inches long to the HID reflector. Use the string to measure the distance between the bulb and plant canopy.

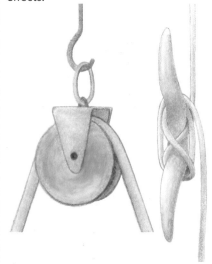

A simple pulley and rope system is the easiest, cheapest way to adjust your lamps.

Some gardeners leave the HID on 24 hours a day. Many plants can efficiently process 16 to 18 hours of light per day, after which they reach a point of diminishing returns, and the electricity is wasted.

I talked with Dutch and Canadian gardeners who claim their plants flower under a 6-hour dark and 12-hour light photoperiod. This expedited, 18-hour photoperiod regimen is supposed to work, but I'm not sold on it. Gardeners say that their harvest is undiminished, and that they are getting 25 percent more produce in the same time. I have not visited their gardens to verify these claims. No electricity is saved by adopting this regimen.

Intensity

High intensity discharge lamps are bright—very, very bright. Gardeners who properly manage this intense brightness have a higher harvest per watt. Intensity is the magnitude of light energy per unit of area. It is greatest near the bulb and diminishes rapidly as it moves away from the source.

For example, plants that are two feet (60 cm) from a lamp receive one-fourth the amount of light received by plants one foot (30 cm) away! An HID that emits 100,000 lumens produces a paltry 25,000 lumens two feet (60 cm) away. A 1000-watt HID that emits 100,000 initial lumens yields 11,111 lumens three feet (90 cm) away.

Couple this meager sum with a poorly designed reflective hood, and beautiful plants suffer big time! The closer a plant is to a light source, the more PAR watts it receives and the better it grows, as long as it is not so close that heat from the lamp burns foliage.

The Inverse Square Law

The relationship between light emitted from a point source (bulb) and distance are defined by the inverse square law. This law affirms that the intensity of light changes in inverse proportion to the square of the distance.

$I = L/D^2$
Intensity = light output/distance^2
For example:
$100,000 = 100,000/1$
$25,000 = 100,000/4$
$11,111 = 100,000/9$
$6250 = 100,000/16$

A 1000-watt standard metal halide emits from 80,000 to 110,000 initial lumens and 65,000 to 88,000 average (mean) lumens. One lumen is equal to the amount of light emitted by one candle that falls on one square foot of surface one foot away. Super halides emit 115,000 initial lumens and 92,000 mean lumens. A 1000-watt HP sodium emits 140,000 initial lumens, and a 600-watt HP sodium emits 90,000; watt for watt, that's seven percent more lumens than the 1000-watt HPS. Lumens emitted are only part of the equation. Lumens received by the plant are much more important.

Lumens received are measured in watts-per-square-foot or in foot-candles (fc). One foot-candle equals the amount of light that falls on one square foot (30 cm^2)of surface that is one foot (30 cm) away from one candle.

Watts-per-square-foot (or m^2) is easy to calculate but is an erroneous way to determine usable light for a garden. It measures how many watts are available from a light source in an area. For example, a 400-watt incandescent bulb emits the same watts-per-square-foot as a 400-watt metal halide. Mounting height is not considered in watts-per-square-foot; the lamp could be mounted at any height from four to eight feet (1.2 x 2.4 m). Nor does it consider PAR watts or efficiency of the bulb.

This Adjust-A-Wing spreads light evenly and plants can be placed very close to the bulb without burning.

Calculating foot-candles or lux is a more accurate way to estimate the amount of light plants receive, but it still lacks the precision of measuring how much light is used by plants. If you start with a bulb that is rated in PAR watts, using a foot-candle or lux meter will suffice.

To demonstrate how dim light intensity retards plant development, check out an outdoor vegetable garden. Have you ever planted 65-day broccoli that took 100 days to mature? Most gardeners have suffered this fate. Did the plants get full sun all day long? The seed vendor assumes seeds were planted under perfect conditions—full sun and ideal temperature range. Plants that received less PAR light matured slowly and produced less than plants getting full sun all day long. It is the same in an indoor garden; plants that receive less light grow poorly.

Gardening Indoors

Lamp Spacing

Light intensity virtually doubles for every six inches (15 cm) closer an HID is to the canopy of a garden. When light intensity is low, plants stretch for it. Low light intensity is often caused by the lamp being too far away from plants. Dim light causes sparse foliage and spindly branches that are further apart on the stem.

Increase yield by giving growing area uniform light distribution. Uneven light distribution causes strong branch tips to grow toward the intense light. Foliage in dimly lit areas is shaded when light distribution is uneven.

Reflective hoods ultimately dictate lamp placement—distance between lamps and above the plants. Nearly all stationary lamps have bright (hot) spots that plants grow toward.

Gardeners prefer high-wattage lamps—400, 600, 1000, or 1100 watts—because they have lumens-per-watt and their PAR rating is higher than smaller bulbs. Plants receive more light when the lamp is closer to the garden. Even though 400-watt lamps produce fewer lumens-per-watt than a 1000-watt bulb, when properly set up, they actually deliver more usable light to plants. The 600-watt bulb has the highest lumen-per-watt conversion (150 LPW) and can be placed closer to the canopy of the garden than 1000 or 1100-watt bulbs. When the 600-watt bulb is closer to plants, they receive more light.

	175w	250w	400w	600w	1000w	
30cm	1200-2000	2000-3500	3500-5500	5400-9000	9000-12000	1 ft
60cm	500-1000	800-1700	1400-3000	3300-4800	5500-8000	2 ft
90cm	250-400	500-800	600-1200	1000-2000	2500-4000	3 ft
1.2m		100-200	300-500	450-800	1500-2000	4 ft
1.5m					500-1200	6.5 ft
1.5m						6.5 ft

- A 175-watt HID yields enough light to grow a 2 × 2-foot (60 × 60 cm) garden well. Notice how fast light intensity diminishes more than a foot from the bulb.
- A 250-watt HID will illuminate up to a 3 × 3-foot (90 × 90 cm) area. Keep the bulb from 12 to 18 inches (30–45 cm) above plants.
- A 400-watt HID delivers plenty of light to illuminate a 4 × 4-foot (1.2 × 1.2 m) area well. Hang the lamp from 12 to 24 inches (30–60 cm) above the canopy of the garden.
- A 600-watt HP delivers enough light to illuminate a 4 × 4-foot (1.2 × 1.2 cm) area well. Hang the lamp from 18 to 24 inches (30–60 cm) above plants.
- A 1000-watt HID delivers enough light to illuminate a 6 × 6-foot (1.8 × 1.8 m) area well. Some reflective hoods are designed to throw light over a rectangular area. Large 1000-watt HIDs can burn foliage if located closer than 24 inches (60 cm) from plants. Move HIDs closer to plants when using a light mover.

A 1000-watt HID emits a lot of light. It also radiates a lot of heat. The bulb must be farther away from the plants to avoid burning them. In many cases it is more effective to use smaller wattage bulbs. For example, two 400-watt bulbs can be placed closer to plants than one 1000-watt bulb, and the 400-watt bulbs emit light from two points. The disadvantage is that two 400-watt systems cost more than one 1000-watt system.

Check out the diagrams that show the difference in usable light in different sized growing areas. Gardeners who use these drawings fine-tune the area with a hand-held light meter.

Look at the simple mathematical examples below to see how much more efficient 400 and 600-watt lamps are than 1000-watt lamps.

For example, a 1000-watt lamp that produces 100,000 lumens at the source produces the following:

The goal is to give plants 10,000 lumens.

If you use three 600-watt HP sodium lamps, you get a total of 270,000 lumens at a cost of $0.18 per hour (cost per kWh = $0.10). If you use two 1000-watt HP sodium lamps, you get a total of 280,000 lumens at a cost of $0.20 per hour.

Use the examples above to see the 1000-watt HP sodium offers more watts per square foot and m² to achieve the desired lumen output of 10,000 lumens. However, the bulb also produces a hot spot near the center of the illuminated area. Plants tend to grow into the hot spot and shade other plants.

Although 400-watt lamps have a lower lumen-per-watt conversion, when used properly they may be more efficient than

The benefits of using lower wattage bulbs include:
More point sources of light
More even distribution of light
Able to place bulbs closer to garden

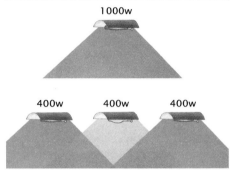

Using three 400-watt bulbs can cover 30 to 40 percent more growing area than one 1000-watt bulb. The 400s can also be hung closer to plants.

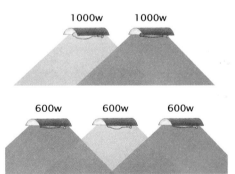

Three 600-watt HIDs deliver more light to plants than two 1000-watt HIDs. Smaller HIDs provide three points of light and can be located closer to plants.

higher wattage bulbs. One 1000-watt halide produces 115,000 initial lumens and a 400-watt halide only 40,000. This means each 400-watt lamp must be located closer to the canopy of the garden to provide a similar amount of light. It also

Gardening Indoors

1000-watt: LPW = 140

1 foot (30 cm) away	140,000 lumens
2 feet (60 cm) away	35,000 lumens
3 feet (90 cm) away	15,555 lumens
4 feet (120 cm) away	9999 lumens

1000-watt HP sodium @ 4 feet = 10,000 lumens
4×4 = 16 square feet, 1000 watts / 16 square feet = 62.5 watts per square foot.
1000 watts / M^2 = 100 watts per cm^2

1000-watt: LPW = 115

1 foot (30 cm) away	115,000 lumens
2 feet (60 cm) away	28,750 lumens
3 feet (90 cm) away	12,777 lumens
4 feet (120 cm) away	8214 lumens

1000-watt metal halide @ 3.25 feet = 10,000 lumens
3.25×3.25 = 12.25 square feet, 1000 watts / 12.25 = 81.6 watts per square foot.
1000 watts / m^2 = 10 watts per cm^2

600-watt: LPW = 150

1 foot (30 cm) away	90,000 lumens
2 feet (60 cm) away	22,500 lumens
3 feet (90 cm) away	9,999 lumens
4 feet (120 cm) away	6428 lumens

600-watt HP sodium @ 3 feet = 10,000 lumens
3×3 = 9 square feet, 600 watts / 9 = 66 watts per square foot
600 watts / m^2 = 6 watts per cm^2

400-watt: LPW = 125

1 foot (30 cm) away	50,000 lumens
2 feet (60 cm) away	12,500 lumens
3 feet (90 cm) away	5555 lumens
4 feet (120 cm) away	3571 lumens

400-watt HP sodium @ 2.25 feet = 10,000 lumens
2.25×2.25 = 5 square feet, 400 watts / 5 square feet = 80 watts per square foot.
400 watts / m^2 = 4 watts per cm^2

400-watt: LPW = 100

1 foot (30 cm) away	40,000 lumens
2 feet (60 cm) away	10,000 lumens
3 feet (90 cm) away	4444 lumens
4 feet (120 cm) away	2857 lumens

400-watt metal halide @ 2 feet = 10,000 lumens
2×2 = 4 square feet, 400 watts / 4 = 100 watts per square foot
400 watts / m^2 = 4 watts per cm^2

means that several different point sources sustain more even, intense light distribution.

Side Lighting

Side lighting is generally not as efficient as lighting from above. Vertically oriented lamps without reflectors are efficient, but require plants to be oriented around the bulb. To promote growth, light must penetrate the dense foliage of a garden. The lamps are mounted where light intensity is marginal—along the walls—to provide sidelight.

Compact fluorescent lamps are not a good choice for side lighting when using HID lamps. (See Compact Fluorescent Lamps for more information.)

Rotating Plants

Rotating the plants will help ensure even distribution of light. Rotate plants every day or two by moving them one-quarter to one-half turn. Rotating promotes even growth and fully-developed foliage.

Move plants around under the lamp so they receive the most possible light. Move smaller plants toward the center and taller plants toward the outside of the garden. Set small plants on a stand to even out the garden profile. Arrange plants in a concave shape (stadium method) under the lamp so all plants receive the same amount of light. Containers with wheels are easier to move.

Take advantage of the different levels of light below the HID. Place seedlings and cuttings requiring low light levels on the perimeter and flowering plants needing higher light levels under bright bulbs.

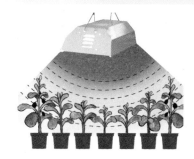

Light intensity is brightest directly under the bulb. To promote even growth, arrange plants under lamps so they receive the same intensity of light.

Plant Spacing

When light shines on a garden, the leaves near the top of plants get more intense light than the leaves at the bottom. The top leaves shade the bottom leaves and absorb light energy, making less light energy available to lower leaves. If the lower leaves do not receive enough light, they will yellow and die. Tall six-foot (1.8 m) plants take longer to grow and have higher overall yields than shorter four-foot (1.2 m) plants, but the yield will be about the same.

At least 99 two-week-old seedlings or cuttings can be huddled directly under a single 400-watt HID. The young plants will need more space as they grow. If packed too closely together, plants sense the shortage of space and do not grow to their maximum potential. Leaves from one plant shade another plant's foliage and slow overall plant growth. It is very important to space young plants just far enough apart so their leaves do not touch or touch very little. This will keep shading to a minimum and growth to a maximum. Check and alter the spacing every few days. Eight to sixteen mature tomato plants three to four months old will completely fill the space under one 1000-watt HID.

A large bed on casters is easy to maintain. The gardener is able to rotate and move plants around within these large elevated garden beds. Wheels on the bed make it easy to rotate or remove entire beds.

Side lighting

Gardening Indoors

Bulb	Model	Mfrg	MH/HPS	Watts	Initial Lumens	Color Deg. K
Sunmaster	Warm Deluxe	V	MH	1100	133000	385 PAR
AgroSun	AgroSun	V	MH	1000	117000	3250
Multivapor	HO	GE	MH	1000	115000	3800
MultiMetal	Super	I	MH	1000	115000	4200
Metal Halide	Metal Halide	Ph	MH	1000	110000	3700
Solarmax	Veg	V	MH	1000	85000	7200
Super Metalarc	Super	O	MH	1000	115000	3600
Sunmaster	Warm Deluxe	V	MH	1000	117000	315 PAR
Sunmaster	Natural Deluxe	V	MH	1000	117000	315 PAR
Sunmaster	Cool Deluxe	V	MH	1000	80000	315 PAR
Solarmax	Veg/Conversion	V	MH	600	55000	7200
Solarmax	Veg	V	MH	400	32000	7200
Sunmaster	Warm Deluxe	V	MH	400	40000	110 PAR
Sunmaster	Natural Deluxe	V	MH	400	40000	110 PAR
Sunmaster	Cool Deluxe	V	MH	400	32500	110 PAR
Super Metalarc	Super	O	MH	400	40000	4200
Super Metal Halide	Super	Ph	MH	400	4000	4300
AgroSun	AgroSun	V	MH	400	4000	3250
Multivapor	HO	GE	MH	400	40000	4200
Sunmaster	Warm Deluxe	V	MH	250	22000	85 PAR
Sunmaster	Natural Deluxe	V	MH	250	23000	85 PAR
Sunmaster	Cool Deluxe	V	MH	250	21500	85 PAR
Super Metalarc	Super	O	MH	250	23000	4200
Super Metal Halide	Super	Ph	MH	250	23000	4300
Multivapor	HO	GE	MH	250	23000	4200
Hortilux	Super		HPS	1000	145000	2100
Solarmax	Super HPS	V	HPS	1000	147000	2100
Lucalox	HPS	GE	HPS	1000	140000	2100
Sunlux	HPS	I	HPS	1000	140000	2100
Lumalux	HPS	O	HPS	1000	140000	2100
Ceramalux	HPS	Ph	HPS	1000	140000	2100
Solarmax	Super HPS	V	HPS	600	95000	2100
Sunmaster	Super HPS Deluxe	V	HPS	600	85000	358 PAR
Lumalux	Super	O	HPS	600	9000	2200
SonAgro	Plus	Ph	HPS	600	9000	2100
Hortilux	Super	I	HPS	430	58500	2100
Hortilux	Super	I	HPS	400	55000	2100
Solarmax	Super HPS	V	HPS	400	55000	2100
Lucalox	HPS	GE	HPS	400	41000	4000
Sunlux	HPS	I	HPS	400	50000	2100
Lumalux	HPS	O	HPS	400	50000	2100
Ceramalux	HPS	Ph	HPS	400	50000	2100
Hortilux	Super	I	HPS	250	32000	2100
Lucalox	HPS	GE	HPS	250	30000	2100
Sunlux	HPS	I	HPS	250	29000	2100
Lumalux	HPS	O	HPS	250	29000	2100
Ceramalux	HPS	Ph	HPS	250	28500	2100

The ballast box is attached to the reflector in this greenhouse fixture.

The Wide reflector from Hortilux was one of the first European reflectors to use a deflector below the bulb.

Double fixture greenhouse fixture has the ballasts between bulbs.

This air-ventilated tube is very inefficient, leaving a hot spot below.

Place Hortilux 1000-watt fixture 4 feet (1.2 m) above garden.

You can put the Super Wide reflector very close to plants.

This fixture is designed to be mounted next to a wall. It reflects light down and away from the wall.

This Ecotechnics Diamond reflector from Spain is very efficient.

Hortilux sets the standard with their line of reflectors. The Deep model is to be mounted high in greenhouses.

The Adjust-A-Wing is one of my favorite reflectors because it delivers the most light! The deflector under bulb allows it to be super close to plants.

Parabolic dome reflectors orient bulbs vertically. Although less efficient these hoods work well to grow vegetative plants.

Gavita invented a lamp with the reflector inside the bulb! The reflector is the most efficient I have seen!

The Medium reflector from Hortilux is a favorite in Europe.

The Hydrofarm reflector is one of the best values in North America. It reflects a lot of light and "breathes" well.

The "cone" reflector is one of the least efficient available. Much reflected light is wasted.

The Butterfly reflector and deflector is one of the most interesting designs I have seen, but I have no idea about its efficiency!

Hortilux Midi reflector spreads light well.

The hammered-finish specular interior of this lamp/ballast fixture diffuses light well.

This vertical reflector is covered in plastic. The bulb hangs between plants.

This reflector from Easy Green has holes for forced-air ventilation and can be placed close to plants.

Gardening Indoors

Plants can absorb light only if it falls on their leaves. Plants must be spaced so their leaves do not overlap too much. Yield increases very little when plants are crowded. Plants also stretch for light, which makes less efficient use of intense light.

Best number of plants per square foot or m² is often a matter of experimenting to find the magic number for your garden. In general, each 40-inch-square (m²) space will hold from 16 to 32 plants.

Reflective Hoods

Some reflective hoods reflect light more evenly than others. A reflector that distributes light evenly—with no hot spots—can be placed closer to plants without burning them. These hoods are most efficient, because the lamp is closer and the light more intense. The farther the lamp is from the garden, the less light plants receive. For example, a 1000-watt reflector with a hot spot must be placed 36 inches (90 cm) above the garden. A 600-watt lamp with a reflector that distributes light evenly can be placed only 18 inches (45 cm) above the garden. When placed closer, the 600-watt lamp shines as much light on the garden as the 1000-watt bulb!

Using reflective walls and the proper reflective hood over the lamp can double the growing area. Gardeners who use the most efficient reflective hoods harvest up to twice as much as those who don't.

Seedlings, cuttings, and plants in the vegetative growth stage need less light than flowering plants, because their growth requirements are different. For the first few weeks of life, seedlings and cuttings can easily survive beneath fluorescent lights. Vegetative growth requires a little more light, easily supplied by a metal halide or compact fluorescent lamp. Review the "Maximum Light Requirements for Plants" chart.

Reflective hoods are made from steel sheet metal, aluminum, even stainless steel. The steel is either cold-rolled or pre-galvanized before a reflective coating is applied. Pre-galvanized steel is more rust resistant than cold-rolled steel. This metal can be polished, textured, or painted, with white being the most common paint color. Premium hood manufacturers apply white paint in a powder-coating process. Note: there are different shades of white, and some whites are whiter than others. Flat titanium white is the most reflective color and diffuses light most effectively. Glossy white paint is easy to clean but tends to create hot spots of light. Sheet metal hoods are less expensive than the same size aluminum hood because of reduced materials expense.

The pebble and hammer-tone surfaces offer good light diffusion and more sur-

Maximum Light Requirements for Plants			
Growth Stage	Foot-candles	Lux	Hrs. of Light
Seedling	375	4000	16–24
Clone	375	4000	18–24
Vegetative	2500	27,000	18
Flowering	10,000	107,500	12

These guidelines will give high light plants all the light they need to grow well. Less light will often cause looser, less-compact buds to form.

Three lights covering 136 pots.

face area to reflect light. Hot spots are commonplace among highly polished, mirror-like surfaces. Mirror-polished hoods also scratch easily and create uneven lighting.

Horizontal Reflective Hoods

Horizontal reflectors are most efficient for HID systems, and are the best value for gardeners. A horizontal lamp yields up to 40 percent more light than a lamp burning in a vertical position. Light is emitted from the arc tube. When horizontal, half of this light is directed downward to the plants, so only half of the light needs to be reflected. Horizontal reflectors are inherently more efficient than vertical lamps/reflectors, because half of the light is direct and only half of the light must be reflected.

Horizontal reflective hoods are available in many shapes and sizes. The closer the reflective hood is to the arc tube, the less

This horizontal reflector system is perfect for light-loving flowering plants.

distance light must travel before being reflected. Less distance traveled means more light reflected.

Gardening Indoors

Horizontal reflective hoods tend to have a hot spot directly under the bulb. To dissipate this hot spot of light and lower the heat it creates, some manufacturers install a light deflector below the bulb. The deflector diffuses the light and heat directly under the bulb. When there is no hot spot, reflective hoods with deflectors can be placed closer to plants.

Horizontally mounted HP sodium lamps use a small reflective hood for greenhouse culture. The hood is mounted a few inches over the horizontal HP sodium bulb. All light is reflected down toward plants, and the small hood creates minimal shadow.

Vertical Reflective Hoods

Reflectors with vertical lamps are less efficient than horizontal ones. Like horizontal bulbs, vertically mounted bulbs emit light from the sides of the arc tube. This light must strike the side of the hood before it is reflected downward to plants. Reflected light is always less intense than original light. Light travels farther before being reflected in parabolic or cone reflective hoods. Direct light is more intense and more efficient.

Parabolic dome reflectors offer the best value for vertical reflectors. They reflect light relatively evenly, though they throw less overall light than horizontal reflectors. Large parabolic dome hoods distribute light evenly and reflect enough light to sustain vegetative growth. The light spreads out under the hood and is reflected downward to plants. Popular parabolic hoods are inexpensive to manufacture and provide a good light value for the money. Four-foot parabolic hoods are usually manufactured in nine parts. The smaller size facilitates shipping and handling. The customer assembles the hood with small screws and nuts.

Four-foot cone hoods are usually manufactured in four parts. The smaller size facilitates shipping and handling. The customer assembles the pieces with small screws and nuts. Cone-shaped reflectors using a vertical bulb waste light and are very inefficient. Gardeners who try to save money by purchasing cone-shaped reflectors pay even more in lost efficiency.

Vertical hood over a mixed variety indoor garden.

For example, say you bought a cone reflective hood for $20 instead of the top-of-the-line horizontal reflector for $40. First, let's look at efficiency. The cone hood produces at 60-percent efficiency and the horizontal reflector at 100-percent, or 40 percent more. Each lamp costs $36 per month to operate 12 hours daily at $0.10 per kilowatt-hour (kWh). If 100 percent = $0.10 per kilowatt-hour, then 60-percent efficiency = $0.06, or a loss of $0.04 for each kilowatt-hour. With this information we can deduce that $36/$0.04 = 900 hours. In 900 hours (75 12-hour days) the horizontal reflector has recouped the extra $20 cost. Not only does the vertical cone yield 40 percent less light, it costs 40 percent more to operate! When this 75-day break-even point is reached, you will be stuck with an inefficient reflective hood that costs more for fewer lumens every second the lamp is using electricity!

Lightweight reflective hoods with open ends dissipate heat quickly. Extra air flows directly through the hood and around the bulb in open-end fixtures to cool the bulb and the fixture. Aluminum dissipates heat more quickly than steel. Train a fan on reflective hoods to speed heat loss.

Artificial light fades as it travels from its source (the bulb). The closer you put the reflector to the bulb, the more intense the light it reflects.

Enclosed hoods with a glass shield covering the bulb operate at higher temperatures. The glass shield is a barrier between plants and the hot bulb. Enclosed hoods must have enough vents; otherwise, heat build-up in the fixture causes bulbs to burn out prematurely. Many of these enclosed fixtures have a special vent fan to evacuate hot air.

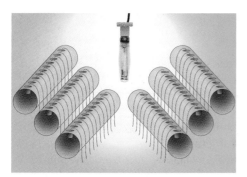

The lamp in this hydroponic garden hangs between plants so foliage receives only direct light.

Air-Cooled Lamp Fixtures

Several air-cooled lights are available. Some use a reflective hood with a protective glass face and two squirrel cage blowers to move air through the sealed reflective hood cavity. The air is forced to travel around corners, which requires a higher velocity of airflow. Other air-cooled reflectors have no airflow turns, so the air is evacuated quickly and efficiently.

Water-cooled Lamp Fixtures

Water-cooled and air-cooled lamp fixtures are somewhat popular in hot climates. These lamps run cooler and can be moved closer to plants. Water-cooled bulbs are difficult for thermal imaging equipment to detect. Air-cooled fixtures are inexpensive to operate and easy to set up. Keep outer jacket clean and avoid scratching.

Gardeners decrease bulb heat by 80 percent with a properly set up water-cooled bulb. The water and outer jacket account for a ten percent lumen loss. Gardeners make up for the loss by moving bulbs closer to plants. On an average day, a 1000-watt bulb uses about 100 gallons of water to keep cool, if the water runs to waste. To recirculate the water requires a big, big reservoir. The water in the reservoir that serves a recirculating cooling system must also be cooled. Reservoir coolers can easily cost $1000.

No Reflective Hood

One option is to remove the reflective hood. With no hood, the lamp burns cooler and emits only direct light.

Reflective Hood Study

I constructed a black room, everything black inside, to measure the amount of light reflective hoods yield. The room was

Gardening Indoors

10 × 10-foot square (3 m²). The floor was covered with black tar paper. Less than three percent light could be reflected from the black surfaces—there was no extra light in this room. Measurements were made every 12 inches (30 cm) on a matrix marked on the floor. The walls had one-foot increments marked.

I tested five different lamps: a 1000-watt clear super metal halide, a 1000-watt HP sodium, a 600-watt HP sodium, a 400-watt super metal halide, and a 400-watt HP sodium. I positioned the bulb exactly three feet from the floor. Every lamp was warmed up for 15 minutes before taking measurements.

The foot-candle readings on the floor were taken every 12 inches (30 cm) and the results posted to a spreadsheet program. I used a simple spreadsheet graph program to present the graphic results.

The studies show a huge difference between reflective hoods. Some companies do not test their hoods before putting them on the market. To protect yourself and your plants, set up tests like the ones I did here to find out which reflector is the best for your needs.

When a reflector distributes light evenly, the lamp can be placed closer to plants.

In general, the larger the wattage of the bulb, the more efficient it is. Since light intensity diminishes so quickly, bulbs must be close to plants. Consequently, more lamps or point sources of light are necessary for even distribution of bright light.

Operating costs for three 600-watt HPS lamps are lower than for two 1000-watt HPS lamps. The 600-watt lamps produce more lumens for the same amount of money, plus they can be closer to plants. There are also three point sources of light, which evens out distribution.

A heat vent outlet around the bulb helps dissipate heat into the atmosphere. Excessive heat around the bulb causes premature burnout.

The studies show the light distribution of several types of light reflectors. The graphs clearly show that horizontal reflectors deliver many more lumens than vertical setups.

Check out the "Light Measurement Handbook" available free on the Internet. The 64-page technical book answers endless light questions. Download the book in a few minutes, photos and all: www.Intl-Light.com/handbook/.

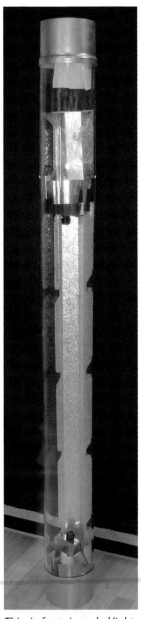

This six-foot air-cooled light tube is available from the Garden Spout and other retailers. It can handle up to a 60-inch bulb.

Move small plants to shelves around the perimeter of the indoor garden. Remember, plants grow wherever light shines!

Reflective Light

Flat white contains little or no light-absorbing pigment, so it absorbs almost no light and reflects almost all light. Do not use glossy white. It contains varnish that inhibits reflective light. A matte texture provides more reflective surface.

Foylon is a reflective material that reflects light and heat in an evenly dispersed pattern. It is durable, and it reflects about 95 percent of the light that hits it. The material is plied with ripstop fiber and is thick enough to act as an insulator. It's also heat and flame resistant. For more information on Foylon, see www.greenair.com.

Reflective Mylar provides one of the most reflective surfaces possible. Mylar looks like a very thin mirror. Unlike light-absorbing paint, Reflective Mylar reflects almost all light. To install Reflective Mylar, simply tape or tack to the wall. To prevent rips or tears, place a piece of tape over

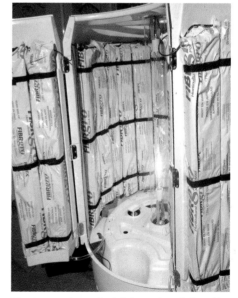

Plants grow in vertical slabs and are irrigated from above in this completely enclosed recirculating garden.

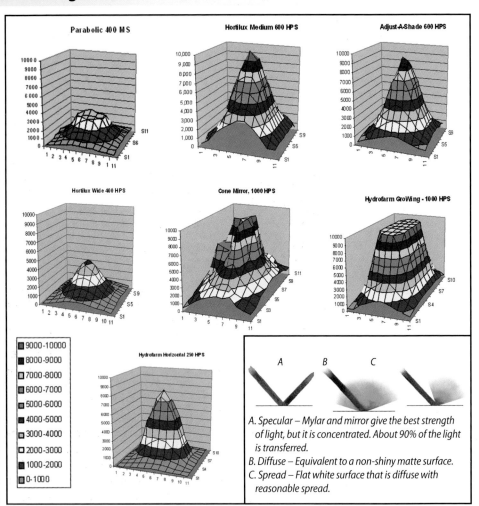

Parabolic 400 MS

Hortilux Medium 600 HPS

Adjust-A-Shade 600 HPS

Hortilux Wide 400 HPS

Cone Mirror, 1000 HPS

Hydrofarm GroWing - 1000 HPS

Hydrofarm Horizontal 250 HPS

Legend:
- 9000-10000
- 8000-9000
- 7000-8000
- 6000-7000
- 5000-6000
- 4000-5000
- 3000-4000
- 2000-3000
- 1000-2000
- 0-1000

A. Specular – Mylar and mirror give the best strength of light, but it is concentrated. About 90% of the light is transferred.

B. Diffuse – Equivalent to a non-shiny matte surface.

C. Spread – Flat white surface that is diffuse with reasonable spread.

Reflective Chart

Material	Percent Reflected
Foylon	94–95
Reflective Mylar	90–95
Flat white paint	85–93
Semigloss white	75–80
Flat yellow	70–80
Aluminum foil	70–75
Black	less than 10

How to add light without using more electricity

Any unused light is wasted. There are several ways to get the most out of your light without adding more watts, including:

Use several 400 or 600-watt lamps instead of 1000s.
Manually rotate plants regularly.
Add a shelf.
Install rolling beds.
Grow a perpetual crop.
Use a light mover.

the spot where the staple, nail or tack will be inserted. Although expensive, Mylar is preferred by many gardeners. The trick is to position it flat against the wall. When loosely affixed to surfaces, light is poorly reflected. To increase its effectiveness, keep Reflective Mylar clean.

Aluminum foil is one of the worst possible reflective surfaces. The foil always crinkles up and reflects light in the wrong directions—actually wasting light. It also reflects more ultraviolet rays than other surfaces, which are harmful to chloroplasts in leaves.

Mirrors also reflect light, but much less than Mylar. Light must first pass through the glass in the mirror, before it is reflected back through the same glass. Light is lost when passing through the glass.

Reflective walls increase light in the growing area. Less intense light on the perimeter of gardens is wasted unless it is reflected back onto foliage. Up to 95 percent of this light can be reflected back toward plants. For example, if 500 foot-candles of light is escaping from the edge of the garden and it is reflected at the rate of 50 percent, then 250 foot-candles will be available on the edge of the garden.

Reflective walls should be 12 inches (30 cm) or less from the plants for optimum reflection. Ideally, take the walls to the plants. The easiest way to install mobile walls is to hang the lamp near the corner of a room. Use the two corner walls to reflect light. Move the two outside walls close to plants to reflect light. Make the mobile walls from lightweight plywood, Styrofoam, or white Visqueen plastic.

Using white Visqueen plastic to "white out" a room is quick and causes no damage to the room. Visqueen plastic is inexpensive, removable, and reusable. It can

Watch out for the following:
Stretched or leggy plants.
Weak or yellowing plants.
Foliage burned directly under the bulb.
Uneven lighting.
Light mover binding or getting hung up.

be used to fabricate walls and partition rooms. Waterproof Visqueen also protects the walls and floor from water damage. Lightweight Visqueen is easy to cut with scissors or a knife and can be stapled, nailed, or taped.

To make the white walls opaque, hang black Visqueen on the outside. The dead air space between the two layers of Visqueen also increases insulation.

The only disadvantages of white Visqueen plastic are that it is not as reflective as flat white paint, it may get brittle after a few years of use under an HID lamp, and it can be difficult to find at retail outlets.

Using flat white paint is one of the simplest, least expensive, most efficient ways to create optimum reflection. Artists' titanium white paint is more expensive but more reflective. While easy to clean, semi-gloss white is not quite as reflective as flat white. Regardless of the type of white used, a nontoxic, fungus-inhibiting agent should be added when the paint is mixed. A gallon of good flat white paint costs less than $25. One or two gallons should be enough to "white out" the average indoor garden. But do not paint the floor white—the reflection is detrimental to tender leaf undersides. Use a primer coat to prevent bleed-through of dark colors or stains or if walls are rough and unpainted. Install the

Gardening Indoors

vent fans before painting. Fumes are unpleasant and can cause health problems. Painting is labor-intensive and messy, but it's worth the trouble.

More Free Growing Light

Even though the lumens-per-watt conversion is lower with 400-watt bulbs than 1000-watt bulbs, hanging ten 400-watt lamps over the same area that four 1000-watt lamps cover, provides more even distribution of light and minimizes shading. Three 600-watt lamps that produce 270,000 lumens from three point sources, instead of two 1000-watt HP sodiums yielding 280,000 lumens from two points, lower total light output by 10,000 lumens but increase the number of sources of light. Lamps can be placed closer to plants, increasing efficiency even more.

Manually rotating plants helps them fill out better, promoting more even development. The longer plants are in the flowering growth stage, the more light they need. During the first three to four weeks of flowering, plants process a little less light than during the last three to four weeks. Plants flowering during the last three to four weeks are placed directly under the bulb where light is the brightest. Plants that have just entered the flowering room can stay on the perimeter until the more mature plants are moved out. This simple trick can easily increase harvests by five to ten percent.

When plants get big it can become laborious to rotate them. Difficult jobs often go undone. Save the strain and use a light mover, or put the containers on wheels.

Add a shallow shelf around the perimeter of the garden to use light that is eaten by the walls. This sidelight is often very bright and very much wasted. Use brackets to put up a four to six-inch-wide shelf around the perimeter of the garden. The shelf can be built on a slight angle and lined with plastic to form a runoff canal. Pack small plants in six-inch pots along the shelf. Rotate them so they develop evenly. These plants can either flower on the short shelf or when moved under the light.

Installing rolling beds will remove all but one walkway from the garden. Greenhouse gardeners learned long ago to save space. We can use the same information to increase usable growing space in an indoor garden. Gardens with elevated growing beds often waste light on walkways. To make use of more growing area place two, two-inch (6 cm) pipes or wooden dowels below the growing bed. The pipe allows the beds to be rolled back and forth, so only one walkway is open at a time. This simple trick usually increases growing space by about 25 percent of the garden.

Growing a perpetual crop and flowering only a portion of the garden allows for more plants in a smaller area and a higher overall yield. More plants receive intense light, and no light is wasted in such a garden.

Light Movers

Replicate the movement of the sun through the sky with a motorized light mover. A light mover is a device that moves lamps back and forth or in circles across the ceiling of an indoor garden. The linear or circular path distributes light evenly. Use a light mover to get lights closer to plants. Keep plants at least 12 inches away from a lamp on a light mover. The closer a lamp is to plants without burning them, the more light plants receive!

Light movers make bright light distribution more even. Uniform light distribution makes plants grow evenly. Plants placed directly under the center of the HID tend to grow toward and around stationary HIDs. These extra-tall plants can shade other plants' foliage. More plants receive more intense light with a lamp moving overhead. This is not a substitute for more lumens from an additional lamp. It is a more efficient way to use each HID, especially 1000-watt lamps. A lamp that is directly overhead casts more direct, intense light to a greater number of plants.

Slower-moving light movers are generally more reliable. Fast-moving light movers can cause lightweight reflectors to wobble or list.

Light from a stationary bulb always shines with the same intensity in the same spot. If upper foliage shades lower leaves, growth slows and is uneven. Light, received by plants from several directions, shines more intensely on more foliage. The light energy is being processed by more foliage and promotes even growth. In nature, as the sun arcs overhead, the entire plant gets full benefit of the light. Some plants grow into a classic Christmas tree shape. This is the most efficient configuration for the plant's growth. Light reaches the center of the plant as well as all outside parts.

Commercial light movers supply more intense light to more plants for less money. Gardeners report that light movers make it possible to use fewer lamps to get the same yield. Light movers increase intense light coverage by 25 to 35 percent. According to some gardeners, three lamps mounted on motorized light mover(s) will do the job of four lamps.

Benefits of a light mover:

Bulbs can be placed closer to the canopy of the garden.

Increases bright light to more plants.

Delivers light from different angles providing even lighting.

Increases intense light coverage 25 percent or more.

Light is closer to plants.

Economical use of light.

Reliable linear light movers offer an exceptional value to indoor gardeners. Light intensity increases exponentially when bulbs are moved closer to the garden using a light mover.

Motorized light movers keep an even garden profile. The HID draws about 9.2 amperes (amps). If this lamp is on a 15- or 20-ampere circuit, you can easily add a light mover that draws one more ampere to the circuit with no risk of overload.

Linear systems move in a straight line simulating the sun's path through the heavens. A linear system increases intense light to plants in a linear oval. The area covered by a light mover depends on the length of the track and the number of lamps. The systems use a track that affixes to the ceiling. The lamp moves back and forth across the ceiling, guided

Gardening Indoors

Setting up a Light Mover Step-by-Step

Step One: Choose the right place.

Step Two: Affix board to the ceiling. Mount light mover track on board. Attach Sun Twist units to a board that is screwed into ceiling joists.

Step Three: Run electrical cord via timer to light mover.

Step Four: Attach supporting electrical wires with cable ties alongside track. You may want to install eyebolts alongside the light track.

Step Five: Reduce vibrations by backing the mounting board with a vibration-absorbing material.

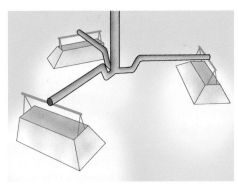

This light mover rotates three lamps above the garden for even distribution.

Affix a sturdy board to the ceiling. Mount a light mover on the board with joist below. Run electrical cord via timer to light mover.

Here is a two-lamp rotary light mover above a 36-container garden. Manufacturers say the light mover illuminates more area for less light.

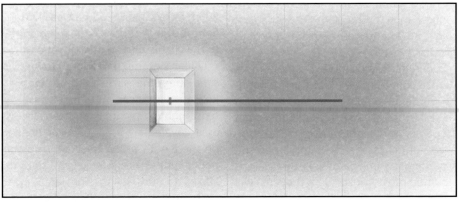

Approximate coverage of a linear light mover. Note the brightest light is close to the reflector.

by the track. The lamp is fastened to the mover with an adjustable chain or cord. These units vary in length and the speed at which the lamp travels. Some are designed for one lamp, while others are able to move six lamps efficiently. A six-foot linear light mover increases optimum coverage of light from 36 to 72 square feet (3.3 m² to 6.5 m²)

Young cuttings and seedlings might stretch and become leggy if the lamp travels too far away. Start using the light movers after the plants are 12 inches (30 cm) tall and have several sets of leaves.

Planter boxes or containers on wheels offer a good alternative to light movers. Containers are rotated daily; wheels make this job a snap. Light reaches every corner of the garden without having to move the lamp. This method has a similar effect as moving the lamp overhead, but is more work because all plants have to be moved, rather than only one or two lamps.

High Intensity Discharge (HID) Lights

Gardeners use HID lamps to replace natural sunlight indoors and grow outstanding plants. High intensity discharge lamps outperform all other lamps in their lumens-per-watt efficiency, spectral balance, and brilliance. The spectrum and brilliance of HIDs help gardeners replicate growth responses induced in plants by natural sunlight. Compare charts on HID spectral emission with the chart on photosynthetic response, chlorophyll synthesis, and positive tropism.

The HID lamp family contains mercury vapor, metal halide, High Pressure (HP) so-dium, and conversion bulbs. Metal halide, HP sodium, and conversion lamps have a spectrum similar to actual sunshine and can be used to grow high-quality plants indoors. Mercury vapor lamps were the first HIDs on the market. Obsolete mercury vapor lamps are electrically inefficient and produce a poor spectrum for plant growth. Now most all mercury vapor lamps have been retrofitted with more efficient HIDs.

Researchers have created a few better bulbs with a higher PAR rating, but there is no new technology in sight. The latest glass covers of the bulbs have become slightly better at letting light through, but there have been very few major technical advances in these bulbs for the last 20 years.

Popular HID wattages include 150, 175, 250, 400, 430, 600, 1000, and 1100. A 1500-watt metal halide is also available but is not practical for growing. The 1500-watt lamp is designed for stadium lighting and generates too much heat and light to be used efficiently indoors. Smaller 150 to 250-watt bulbs are popular for small gardens measuring up to up to three feet square (90 cm²). Brighter 400 to 1000-watt lamps are favorites for larger gardens. The 400 and 600-watt bulbs are most popular among European gardeners. North American gardeners favor 600 and 1000-watt bulbs. Super efficient 1100-watt metal halides were introduced in 2000.

Incandescent bulbs are the least efficient; 600-watt HP sodium lamps are the most efficient. The brightest bulbs measured in lumens-per-watt are the metal halide and HP sodium bulbs.

Originally developed in the 1970s, metal halides and HP sodium bulbs were

Gardening Indoors

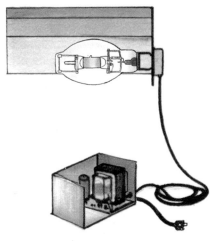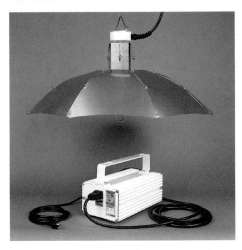

A cutaway drawing of a metal halide reveals the transformer and capacitor in a protective metal box. The bulb and hood are attached to the ballast with 14/3-wire and a mogul socket.

characterized by one main technical limitation—the larger the bulb, the higher the lumens-per-watt conversion. For example, watt for watt, a 1000-watt HP sodium produces about 12 percent more light than a 400-watt HPS and about 25 percent more light than a 150-watt HPS. Scientists overcame this barrier when they developed the 600-watt HP sodium. Watt for watt, a 600-watt HPS produces seven percent more light than the 1000-watt HPS. The "pulse start" metal halides are also brighter and much more efficient than their predecessors.

High intensity discharge lamps produce light by passing electricity through vaporized gas enclosed in a clear ceramic arc tube under very high pressure. The dose, or combination of chemicals sealed in the arc tube, determines the color spectrum produced. The mix of chemicals in the arc tube allows metal halide lamps to yield the broadest and most diverse spectrum of light. The spectrum of HP sodium lamps is somewhat limited because of the nar-

rower band of chemicals used to dose the arc tube. The arc tube is contained within a larger glass bulb. Most of the ultraviolet (UV) rays produced in the arc tube are filtered by the outer bulb. Never look at the arc tube if the outer bulb breaks. Turn off the lamp immediately. Some bulbs have a phosphor coating inside the bulb. This coating makes them produce a little different spectrum and fewer lumens.

General Electric, Iwasaki, Lumenarc, Osram/Sylvania, Philips, and Venture (SunMaster) manufacture HID bulbs. These companies construct many bulbs with the exact same technical statistics. According to some gardeners, certain brands of bulbs are better than others because of where they are manufactured. They usually came to this conclusion because they purchased two different brands of (1000-watt) bulbs and had better luck using one brand. What these gardeners don't know is that many of the manufacturers buy and use the same components, often manufactured by competitors!

Pulse-start metal halides commonly use 240 volts and harbor the starter in the ballast box, not in the arc tube. These systems employ physically smaller reactor ballasts that keep original line voltage within ten percent of the voltage in the arc tube.

HID Ballasts

A ballast regulates specific starting requirements and line voltage for specific HID lamps. Wattages from 150–1100 use old-fashioned coil transformer-type ballasts. Smaller wattages—below 100—use energy-efficient electronic ballasts. Electronic ballasts run cool and quiet. Scientists continue to develop electronic ballasts for larger wattage HIDs, but the failure rate is still very high. It is important to buy the proper ballast for your HID. Smart gardeners buy the entire HID system—ballast, lamp, socket, connecting wiring, and timer—at the same time from a reputable supplier to ensure the ballast and lamp go together.

Place ballasts up on shelves so they stay out of the way and out of the splash-range of water.

New ballast designs are very simple and efficient.

Be careful when purchasing ballasts made in China, or Asia in general. Many of these ballasts are poorly made and do not meet local safety standards. Do not be tricked by misleading sales phrases such as "all components UL or CSA approved." Of course, each of the components could be UL or CSA approved, but when the components are used together to operate a lamp, they are not UL or CSA approved. Furthermore, chances are that if components are approved, they are not approved for the specific application. Cheap transformers, capacitors, and starters are cheap because they are of inferior quality.

Do not try to mix and match ballasts and lamps. Just because a lamp fits a socket attached to a ballast does not mean it will work properly in it. If you use the wrong ballast, capacitor, or starter with a lamp, the lamp will not produce the rated amount of light, and it will burn out sooner. The wrong lamp plugged into the wrong ballast adds up to a burnout!

Gardening Indoors

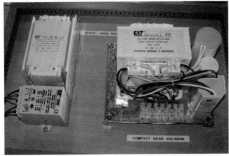

Ballast designs are more simple now than ever before. Above, you see two new European ballast designs.

The ballast is attached to the bulb and reflective hood in this greenhouse fixture.

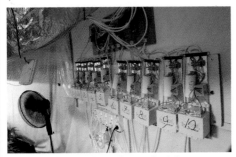

Attach ballasts to the wall on a plank for easy inspection and troubleshooting.

The "core," or transformer, consists of metal plates stuck together by resin and wound with copper wire. The capacitor can is on the right under the connecting wires.

More economical ballast kits contain a transformer core, capacitor (HPS and some metal halides), starter, containing box, and, sometimes, wire. You can purchase components separately from an electrical supply store, but it's a bigger hassle than it's worth.

If unfamiliar with electrical component assembly and reading wiring diagrams, purchase the assembled ballast in a package containing the lamp and hood from one of the many HID distributors.

Do not buy used parts from a junkyard or try to use a ballast if unsure of its capacity. Again, just because a bulb fits a socket attached to a ballast does not mean that it is the proper system.

Even though HIDs have specific ballasting requirements, the ballasts have a good deal in common. The most common characteristics ballasts share are noise and heat. This noise could drive some people to great fits of paranoia! Ballasts operate at 90–150°F (32–60°C). Touch a "strike anywhere" kitchen match to the side to check if it is too hot. If the match lights, the ballast is too hot and should be taken into the shop for assessment. A ballast that runs too hot is noisy and could cause problems or burn out. Heat is the number one ballast destroyer. Many ballasts are manufactured with a protective metal box. This outer shell safely contains the core, capacitor (starter), and wiring. If you build another box around a ballast to dampen noise, make sure there is plenty of air circulation. If the ballast runs too hot, it will be less efficient, burn out prematurely, and may even start a fire!

More expensive ballasts are equipped with ventilation fans to maintain cool operating temperatures. Air vents allow a ballast to run cooler. The vents should protect the internal parts and prevent water from splashing in.

Some industrial ballasts are sealed in fiberglass or similar material to make them weatherproof. These ballasts are not recommended. They were designed for outdoor use where heat buildup is not a problem. Indoors, the protection of the sealed unit from weather is unnecessary and creates excessive heat and inefficient operation.

A handle will make the ballast easy to move. A small 400-watt halide ballast weighs about 30 pounds (14 kg), and a large 1000-watt HP sodium ballast tips the scales at about 55 pounds (25 kg). This small, heavy box is very awkward to move without a handle.

Most ballasts sold by HID stores are "single tap" and set up for 120-volt house-hold current in North America or 240-volts in Europe, Australia, and New Zealand. North American ballasts run at 60 cycles per minute, while European, Australian, and New Zealand models run at 50 cycles per minute. A ballast from Europe, Austra-lia, or New Zealand will not work properly at 60 cycles per minute. Some "multi-tap" or "quad-tap" ballasts are ready for 120 or 240-volt service. Single-tap ballasts ac-commodate only one voltage, usually 120. Multi-tap ballasts accommodate either 120 or 240-volt service.

It is generally easiest to use the regular 120-volt systems, because their outlets are more common. The 240-volt systems are normally used in Europe, Australia, and New Zealand or in North America when several lamps are already taking up space on other 120-volt circuits. Changing a "multi-tap" ballast from 120 volts to 240 volts is a simple matter of moving the wire from the 120-volt tap to the 240-volt tap. "Single-tap" ballasts cannot change oper-ating voltages. Consult the wiring diagram found on each transformer for specific instructions. There is no difference in the electricity consumed by using either 120 or 240-volt systems. The 120-volt system draws about 9.6 amperes, and an HID on a 240-volt current draws about 4.3 amperes. Both use the same amount of electricity.

This gardener lost the crop and almost lost his life! Pay attention to electrical connections, ampere ratings for wire, breaker switches, and connectors.

Some people have a way of making simple things complex.

Work out the details yourself using the chart below.

The ballast has a lot of electricity flow-ing through it. Do not touch the ballast when operating. Do not place the ballast directly on a damp floor or any floor that

Gardening Indoors

might get wet and conduct electricity. Always place it up off the floor, and protect it from possible moisture. The ballast should be suspended in the air or on a shelf attached to the wall. It does not have to be very high off the ground, just far enough to keep it dry.

Place the ballast on a soft foam pad to absorb vibrations and lower decibel sound output. Loose components inside the ballast can be tightened to further deaden noise caused by vibrations. Train a fan on ballasts to cool them. Cooler ballasts are more efficient, and bulbs burn brighter.

Ballasts can be attached to the light fixture remote. The remote ballast offers the most versatility and is the best choice for most indoor gardens. A remote ballast is easy to move. Help control heat by placing it on or near the floor to radiate heat in a cool portion of the indoor garden, or move the ballast outside the garden to cool the room. Attached ballasts are fixed to the hood; they require more overhead space,

Some indoor gardeners run flowering rooms 24 hours a day with half as many ballasts. This box is made for three transformers, capacitors, and starters to run six 1000-watt HP sodiums. Three lamps run for 12 hours; the other three lamps run for the next 12 hours.

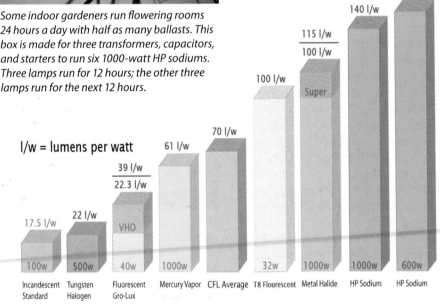

The above bar graph shows the lumens-per-watt conversion of different lamps. Notice that except for the 600-watt HPS, the lumens-per-watt conversion factor increases with higher wattage bulbs. The lumens-per-watt formula is used to measure the lamps' efficiency–the amount of lumens produced for the quantity of watts (electricity) consumed.

are very heavy, and tend to create more heat around the lamp.

Ballasts may be manufactured with an attached timer. These units are very convenient, but the timer should be constructed of heavy-duty, heat-resistant materials. If it is lightweight plastic, it could easily melt under the heat of the ballast.

Ballasts with a switch allow gardeners to use the same ballast with two different sets of lights. This wonderful invention is perfect for running two flowering garden rooms. The lights go on for 12 hours in one indoor garden room while they are off in a second room. When the lights turn off in the first room, the same ballast switches on another set of lights in the second room. This setup is very popular in Canada.

There are also ballasts to run both metal halide and HP sodium systems. These dual-purpose ballasts are not a good idea. They will work, but they generally overdrive the metal halide bulb causing it to burn out prematurely after accelerated lumen output loss. I do not recommend these types of ballasts. If you have a limited budget and can only afford one transformer, use conversion bulbs to change spectrum. (See "Conversion Bulbs")

HID Bulbs

Many new HID bulbs have been developed in the last few years. The most notable have been the 430-watt HP sodium, pulse start metal halides, the AgroSun, SunMaster PAR bulbs, and the 1100-watt metal halide. These HID bulbs are also available with many different outer envelopes, so bulbs can fit into more confining reflective hoods.

High intensity discharge bulbs are rated by wattage and by the size of the outer

envelope or bulb.

High intensity discharge bulbs come in different shapes and sizes. Below each bulb are the numbers industry uses to define their shape and size.

In general, HID bulbs are designed to be tough and durable. New bulbs are tougher than used bulbs. Once the bulb has been used a few hours, the arc tube blackens, and the internal parts become somewhat brittle. After a bulb has been used several hundred hours, a good bump will substantially shorten its life and lessen its luminescence.

Never remove a warm lamp. Heat expands the metal mogul base within the socket. A hot bulb is more difficult to remove, and it must be forced. Special electrical grease is available to lubricate sockets (Vaseline works, too). Lightly smear a dash of the lubricant around the mogul socket base to facilitate bulb insertion and extraction.

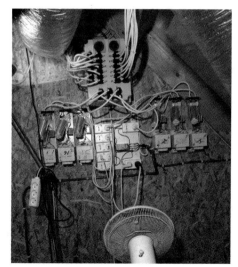

The switch at the top of this photo is running twelve 600-watt lamps in a zigzag pattern. A fan is trained on the ballasts and switch to keep them cool.

Gardening Indoors

The outer arc tube contains practically all the ultraviolet light produced by HIDs. If an HID should happen to break when inserting or removing, unplug the ballast immediately and avoid contact with metal parts to prevent electrical shock.

Always keep the bulb clean. Wait for it to cool before wiping it off with a clean cloth every two to four weeks. Dirt will lower lumen output substantially. Bulbs get covered with insect spray and salty water vapor residues. This dirt dulls lamp brilliance just as clouds dull natural sunlight.

Hands off bulbs! Touching bulbs leaves them with your hand's oily residue. The residue weakens the bulb when it is baked onto it. Most gardeners clean bulbs with Windex or rubbing alcohol and use a clean cloth to remove filth and grime, but Hortilux Lighting advises cleaning bulbs with a clean cloth only.

Lumen output diminishes over time. As the bulb loses brilliance, it generates less heat and can be moved closer to the garden. This is not an excuse to use old bulbs; it is always better to use newer bulbs. However, it is a way to get a few more months out of an otherwise worthless bulb.

Write down the day, month, and year you start using a bulb so you can better calculate when to replace it. For best results, replace metal halides after 12 months of operation and HP sodium bulbs after 18 months. Many gardeners replace them sooner.

Always keep a spare bulb in its original box available to replace old bulbs. You can go blind staring at a dim bulb trying to decide when to replace it. Remember, your pupils open and close to compensate for different light levels! One way to determine when to replace a bulb is to examine the arc tube. When the arc tube is very cloudy or very blackened, it is most likely time to replace it.

1. Place the bulb in a dry container, and set it out for hazardous waste garbage pickup.
2. Lamps contain materials that are harmful to the skin. Avoid contact, and use protective clothing.
3. Do not place the bulb in a fire.

Metal Halide Bulbs

Metal Halide Systems

The metal halide HID lamp is the most efficient source of artificial white light available to gardeners today. It comes in 175, 250, 400, 1000, 1100, and 1500-watt sizes. They may be either clear or phosphor coated, and all require a special ballast. The smaller 175 or 250-watt halides are very popular for closet indoor gardens. The 400, 1000, and 1100-watt bulbs are very popular with most indoor gardeners. The 1500-watt halide is avoided due to its relatively short 2000 to 3000-hour life and incredible heat output. American gardeners generally prefer the larger 1000-watt lamps, and Europeans almost exclusively favor 400-watt metal halide lamps.

The main metal halide manufacturers include General Electric (Multivapor), Osram/Sylvania (Metalarc) and Westinghouse (Metal Halide), Iwasaki (Eye), Venture (SunMaster), and Philips (Son Agro). Each manufacturer makes a super halide which fits and operates in standard halide ballasts and fixtures. Super metal halides produce about 15 percent more lumens than standard halides. Super halides cost a few dollars more than standards but are well worth the money.

SunMaster, a division of Venture Lighting, has developed new horticultural metal halide bulbs. The new bulbs are brighter and provide a spectrum better suited to plant growth. Gardeners prefer the Warm Deluxe bulbs. Check out their web site: www.sunmastergrowlamps.com.

Clear halides are most commonly used by indoor gardeners. Clear super metal halides supply the bright lumens for plant growth. Clear halides work well for seedling, vegetative, and flower growth.

Phosphor-coated 1000-watt halides give off a more diffused light and are easy on the eyes, emitting less ultraviolet light than the clear halides. They produce the same initial lumens and about 4000 fewer lumens than the standard halide and have a slightly different color spectrum. Phosphor-coated halides have more yellow, less blue and ultraviolet light. Phosphor-

coated bulbs used to be popular among gardeners, but this trend has waned over the last ten years because they are not as bright as clear bulbs.

The 1000-watt super clear halides are the most common halides used in indoor gardens in North America. Compare energy distribution charts and lumen output of all lamps to decide which lamp offers the most light for your garden. Typically, a home gardener starts with one super metal halide.

Construction and Operation

Metal halide lamps produce light by passing or arcing electricity through vaporized argon gas, mercury, thorium iodide, sodium iodide, and scandium iodide within the quartz arc tube. After they are in their proper concentrations in the arc tube, the characteristic bright white light is emitted. This process takes about three to five minutes. The metal halide arc system is very complex and requires a seasoning period of 100 hours operation for all its components to stabilize. If a power surge occurs and the lamp goes out or is turned off, it will take five to fifteen minutes for the gases inside the arc tube to cool before restarting.

The outer bulb functions as a protective jacket that contains the arc tube and starting mechanism, keeping them in a constant environment as well as absorbing ultraviolet radiation. Protective glasses that filter out ultraviolet rays are a good idea if you spend much time in the indoor garden, or if you are prone to staring at the HID!

When the lamp is started, incredible voltage is necessary for the initial ionization process to take place. Turning the lamp on and off more than once a day causes unnecessary stress on the HID system and will shorten its life. It is best to start the lamp only once a day, and always use a timer.

The metal halides operate most efficiently in a vertical ± 15-degree position (see diagram). When operated in positions other than ± 15-degrees of vertical, lamp wattage, lumen output, and life decrease; the arc bends, creating non-uniform heating of the arc tube wall, resulting in less efficient operation and shorter life. There are special lamps made to operate in the horizontal or any other position other than ± 15 degrees (see diagram). These bulbs have "HOR" stamped on the crown or base which refers to horizontal.

Lumen Maintenance and Life

The average life of a halide is about 12,000 hours, almost two years of daily operation at 18 hours per day. Many will last even longer. The lamp reaches the end of its life when it fails to start or come up to full brilliance. This is usually caused by deterioration of lamp electrodes over time, loss of transmission of the arc tube from blackening, or shifts in the chemical balance of the metals in the arc tube. Do not wait until the bulb is burned out before changing it. An old bulb is inefficient and costly. Replace bulbs every 10–12 months or 5000 hours. Electrode deterioration is greatest during start-up. Bulbs are cheap! Throw another one in, and you will be happy!

The halide may produce a stroboscopic (flashing) effect. The light will appear bright, then dim, bright, dim, etc. This flashing is the result of the arc being extinguished 120 times every second. Illumination usually remains constant, but it may pulsate a little. This is normal and nothing to worry about.

Metal Halide Ballasts

Read "About Ballasts." The ballast for a 1000-watt halide will operate standard, clear, and phosphor-coated, as well as super, clear, and phosphor-coated halides on a 120 or 240-volt current. Different ballasts are required for each lamp wattage; 150, 250, 400, 1000, 1100, and 1500. The ballast for each wattage will operate all halides (super or standard, clear or phosphor coated) of the same wattage. Each ballast must be specifically designed for the 150, 250, 400, 1000, 1100, or 1500-watt halides, because their starting and operating requirements are unique.

Metal Halide Bulbs

Universal metal halide bulbs designed to operate in any position, vertical or horizontal, supply up to ten percent less light and often have a shorter life.

SunMaster Warm Deluxe Grow Lamps emit balanced light similar to a 3000 kelvin source. The enhanced orange-red component promotes germination, stem elongation, and flowering while a rich blue content assures healthy vegetative growth.

Venture manufactures the AgroSun for Hydrofarm. It is an enhanced metal halide bulb with more yellow/orange in the spectrum. To find out more about this lamp, hit the site www.growlights.com.

High Pressure Sodium Systems

The most impressive fact about the 600-watt high-pressure sodium lamp is that it produces 90,000 initial lumens. The HP sodium is also the most efficient HID lamp

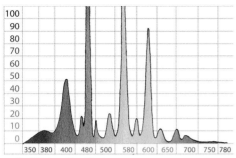

Cool Deluxe SunMaster

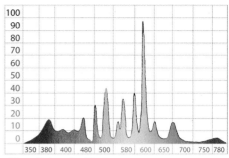

Warm Deluxe SunMaster

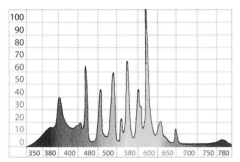

Neutral Deluxe SunMaster

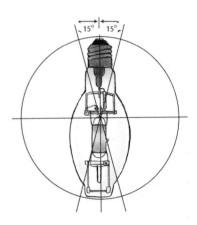

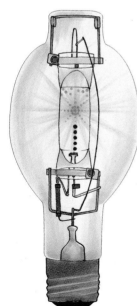

Metal Halide bulb showing reaction.

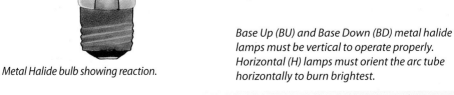

Base Up (BU) and Base Down (BD) metal halide lamps must be vertical to operate properly. Horizontal (H) lamps must orient the arc tube horizontally to burn brightest.

HPS + Reaction

available. It comes in 35, 50, 70, 100, 150, 200, 250, 310, 400, 600, and 1000 wattages. Nearly all HP sodium bulbs used in indoor gardens are clear. All HP sodium vapor lamps have their own unique ballast. High pressure sodium lamps are manufactured by: GE (Lucalox), Sylvania (Lumalux), Westinghouse (Ceramalux), Philips (Son Agro), Iwasaki (Eye), and Venture (High Pressure Sodium). American gardeners use 1000 and 600-watt HP sodiums most often, while European gardeners love 400 and 600-watt HPS lamps.

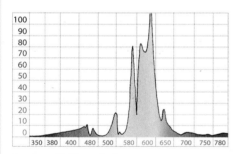

Spectrum HPS Super bulb

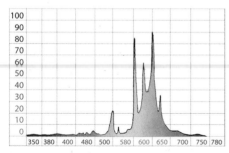

Color spectrum of Son Agro bulb

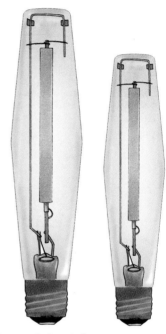

High Pressure Sodium Bulbs

High pressure sodium lamps emit an orange-tinged glow that could be compared to the harvest sun. The color spectrum is highest in the yellow, orange, and red end. For many years, scientists believed this spectrum promoted flower production.

However, with the new PAR technology, scientists are rethinking old theories. A plant's light needs change when flowering; it no longer needs to produce so many vegetative cells. Vegetative growth slows and eventually stops during blooming. All the plant's energy and attention is focused on flower production so it can complete its annual life cycle. Light from the red end of the spectrum stimulates floral hormones within the plant, promoting flower production. According to some gardeners, flower volume and weight increase when using HP sodium lights. Other compelling evidence shows the SunMaster halides to be superior. Gardeners using a 10×10-foot ($3 m^2$) room often retain the 1000-watt halide and add a 1000-watt sodium during flowering. Adding an HP sodium lamp not only doubles available light, it increases the red end of the spectrum. This 1:1 ratio (1 halide and 1 HP sodium) is a popular combination for flowering.

Operation and Construction

High pressure sodium lamps produce light by passing electricity through vaporized sodium and mercury within an arc tube. The HP sodium lamp is totally different from the metal halide in its physical, electrical, and color spectrum characteristics. An electronic starter works with the magnetic component of the ballast to supply a short, high-voltage pulse. This electrical pulse vaporizes the xenon gas and initiates the starting process that takes three to four minutes. Electricity passes, or arcs, between the two main electrodes. If the lamp is turned off, or power surge occurs and the lamp goes out, the gases in the tube will usually need to cool three to fifteen minutes before restarting is possible.

Similar to the metal halide, the HP sodium has a two-bulb construction, with an outer protective bulb and inner arc tube. The outer bulb, or jacket, protects the arc tube from damage and contains a vacuum, reducing heat loss from the arc tube. The sodium, mercury, and xenon gas are contained within the arc tube and have a constant operating temperature. The lamp may be operated in any position (360 degrees). However, most prefer to hang the lamp overhead in a horizontal operating position.

Life and Lumen Maintenance

High pressure sodium lamps have the longest life and best lumen maintenance of all HIDs. Eventually, the sodium bleeds out through the arc tube. Over a long period of daily use, the sodium to mercury ratio changes, causing the voltage in the arc to rise. Finally, the arc tube's operating voltage will rise higher than the ballast is able to sustain. At this point, the lamp will start, warm-up to full intensity, and go out. This sequence is then repeated over and over, signaling the end of the lamp's life. The life of a 1000-watt HP sodium lamp will be about 24,000 hours, or five years, operating at 12 hours per day. Replace HPS bulbs after 18 to 24 months to keep the garden bright.

HP Sodium Ballasts

Read "About Ballasts." A special ballast is specifically required for each wattage of HP sodium lamp. Each wattage lamp has unique operating voltages and currents during start-up and operation. These voltages and currents do not correspond to similar wattages of other HID lamps. Sodium ballasts contain a transformer that is larger than that of a metal halide, a capacitor, and an igniter or starter. Purchase complete HID systems rather than a component kit.

HP Sodium Bulbs

High pressure sodium bulbs are used for industrial, residential, and horticultural lighting. The bulbs are inexpensive and readily available. Discount building stores often carry 250- and 400-watt lamps. All HP sodium lamps will grow indoor vegetables, flowers, and ornamental plants. Even though they are brighter, the spectrum contains little blue and more yellow/orange. Lack of color balance makes plants stretch between internodes but does not necessarily diminish overall harvest.

Philips designed and manufactures the 430-watt Son Agro specifically to augment natural sunlight and grow plants. The bulb produces a little more blue light in the spectrum. Adding a touch more blue light helps prevent most plants from becoming leggy. The other enhanced performance HP sodium bulb is the Hortilux by Eye (Iwasaki).

The 600-watt HP sodium increased the lumens-per-watt (LPW) efficiency of high intensity bulbs by seven percent. The 600-watt HP sodium is the most efficient lamp on the market. The 430-watt Son Agro HP sodium bulbs have more blue in the spectrum and run a little hotter than their 400-watt counterpart. The Son Agro bulbs are the choice of European gardeners.

Conversion Bulbs

Conversion, or retrofit, bulbs increase flexibility. One type of conversion bulb allows you to utilize a metal halide (or mercury vapor) system with a bulb that emits light similar to an HP sodium bulb. The bulb looks like a blend between a metal

halide and an HP sodium. While the outer bulb looks like a metal halide, the inner arc tube is similar to that of an HP sodium. A small igniter is located at the base of the bulb. Other conversion bulbs retrofit HP sodium systems to convert them into virtual metal halide systems.

Conversion bulbs are manufactured in 150, 215, 360, 400, 880, 940, and 1000-watt sizes. You do not need an adaptor or any additional equipment. Simply screw the bulb into a compatible ballast of comparable wattage. Conversion bulbs operate at a lower wattage and are not as

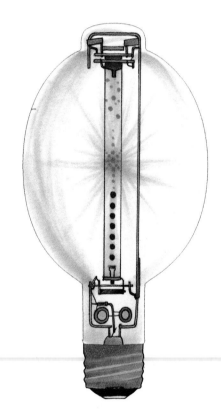

Conversion bulbs make it possible to have both metal halide and HP sodium spectrums at the expense of electrical efficiency.

bright as HP sodium bulbs. Although conversion bulbs have less blue, they are up to 25 percent brighter than metal halide systems and their lumens-per-watt conversion is better than that of super metal halides. The 940-watt conversion bulb has a lumens-per-watt rating of 138. Similar to the HP sodium lamp, the conversion bulb has a life expectancy of up to 24,000 hours. Unlike most HP sodium lamps, which flicker on and off near the end of their lives, conversion bulbs go off and remain off at the end of their lives.

Although conversion bulbs are not inexpensive, they are certainly less expensive than an entire HP sodium system. For gardeners who own a metal halide system, or who deem metal halide the most appropriate investment for their lighting needs, conversion bulbs offer a welcome alternative for bright light. In the United States of America, CEW Lighting distributes Iwasaki lights. Look for their Sunlux Super Ace and Sunlux Ultra Ace lamps.

Venture, Iwasaki, and Sunlight Supply manufacture bulbs for conversion in the opposite direction, from HP sodium to metal halide. Venture's White-Lux and Iwasaki's White Ace are metal halide lamps which will operate in an HP sodium system. The 250, 400, 1000-watt conversion bulbs can be used in compatible HPS systems with no alterations or additional equipment. If you own a high-pressure sodium system but need the added blue light which metal halide bulbs produce, these conversion bulbs will suit your needs.

Many gardeners have great success using conversion bulbs. If you have a metal halide system but want the extra red and yellow light of an HP sodium lamp to promote flowering, simply buy a conversion bulb. Instead of investing in both a metal

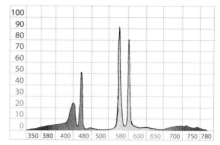

Mercury Vapor Spectrum

Full Spectrum?

The term "full-spectrum" was coined in the 1960s by photo-biologist Dr. John Ott to describe electric light sources that simulate the visible and UV spectrum of natural light.

Today there are many fluorescent lamps advertised as "full-spectrum." All fluorescent bulbs marketed as "full-spectrum" grow lights are tri-phosphor-coated. Until Dr. John Ott began producing and selling the first "color-corrected" bulbs, all fluorescent lamps were halo-phosphor or deluxe halo-phosphor blends, which did not render the reds well. Tri-phosphor-coated lamps emit the visible light spectrum in spectrums from 2700 K to 6400 K. They simulate colors by mixing the three colors associated with the three cone types in our eyes "specially formulated to replicate all the wavelengths in the visible spectrum."

The term "full-spectrum" has been successful to help sell overpriced lights. Now the market is rampant with hype about the lights. Resellers purchase tri-phosphor bulbs from manufacturers and market them as "Grow Lites." Major lamp manufacturers do not sell tri-phosphor-coated lights as "full-spectrum."

halide and an HP sodium system, you can rely on a metal halide system and use conversion bulbs when necessary, or vice versa.

Gardening Indoors

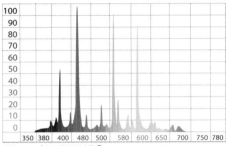

Warm white (2700 K) fluorescent spectrum

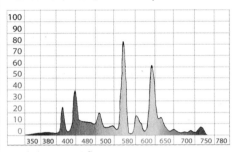

Daylight (6400 K) fluorescent spectrum

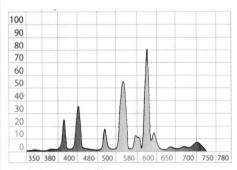

Cool white (4100 K) fluorescent spectrum

Watts	Initial Lumens
26	1800
55	3500
60	4000
65	4500
85	6000
95	7600
12	9000
125	9500
150	12,000
200	15,000

HP Sodium to Metal Halide

The Sunlux Super Ace and Ultra Ace (Iwasaki) and Retrolux (Philips) produce an HP sodium spectrum with a metal halide system. These bulbs make it possible to use a metal halide ballast and get the same spectrum as an HP sodium lamp. Lumens-per-watt efficiency is traded for the convenience of using these bulbs. A 1000-watt HP sodium bulb produces 140,000 initial lumens. A MH to HPS conversion bulb produces 130,000 initial lumens. If you only want one lamp, a conversion bulb is a fair choice.

Metal Halide to HP Sodium

The White Ace (Iwasaki) and White Lux (Venture) are conversion bulbs. They have a metal halide spectrum and are used in an HPS system. The bulb converts from HPS to MH and produces 110,000 initial metal halide lumens.

Mercury Vapor Lamps

The mercury vapor lamp is the oldest and best-known member of the HID family. The HID principle was first used with the mercury vapor lamp around the turn of the 20th century, but it was not until the mid 1930s that the mercury vapor lamp was really employed commercially.

Mercury vapor lamps produce only 60 lumens-per-watt. A comparison of the spectral energy distribution of the mercury vapor and the photosynthetic response chart will show this is a poor lamp for horticulture. It is expensive to operate and produces a spectrum with a low PAR value.

Lamps are available in sizes from 40 to 1000-watts. Bulbs have fair lumen maintenance and a relatively long life. Most wattages last up to three years at 18 hours of daily operation.

Bulbs usually require separate ballasts; however, there are a few low wattage bulbs with self-contained ballasts. Uninformed gardeners occasionally try to scrounge mercury vapor ballasts from junkyards and use them in place of the proper halide or HP sodium ballast. Trying to modify these ballasts for use with other HIDs will cause problems.

Fluorescent Lamps

Fluorescent lamps have gone through major changes in recent years. New bulbs produce more light. Most gardeners use fluorescents to grow cuttings and small vegetative plants. Some gardeners even use them to flower a crop. Fluorescents are available in many different spectrums, some almost identical to natural sunlight.

Fluorescent lamps are long glass tubes that come in a wide variety of lengths, from one to twelve feet. The two- and four-foot tubes are the easiest to handle and most readily available. Two four-foot fluorescent bulbs in a shop light fixture cost from $20 to $30.

Fluorescent lamps work very well for rooting cuttings. They supply cool, diffused light in the proper color spectrum to promote root growth. Use any "daylight spectrum" fluorescent lamp to root cuttings. Fluorescents produce much less light than HIDs and must be very close (two to four inches) to the plants for best results.

Using fluorescents along with

HIDs is awkward and problematic. When using them in conjunction with HIDs, fluorescents must be very close to plants to provide enough intense light to do any good. Fixtures may also shade plants from HID light and generally get in the way.

Plants will flower under fluorescent lights. The flowers will be small, but, with enough fluorescent light, the plants will mature. The garden will have to literally be lined with fluorescents to supply enough light.

Fluorescent tubes are available in so many different wattages or outputs that they are hard to track! All fluorescents require specific ballasts. The old standard (T12) tubes use about ten watts per linear foot. A two-foot tube uses about 20 watts, four-foot: 40 watts, etc. The most common bulbs used for growing are available in lengths from 15 inches (38 cm) to four feet (120 cm). Lamps are available in very low to more than 50 watts. Circular fluorescent tubes are also available but used by few gardeners.

Power twist, or groove type, lamps offer additional lumens in the same amount of linear space. The deep wide grooves give more glass surface area and more light output. Several companies market variations of power twist fluorescents.

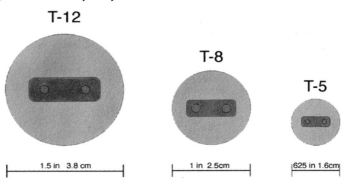

T-12

T-8

T-5

1.5 in 3.8 cm

1 in 2.5cm

.625 in 1.6cm

This end view of different sized fluorescent lamps shows their diameters.

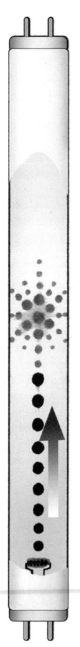

The arc tube of a fluorescent lamp is long, emitting light along its entire length.

Blacklight fluorescent lamps emit ultraviolet (UV) rays through a dark filter glass bulb, but they are not used to grow warm-season annual vegetables and flowers.

Most major lighting manufacturers—GE, Osram/Sylvania, and Philips—make fluorescent lamps in a variety of spectrums. The most common are Warm White, White, Cool White, Full Spectrum, and Daylight. See chart for kelvin temperatures. Sylvania has the GroLux and the Wide Spectrum GroLux. The Standard GroLux is the lamp to use for starting cuttings or seedlings. It is designed for use as the only source of light, having the full spectrum necessary for photosynthesis and chlorophyll production. The Wide Spectrum GroLux is designed to supplement natural light and covers the blue to far-red regions. Westinghouse has the AgroLight that produces a very similar spectrum to the sun. Warm White and Cool White bulbs used together make excellent lamps to root cuttings.

Fluorescent bulbs are further classified by diameter and come in the sizes T12 (1.5 inch [5 cm]), T8 (1 inch [3 cm]), T5 (0.625 inch [1.5 cm]) and CFL (see "Compact Fluorescent Lamps"). The T12 uses old-fashioned magnetic ballasts. The T8 and the T5 (technically CFLs) use electronic ballasts. Gardeners prefer slimmer T8 and T5 bulbs with electronic ballasts because they run cooler, electricity cycles faster, and lights do not flicker.

The average lumen output of a 40-watt T12 is 2800 lumens, about 68 lumens per watt.

A 32-watt T8 bulb yields 100 lumens per watt and cranks out 100 average lumens.

A 54-watt T5 throws 5000 average lumens, which means it produces 92 lumens per watt.

Construction and Operation

Fluorescent lamps create light by passing electricity through gaseous vapor under low pressure.

Like the HID family, fluorescents require an appropriate fixture containing a small ballast to regulate electricity and household electrical current. The fixture is usually integrated into the reflective hood. There are several types of fixtures. The most common fluorescent bulbs used for growing are hooked to sockets with bi-pin connectors. If purchasing new tubes, make sure the bulb fits the fixture. The fixture may contain one, two, or four tubes.

A ballast radiates almost all heat produced by the system. The ballast is located far enough away from fluorescent tubes that plants can actually touch them without being burned.

Ballasts will normally last 10–12 years. Used fluorescent fixtures are generally acceptable. The end of a magnetic ballast's life is usually accompanied by smoke and a miserable chemical odor. Electronic ballasts simply stop. When the ballast burns out, remove it and buy a new one to replace it. Be very careful if the ballast has brown slime or sludge on or around it. This sludge could contain carcinogenic PCBs. If the ballast contains the sludge, dispose of it in an approved location. Most modern fluorescents are self-starting, but older fluorescents require a special starter. This starter may be integrated into the body of the fixture and hidden from view, or be a small metal tube (about one inch [3 cm] in diameter and one-half inch long [1 cm]), located at the end of the fixture on the underside. The latter starters are replaceable, while the former require a trip to the electrical store.

If your fluorescent fixture does not work, and you are not well versed in fluorescent troubleshooting, take it to the nearest electrical store and ask for advice. Make sure they test each component and tell you why it should be replaced. It might be less expensive to buy another fixture.

The tubular glass bulb is coated on the inside with phosphor. The mix of phosphorescent chemicals in the coating and the gases contained within determine the spectrum of colors emitted by the lamp. Electricity arcs between the two electrodes located at each end of the tube, stimulating the phosphor to emit light energy. The light emission is strongest near the center of the tube and somewhat less at the ends. If rooting just a few cuttings, place them under the center of the fixture for best results.

Once the fluorescent is turned on, it will take a few seconds for the bulb to warm-up before an arc can be struck through the tube. Fluorescents blacken with age, losing intensity. Replace bulbs when they reach 70 percent of their stated service life listed on the package or label. A flickering light is about to burn out and should be replaced. Life expectancy ranges from 9000 hours (15 months at 18 hours daily operation).

Compact Fluorescent Lamps

Available since the early 1990s, compact fluorescent lamps (CFLs) are finally available in larger wattages. The larger CFLs are having a major impact on small indoor gardens. CFLs are similar to long-tube fluorescents but boast increased power, smaller size, and an electronic ballast that ensures longevity and precise spectrum rendition. Although not as bright as HIDs, they are available in Cool White and Warm White spectrums and generate little heat. Compact fluorescent lamps are perfect for gardeners with a limited budget and a small space. They run cooler than HIDs and require minimal ventilation.

When CFLs were first introduced, wattages were too small, and bulbs did not emit enough light to grow plants. New large-wattage CFLs are much brighter than smaller, low-wattage CFLs. Several years ago, European companies started selling 55-watt CFLs, and Home Depot began to sell a 65-watt CF flood light for $30. Soon afterward 95, 125, and 200-watt CF lamps made in China became available in North America and Europe. The new lamps changed the way gardeners looked at CFLs. The new CFLs provide enough light to grow plants from seed to harvest.

Gardening Indoors

Compact fluorescent lamp box shows 65 actual watts. That is comparable to a 500-watt incandescent.

Each of these 20-inch (50 cm) bulbs uses 55 watts of electricity.

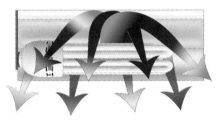

A horizontal reflector is not as efficient as vertical operation with no reflector with this bulb.

The ballast is attached to the lamp in this compact fluorescent.

The inside of an electronic CFL ballast is compact and creates very little heat.

Compact fluorescent lamps used to grow plants are available in two basic styles and shapes. Modular CFLs have independent bulbs and ballasts that can be replaced separately. The bulb is shaped like a long "U" with a two- or four-pin fixture (these lamps are designated "1U"). The 20-inch (50 cm) long "1U" 55-watt, dual-pin base bulbs are common in Europe. Normally, two 55-watt lamps are placed in a reflective hood. Shorter U-shaped bulbs are common in North America, the United Kingdom, Europe, Australia, and New Zealand.

The second type consists of miniaturized fluorescent tubes packaged with an attached (electronic) ballast. The short lamps consist of several U-shaped tubes (designated 4U, 5U, 6U, etc., for the number of U-shaped tubes) that measure from eight to twelve inches (20–30 cm) not including the two- to four-inch (5–10 cm) attached ballast and threaded base. Smaller wattages fit into household incandescent lightbulb sockets. Larger 95, 125, 150, and 200-watt bulbs require a larger mogul socket. Common wattages used for growing plants include 55, 60, 65, 85, 95, 120, 125, 150, and 200.

Lighting and specialty stores sell CF lamps but often charge more than discount warehouse stores. Look for deals at Home Depot and other similar discount stores. Check the Internet, too. For example, www.lightsite.net is an outstanding site that also has a retail store locator. Philips is producing some of the higher wattage lamps. Their PL-H bulb is a 4U bulb available in 60, 85, and 120 wattages with kelvin ratings from 3000 to 4100.

Beware of manufacturer and reseller web sites making outrageous claims about CFL performance. The most common exaggerated claim is found at the Lights of America site about the 65-watt Florex security light. The package claims the lamp produces 6825 lumens, but an asterisk directs you to the bottom of the box and explains these are "brightness lumens" not "photometric lumens." Their web site www.lightsofamerica.com claims the 65-watt Florex produces 4550 lumens. We tested them, and we can agree with 4500 lumens.

Furthermore, manufacturers commonly compare the output of CFLs with that of incandescent lamps. But the comparison is misleading. They claim the 65-watt CFL is equivalent to a 500-watt incandescent. A 65-watt CFL produces the same number of lumens as a 500-watt incandescent bulb. Given this information many people assume that a 65-watt lamp produces as much light as all 500-watt bulbs. Not true.

Cool White CFLs have a kelvin (K) temperature of 4100, with more blue in the spectrum, which lessens internodal branching space in plants. Cool White CFLs are perfect to grow short, stout seedling and vegetative plants. Warm White CFLs (2700 K) have more red in the spectrum and can be used alone but are best used in conjunction with Cool White lamps to avoid internodal stretching during flowering. A 95- to 120-watt lamp will illuminate a space of about two square feet (60 cm²).

Light from CFLs fades fast and must be placed close to the plants. The bulb produces very little heat and can be mounted about two inches (5 cm) away from foliage to achieve the best results.

Short U-shaped bulbs are most efficient when vertically oriented. When mounted horizontally under a reflective hood, much light is reflected back and forth between the bulb's outer envelope and the hood, which markedly lowers efficiency. Heat also builds up from the ballast. Both conditions lessen efficiency.

Save electricity in the indoor garden and replace incandescent bulbs with compact fluorescents. Compact fluorescents use about 75 percent less energy than incandescent lamps, and emit 90 percent less heat for the same amount of light. If you replace ten 100-watt incandescent bulbs, you will save 750 watts of electricity!

Construction and Operation

Compact fluorescent lamps create light by passing electricity through gaseous vapor under low pressure. Compact fluorescent bulbs are coated inside with tri-phosphor, which further expands light emission. CFLs must warm up about five minutes so the chemicals become stable before they come to full brightness. Like all fluorescents, CFLs require an appropriate fixture containing a small electronic ballast to regulate electricity and household electrical current. Ballasts are either attached to the lamp (self-ballasted) or integrated into the reflective hood. Smaller self-ballasted lamps screw into a household incandescent bulb socket. Larger bulbs screw into a mogul socket. Each 1-U bulb is hooked to sockets with bi-pin connectors.

Compact fluorescent lamps will normally last 10–20,000 hours (18–36 months at 18 hours daily use). The life of a CF ballast is from 50,000 to 60,000 hours (seven to nine years at 18 hours daily use). Lamps with an attached ballast burn out three to six times faster than the ballast. When the lamp's life is over, the lamp and the attached ballast are both thrown away, which means you are throwing away a perfectly good ballast! My preference is to use the long CFLs that are not attached to

Gardening Indoors

a ballast.

Compact fluorescent lamps can also be used to supplement the reddish-yellow spectrum from HP sodium lamps. However, the outer case covering the attached ballast is susceptible to deterioration from UV light. When used in conjunction with other HID lamps that produce UV rays, the ballast case deteriorates more quickly. Attached ballasts are not designed for humid indoor garden applications. Couple this weakness to humidity with a bit of UV light, and bulbs burn out more quickly.

The end of ballast life is signaled when it stops. When the ballast burns out, remove and replace it.

Although CFLs are not considered hazardous waste, they still contain a little mercury and should be disposed of properly to avoid contaminating the environment. Place CFL bulbs in a sealed plastic bag and dispose the same way you do batteries, oil-based paint, motor oil, etc., at your local Household Hazardous Waste (HHW) Collection Site.

This 125-watt CFL can be used with or without a reflective hood.

Other Lamps

Several other lamps deserve a mention; however, they grow plants poorly. Incandescent lamps are inefficient; tungsten halogen lamps are bright but inefficient; and low-pressure sodium lamps are efficient but have a limited spectrum.

Incandescent Lamps

Incandescent lamps were invented by Thomas Edison. Light is produced by sending electricity through the filament, a super fine wire inside the bulb. The filament resists the flow of electricity, heating it to incandescence, causing it to glow and emit light. The incandescent bulbs work on ordinary home current and require

no ballast. They come in a wide range of wattages and constructions.

Most incandescent lamps have a spectrum in the far-red end, but there are some incandescent grow lamps that have an enhanced blue spectrum. They are expensive to operate and produce few lumens-per-watt. They are most efficiently used as a source of rooting medium heat for cuttings rooting under cool fluorescents.

LP Sodium Lamps

Low Pressure (LP) sodium lamps are monochromatic. Do not use these lamps to grow plants. They produce light in a very narrow portion of the spectrum, at 589 nanometers, and emit a yellow glow. They are available in wattages from 55 to 180. Their lumens-per-watt conversion is the highest of all lamps on the market to-day. Their main use in industry has been for security or warehouse light.

Lamps require specific ballasts and fixtures according to wattage. The fixture for a 180-watt lamp is just a little larger than a fixture for two 40-watt, four-foot (120 cm) fluorescent tubes.

After visiting hundreds and hundreds of indoor gardens over the last 20 years, I have seen only one LP sodium lamp in use.

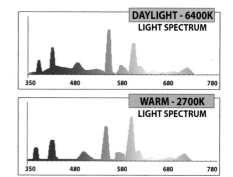

CFL light spectrums are perfect for growing plants!

Tungsten Halogen Lamps

The tungsten halogen lamp is a poor grow light. It was originally called Iodine Quartz lamp. The outer tube is made of heat-resistant quartz. The main gas inside the quartz tube was iodine, one of the five halogens. Today, Bromine is used most often in the lamps. Similar to incandescent lamps, they use a tungsten wire filament and a sealed bulb and are very expensive to operate. Their lumens-per-watt output is very low. They run on a household current and require no ballast. Tungsten bulbs are as inefficient to operate as are the incandescent lamps. Their color spectrum is in the far-red end with 10–15 percent in the visible spectrum.

Electricity & Safety

You don't need to understand the basics of electricity to grow indoors or in a greenhouse, but understanding the basics will save you money, time, and possibly the shock of your life.

Before you touch anything electrical, please remember to work backward when installing electrical components or doing wiring. Start at the bulb, and work toward the plug-in. Always plug in the cord last!

Safety is very important when using electricity around water.

All electrical outlets, fuses, and connec-

Overload Chart

Rating	Available	Overload
15	13	14
20	16	17
25	20	21
30	24	25
40	32	33

Connect only one 1000-watt HID to a 15, 20, or 25-ampere 120-volt (North American) circuit.
Connect two 1000-watt HIDs to a 15-ampere 240-volt (European) circuit.

Type/model	Kelvin Temperature
Warm White	2700 K
White	3000 K
Neutral	3500 K
Cool White	4100 K
Full Spectrum	5000 K
Daylight	6500 K

tions must be grounded. Inspect electrical connections for signs of heat-blackened wires, melted connections, and smelly wiring.

Have a current fire extinguisher on hand, one rated to put out wood, paper, grease, oil, and electrical fires.

Ampere (amp): is the measure of electricity in motion. Electricity can be looked at in absolute terms of measurement just as water can. A gallon is an absolute measure of a portion of water; a coulomb is an absolute measure of a portion of electricity. Water in motion is measured in gallons per second, and electricity in motion is measured in coulombs per second. When an electrical current flows at one coulomb per second, we say it has one ampere.

Breaker Switch: ON/OFF safety switch that will turn the electricity OFF when the circuit is overloaded. Look for breaker switches in the breaker panel or breaker box.

Circuit: the circular path that electricity travels. If this path is interrupted, the power will go off. If this circuit is given a chance, it will travel a circular route through your body!

Conductor: something that is able to carry electricity easily. Copper, steel, water, and your body are good electrical conductors.

Fuse: electrical safety device consisting of a fusible metal that melts and interrupts the circuit when overloaded. Never replace fuses with pennies or aluminum foil! They will not melt and interrupt the circuit when overloaded. This is an easy way to start a fire.

Ground: means to connect electricity to the ground or earth for safety. If a circuit is properly grounded and the electricity travels somewhere it is not supposed to, it will go via the ground wire into the ground (earth) and be rendered harmless. Electric-

ity will travel the path of least resistance. This path must be along the ground wire.

The ground is formed by a wire (usually green, brown, or bare copper) that runs parallel to the circuit and is attached to a metal ground stake. Metal water and sewer pipes also serve as excellent conductors for the ground. Water pipes conduct electricity well and are all in good contact with the ground. The entire system—pipes, copper wire, and metal ground stake—conducts any misplaced electricity safely into the ground.

The ground wire is the third wire with the big round prong. The ground runs through the ballast all the way to the hood. High intensity discharge systems must have a ground that runs a continual path from the socket through the ballast to the main fuse box, then to the house ground.

GFI: Ground Fault Interrupt outlets are required anywhere water is used in a home or business. Install GFI outlets in indoor gardens to provide an instant, safe electrical shut-off when necessary.

Hertz: irregular fluctuations or cycles in electricity within a conductor (wire). In the USA, electricity runs at 60 hertz (Hz), or cycles, per second.

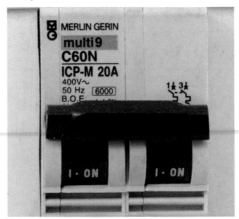

Breaker switches have their ampere rating printed on the face.

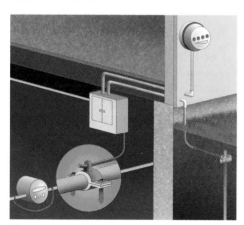

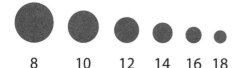

Water and electricity don't mix. Always work with a grounded system, and keep all standing water off the floor!

Electrical ground

The diameter of electrical wire grows thicker as the gauge number decreases. Notice how much thicker 14-gauge wire is than 16-gauge.

A ground fault interrupt (GFI) outlet contains a breaker switch and will turn off electricity when tripped.

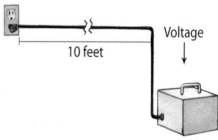

The voltage drops if electricity travels more than ten feet (3 m) from the outlet to the ballast. The longer the distance, the greater the voltage drop. Ballasts are underpowered when voltage is low, causing the bulb to dim.

Avoid scenes like this, and never operate lamps on an overloaded circuit.

Gardening Indoors

Ohm's Power Law: a law that expresses the strength of an electric current: volts × amperes = watts.

Short Circuit: a short or unintentional circuit formed when conductors (wires) cross. A short circuit will normally blow fuses and turn off breaker switches.

Volts: electricity is under pressure or electrical potential. This pressure is measured in volts. Most home wiring is under the pressure of approximately 120 or 240 volts.

Watts: are a measure of work. Watts measure the amount of electricity flowing in a wire. When amperes, (units of electricity per second) are multiplied by volts (pressure), we get watts. 1000 watts = 1 kilowatt.

A halide lamp that draws about 9.2 amperes × 120 volts = 1104 watts. Remember Ohm's Power Law: amps × watts = volts. This is strange; the answer was supposed to be 1000 watts. What is wrong? The electricity flows through the ballast, which uses energy to run. The energy drawn by the ballast must amount to 104 watts.

watt-hour is equal to one watt used for one hour. A kilowatt-hour (kWh) is 1000 watt-hours. A 1000-watt HID will use roughly one kilowatt per hour, and the ballast will use about 100 watts. Electrical bills are charged out in kWh.

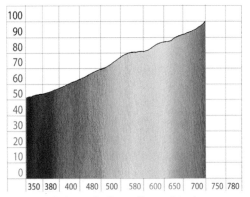

Tungsten halogen bulbs really crank in the red end of the spectrum. Too bad they are so inefficient.

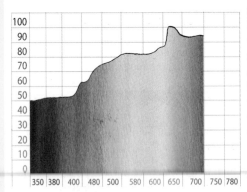

The light spectrum of an incandescent lamp will grow plants but is best suited to generating heat.

Watt-hours: measure the amount of watts that are used during an hour. One

Electrical wire comes in many thicknesses (gauges) indicated by number. Higher numbers indicate smaller wire and lower numbers indicate larger wire. Most household circuits are connected with 14-gauge wire. Wire thickness is important for two reasons—ampacity and voltage drop. Ampacity is the amount of amperes a wire is able to carry safely. Electricity flowing through wire creates heat. The more amps flowing, the more heat created. Heat is wasted power. Avoid wasting power by using the proper thickness of well-insulated wire (14-gauge for 120-volt applications and 18-gauge for 240-volts) with a grounded wire connection.

Using too small of a wire forces too much power (amperes) through the wire, which causes voltage drop. Voltage (pressure) is lost in the wire. For example: by forcing an 18-gauge wire to carry 9.2 amperes at 120 volts, it would not only heat up, maybe even blowing fuses, but the voltage at the outlet would be 120 volts, while the voltage ten feet away could be as low as 108. This is a loss of 12 volts that you are paying for. The ballast and lamp run less efficiently with fewer volts. The further the electricity travels, the more heat that is generated and the more voltage drops.

A lamp designed to work at 120 volts that only receives 108 volts (90 percent of the power it was intended to operate at) would produce only 70 percent of the normal light. Use at least 14-gauge wire for any extension cords, and if the cord is to carry power over 60 feet, use 12-gauge wire.

When wiring a plug-in or socket:

The hot wire attaches to the brass or gold screw.

The common wire attaches to the aluminum or silver screw.

The ground wire always attaches to the ground prong.

Take special care to keep the wires from crossing and forming a short circuit.

Plugs and outlets must have a solid connection. If they are jostled around and the electricity is allowed to jump, electricity is lost in the form of heat; the prongs will burn, and a fire could result. Periodically check plugs and outlets to ensure they have a solid connection.

If installing a new circuit or breaker box, hire an electrician or purchase *Wiring Simplified* by H. P. Richter and W. C. Schwan. It costs about $10 and is available at most hardware stores in the USA. Installing a new circuit in a breaker box is very easy, but installing another fuse in a fuse box is more complex. Before trying anything of this scope, read about it and discuss it with several professionals.

Cost of Electricity Chart

Cost per 12-hour days 18-hour days

kWh	day	month	day	month
$0.05	$0.60	$18.00	$0.90	$27.00
$0.06	$0.72	$21.60	$1.08	$32.40
$0.07	$0.84	$25.20	$1.26	$37.80
$0.08	$0.96	$28.80	$1.44	$43.20
$0.09	$1.08	$32.40	$1.62	$48.60
$0.10	$1.20	$36.00	$1.80	$54.00
$0.15	$1.80	$54.00	$2.70	$81.00
$0.20	$2.40	$72.00	$3.60	$108.00
$0.25	$3.00	$90.00	$4.50	$135.00

(In US dollars)

A circuit with a 20-amp fuse, containing the following items
1400-watt toaster oven
100-watt incandescent light bulb
+ 20 watt radio
=1520 total watts
1520/120 volts = 12.6 amps in use
or
1520/240 volts = 6.3 amps in use

The above example shows 12.6 amps are being drawn when everything is on. By adding 9.2 amps, drawn by the HID to the circuit, we get 21.8 amps, an overloaded circuit!

There are three solutions:
1. Remove one or all of the high-amp–drawing appliances and plug them into another circuit.
2. Find another circuit that has few or no amps drawn by other appliances.
3. Install a new circuit. A 240-volt circuit will make more amps available per circuit.

Gardening Indoors

Electricity Consumption

There are many ways to deal with the increase in consumption of electricity. One gardener moved into a home that had all electric heat and a fireplace. He installed three HID lamps in the basement that also generated heat. The excess heat was dispersed via a vent fan attached to a thermostat/humidistat. He turned off the electric heat, bought a fireplace insert, and started heating with wood. Even running three lamps, consuming three kilowatts per hour, the electric bill was less than it had been with electric heat!

Electric bills are controlled with and generated by a computer system. Monthly energy consumption is often displayed on a bar graph for the previous 12 months. This graph makes it easy to see fluctuations in electricity consumption.

A one- to three-bedroom home can run two to three 1000-watt lamps, and a four- to five-bedroom home can operate three to five lamps. Powering any more lamps usually requires adding new incoming circuits, or the use of present circuits will be severely limited.

The amount of electricity consumption and the size of the home are proportional. Often, an increase in electric consumption is normal. For example, electric bills always increase if there is a baby in the home or if there are more residents living there. Changing to gas or wood heat and a gas stove and water heater will also lower the electricity bill. Some friends bought a new, efficient water heater and saved $17 per month! Just by changing water heaters, they were able to add another 600-watt lamp. Another gardener set her water heater for 130°F (54°C) instead of 170°F (77°C). This simple procedure saved about 25 kWh per month. But do not turn the water heater any lower than 130°F. Harmful bacteria can grow below this safe point.

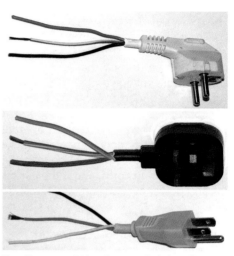

Top: European 240-volt grounded plug. Center UK 240-volt grounded plug that contains a fuse. Bottom: Grounded US and Canadian plug. The green or green-striped wires are ground wires.

This generator produces 4000 watts at full capacity.

For more information on indoor horticulture safety issues, check out the web sites listed earlier in this chapter.

Generators

Generators can supply all the electricity necessary for an indoor garden, and you can grow "off the power grid." Reliability, ampere output, and noise are important to consider when shopping for a generator.

Buy the generator new. It should be water-cooled and fully automated. Start it up, and check its noise output before purchasing. Always buy a generator that is big enough to do the job. A little extra cushion will be necessary to allow for power surges. If it fails, the crop could fail! Allow about 1300 watts per lamp to be run by the generator. The ballast consumes a few watts as does the wire, etc. A 5500-watt Honda generator will run four lamps.

Honda generators are used most often because they are reasonably priced, dependable, and quiet. But, they are not designed to work for long periods. Always make sure gasoline or diesel-powered generators are vented properly. The exhaust produces carbon monoxide, which is toxic to plants and humans.

Gasoline generator motors can be converted to propane, which burns much cleaner, and the exhaust may be used as a source of CO_2.

Diesel generators for truck and train car refrigerators are fairly easy to acquire and last for years. Once set up, one of these "Big Bertha" generators can run many, many lights. Check with wholesale railway and truck wrecking yard outlets for such generators. The generators are usually moved to a belowground location- and covered with a building. With a good

If you must wire your own indoor garden electricity, make sure to plan ahead. Attach junction boxes, timers, etc., to a board, and mount the board on the wall once the appliances are in place.

Indoor garden controllers make dialing in the exact temperature and humidity for your garden easy.

The timer on the right controls the entire lighting system in the indoor garden.

exhaust system and baffling around the motor, the sound is soon dissipated. Muffling the exhaust and expelling the fumes is a little complex but very effective. The exhaust must be able to escape freely into the atmosphere.

Maintaining a generator that runs 12 hours a day is a lot of work. The generator will need fuel and must be monitored regularly. If the generator shuts down prematurely, plants stop growing.

I once interviewed a gardener who ran a generator for six years. He seemed to know a lot about the idiosyncrasies of the machine. He also had the innate feeling that the machine would do something outrageous if he were not there to make it right. This underlying theme dominated the entire interview. Running the generator motor—making sure it had oil, fuel, and ran quietly—was all he thought about when he was growing in the country with "Big Bertha," who produced 20 kilovolts of electricity. Check this site for more information, www.hardydiesel.com.

This generator on wheels provides complete "off the grid" security. Check into consumption and maintenance before purchasing. Some models make quite a bit of noise that must be muffled. You can park it anywhere!

Timers

A timer is an inexpensive investment that turns lights and other appliances on and off at regular intervals. Using a timer ensures that your garden will receive a controlled light period of the same duration every day.

Purchase a heavy-duty grounded timer with an adequate amperage and tungsten rating to meet your needs. Some timers have a different amperage rating for the switch; it is often lower than that of the timer. Timers that control more than one lamp are more expensive because they require the entire force of electricity to pass through them. Many pre-wired timers are available at stores that sell HID lights.

How many lights (total watts) will the timer handle? If you are running more than 2000 or 3000 watts, you may want to attach the lamps to a relay, and control the relay with a timer. The advantage of a relay is it offers a path for more electricity without having to change the timer. There are numerous sophisticated timers on the market that will solve every last need you have.

Setting up the HID System – Step-by-Step

Step One: Before setting up the HID system, read "Setting Up the Indoor Garden" in Chapter Six, and complete the step-by-step instructions.

Step Two: Both the lamp and ballast radiate quite a bit of heat. Take care when positioning them so they are not so close to plants or flammable walls and ceiling that they become hazardous. If the room has limited space with a low ceiling, place a protective, nonflammable material like metal between the lamp and ceiling to protect from heat. An exhaust fan will be necessary to keep things cool. It is most effective to place the remote ballast near the floor to keep things cool. Place it outside the indoor garden if the room is too hot.

When hanging the lamp on the overhead chain or pulley system, make sure electrical cords are unencumbered and not too close to any heat source.

Step Three: Buy and use a good timer to keep the photoperiod consistent. A decent timer costs from $20 to $30 and is worth its weight in harvest yields!

Step Four: To plug in the HID lamp, it will be necessary to find the proper outlet. A 1000-watt HID lamp will use about 9.5 amps of electricity on a regular 120-volt house current.

Place ballasts on shelves so they are up and out of the way.

A typical home has a fuse box or a breaker box. Each fuse or breaker switch controls an electrical circuit in the home. The fuse or breaker switch will be rated for 15, 20, 25, 30, or 40-amp service. Circuits are considered overloaded when more than 80 percent of the amps are being used. (See "Overload Chart"). The fuse will have its amp rating printed on its face, and the breaker switch will have its amp rating printed on the switch or on the breaker box. To find out which outlets are controlled by a fuse or breaker switch, remove the fuse or turn the breaker switch off. Test each and every outlet in the home to see which ones do not work. All the outlets that do not work are on the same circuit. All outlets that work are on another circuit. When you have found a circuit that has few or no lights, ra-

dios, TVs, stereos, etc., plugged into it, look at the circuit's amp rating. If it is rated for 15 amps, you can plug one 1000-watt HID into it. A leeway of 5.5 amps is there to cover any power surges. If the circuit is rated for 20 or more amps, it may be used for the 1000-watt HID and a few other low-amp appliances. To find out how many amps are drawn by each appliance, add up the number of total watts they use, and divide by 120.

Never put a larger fuse in the fuse box than it is rated for. The fuse is the weakest link in the circuit. If a 20-amp fuse is placed into a 15-amp circuit, the fuse is able to conduct more electricity than the wiring. This causes wires to burn rather than the fuse. An overloaded circuit may result in a house fire.

Use an extension cord that is at least 14-gauge wire or heavier if the plug will not reach the outlet desired. Thick 14-gauge extension cord is more difficult to find and may have to be constructed. Smaller 16- or 18-gauge cord will not conduct adequate electricity and will heat up, straining the entire system. Cut the 14-gauge extension cord to the exact length. The further electricity travels, the weaker it gets and the more heat it produces, which also strains the system.

Step Five: Always use a three-prong grounded plug. If your home is not equipped with working three-prong grounded outlets, buy a three-prong grounded plug and outlet adapter. Attach the ground wire to a grounded ferrous metal object like a grounded metal pipe or heavy copper wire driven into the earth to form a ground, and screw the ground into the plug-in face. You will be working with water under and around the HID system. Water conducts electricity about as well as the human body.

Gardening Indoors

Step Six: Once the proper circuit is selected, the socket and hood are mounted overhead, and the ballast is in place (but not plugged in), screw the HID bulb finger-tight into the socket. Make sure the bulb is secured in the socket tightly, but not too tight, and make certain there is a good connection. When secure, wipe off all smudges on the bulb to increase brightness.

Step Seven: Plug the three-prong plug into the timer that is in the OFF position. Plug the timer into the grounded outlet, set the timer at the desired photoperiod, and turn the timer on. Shazam! The ballast will hum and the lamp will flicker and slowly warm up, reaching full brilliance in about five minutes.

Attach ballasts to the wall so they are out of the way in the garden.

This timer is ideal to control a single lamp.

The mechanical time switch above is easily setup and can be found in most garden outlets.

Fixing all wiring and electrical devices to a control panel makes control and troubleshooting easy.

Rich, healthy soil is the key to success, whether gardening outdoors or in containers.

This cutaway drawing shows how the roots penetrate the soil. Note: There must be enough air trapped in the soil to allow biological activity and absorption of nutrients.

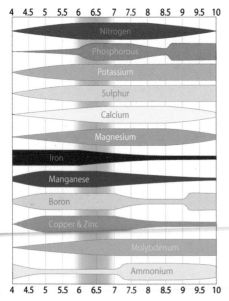

This pH Chart shows the Safe Zone is between 5.8 and 6.8.

Introduction

Soil is made up of many mineral particles mixed together with living and dead organic matter that incorporates air and water. Three basic factors contribute to the plant root's ability to grow in a soil: texture, pH, and nutrient content.

Soil texture is governed by the size and physical makeup of the mineral particles. Proper soil texture is required for adequate root penetration, water and oxygen retention, and drainage as well as many other complex chemical processes.

Clay or adobe soil is made up of very small, flat mineral particles; when it gets wet, these minute particles pack tightly together, slowing or stopping root penetration and water drainage. Roots are unable to breathe because very little or no space is left for oxygen. Water has a very difficult time penetrating these tightly packed soils, and once it does penetrate, drainage is slow.

Sandy soils have much larger particles. They permit good aeration (supply of air or oxygen) and drainage. Frequent watering is necessary because water retention is very low. The soil's water- and air-holding ability and root penetration are a function of texture.

Loam soil is ideal for gardens. It contains a mix of clay, silt, and sand. The different sized particles allow a large combination of pore spaces, so it drains well and still retains nutrients and moisture.

To check soil texture, pick up a handful of moist (not soggy) soil and gently squeeze it. The soil should barely stay together and have a kind of sponge effect when you slowly open your hand to release the pressure. Indoor soils that do not fulfill these requirements should be thrown out or amended. See "Soil Amendments."

pH

The pH scale, from 1 to 14, measures acid-to-alkaline balance. The number 1 is the most acidic, 7 is neutral, and 14 most alkaline. Every full-point change in pH signifies a ten-fold increase or decrease in acidity or alkalinity. For example, soil or water with a pH of 5 is ten times more acidic than water or soil with a pH

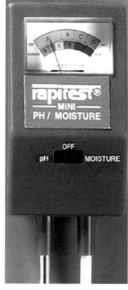

An inexpensive electronic pH tester is easy to use.

of 6. Water with a pH of 5 is one hundred times more acidic than water with a pH of 7. With a ten-fold difference between each point on the scale, accurate measurement and control is essential to a strong, healthy garden.

Most plants grow best in soil with a pH from 6.5 to 7. Within this range plants can properly absorb and process available nutrients most efficiently. If the pH is too low (acidic), acid salts chemically bind nutrients, and the roots are unable to absorb them. An alkaline soil with a high pH causes nutrients to become unavailable. Toxic salt buildup that limits water intake by roots also becomes a problem. Hydroponic solutions perform best in a pH range a little lower than for soil. The ideal pH range for hydroponics is from 5.8 to 6.8. Some gardeners run the pH at lower levels and report no problems with nutrient uptake. The pH of organic soil mixes is very

important because it dictates the ability of specific pH-sensitive bacteria.

Measure the pH with a soil test kit, litmus paper, or electronic pH tester, all of which are available at most nurseries. When testing pH, take two or three samples and follow instructions supplied by the manufacturer "to the letter." Soil test kits measure soil pH and primary nutrient content by mixing soil with a chemical solution and comparing the color of the solution to a chart. Every one of these kits I have seen or used is difficult for novice gardeners to achieve accurate measurements. Comparing the color of the soil/chemical mix to the color of the chart is often confusing. If you use one of these kits, make sure to buy one with good, easy-to-understand directions, and ask the sales clerk for exact recommendations on using it.

When planting, add one cup of fine dolomite lime to each cubic foot (one ounce per gallon) of planting medium to stabilize the pH and provide calcium and magnesium.

For an accurate pH test with an electronic pH meter:
- Clean the probes of the meter after each test and wipe away any corrosion.
- Pack the soil around the probes.
- Water soil with distilled or neutral pH water before testing.

If using litmus paper, collect samples that demonstrate an average for the soil. Place the samples in a clean jar, and moisten the soil samples with distilled water. Place two pieces of litmus paper in the muddy water. After ten seconds, remove one strip of litmus paper. Wait a minute before removing the other one. Both pieces of litmus paper should register the same color. The litmus paper container should have a pH-color chart on the side. Match the color of the litmus paper with the colors on the chart to get a pH reading. Litmus paper will accurately measure the acidity of the substance to within one point. The pH readings will not be accurate if altered by water with a high or low pH, and the litmus paper could give a false reading if the fertilizer contains a colored tracing agent.

Electronic pH testers are economical and convenient. Less-expensive pH meters are accurate enough for casual use. More-expensive models are quite accurate. Pay special attention to the soil moisture when taking a pH test with an electronic meter. The meters measure the electrical current between two probes and are designed to work in moist soil. If the soil is dry, the probes do not give an accurate reading. I prefer electronic pH meters over the reagent test kits and litmus paper because they are convenient, economical, and accurate. Once purchased, you can measure pH thousands of times with an electronic meter, while the chemical test kits are good for about a dozen tests. Perpetual pH-metering devices are also available and most often used to monitor hydroponic nutrient solutions.

Check the pH of irrigation water. In dry climates, such as the desert Southwest United States, Spain, and Australia, irrigation water is often alkaline with a pH above 6.0. The water in rainy climates, such as the Pacific Northwest of North America, the United Kingdom, Netherlands, and maritime Northern Europe is often acidic with a pH below 6.0. The pH and EC of water supplies in municipalities and cities can also change throughout the year in some countries. After repeated watering, water with a pH that is too high or low will change the pH of the growing medium, especially in organically amended soils. Raw-water pH above 6.0 helps keep fertilizer mixes from becoming too acidic. Climatic conditions can also affect irrigation water pH. For example, the pH can become more acidic in late autumn, when leaves fall and decompose. Large municipalities carefully monitor and correct the pH, and there are few water-quality problems. Check the pH at least once a week.

Plants will grow in almost any soil but will flourish when the pH is between 6.5 and 7. Commercial potting soil almost never has a pH above 7.5. A lower pH is more common, even as low as 5.5. Some potting soils purchased at a nursery are pH balanced and near a neutral 7. However, most potting soils have a tendency to be acidic. The easiest way to stabilize soil pH is to mix in one cup of fine dolomite lime per cubic foot (0.25 liters) of potting soil. Mix dolomite lime thoroughly into dry soil. Remix the soil in the container after it has been watered.

Fine dolomite lime has long been a favorite pH stabilizer for gardeners. It is difficult to apply too much as long as it is thoroughly mixed into soil. Dolomite has a neutral pH of 7, and it can never raise the pH beyond 7.0. It stabilizes the pH safely.

Compensate for acidic soil by mixing dolomite with soil before planting. It will help keep the pH stable and maintain the correct pH when applying mild acidic fertilizers. Dolomite, a compound of magnesium (Mg) and calcium (Ca), is popular among indoor and outdoor gardeners in rainy climates with acidic soil. Dolomite does not prevent toxic-salt accumulation caused by impure water and fertilizer buildup. A proper fertilizer regimen and regular leaching help flush away toxic salts. When purchasing, look for dolomite flour, the finest fast-acting dust-like grade available. Coarse dolomite could take a year or more to become available for uptake by roots. Mix dolomite flour thoroughly with the growing medium before planting. Improperly mixed dolomite will stratify, forming a cake or layer that burns roots and repels water.

Hydrated lime contains only calcium and no magnesium. As the name hydrated implies, it is water-soluble. Fast-acting hydrated lime alters the pH quickly. Mix it thoroughly with warm water and apply with each watering for fast results. Many gardeners use a mix of 0.25-cup (6 cl) hydrated lime and 0.75-cup (18 cl) dolomite lime. Hydrated lime is immediately available, whereas the slower-acting dolomite buffers the pH over the long term. Do not use more than 0.5-cup (12 cl) of hydrated lime per cubic foot of soil. The larger quantity is released so fast that it can toxify soil and stunt or even kill plants. The beauty of hydrated lime is that it washes out of the soil in about two weeks. Leach it more quickly by flushing pots with copious quantities of water. Hydrated lime is also used as an indoor garden fungicide. Sprinkle it on the floor and around the room. It kills fungus on contact.

Do not use quicklime; it is toxic to plants. Calcic lime (quicklime) contains only calcium and is not a good choice. It does not have the buffering qualities of dolomite nor does it contain magnesium.

Raise the pH of a growing medium or irrigation water by adding some form of alkali, such as calcium carbonate, potassium hydroxide, or sodium hydroxide. Both hydroxides are caustic and require special care when handling. These compounds are normally used to raise the pH of hydroponic nutrient solutions but can be used to treat acidic nutrient solutions when applied to soil. The easiest and most convenient way to raise and stabilize soil pH is to add fine dolomite lime and hydrated lime before planting. To raise the pH one point, add three cups (60 cl) of fine dolomite lime to one cubic foot (30 L) of soil. An alternate fast-acting mix would be to add two and one half cups (590 cl) of dolomite and one-half cup (12 cl) of hydrated lime to one cubic foot (30 L) of soil.

Pulverized eggshells, clam or oyster shells, and wood ashes have a high pH and help raise soil pH. Eggshells and oyster shells take a long time to decompose enough to affect the pH; wood ashes have a pH from 9.0–11.0 and are easy to overapply. Ashes are often collected from fireplaces or woodstoves that have been burning all kinds of trash and are, therefore, unsafe. Do not use wood ashes on indoor gardens unless you know their origin, pH, and nutrient content. You can add cottonseed meal, lemon peels, coffee grounds, or a high-acidity fertilizer to lower pH in soil to below 7.0.

Commercial potting soils and soilless mixes are often acidic, and the pH seldom needs to be lowered. If new soil pH is under 6 or above 8, it is easier and less expensive in the long run to change soil rather than experiment with changing the pH. Fertilizers are naturally acidic and will lower the pH of the growing medium. Sulfur will lower the pH, if necessary, but it is tricky to use. I advise using an acid to alter the pH. Add distilled white vinegar at the rate of one teaspoon per gallon (1.2 ml per L) of irrigation water, allow the water to sit for a few minutes, and then recheck it. The pH should drop by a full point. If it does not, add more vinegar in small increments. Often when using vinegar, the pH drifts up overnight. Check the pH the next day. Hydroponic gardeners use phosphoric and nitric acid to lower pH. Calcium nitrate can also be used but is less common. Keep a close eye on the pH and control it accordingly. After altering the pH, check it, and then check it again daily to make sure it remains stable.

Aspirin also lowers the pH. However, hormonal reactions appear to be triggered by aspirin. Some gardeners have reported more hermaphrodites when using aspirin to alter the pH.

Humates Chelate

Humic and fulvic acids chelate metallic ions, making them readily transportable by water. This ability is dependent upon the pH level. Copper, iron, manganese, and zinc are difficult to dissolve. When mixed in a chelated form, they become readily available for absorption.

Soil Temperature

Soil temperature should stay between 65°F and 70°F (18–24°C) for best results.

Raising the soil temperature speeds the chemical process and can hasten nutrient uptake. Ideally, the soil temperature should range from 65–70°F (18–24°C) for the most chemical activity. Warm the soil with soil-heating cables or a heating pad. Fasten heating cables to a board or table and set a heat-conducting pad on top of the cables to distribute heat evenly. Set cuttings and seedlings in shallow flats or growing trays on top of the heat-conducting pad. The added heat speeds root growth when soil temperature is below 65°F (18°C).

Soil-heating cables cost much less than soil-heating pads but must be installed, whereas the pads are ready to use. Most commercial nurseries carry cables, and hydroponic stores carry heating pads. When rooting cuttings, a heating pad or cables virtually ensures success and expedites root growth.

Cold soil slows water and nutrient uptake and stifles growth. Gardeners often overwater when the soil is too cold or the room cools unexpectedly, which further slows growth. Pots on cold concrete floors stay as cold as the concrete, which is always colder than the ambient temperature. Increase soil temperature by moving pots up off the floor a few inches. Set them on an insulating board or piece of Styrofoam™.

Outdoors, the soil temperature can climb quickly when sunshine warms the containers.

Soil temperatures that climb above 75°F (39°C) dehydrate roots, and at higher temperatures the roots actually cook! It is relatively easy to heat the soil in a pot. If the light or any heat source is too close to small pots, it can easily heat up the outside layer of soil where the majority of the feeder roots are located. Once destroyed, roots take one or two weeks to grow back. Two weeks accounts for one-quarter of the flowering cycle!

The more feeder root hairs there are to absorb water and nutrients, the faster and stronger plants will grow. Once roots go beyond their comfort zone, they send stress signals to foliage and stomata via hormones to close and conserve moisture.

Oxygen is essential for cuttings that are growing roots. Water holds under one percent dissolved oxygen at 70°F (21°C). Bump the temperature up to 85°F (29°C) and it holds less than 0.5 percent oxygen.

Root temperatures below 40°F (4°C) make water expand, which causes cell damage. Temperatures above 92°F (33°C) cause excessive vapor pressure within the roots, which can cause damage. At high temperatures, roots send stress signals to shut the leaves down before damage can occur.

Potting Soil

Potting soil fresh out of the bag often fulfills all requirements for a growing medium: good texture that allows good root penetration, water retention, and good drainage; a stable pH between 6 and 7; and a minimum supply of nutrients.

Premium fast-draining soils with good texture that will not break down quickly are the best choice. Potting soils found at nurseries are often formulated with a wetting agent to help them retain water and air evenly, drain well, and allow easy root penetration. Organic potting soils are very popular. These soils are often fortified with organic nutrients including readily available high-nitrogen worm castings. Potting soils are very heavy, and transportation costs tend to keep them somewhat localized. There are many good brands of high-quality potting soil. Ask your nursery person for help in selecting one for fast-growing vegetables.

Stay away from discount brands of low-quality potting soil. These soils can be full of weed seeds and diseases, hold water unevenly, and drain poorly. Ultimately, saving a few pennies on soil will cost many headaches and a low yield later.

Many potting soils supply seedling transplants and cuttings with enough food (fertilizer) for the first two to four weeks of growth. After that, supplemental fertilization is necessary to retain rapid, robust growth. Add fine-grade dolomite lime to buffer and stabilize the pH. Trace

Quality potting soil   *Quality organic potting soil*   *Mushroom compost*

elements in fortified soil and soilless mixes can leach out and should be replenished with chelated nutrients, if deficiency signs occur. Organic gardeners often add their own blends of trace elements in mixes that contain seaweed, guanos, and manures.

Although some gardeners reuse their potting soil, I do not recommend it. If used for more than one crop, undesirable microorganisms, insects, and fungi start growing; nutrients are depleted; water- and air-retention are poor, causing compaction and poor drainage. Some gardeners mix their old potting soil with new potting soil to stretch their mix. Cutting corners this way most often costs more in production than is saved in soil.

Potting soil or soilless mix that contains more than 30 percent lightweight pumice or perlite may float and stratify when saturated with water before planting. Mix water-saturated soil with your hands until it is evenly mixed before planting or transplanting, if necessary.

Mushroom Compost

Mushroom compost is an inexpensive potting soil and soil amendment that is packed with organic goodies. Mushroom compost is sterilized chemically to provide a clean medium for mushroom growth. After serving its purpose as a mushroom growing medium, it is discarded. Laws usually require that it sit fallow for two years or more to allow all harmful sterilants to leach out. After lying fallow for several years, mushroom compost is very fertile and packed with beneficial microorganisms. This high-powered compost could also foster antifungal and antibacterial properties in foliage and below the soil line, which helps guard against disease. Mushroom compost is loaded with beneficial bacteria that hasten nutrient uptake. The texture, water-holding ability, and drainage in some mushroom compost should be amended with perlite to promote better drainage. Check your local nursery or extension service for a good source of mushroom compost. Some of the most abundant harvests I have seen were grown in mushroom compost.

Soilless Mix

Soilless mixes are popular, inexpensive, lightweight, and sterile growing mediums.

Commercial greenhouse gardeners have been using them for decades. The mixes contain some or all of the following: pumice, vermiculite, perlite, sand, peat moss, and coconut coir. Premixed commercial soilless mixes are favorites of countless gardeners. These mixes retain moisture and air while allowing strong root penetration and even growth. The fertilizer concentration, moisture level, and pH are very easy to control with precision in soilless mix.

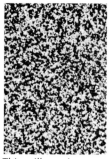

Lightweight horticultural perlite is available in large bags.

This soilless mix contains 50 percent perlite and 50 percent coco. Drainage is rapid and water retention is good. This mix must be watered daily.

Pro-Mix is a good value and one of the most readily available soilless mixes.

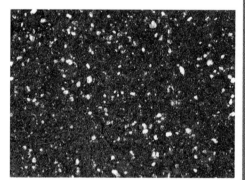

This soilless mix contains 10 percent perlite and 90 percent peat moss. It holds water very well and the perlite assists drainage.

Soilless mixes are the preferred substrate for many bedding plant and vegetable seedling commercial gardeners. Soilless mixes have good texture, hold water, and drain well. Unless fortified with nutrient, soilless mixes contain no nutrients and are pH-balanced near 6.0 to 7.0.

Make a seedbed from fine-screened soil.

Coarse soilless mixes drain well and easily push plants into growing faster with heavy fertilization. The fast-draining mixes can be leached efficiently so nutrients have little chance of building up to toxic levels. Look for ready-mixed bags of fortified soilless mixes such as Jiffy Mix®, Ortho Mix®, Sunshine Mix®, Terra-Lite®, and ProMix®. To improve drainage, mix with 10–30 percent coarse perlite before planting. Fortified elements supply nutrients up to a month, but follow directions on the package.

Soilless components can be purchased separately and mixed to the desired consistency. Ingredients always blend together best when mixed dry and wetted afterward using a wetting agent to make water more adhesive. Mix small amounts right in the bag. Larger batches should be mixed in a wheelbarrow, concrete slab, or in a cement mixer. Blending your own soil or soilless mix is a dusty, messy job but one that takes little space. To cut down on dust, lightly mist the pile with water several times when mixing. Always wear a respirator to avoid inhaling dust.

The texture of soilless mixes for rapid-growing plants should be coarse, light, and spongy. Such texture allows drainage with sufficient moisture and air retention, as well as providing good root-penetration qualities. Fine soilless mix holds more moisture and works best in smaller containers. Soilless mixes that contain more perlite and sand drain faster, making them easier to fertilize heavily without excessive fertilizer salt buildup. Vermiculite and peat hold water longer and are best used in small pots that require more water retention.

The pH is generally near neutral, 7.0. If using more than 15 percent peat, which is acidic, add appropriate dolomite or hy-drated lime to correct and stabilize the pH. Check the pH regularly every week. Soilless mixes are composed mainly of mineral particles that are not affected by organic decomposition, which could change the pH. The pH is affected by acidic fertilizers or by water with a high or low pH. Check the pH of the runoff water to ensure the pH in the medium is not too acidic.

Seedling trays are easy to use.

Small rockwool plugs are fast to plant and easy to maintain.

Rockwool plugs grow strong root systems in about two weeks.

Cutting and Seedling Cubes and Mixes

Rockwool root cubes, peat pellets, and Oasis® blocks are preformed containers that make rooting cuttings, starting seedlings, and transplanting them easy. Root cubes and peat pots also help encourage strong root systems. Peat pots are small, compressed peat moss containers with an outer wall of expandable plastic netting. The flat pellets pop up into a seedling pot when watered.

Place a seed or cutting in a moist peat pot or root cube. If the little container does not have a planting hole, make one with a chopstick, large nail, or something similar. Set the seed or cutting stem in the hole. Crimp the top over the seed or around the stem so it makes constant contact with the medium. In one to three weeks, roots grow and show through the side of the cube. Cut the nylon mesh from peat pots before it gets entangled with roots. To transplant, set the peat pot or root cube in a pre-drilled hole in a rockwool block or into a larger pot. Cuttings and seedlings suffer little or no transplant shock when transplanted properly.

Check moisture levels in peat pots and root cubes daily. Keep them evenly moist but not drenched. Root cubes and peat pots do not contain any nutrients. Seedlings do not require nutrients for the first week or two. Feed seedlings after the first week, and feed cuttings as soon as they are rooted.

Coarse sharp sand, fine vermiculite, and perlite work well to root cuttings. Sand and perlite are fast-draining, which helps prevent damping-off. Vermiculite holds water longer and makes taking cuttings easier. A good mix is one third of each: sand, fine perlite, and fine vermiculite. Premixed seed starter mixes sold under such brand names as Sunshine Mix and Terra-Lite are the easiest and most economical mediums in which to root cuttings and start seedlings. Soilless mix also allows for complete control of critical nutrient and root-stimulating hormone additives, which are essential to asexual propagation.

Soil Amendments

Soil amendments increase the soil's air-, water-, and nutrient-retaining abilities. Soil amendments fall into two categories: mineral and organic.

Mineral amendments are near neutral on the pH scale and contain few, if any, available nutrients. Mineral amendments decompose through weathering and erosion. Add mineral amendments to augment air and increase drainage. They have the advantage of creating no bacterial activity to alter nutrient content and pH of the growing medium. Dry mineral amendments are also very lightweight and much easier to move in and out of awkward spaces.

Perlite is sand or volcanic glass expanded by heat. It holds water and nutrients on its many irregular surfaces, which works especially well for aerating the soil. This is a good medium to increase drainage during vegetative and flowering growth, and it does not promote fertilizer-salt buildup.

Versatile perlite is available in three main grades: fine, medium, and coarse. Most gardeners prefer the coarse grade as a soil amendment. Perlite should make up one-third or less of any mix to keep it from floating and stratifying the mix.

Coco bricks are ideal for some growers. They expand to nine times their original size when wet.

Pumice is lightweight.

Vermiculite is lightweight and absorbent.

Coconut peat is becoming very popular among indoor gardeners.

LEFT: Some growers use organic potting soil as a soil amendment. RIGHT: This bag of soil amendments contains well-rotted mulch and chicken manure.

Rent a commercial cement mixer to mix large quantities of soil.

Pumice, volcanic rock, is very light and holds water, nutrients, and air in its many catacomb-like holes. It is a good amendment for aerating the soil and retaining moisture evenly. But like perlite, pumice floats and should constitute less than one-third of any mix to avoid problems.

Hydroclay is used more and more as a soil amendment in containers. The large expanded-clay pellets expedite drainage and hold air within the growing medium. See Chapter Ten "Hydroponics" for more information.

Vermiculite is mica that has been processed and expanded by heat. It holds water, nutrients, and air within its fiber and gives body to fast-draining soils. Fine vermiculite holds too much water for cuttings but does well when mixed with a fast-draining medium. This amendment holds more water than perlite or pumice. Used in hydroponic wick systems, vermiculite holds and wicks much moisture. Vermiculite comes in three grades: fine, medium, and coarse. Use fine vermiculite as an ingredient in mixes used when taking cuttings. If fine vermiculite is not available, crush coarse or medium vermiculite between your hands, rubbing palms back and forth. Coarse is the best choice as a soil amendment.

Organic soil amendments contain carbon and break down through bacterial activity, slowly yielding humus as an end product. Humus is a soft, spongy material that binds minute soil particles together, improving the soil texture. New, actively-composting, organic soil amendments require nitrogen to carry on bacterial decomposition. If they do not contain at least 1.5 percent nitrogen, the organic amendment will get it from the soil, robbing roots of valuable nitrogen. When using organic amendments,

make sure they are thoroughly composted (at least one year) and releasing nitrogen rather than stealing it from the soil. A dark, rich color is a good sign of fertility.

Rich, thoroughly composted organic matter amends texture and supplies nutrients. Leaf mold, garden compost (at least one year old), and many types of thoroughly composted manure usually contain enough nitrogen for their decomposition needs and release nitrogen rather than using it. Purchase quality organic amendments at a reputable nursery. Look carefully at the descriptive text on the bag to see if it is sterilized and is guaranteed to contain no harmful insects, larvae, eggs, and fungi or bad microorganisms. Contaminated soil causes many problems that are easily averted by using a clean mix.

Garden compost and leaf mold are usually rich in organic nutrients and beneficial organisms that speed nutrient uptake, but they can be full of harmful pests and diseases, too. For example, compost piles are a favorite breeding ground for cutworms and beetle larvae. Just one cutworm in a container means certain death for the defenseless plant. Garden compost is best used in outdoor gardens and not indoors. See below for more information on garden compost.

Manure: Barnyard manure, a great fertilizer for outdoor gardens, often contains toxic levels of salt and copious quantities of weed seeds and fungus spores that disrupt an indoor garden. If using manure, purchase it in bags that guarantee its contents. There are many kinds of manure: cow, horse, rabbit, and chicken, etc. See Chapter Nine for a complete rundown on manures, all of which help retain water and improve soil texture when used as soil amendments. When mixing manures as amendments, do not add more than 10–15 percent, to avoid salt buildup and overfertilization. The nutrient content of manures varies, depending upon the animal's diet and the decomposition factors.

Peat moss is available in bags or compressed bales.

Peat is the term used to describe partially decomposed vegetation. The decay has been slowed by the wet and cold conditions of the northern USA and Canada where it is found in vast bogs. The most common types of peat are formed from sphagnum and hypnum mosses. These peats are harvested and used to amend soil and can be used as a growing medium. Peat moss is very dry and difficult to wet the first time, unless you bought it wet. Wet peat is heavy and awkward to transport. When adding peat moss as a soil amendment, cut your workload by dry-mixing all the components before wetting. Use a wetting agent. Another trick to mixing peat moss is to kick the sack a few times to break up the bale before opening.

Peat tends to break down and should be used for only one crop.

Sphagnum peat moss is light brown and is the most common peat found at commercial nurseries. This bulky peat gives soil body and retains water well, absorbing 15 to 30 times its own weight. It contains essentially no nutrients of its own, and the pH ranges from 3.0 to 5.0. After decomposing for several months, the pH could continue to drop and become very acidic. Counter this propensity for acidity and stabilize the pH by adding fine dolomite lime to the mix.

Hypnum peat moss is more decomposed and darker in color with pH from 5.0 to 7.0. This peat moss is less common and contains some nutrients. Hypnum peat is a good soil amendment, even though it cannot hold as much water as sphagnum moss.

Coconut fiber is also called palm peat, coco peat, cocos, kokos, and coir. Coir is coconut pith, the fibrous part just under the heavy husk. Pith is soaked in water for up to nine months to remove salts, natural resins, and gums in a process called retting. Next, they beat the straw-brown coir to extract the husk.

Coir is biodegradable and a good medium for propagation through to the flowering and fruit growth stages. Coir holds lots of water while maintaining structure. It is durable, rot-resistant, and a good insulator, too. It is inexpensive, easy to control, and holds lots of air.

Washed, pressed blocks or bricks of coir are virtually inert. Bricks weigh about 1.3–2.2 pounds (0.6–1 kg). The pH is between 5.5 and 6.8. Some of the best coconut coir is from the interior of the Philippine Islands, where the environment is not packed with coastal salts. Quality coconut coir is guaranteed to have sodium content of less than 50 ppm.

Gardeners use coir by itself or mixed 50/50 with perlite or expanded clay to add extra drainage to the mix. Some gardeners sprinkle coconut coir on top of rockwool blocks to keep the tops from drying out.

Flake dry bricks of coconut coir apart by hand or soak the bricks in a bucket of water for 15 minutes to expand and wet. One brick will expand to about nine times its original size. Growing in coconut coir is similar to growing in any other soilless medium. Coconut coir may stay a little too wet and require more ventilation and air circulation.

Soil Mixes

Outdoor soil mixes that incorporate garden soil, compost, manure, coco peat, and rock powders grow some of the best plants in the world. Outdoor soil mixes can be mixed a few months early and left in the hole to blend and mature. Outdoor organic soil mixes are alive, and controlling the soil life is a matter of paying attention to a few details.

Indoors, outdoor soil mixes often create more trouble than they are worth. Too often, misguided novices go out to the backyard and dig up some good-looking dirt that drains poorly and retains water and air unevenly. The problems are compounded when they mix the dirt with garden compost packed with harmful microorganisms and pests. This lame soil mix grows bad plants. By saving a few bucks on soil, such gardeners create unforeseen problems and pay for their savings many times over with low harvest yields. Avert problems with soil mixes by purchasing all the components. Use garden soil or compost only if top quality and devoid of harmful pests and diseases. Use only the richest, darkest garden soil with good texture. Amend the soil by up to 80 percent

to improve water retention and drainage. Even a soil that drains well in the outdoor garden needs amending to drain properly indoors. Check the pH of garden soil before digging to ensure it is between 6.0 and 7.0. Add fine dolomite to stabilize and buffer pH. Check pH several times after mixing to ensure it is stable.

Solarize garden soil by putting it out in the sun in a plastic bag for a few weeks. Turn the bag occasionally to heat it up on all sides. Make sure the bag receives full sun and heats up to at least 140°F (60°C). This will kill the bad stuff and let the beneficial bacteria live.

You can also sterilize soil by laying it out on a Pyrex plate and baking it at 160°F for ten minutes or by microwaving it for two minutes at the highest setting. It is much easier and more profitable in the end to purchase good potting soil at a nursery.

Compost

Compost is outstanding. It solves most outdoor growing problems. Compost is an excellent soil amendment. It holds

Soil mixes with compost:

0.5 compost
0.5 soilless mix

0.3 compost
0.3 soilless mix
0.3 coco coir

0.5 compost
0.5 coco coir

0.3 compost
0.3 soilless mix
0.16 worm castings
0.16 perlite

Visible Signs of Grow Medium Stress

Dry, crispy, brittle leaves

Patchy or inconsistent leaf color

Yellow leaf edges that worsen

Crispy, burnt leaf edges

Chlorosis—yellowing between veins while veins remain green

Irregular blotches on leaves

Purple stems and leaf stems

Leaf edges curl up or down

Leaf tip curls down

Super-soft, pliable leaves

Branch tips stop growing

Leggy growth

Used Soil

Let soil dry.

Screen to separate roots, stems, and foliage from the soil.

Pack in plastic bags.

Remove soil from property.

Dispose of properly.

Compost piles must be at least 3 feet (90 cm) square in order to retain more heat than they give off.

CEC of popular growing mediums measured in Milli-Eq/100 grams

Compost	90
Sunshine Mix	90
Peat moss	80
Garden soil	70
Expanded clay	20
Vermiculite	20
Perlite	0
Rockwool	0

This chart shows different growing mediums' ability to hold positive charges that are ready for root uptake. Note the zero CEC of perlite and rockwool. Roots must be constantly bathed in nutrients. Other mediums do not provide a constant flow of nutrients and the CEC regulates the ability to hold a positive charge to make nutrients available for root uptake.

nutrients and moisture within its fibers. However, using backyard compost indoors is tricky.

Some gardeners have no trouble with organic composts, but others have bad luck and even lose their entire crop when growing in backyard compost. Good compost recipes are available from monthly publications such as *Sunset*, *Organic Gardening*, and *National Gardening*, or from companies specializing in organic composts. Outdoor gardeners love compost. It is inexpensive, abundant, and works wonders to increase water retention and drainage. It also increases nutrient uptake because of biological activity. Indoors, compost is not very practical to use in containers. It could also have unwanted pests. If using compost indoors, make sure it is well-rotted and screened.

A good compost pile includes manure—the older the better. Manure from horse stalls or cattle feedlots is mixed with straw or sawdust bedding. Sawdust uses available nitrogen and is also acidic and not recommended. Look for the oldest and most-rotted manure. Well-rotted manure is less prone to have viable weed seeds and pests. Fresh nitrogen-packed grass clippings are one of my favorites to use in a compost pile. Put your hand down deep into a pile of grass clippings. The temperature one or two feet down in such a pile ranges from 120–180°F (49–82°C). Heat generated by chemical activity kills pests, breaks down foliage, and liberates nutrients.

Build compost piles high, and keep turning them. Good compost pile recipes include the addition of organic trace elements, enzymes, and the primary nutrients. The organic matter used should be ground up and in the form of shredded leaves and grass. Do not use large woody branches that could take years to decompose.

Before using compost indoors, pour it through 0.25-inch mesh hardware cloth (screen) to break up the humus before mixing with soil. Place a heavy-duty framed screen over a large garbage can or a wheelbarrow to catch the sifted compost. Return earthworms found on the screen to the medium, but kill cutworms. Make sure all composts are well-rotted and have cooled before mixing with indoor soil. For more information about composting, see *Let It Rot!*, Third Edition, by Stu Campbell, Storey Press, Prowal, VT.

Some gardeners mix up to 30 percent perlite into organic potting soil that contains lots of worm castings. Heavy worm castings compact soil and leave little space for air to surround roots. Adding perlite or similar amendments aerates the soil and improves drainage.

Solarize used soil to kill pests and diseases.

Growing Medium Disposal

Disposing of used growing medium can be as big a problem as finding the proper soil. Most soilless mixes and soils contain perlite, which is environmentally okay, but unsightly if reused in backyard gardens.

Dry soil is easier to work and transport. Press and rub dry soil through a one-fourth to one-half–inch screen to remove roots, stems, and foliage. Screening also transforms the cast-container shape of the soil to an innocuous form. Once the roots are removed, dry used soil can be bagged up or compacted. Place the dry soil in a trash compactor to make it smaller and more manageable. Used indoor growing mediums make excellent outdoor amendments when mixed with compost and garden soil. Do not reuse the depleted soil in outdoor pots. Many of the same problems that occur indoors will happen in outdoor pots.

Growing Medium Problems

These maladies are caused by growing medium problems but manifest as nutrient problems. The solution is found within the growing medium.

When water is abundant in the growing medium, roots easily absorb it. Roots use more energy to absorb more water as it becomes scarce. Finally, the point comes when the substrate retains more moisture than it surrenders, and the roots receive no water. A good growing medium readily yields its bank of stored water and nutrients. A poor medium does not pass enough nutrients to a plant's roots. The more easily plants absorb nutrients, the higher the yield.

Containers on casters are easy to move and stay warmer when up off the floor.

The cation-exchange-capacity (CEC) of a growing medium is its capacity to hold cations that are available for uptake by the roots. The CEC is the number of cation charges held in three and one-half ounces (100 gm) or 100 cc of soil and is measured in milli-Equivalents (mEq) or Centi-Moles/kg on a scale from 0–100. A CEC of zero means the substrate holds no available cations for roots. A CEC of 100 means the medium always holds cations available for root uptake. Growing mediums that carry a negative electrical charge are the best.

Woven coco fiber pots from General Hydroponics breathe well, do not compact, can be used several times, and are biodegradable.

Containers

Container preference is often a matter of convenience, cost, and availability. But the size, shape, and color of a container can affect the size and health of a plant as well as the versatility of the garden. Containers come in all shapes and sizes and can be constructed of almost anything—clay, metal, plastic, wood, and wood fiber are the most common. Plants will grow in any clean container that has not been used for petroleum products or deadly chemicals.

Clay, fiber, and wood containers breathe better than plastic or metal pots. Heavy clay pots are brittle and absorb moisture from the soil inside, causing the soil to dry out quickly. Metal pots are also impractical for indoor gardens because they oxidize (rust) and can bleed off harmful elements and compounds. Wood, although some-

> **Containers must:**
> Be clean
> Have adequate drainage holes
> Be big enough to
> accommodate plant

Individual plants are easily quarantined or dipped in a medicinal solution. Weak, sick, and problem plants are easy to cull from the garden.

White pots reflect light and heat. Black pots set inside the white pots keep roots in a dark environment.

what expensive, makes some of the best containers, especially large raised beds and planters on wheels. Plastic containers are inexpensive, durable, and offer the best value to indoor gardeners.

Ceramic containers are durable but heavy.

Rigid plastic pots are the most commonly used containers in indoor gardens. Growing in inexpensive, readily available containers is brilliant because they allow each plant to be cared for individually. You can control each plant's specific water and nutrient regimen. Individual potted plants can also be moved. Turn pots every few days, so plants receive even lighting and foliage will grow evenly. Huddle small, containerized plants tightly together under the brightest area below the HID lamp, and move them further apart as they grow. Set small plants up on blocks to move them closer to the HID.

Grow bags are economical, lightweight, and reusable.

Grow bags are among my favorite containers. Inexpensive, long-lasting grow bags take up little space and are lightweight. A box of 100 three-gallon (13 L) bags weighs less than five pounds (2.3 kg) and measures less than a foot square. One hundred three-gallon (13 L) grow bags can

Planting directly in the floor of a basement or building gives roots plenty of space to expand.

be stored in two three-gallon (13 L) bags. Imagine storing 100 rigid pots in the same space!

Grow bags are very easy to wash and reuse. Empty out the soilless mix and submerge bags in a big container of soapy water overnight. Wash each one by hand the next day and fill with soil. I like them much better than rigid pots because they are so practical.

The potting soil bag can also be used as a container.

The potting soil sack can be used as a container. The moist soil inside the bag holds its shape well, and the bags expand and contract with the soil, lessening the chance of burned root tips that grow down the side of pots.

Fiber and paper-pulp pots are popular with gardeners who move their plants outdoors, but the bottoms of the pots habitually rot out. Painting the inside of the fiber container with latex paint will keep the bottom from rotting for several crops.

Set large pots on blocks or casters to allow air circulation underneath. The soil stays warmer, and maintenance is easier. Planters should be as big as possible but still allow easy access to plants. The roots have more room to grow and less container surface for roots to run into and grow down. With large pots, roots are able to intertwine and grow like crazy.

Garden beds can be installed right on the earthen floor of a garage or basement. If drainage is poor, a layer of gravel or a dry well can be made under the bed. Some gardeners use a jackhammer to remove the concrete floor in a basement to get better drainage. An easier option is to cut a hole in the basement floor and install a dry well. Knocking holes in basement floors could cause water seepage where water tables are high. When it rains, the water may collect underneath; the garden seldom needs watering, but plants are kept too wet.

A raised bed with a large soil mass can be built up organically after several crops. To hasten organic activity within the soil, add organic seaweed, manure, and additives. When mixing soil or adding amendments, use the best possible organic components and follow organic principles. There should be good drainage, and the soil should be as deep as possible, 12–24 inches (30–60 cm).

Some gardeners in Amsterdam, Netherlands, grow in large soil beds set on a concrete floor. The basement beds are below sea level and filled with outstanding plants. They are able to treat the beds similarly to outdoor soil beds, but when watered heavily, water runs out on the floor and must be mopped up. They also have problems with ventilation. The ambient climate is naturally humid, and the extra water in the large basement increases humidity to above 90 percent, day and night. They employ a large extraction fan and a relatively small intake fan. Air is pulled through the long narrow basement room quickly and efficiently to evacuate moisture and lower the humidity. Even with this much soil, they have to flush individual beds at least once every four weeks to avoid nutrient buildup.

Much heat can be generated by decomposing organic matter, and it warms the room. Ventilation lowers heat and humidity and helps keep the room free of pests and diseases. An organic indoor garden sounds great, but it is a lot of work to replicate the great outdoors. Most or-

Flush containers with a mild nutrient solution every month.

Flush containers with three times as much water volume of soil to leach out excess fertilizer salts. Flush containers every month to avoid many problems.

ganic gardeners opt for organic liquid fertilizers and a bagged commercial organic soil mix.

Another drawback to raised beds is that the crop will take a few days longer to mature than if it were grown in containers. But the longer wait is offset by a larger harvest.

Drainage

All containers need some form of drainage. Drainage holes allow excess water and nutrient solution to flow freely out the bottom of a container. Drainage holes should let water drain easily but not be so big that growing medium washes out onto the floor. Containers should have at least two half-inch (1.2 cm) holes per square foot of bottom. Most pots have twice this amount. To slow drainage and keep soil from washing out of the large holes, add a one-inch (3 cm) layer of gravel in the bottom of the pot. Surface tension created by the varying sizes of soil and rock particles cause water to be retained at the bottom of the container. Line pots with newspaper if drainage is too fast or if soil washes out drain holes. This will slow drainage, so be wary!

Large pots hold a lot of soil and require irrigation less frequently.

Put trays under containers to catch excess water. Leaving water-filled saucers under pots often causes root rot. To avoid waterlogging soil and roots, set containers up an inch or two on blocks when using trays.

Nursery trays used for rooting cuttings and growing seedlings must have good drainage throughout the entire bottom. Once cuttings and seedlings are in place in the tray, the tray should always drain freely with no standing water in the bottom.

Container Shape, Size, and Maintenance

Popular pot shapes include rectangular and cylindrical. Gardeners prefer taller pots rather than wide, squat containers because many plant root systems penetrate deeply. Of all the gardens I have visited, squat pots were few and far between. Gardeners I queried said squat pots may hold more soil for their stature, but they do not produce as extensive a root system.

The volume of a container can easily dictate the size of a plant. For example, annual flowers and vegetables grow very fast and require a lot of root space for sustained, vigorous development. Containers should be big enough to allow for a strong root system, but just big enough to contain the root system before harvest. If the container is too small, roots are confined, water and nutrient uptake is limited, and growth slows to a crawl. But if the container is too big, it requires too much expensive growing medium and becomes heavy and awkward to move.

Fast-growing annuals' roots develop and elongate quickly, growing down and out, away from the main taproot. For example, about midsummer, nurseries have unsold tomato plants that are still in small four-inch (10 cm) pots and one-gallon (4 L) containers. The stunted plants have blooming flowers and ripe fruit. But few branches extend much beyond the sides of the container; the plants are tall and leggy with curled-down leaves and an overall stunted, sickly appearance. These plants are potbound, or rootbound. Once a plant deteriorates to this level, it is often easier and more efficient to toss it out and replace it with a healthy one.

Install a dry well to evacuate excess runoff.

Deep containers are ideal for seedlings that will be planted outdoors.

Roots soon hit the sides of containers where they grow down and mat up around the bottom. The unnatural environment inside the container often causes a thick layer of roots to grow alongside the container walls and bottom. This portion of the root zone is the most vulnerable to moisture and heat stress and is the most exposed.

Plant age	Container size
0 – 3 weeks	root cube
2 – 6 weeks	4-inch pot
6 – 8 weeks	2-gallon pot
2 – 3 months	3-gallon pot
3 – 8 months	5-gallon pot
6 – 18 months	10-gallon pot

Allow one or one and one-half gallons (4–7 L) of soil or soilless mix for each month the plant will spend in the container. A two- to three-gallon (7.5–11 L) pot supports a plant for up to three months. Three- to six-gallon containers are good for three to four months of rapid plant growth.

When soil dries in a pot, it becomes smaller, contracting and separating from the inside of the container wall. This condition is worst in smooth plastic pots. When this crack develops, frail root hairs located in the gap quickly die when they are exposed to air whistling down this crevice. Water also runs straight down this crack and onto the floor. You may think the pot was watered, but the root ball remains dry. Avoid such killer cracks by cultivating the soil surface and running your finger around the inside lip of the pots. Cultivate the soil in pots every few days and maintain evenly moist soil to help keep root hairs on the soil perimeter from drying out.

Do not place containers in direct heat. If soil temperature climbs beyond 75°F (24°C), it can damage roots. Pots that are in direct heat should be shaded with a piece of plastic or cardboard.

Cultivate the top layer of soil with a fork to break up the crusty surface.

Feeder roots grow near the soil surface, just under the expanded clay mulch.

A one- to two-inch (3–5 cm) layer of hydroclay mulch on soil surface keeps soil surface moist. Roots are able to grow along the surface, and the soil does not need to be cultivated. The mulch also decreases evaporation and helps keep irrigation water from damaging roots or splashing.

Roots turn green and grow poorly when they receive direct light.

Green Roots

White containers reflect light and keep soil cooler. Always use thick, white containers so light does not penetrate and slow root growth. If roots around the outside of the root ball start turning green, you know they are receiving direct light. Remedy the problem by painting the inside of the container with a non-toxic latex paint.

Fresh water is essential to all plant growth.

Introduction

Water provides a medium to transport nutrients necessary for plant life and make them available for absorption by the roots. Water quality is essential for this process to work at maximum potential. The laws of physics govern plant water uptake. Applying these laws, a gardener can provide precise, properly balanced components to grow outstanding plants indoors.

Microscopic root hairs absorb water and nutrients in the oxygen present in the growing medium and carry them up the stem to the leaves. This flow of the water from the soil through the plant is called the transpiration stream. A fraction of the water is processed and used in photosynthesis. Excess water evaporates into the air, carrying waste products along with it via the stomata in the leaves. This process is called transpiration. Some of the water also returns manufactured sugars and starches to the roots.

Look at a rooting cutting. Check out the fine, fuzzy roots closely. You can see the minute hairlike feeder roots.

The roots support the plants, absorb nutrients, and provide the initial pathway into the vascular system. A close-up look at a root reveals the xylem and phloem core, vascular tissue that is enveloped by a cortex tissue or the layer between the internal vascular and the external epidermal tissue. The microscopic root hairs are located on the epidermal tissue cells. These tiny root hair follicles are extremely delicate and must remain moist. Root hairs must be protected from abrasions, drying out, extreme temperature fluctuations, and harsh chemical concentrations. Plant health and well-being is contingent upon strong, healthy roots.

The nutrient absorption begins at the root hairs, and the flow continues throughout the plant via the vascular system. Absorption is sustained by diffusion. In the process of diffusion, water and nutrient ions are uniformly distributed throughout the plant. The intercellular spaces—apoplasts and connecting protoplasm, symplast—are the pathways that allow water and nutrient ions and molecules to pass through the epidermis and the cortex to the xylem and phloem's vascular bundles. Xylem channels the solution through the plant while phloem tissues distribute the food manufactured by the plant. Once the nutrients are transferred to the plant cells, each cell accumulates the nutrients it requires to perform its specific function.

The solution that is transported through the vascular bundles or veins of a plant has many functions. This solution delivers nutrients and carries away the waste products. It provides pressure to help keep the plant structurally sound. The solution also cools the plant by evaporating the water via the leaves' stomata.

Water Quality
Hard Water

The concentration of calcium (Ca) and magnesium (Mg) indicate how "hard" the water is. Water containing 100 to 150 milligrams of calcium ($CaCO_3$) per liter is acceptable to grow plants. "Soft" water contains less than 50 milligrams of calcium per liter and should be supplemented with calcium and magnesium.

Check the pH of the irrigation water and adjust when necessary.

Sodium Chloride

Water with high levels of chloride frequently contains high levels of sodium, but the opposite is not true. Water with high levels of sodium does not necessarily contain excessive levels of chloride (chlorine).

At low levels sodium appears to bolster yields, possibly acting as a partial substitute to compensate for potassium deficiencies. But when excessive, sodium is toxic and induces deficiencies of other nutrients, primarily potassium, calcium, and magnesium.

Chloride (chlorine) is essential to the use of oxygen during photosynthesis, and it is necessary for root and leaf cell division. Chloride is vital to increase the cellular osmotic pressure, modify the stomata regulation, and augment the plant's tissue and moisture content. A solution concentration of less than 140 parts per million (ppm) is usually safe for plants, but some varieties may show sensitivity when foliage turns pale green and wilts. Excessive chlorine causes the leaf tips and margins to burn and causes the leaves to turn a bronze color.

Simple water filters do not clean dissolved solids from the water. Such filters remove only debris emulsified (suspended) in water; releasing dissolved solids from their chemical bond is more complex. A reverse-osmosis machine uses small polymer, semipermeable membranes that allow pure water to pass through and filter out the dissolved solids from the water. Reverse-osmosis machines are the easiest and most efficient means to clean raw water.

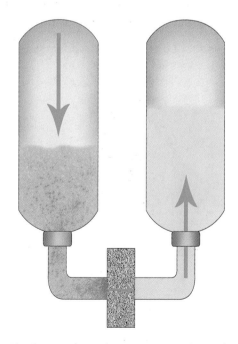

The drawing shows that pure water with no salts or dissolved solids migrates to the solution with more dissolved solids.

Osmosis

Roots draw the nutrient solution up the plant by the process of osmosis. Osmosis is the tendency of the fluids to pass through a semipermeable membrane and mix with each other until the fluids are equally concentrated on both sides of the membrane. Semipermeable membranes located in the root hairs allow specific nutrients that are dissolved in the water to enter the plant while other nutrients and impurities are excluded. Since salts and sugars are concentrated in the roots, the electrical conductivity (EC) inside the roots is (almost) always higher than that outside the roots. Transporting the nutrients by osmosis works because it depends on relative concentrations of each individual nutrient on each side of the membrane; it does not depend on the total dissolved solids (TDS) or EC of the solution. For nutrients to be drawn in by the roots via osmosis, the strength of the individual elements must be greater than that of the roots.

Typical bottled water analysis	mg per liter
Calcium	25.6
Magnesium	6.4
Potassium	<1.0
Sodium	6.4
Bicarbonate	98.3
Sulphate	10.1
Nitrate	<2.5
Fluoride	<0.1
Chloride	6.8
Silicate	7.6
Dry residue at 180°C	109.1
pH	4.6

The dissolved solids in bottled water are measured in milligrams per liter (m/L). Before the year 2000, bottlers in the USA were required by law to print a detailed analysis of the dissolved solids on their product's label. Relaxed rules now simply allow them to direct consumers to where that knowlege can be obtained, usually an Internet web site.

But, the transport of water (instead of nutrients) across the semipermeable membrane depends on EC. For example, if the EC is greater outside the roots than inside, the plant dehydrates as the water is drawn out of the roots. In other words, salty water with a high EC can dehydrate plants.

Reverse-osmosis

Reverse-osmosis machines are used to separate the dissolved solids from the water. These machines move the solvent (water) through the semipermeable membrane, but the process is reversed. It moves from lower concentrations to higher. The process is accomplished by applying pressure to the "tainted" water to force only "pure" water through the membrane. The water is not totally "pure" with an EC of zero, but most of the dissolved solids are removed. The efficiency of reverse osmosis depends on the type of membrane, the pressure differential on both sides of the

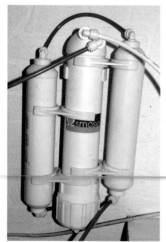

This reverse osmosis machine transforms water with a high ppm or EC into water with less than 10 ppm.

membrane, and the chemical composition of the dissolved solids in the tainted water.

Unfortunately, common tap water often contains high levels of sodium (Na), calcium (Ca), alkaline salts, sulfur (S), and chlorine (Cl). The pH could also be out of the acceptable 6.5 to 7 range. Water containing sulfur is easily smelled and tasted. Saline water is a little more difficult to detect. Water in coastal areas is generally full of salt that washes inland from the ocean. Dry regions that have less than 20-inches-annual rainfall also suffer from alkaline soil and water that is often packed with alkaline salts.

Table salt, sodium chloride (NaCl), is added to many household water systems. A small amount of chlorine, below 140 ppm, does not affect most plants' growth, but higher levels cause foliage chlorosis and stunt growth. Do not use salt-softened water. Salty, brackish, salt-softened water is generally detrimental to most plants. Chlorine also tends to acidify soil after repeated applications. The best way to get chlorine out of the water is to let it sit one or two days in an open container. The chlorine will evaporate (volatilize) as a gas when it comes in contact with the air. If chlorine noticeably alters soil pH, adjust it with a commercial "pH UP" product or hydrated lime.

The metric system facilitates the measurement of "dry residue per liter." Measure the dry residue per liter by pouring a liter of water on a tray and allowing it to evaporate. The residue of dissolved solids that remains after all of the water evaporates is the "dry residue per liter." The residue is measured in grams. Try this at home to find out the extent of impurities. Fertilizers have a difficult time penetrating root tissue when they must compete with resident dissolved solids.

Water that is loaded with high levels of dissolved solids (salts in solution) is possible to manage but requires different tactics. Highly saline water that contains sodium will block the uptake of potassium, calcium, and magnesium. Salt-laden water will always cause problems. If water contains 300 ppm or less dissolved solids, allow at least 25 percent of the irrigation water to drain out of the bottom of containers with each watering. If raw water contains more than 300 ppm of dissolved solids, use a reverse-osmosis device to purify the water. Add nutrients to pure water as a way to avoid many nutrient problems.

Dissolved salts, caused by saline water and fertilizer, quickly build up to toxic levels in container gardens. Excessive salts inhibit seed germination, burn the root hairs and tips or edges of leaves, and stunt the plant. Flush excess salt buildup from grow-

Flush your plants regularly to avoid salt and excess nutrient buildup.

ing mediums by applying two gallons of water per gallon of medium, and repeat leaching process using a mild pH-corrected fertilizer solution. Leach growing medium every two to four weeks if using soft water or saline water. Hard water and well water in dry climates are often alkaline and usually contain notable amounts of calcium and magnesium. Many fast-growing annual flowers and vegetables use large quantities of both nutrients, but too much calcium and magnesium can build up in soil. In general, water that tastes good to people also tastes good to plants.

Irrigation

Large plants use more water than small plants, but there are many more variables than size that dictate a plant's water consumption. The age of the plant, container size, soil texture, temperature, humidity, and ventilation all contribute to water needs. Change any one of these variables, and the water consumption will change. Good ventilation is essential to promote a free flow of fluids, transpiration, and rapid growth. The healthier a plant, the faster it grows and the more water it needs.

Small plants with small root systems in small containers must be watered often. Water frequently—as soon as the soil surface dries out. If exposed to wind, the small plants will dry out very quickly.

Irrigate soil and soilless mixes when they are dry one-half inch below the surface. As long as the drainage is good, it is difficult to overwater fast-growing plants. Four-week-old cuttings flowering in two- to three-gallon (7.5 to 11 L) containers need to be irrigated once or twice daily. In fact, most gardeners prefer smaller containers because they are easier to control.

Irrigate larger plants in the vegetative and flowering stages when soil is dry one-half inch below the surface. Flowering annuals use high levels of water to carry on rapid floral formation. Withholding water stunts flower formation.

Plants that are exposed to wind dry out much faster. Outdoor, terrace, and patio plants will use up to three or four times more water on a hot, windy day. Keeping up with the watering is difficult and time-consuming. Use an automated watering system or break the wind to lessen its impact on the plants. Mulch will also lessen the evaporation from the soil.

A water meter takes the guesswork out of watering. Remember to keep probes clean for an accurate reading.

Use plenty of water, and allow up to ten percent runoff during each watering. The runoff will prevent the fertilizer from building up in the soil. Water early in the day so excess water will evaporate from the soil surface and the leaves. Leaving the foliage and the soil wet overnight invites a fungal attack.

Moisture meters take most of the guesswork out of irrigating. They can be purchased for less than $30 and are well worth the money. These meters measure exactly how much water soil contains at any level or point. Often soil will not hold water evenly, and it develops dry pockets. Checking the moisture with a finger provides an educated guess but disturbs the root system. A moisture meter will give an exact moisture reading without disturbing the roots.

Cultivate the soil surface to allow the water to penetrate evenly and guard against dry soil pockets. It also keeps the water from running down the crack between the inside of the pot and the soil and out the drain holes. Gently break up and cultivate the top half-inch of soil with your fingers or a salad fork. Be careful not to disturb tiny surface roots.

After you develop some skill at knowing when the plants need water, you can check to see how heavy they are simply by tipping them. Once you get the hang of it, all you will have to do is tip each container.

It is easier to keep pots in straight lines when growing and watering, and it is much easier to keep track of watered pots when they are in a straight line.

Overwatering is a common problem, especially with small plants. Too much water drowns the roots by cutting off their supply of oxygen. If you have symptoms of overwatering, buy a moisture meter! It will let both you and your garden breathe easier. Sometimes, parts of the soil are overwatered and other soil pockets remain bone-dry. Cultivating the soil surface, allowing even water penetration, and using a moisture meter will overcome this problem. If you are using trays to catch runoff water, use a turkey baster, large syringe, or sponge to draw excess water from the trays.

One of the main causes of overwatering is poor air ventilation. Plants need to transpire water into the air. If there is nowhere for this wet, humid air to go, gallons of water are locked in the indoor garden air. Well-ventilated air carries this moist air away, replacing it with fresh, dry air.

Signs of overwatering: leaves curl down and yellow, waterlogged and soggy soil, fungal growth, and slow growth. Symptoms of overwatering can be subtle; inexperienced gardeners may not see blatant symptoms for a long time.

Fast-growing annuals do not like soggy soil. Soil kept too wet drowns the roots, squeezing out the oxygen. This causes slow growth and possible fungal attack. Poor drainage is most often the cause of soggy soil. It is compounded by poor ventilation and high humidity.

Underwatering is less of a problem; however, it is fairly common if small (1–2 gallon) pots are used and the gardener does not realize the water needs of fast-growing plants. Small containers dry out quickly and may require daily watering. If forgotten, water-starved plants become stunted. Once tender root hairs dry out, they die. Most gardeners panic when they see their prized plants wilt in bone-dry soil. Dry soil, even in pockets, makes root hairs dry up and die. It seems to take forever for affected roots to grow new root hairs and resume rapid growth.

Add a few drops (one drop per pint) of a biodegradable, concentrated liquid soap like Palmolive® or Ivory® to the water. It will act as a wetting agent by helping the water penetrate the soil more efficiently, and it will guard against dry soil pockets. Most soluble fertilizers contain a wetting agent. Apply about one-quarter to one-half as much water/fertilizer as the plant is expected to need, and then wait 10 to 15 minutes for it to totally soak in. Apply more water/fertilizer until the soil is evenly moist. If trays are underneath the pots, let excess water remain in the trays a few hours or even overnight before removing it with a large turkey baster.

Add a few drops of biodegradable liquid dish soap concentrate to irrigation water. Detergent helps water penetrate the soil more thoroughly.

Another way to thoroughly wet soil is to soak containerized plants in water. This is easy to do with small pots. Simply fill a five-gallon (19 L) bucket with three gallons (11 L) of water. Submerge the smaller pot for a minute or longer, until the growing medium is saturated. Thorough wetting insures against dry soil pockets.

Having a readily accessible water source is very convenient, and it saves time and labor. A 4 × 4-foot garden containing 16 healthy plants in three-gallon (11 L) pots needs 10–25 gallons (40–100 L) of water per week. Water weighs eight pounds a gallon (1 kg per L). That's a lot of containers to fill, lift, and spill. Carrying water in containers from the bathroom sink to the garden is okay when plants are small, but when they are large, it is a big, sloppy, regular job. Running a hose into the garden saves much labor and mess. A lightweight, half-inch hose is easy to handle and is less likely to damage the plants. If the water source has hot and cold water running out of the same tap, and it is equipped with threads, attach a hose and irrigate with tepid water. Use a dishwasher coupling if the faucet has no threads. The hose should have an on/off valve at the outlet so water flow can be controlled while watering. A rigid water wand will save many broken branches while leaning over to water in tight quarters. Buy a water wand at a nursery or construct one from plastic PVC pipe. Do not leave water under pressure in the hose for more than a few minutes. Garden hoses are designed to transport water, not hold it under pressure, which may cause hose to rupture.

Place a pump attached to a garden hose and watering wand with an on/off valve to water individual plants by hand.

Use a filter with drip systems!

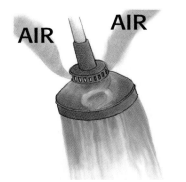

AIR AIR

A water wand with a breaker head mixes air with irrigation water just before applying.

To make a siphon or gravity-fed water system, place a barrel (at least four feet high) in the indoor garden. Make sure it has a lid to reduce evaporation and humidity. If the indoor garden is too small for the barrel, move it to another room. The attic is a good place because it promotes good pressure. Place a siphon hose in the top of the tank, or install a PVC on/off valve near the bottom of the barrel. It is easy to walk off and let the barrel overflow. An inexpensive device that measures the gallons

of water added to the barrel is available at most hardware stores. You can also install a float valve in the barrel to meter out water and retain a constant supply.

Drip systems deliver nutrient solution one drop at a time or in low volume via a low-pressure plastic pipe with friction fittings. Water flows down the pipe and out the emitter one drop at a time or at a very slow rate. The emitters that are attached to the main hose are either spaghetti tubes or a nozzle dripper actually emitting from the main hose. Drip irrigation kits are available at garden stores and building centers. You can also construct your own drip system from component parts.

Drip Systems

Drip systems offer several advantages. Once set up, drip systems lower watering maintenance. Fertilizer may also be injected into the irrigation system (fertigation); naturally, this facilitates fertilization but gives the same amount of water and nutrient to each plant. If setting up a drip system, make sure the growing medium drains freely to prevent soggy soil or salt buildup. If you are growing cuttings that are all the same age and size, a drip system would work very well. However, if you are growing many different varieties of plants, they may need different fertilizer regimens.

I interviewed several gardeners who loved the convenience and constant feeding-ability of their drip systems. All the gardeners irrigated (fertigated) with mild nutrient solution. They mixed the nutrient solution in a reservoir and pumped it through plastic feeder hoses. They also grew cuttings in smaller containers and held root growth to a minimum by keeping

COMMON CULTURAL PROBLEMS

Here is a short list of some of the most common cultural problems, some of which result in nutrient deficiencies.

1. Lack of ventilation: Leaves are stifled and unable to function, causing slow growth and poor consumption of water and nutrients.

2. Lack of light: Nutrients are used poorly, photosynthesis is slow, stems stretch, and growth is scrawny.

3. Humidity: High humidity causes plants to use less water and more nutrients. Growth is slow because stomata are not able to open and increase the transpiration. Low humidity stresses the plants because they use too much water.

4. Temperature: Both low and high temperatures slow the growth of plants. Large fluctuations in temperature—more than 15–20°F (8–10°C)—retard growth and slow the plant's processes.

5. Spray application damage: Sprays are phytotoxic. They can burn the foliage if the spray is too concentrated or if sprayed during the heat of the day.

6. Ozone damage: See Chapter Eleven "Air," for more information on ozone damage.

7. Overwatering: Soggy soil causes a menagerie of problems. It cuts the air from the roots, which retards nutrient intake and weakens the plant's defenses. Roots rot when overwatering is severe.

8. Underwatering: Dry soil causes nutrient transport to slow severely. It causes nutrient deficiencies and sick foliage, and the roots ultimately die.

9. Light burn: Burned foliage is susceptible to pest and disease attacks.

10. Indoor air pollution: This causes very difficult-to-solve plant problems. Always be aware of chemicals leaching or vaporizing from pressboard and other building materials. Such pollution causes plant growth to slow to a crawl.

11. Hot soil: Soil over 90°F (32°C) will harm the roots. Often, outdoor soil that is used in containers warms up to well over 100°F (38°C).

12. Roots receiving light: Roots turn green if light shines through the container or the hydroponic system. Roots require a dark environment. Their function slows substantially when they turn green.

nutrients and water in constant supply.

A drip system attached to a timer disperses nutrient solution at regular intervals. If using such a system, check the soil for water application daily. Check several pots daily to ensure they are watered evenly and that all the soil gets wet. Drip systems are very convenient and indispensable when you have to be away for a few days. However, do not leave a drip system on its own for more than four consecutive days, or you could return to a surprise!

Drip systems cost a few dollars to set up, but with the consistency they add to a garden, their expense is often paid off by a bountiful yield. Be careful! Such an automated system could promote negligence. Remember that gardens need daily care. Even if everything is automated, the garden still needs monitoring. All vital signs—moisture, pH, ventilation, humidity, etc.,—need to be checked and adjusted daily. Automation, when applied properly, adds consistency, uniformity, and usually a higher yield.

One indoor gardener I met was out of town for five consecutive days every week. He put containerized plants in a tray with two-inch-tall (6 cm) sides and fertigated the plants from above until the tray was full of water. He left for five days, and the plants needed no watering while he was gone. He used regular potting soil and added about ten percent perlite. His plants needed maintenance when he returned, but the plants grew quite well.

Misdiagnosed Disorders

Many indoor garden problems, and to a lesser degree outdoor problems, are misdiagnosed as a lack of fertilizer. Often, disease and insects cause such problems. Other times, problems are caused by an imbalanced pH of the growing medium and water. A pH between 6.5 and 7 in soil and 5.8 to 6.5 in hydroponics will allow nutrients to be chemically available; above or below this range, several nutrients become less available. For example, a full point movement in pH represents a tenfold increase in either alkalinity or acidity. This means that a pH of 5.5 would be ten times more acidic than a pH of 6.5. In soil, a pH below 6.5 may cause a deficiency in calcium, which causes root tips to burn and leaves to get fungal infections and dead spots on foliage. A pH over 7 could slow down the plant's iron intake and result in chlorotic leaves causing veins to yellow.

Incorrect pH contributes to most serious nutrient disorders in organic-soil gardens. Many complex biological processes occur between organic fertilizers and the soil during nutrient uptake. The pH is critical to the livelihood of these activities. When the pH fluctuates in a hydroponic garden, the nutrients are still available in the solution for uptake, and the pH is not as critical. Electrical conductivity is the most critical indicator of plant health and nutrient uptake in hydroponics.

Once a plant shows symptoms, it has already undergone severe nutritional stress. It will take time for the plant to resume vigorous growth. Correct identification of each symptom as soon as it occurs is essential to help plants retain vigor. Indoor, greenhouse, and some outdoor crops are harvested so fast that plants do not have time to recover from nutrient imbalances. One small imbalance could cost a week of growth. That could be more than ten percent of the plant's life!

Do not confuse nutrient deficiencies or toxicities with insect and disease damage or poor cultural practices.

The temperature within leaves can climb to an excess of 110°F (43°C). It happens easily because leaves store heat radiated by the lamp. At 110°F (43°C), the internal chemistry of a leaf is disrupted. The manufactured proteins are broken down and become unavailable to the plant. As the internal temperature of the leaves climbs, they are forced to use and evaporate more water. About 70 percent of the plant's energy is used in this process.

The basic elements of the environment must be checked and maintained at specific levels to avoid problems. Check each of the vital signs—air, light, soil, water, temperature, humidity, etc.—and fine-tune the environment, especially ventilation, before deciding that plants are nutrient deficient.

Nutrient deficiencies are less common when using fresh potting soil fortified with micronutrients. If the soil or water supply is acidic, add dolomite lime to buffer the soil pH and to keep it sweet. Avoid nutrient problems by using fresh planting mix, clean water, and a complete nutrient solution. Maintain the EC and pH at proper levels, and flush the system with mild nutrient solution every four weeks.

Nutrients

Nutrients are elements that the plant needs to live. Carbon, hydrogen, and oxygen are absorbed from air and water. The rest of the elements, called nutrients, are absorbed from the growing medium and nutrient solution. Supplemental nutrients supplied in the form of a fertilizer allow plants to reach their maximum potential. Nutrients are grouped into three categories: macronutrients or primary nutrients, secondary nutrients, and micronutrients or trace elements. Each nutrient in the above categories can be further classified as either mobile or immobile.

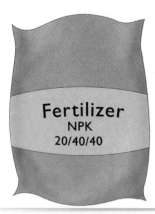

The numbers on the fertilizer bag above represent the Nitrogen, Phosphorus, and Potassium amounts in the fertilizer.

Mobile nutrients—nitrogen (N), phosphorus (P), potassium (K), magnesium (Mg), and zinc (Zn)—are able to translocate, move from one portion of the plant to another, as needed. For example, nitrogen accumulated in older leaves translocates to younger leaves to solve a deficiency. The result: deficiency symptoms appear on the older, lower leaves first.

Immobile nutrients—calcium (Ca), boron (B), chlorine (Cl), cobalt (Co), copper (Cu), iron (Fe), manganese (Mn), molybdenum (Mo), silicon (Si) and sulfur (S)—do not translocate to new growing areas as needed. They remain deposited in their original place in older leaves. This is the reason deficiency symptoms appear first in the upper, new leaves on top of the plant.

Macronutrients

Chart of Mobile and Immobile Nutrients	
Nitrogen (N)	mobile
Phosphorus (P)	mobile
Potassium (K)	mobile
Magnesium (Mg)	mobile
Zinc (Zn)	mobile
Calcium (Ca)	immobile
Boron (B)	immobile
Chlorine (Cl)	immobile
Cobalt (Co)	immobile
Copper (Cu)	immobile
Iron (Fe)	immobile
Manganese (Mn)	immobile
Molybdenum (Mo)	immobile
Selenium (Se)	immobile
Silicon (Si)	immobile
Sulfur (S)	immobile

Macronutrients are the elements that plants use most. The fertilizers usually show nitrogen (N), potassium (P), and phosphorus (K) as (N-P-K) percentages in big numbers on the front of the package. They are always listed in the same N-P-K order. These nutrients must always be in an available form to supply plants with the building blocks for rapid growth.

Nitrogen (N) – mobile

Practical information: flowers and vegetables love nitrogen and require high levels of it during vegetative growth but lower levels during the balance of life. Nitrogen is easily washed away and must be replaced regularly, especially during vegetative growth.

Beginning of nitrogen deficiency.

Technical information: Nitrogen regulates a plant's ability to make proteins essential for new protoplasm in its cells. Electrically charged nitrogen allows the plant to tie proteins, hormones, chlorophyll, vitamins, and enzymes together. Nitrogen is essential for the production of amino acids, enzymes, nucleic acids, chlorophyll, and alkaloids. This important nutrient is mainly responsible for leaf and stem growth, as well as overall size and vigor. Nitrogen is most active in young buds, shoots, and leaves. Ammonium (NH_4^+) is the most readily available form of nitrogen. Be careful when using too much of this form; it can burn the plants. Nitrate (NO_3^-)—the nitrate form of nitrogen—is much slower to assimilate than ammonium. Hydroponic fertilizers use this slower-acting nitrogen compound and mix it with ammonium.

Progression of nitrogen deficiency.

Deficiency: Nitrogen is the most common nutrient deficiency. The symptoms include slow growth. Lower leaves cannot produce chlorophyll, so they become yellow between the veins while the veins remain green. Yellowing progresses through the entire leaf, eventually causing it to die and drop off. Stems and the leaves' undersides may turn reddish-purple, but this can also be a sign of phosphorus deficiency. Nitrogen is very mobile, and it dissipates into the environment quickly. It must be added regularly to sustain fast-growing gardens.

Progression of nitrogen deficiency symptoms at a glance:
Older leaves yellow between the veins (interveinal chlorosis).
Older bottom leaves turn entirely yellow.
More and more leaves yellow. Severely affected leaves drop.
Leaves might develop reddish-purple stems and veins on leaf undersides.

Progressively younger leaves develop interveinal chlorosis.

Later stage of nitrogen deficiency.

Beginning of phosphorus deficiency.

Progression of phosphorus deficiency.

Later stage of phosphorus deficiency.

All foliage yellows, and leaf drop is severe.

Treat deficiency by fertilizing with N or a complete N-P-K fertilizer. You should see results in four to five days. Fast-acting organic sources of nitrogen include seabird guano, fish emulsion, and blood meal. Gardeners also report excellent results by adding bio-fertilizers (see "Additives" below) to stimulate the uptake of nitrogen.

Toxicity: An overdose of nitrogen will cause excessively lush foliage that is soft and susceptible to stress, including insect and fungal attacks. The stems become weak and may fold over easily. The vascular transport tissue breaks down, and water uptake is restricted. In severe cases, leaves turn a brownish-copper color, dry out, and fall off. Roots develop slowly, and they tend to darken and rot. Flowers are smaller and sparse. Ammonium toxicity is most common in acidic soils, and nitrate toxicity is more prevalent in alkaline soil.

Progression of nitrogen toxicity symptoms at a glance:

Excessively lush, green foliage.

Weak stems that fold over.

Slow root development.

Flowers become wispy.

Leaves brown, dry, and fall off.

Treat toxicity by flushing the growing medium of the affected plants with a very mild, complete fertilizer. Severe problems require that more water be flushed through the growing medium to carry away the toxic elements. Flush a minimum of three times the volume of water for the volume of the growing medium. Do not add more fertilizer that contains nitrogen for one week so the excess nitrogen in foliage can be used. If the plants remain excessively green, cut back on the nitrogen dose.

Phosphorus (P) – mobile

Practical information: Fast-growing annuals use the highest levels of phosphorus during germination, seedling, the taking of cuttings, and flowering. "Super Bloom" fertilizers, designed for flowering, have high levels of phosphorus.

Technical information: Phosphorus is necessary for photosynthesis and provides a mechanism for the energy to transfer within the plant. Phosphorus—one of the components of DNA, many being enzymes and proteins—is associated with overall vigor, and seed production. The highest concentrations of phosphorus are found in root growing tips, growing shoots, and vascular tissue.

Deficiency: A lack of phosphorus causes stunted growth and smaller leaves; leaves turn bluish-green and blotches often appear. Stems, leaf stems (petioles), and main veins turn reddish-purple starting on the leaf's underside. NOTE: Reddening of stems and veins is not always well pronounced. The leaf tips of older leaves turn dark and curl downward. Severely affected leaves develop large purplish-black necrotic (dead) blotches. These leaves later become bronzish purple, dry, shrivel up, contort, and drop off. Flowering is often delayed, buds are uniformly smaller, seed yield is poor, and plants become very vulnerable to fungal and insect attack. Phosphorus deficiencies are aggravated by clay, acidic, and soggy soils. Zinc is also necessary for proper utilization of phosphorus.

Deficiencies are somewhat common and are often misdiagnosed. Deficiencies are most common when the growing-medium pH is above 7 and phosphorus is unable to be absorbed properly; the soil is acidic (below 5.8) and/or there is an excess of iron and zinc; the soil has become fixated (chemically bound) with phosphates.

Progression of phosphorus deficiency symptoms at a glance:

Stunted and very slow-growth plants.

Dark bluish-green leaves, often with dark blotches.

Plants are smaller overall.

When blotches overcome leaf stem, leaf turns bronzish purple, contorts, and drops.

Treat deficiency by lowering the pH to 5.5–6.2 in hydroponic units; 6 to 7 for clay soils; and 5.5–6.5 for potting soils so phosphorus will become available. If the soil is too acidic and an excess of iron and zinc exists, phosphorus becomes unavailable. If you are growing in soil, mix a complete fertilizer that contains phosphorus into the growing medium before planting. Fertigate with an inorganic, complete hydroponic fertilizer that contains phosphorus. Mix in the organic nutrients—bat guano, steamed bone meal, natural phosphates, or barnyard manure—to add phosphorus to soil. Always use finely ground organic components that are readily available to the plants.

Toxic signs of phosphorus may take several weeks to surface, especially if excesses are buffered by a stable pH. Most annual flowers and vegetables use a lot of phosphorus throughout their life cycle, and many varieties tolerate high levels. Excessive phosphorus interferes with calcium, copper, iron, magnesium, and zinc stability and uptake. Toxic symptoms of phosphorus manifest as a deficiency of zinc, iron, magnesium, calcium and copper; zinc is the most common.

Treat toxicity by flushing the growing medium of affected plants with a very mild and complete fertilizer. Severe problems require more water to be flushed through the growing medium. Flush a minimum of three times the volume of water for the volume of the growing medium.

Potassium (K) – mobile

Practical information: Potassium is used at all stages of growth. Soils with a high level of potassium increase a plant's resistance to bacteria and mold.

Technical information: Potassium helps combine sugars, starches, and carbohydrates and is essential to their production and movement. It is essential to growth by cell division. It increases the

Beginning of potassium deficiency.

Progression of potassium deficiency.

Later stage of potassium deficiency.

chlorophyll in foliage and helps to regulate stomata openings so plants make better use of light and air. Potassium is essential in the accumulation and translocation of carbohydrates. It is necessary to make the proteins that augment the oil content and improve the flavor in some vegetables and herbs. It also encourages strong root growth and is associated with disease resistance and water intake. The potash form of potassium oxide is (K_2O).

Deficiency: Potassium-starved plants initially appear healthy. Deficient plants are susceptible to disease. Symptoms include the following: older leaves (first tips and margins, followed by whole leaves) develop spots, turn dark yellow, and die. Stems often become weak and sometimes brittle. Potassium is usually present in the soil, but it is locked in by high salinity. First, leach the toxic salt out of the soil and then apply a complete N-P-K fertilizer. Potassium deficiency causes the internal temperature of foliage to climb and the protein cells to burn or degrade. Evaporation is normally highest on leaf edges, and that's where the burning takes place.

Progression of potassium deficiency symptoms at a glance:
Plants appear healthy with dark green foliage.
The leaves lose their luster.
Branching may increase, but branches are weak and scrawny.
Leaf margins turn grey and progress to a rusty-brown color, and then curl up and dry.
Yellowing of older leaves is accompanied by rust-colored blotches.
Leaves curl up, rot sets in, and older leaves drop.
Flowering is retarded and greatly diminished.

Treat deficiency by fertilizing with a complete N-P-K fertilizer. Occasionally, a gardener will add potassium directly to the nutrient solution. Organic gardeners add potassium in the form of soluble potash (wood ashes) mixed with water. Be careful when using wood ash; the pH is normally above 10. Use a pH-lowering mix to bring the pH to around 6.5 before application. Foliar feeding to cure a potassium deficiency is not recommended.

Toxicity occurs occasionally and is difficult to diagnose because it is mixed with the deficiency symptoms of other nutrients. Too much potassium impairs and slows the absorption of magnesium, manganese, and sometimes zinc and iron. Look for signs of toxic potassium buildup when symptoms of magnesium, manganese, zinc, and iron deficiencies appear.

Treat toxicity by flushing the growing medium of affected plants with a very mild and complete fertilizer. Severe problems require that more water be flushed through the growing medium. Flush with a minimum of three times the volume of water for the volume of the growing medium.

Secondary Nutrients

The secondary nutrients—magnesium, calcium, and sulfur—are also used by the plants in large amounts. Rapid-growing indoor vegetable and flower crops are able to process more secondary nutrients than most general-purpose fertilizers are able to supply. Many gardeners opt to use high quality two- and three-part hydroponic fertilizers to supply all necessary secondary and trace elements. But be careful; these three nutrients may be present in high levels in the ground water. It is important to consider these values when adding nutrient supplements. If growing in a soil or soilless mix with a pH below 7 such as Peat-Lite, incorporating one cup of fine (flour) dolomite lime per gallon of medium ensures adequate supplies of calcium and magnesium.

Beginning of magnesium deficiency.

Magnesium (Mg) – mobile

Practical information: Fast-growing annuals use a lot of magnesium, and deficiencies are common, especially in acidic (pH below 7) soils. Adding dolomite lime to acidic potting soils before planting will stabilize the pH, plus it will add magnesium and calcium to the soil. Add Epsom salts with each watering to correct magnesium deficiencies, if no dolomite was added when planting. Use Epsom salts designed specifically for plants rather than the supermarket-type.

Progression of magnesium deficiency.

Technical information: Magnesium is found as a central atom in every chlorophyll molecule, and it is essential to the absorption of light energy. It aids in the utilization of nutrients. Magnesium helps enzymes make carbohydrates and sugars that are later transformed into flowers. It also neutralizes the soil acids and toxic compounds produced by the plant.

Deficiency: Magnesium deficiency is common indoors. The lower leaves, and later the middle leaves, develop yellow patches between dark green veins. Rusty-brown spots appear on the leaf margins, tips, and between the veins, as the deficiency progresses. The brownish leaf tips usually curl upward before dying. The entire plant could discolor in a few weeks, and if severe, turn a yellow-whitish tinge before browning and dying. A minor deficiency will cause little or no problem with growth. However, minor deficiencies escalate and cause a diminished harvest as

Later stage of magnesium deficiency.

flowering progresses. Most often, magnesium is in the soil but is unavailable to the plant because the root environment is too wet and cold or too acidic and cold. Magnesium is also bound in the soil if there is an excess of potassium, ammonia (nitrogen), and calcium (carbonate). Small root systems are also unable to take in enough magnesium to supply heavy demand. A high EC slows the water evaporation and will also diminish magnesium availability.

Progression of magnesium deficiency symptoms at a glance:

No deficiency symptoms are visible during the first three to four weeks.

In the fourth to sixth week of growth, the first signs of deficiency appear. Interveinal yellowing and irregular rust-brown spots appear on older and middle-aged leaves. Younger leaves remain healthy.

Leaf tips turn brown and curl upward as the deficiency progresses.

Rust-brown spots multiply, and interveinal yellowing increases.

Rust-brown spots and yellowing progress, starting at the bottom and advancing to the top of the entire plant.

Younger leaves develop rust-colored spots and interveinal yellowing.

The leaves dry and die in extreme cases.

Treat deficiency by watering with two teaspoons of Epsom salts (magnesium sulfate) per gallon of water. For fast results, spray the foliage with a two-percent solution of Epsom salts. If the deficiency progresses to the top of the plant, it will turn green there first. In four to six days, it will start moving down the plant, turning lower leaves progressively more green. Continue a regular watering schedule with Epsom salts until the symptoms totally disappear. Adding Epsom salts regularly is not necessary when the fertilizer contains available magnesium. Use a foliar spray of Epsom salts for a fast cure. Another option is to apply magnesium sulfate monohydrate in place of Epsom salts. Add fine dolomite lime to soil and soilless mix to add a consistent supply of both calcium and magnesium over the long term. Always use the finest dolomite available.

Control the room and root-zone temperatures, humidity, pH, and EC of the nutrient solution. Keep root zone and nutrient solution at 70–75°F (21–24°C). Keep ambient air temperature at 75°F (21°C) day and 65°F (18°C) night. Use a complete fertilizer with an adequate amount of magnesium. Keep the soil pH above 6.5, the hydroponic pH above 5.5, and reduce high EC for a week.

The extra magnesium in the soil is generally not harmful, but it can inhibit calcium uptake. Signs of excess magnesium are described below.

Toxicity: Magnesium toxicity is rare and difficult to discern with the naked eye. If extremely toxic, magnesium develops a conflict with other fertilizer ions, usually calcium, especially in hydroponic nutrient solutions. Toxic buildup of magnesium is uncommon in soil that is able to grow most fast-growing annuals.

Calcium (Ca) – immobile

Practical information: Fast-growing flowers and vegetables require nearly as much calcium as other macronutrients. Avert deficiencies in the soil and in most soilless mixes by adding fine dolomite lime or using soluble hydroponic fertilizers containing adequate calcium.

CHELATES

A chelate (Greek for claw) is an organic molecule that forms a clawlike bond with free electrically charged metal particles. This property keeps metal ions such as zinc, iron, and manganese, etc., soluble in water, and the chelated metal's reactions with other materials is suppressed. Roots take in the chelated metals in a stable, soluble form that is used immediately.

Natural chelates such as humic acid and citric acid can be added to organic soil mixes. Roots and bacteria also exude natural chelates to promote uptake of metallic elements. Man-made chelates are designed for use in different situations. DTPA is most effective in a pH below 6.5, EDDHA is effective up to a pH

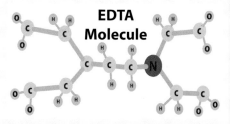

EDTA Molecule

of 8, and EDTA chelate is slow to cause leaf burn.

Chelates decompose rapidly in low levels of ultraviolet (UV) light including light produced by HID bulbs and sunlight. Keep chelates out of the light to protect them from rapid decomposition.

Chelate – combining nutrients in an atomic ring that is easy for plants to absorb.

Technical information: Calcium is fundamental to cell manufacturing and growth. Calcium is necessary to preserve membrane permeability and cell integrity, which ensures proper flow of nitrogen and sugars. It stimulates enzymes that help build strong cell and root walls. Plants must have some calcium at the growing tip of each root.

Deficiency of calcium is somewhat uncommon indoors, but not uncommon in fibrous plants. Frequently, plants can process more calcium than is available. It also washes out of the leaves that are sprayed with water. Deficiency signs may be difficult to detect. They start with weak stems, very dark green foliage, and exceptionally slow growth. Young leaves are affected, and they show the signs first. Severe calcium deficiency causes new, growing shoots to develop yellowish to purple hues and to disfigure before shriveling up and dying. Flower development is inhib-

ited, plants are stunted, and harvest is diminished. Growing tips could show signs of calcium deficiency if humidity is maxed out. At 100 percent humidity the stomata close, which stops transpiration to protect the plant. The calcium that is transported by transpiration becomes immobile.

Treat deficiencies by dissolving one-half teaspoon of hydrated lime per gallon of water. Water the deficient plants with calcium-dosed water as long as the symptoms persist. Or use a complete hydroponic nutrient that contains adequate calcium. Keep the pH of the growing medium stable.

Progression of calcium deficiency symptoms at a glance:

Slow growth, and young leaves turn very dark green.

New growing shoots discolor.

New shoots contort, shrivel, and die.

Bud development slows dramatically.

Toxicity is difficult to see in the foli-

Beginning of sulfur deficiency.

Progression of sulfur deficiency.

Later stage of sulfur deficiency.

age. It causes wilting. Toxic levels also exacerbate deficiencies of potassium, magnesium, manganese, and iron. The nutrients become unavailable, even though they are present. If excessive amounts of soluble calcium are applied early in life, it can also stunt the growth. If growing hydroponically, an excess of calcium will precipitate with sulfur in the solution, which causes the nutrient solution to suspend in the water and to aggregate into clumps causing the water to become cloudy (flocculate). Once the calcium and sulfur combine, they form a residue (gypsum $Ca(SO_4) \cdot 2(H_2O)$) that settles to the bottom of the reservoir.

Sulfur (S) – immobile

Practical information: Many fertilizers contain some form of sulfur, and for this reason, sulfur is seldom deficient. Gardeners avoid elemental (pure) sulfur in favor of sulfur compounds such as magnesium sulfate. The nutrients combined with sulfur mix better in water.

Technical information: Sulfur is an essential building block of many hormones and vitamins, including vitamin B_1. Sulfur is also an indispensable element in many plant cells and seeds. The sulfate form of sulfur buffers the water pH. Virtually all ground, river, and lake water contains sulfate. Sulfate is involved in protein synthesis and is part of the amino acids, cystine and thiamine, which are the building blocks of proteins. Sulfur is essential in the formation of oils and flavors, as well as for respiration and the synthesis and breakdown of fatty acids. Hydroponic fertilizers separate sulfur from calcium in an "A" container and a "B" container. If combined in a concentrated form, sulfur and calcium will form crude, insoluble gypsum (calcium sulfate) and settle as residue to the bottom of the tank.

Deficiency: Young leaves turn lime-green to yellowish. As shortage progresses, leaves yellow interveinally and lack succulence. Veins remain green, and leaf stems and petioles turn purple. Leaf tips can burn, darken, and hook downward. According to literature, youngest leaves should yellow first. Sulfur deficiency resembles a nitrogen deficiency. Acute sulfur deficiency causes elongated stems that become woody at the base.

Sulfur deficiency occurs indoors when the pH is too high or when there is excessive calcium present and available.

Progression of sulfur deficiency symptoms at a glance:
Similar to nitrogen deficiency: older leaves turn pale green.
Leaf stems turn purple, and more leaves turn pale green.
Entire leaves turn pale yellow.
Interveinal yellowing occurs.

MICRONUTRIENTS

Zinc, iron, and manganese are the three most common micronutrients found deficient. Deficiencies of these three micronutrients plague many more indoor gardens than I had imagined. Often, deficiencies of all three occur concurrently, especially when the soil or water pH is above 6.5. Deficiencies are most common in arid climates—Spain, the Southwestern United States, Australia, etc.—with alkaline soil and water. All three have the same initial symptom of deficiency: interveinal chlorosis of young leaves. It is often difficult to distinguish which element—zinc, iron, or manganese—is deficient, and all three could be deficient. This is why treating the problem should include adding a chelated dose of all three nutrients.

Acute deficiency causes more and more leaves to develop purple leaf stems and yellow leaves.

Treat deficiency by fertilizing with a hydroponic fertilizer that contains sulfur. Lower the pH to 5.5–6. Add inorganic sulfur to a fertilizer that contains magnesium sulfate (Epsom salts). Organic sources of sulfur include mushroom composts and most animal manures. Make sure to apply only well-rotted manures to avoid burning the roots.

Toxicity: An excess of sulfur in soil causes no problems if EC is relatively low. At a high EC, plants tend to take up more available sulfur which blocks uptake of other nutrients. Excess sulfur symptoms include overall smaller plant development and uniformly smaller, dark-green foliage. Leaf tips and margins could discolor and burn when severe.

Treat toxicity by flushing the growing medium of affected plants with a very mild and complete fertilizer. Check the pH of the drainage solution. Correct the input pH to 6. Severe problems require more water to be flushed through the growing medium. Flush a minimum of three times the volume of water for the volume of the growing medium.

Micronutrients

Micronutrients, also called trace elements or trace nutrients, are essential to chlorophyll formation and must be present in minute amounts. They function mainly as catalysts to the plant's processes and utilization of other elements. For best results, and to ensure a complete range of trace elements is available, use fertilizers designed for hydroponics. High-quality hydroponic fertilizers use food-grade ingredients that are completely soluble and leave no residues. If using an inexpensive fertilizer that does not list a specific analysis for each trace element on the label, it's a good idea to add soluble trace elements in chelated form. Chelated micronutrients are available in powdered and liquid form. Thoroughly mix micronutrients into the growing medium before planting. Micronutrients are often impregnated in commercial potting soils and soilless mixes. Check the ingredients list on the bag to ensure that trace elements were added to the mix. Trace elements are necessary in minute amounts but can easily reach toxic levels. Always follow the manufacturer's instructions to the letter when applying micronutrients, because they are easy to overapply.

Beginning of zinc deficiency.

Progression of zinc deficiency.

Later stage of zinc deficiency.

Zinc (Zn) – mobile

Practical information: Zinc is the most common micronutrient found deficient in arid climates and alkaline soils.

Technical information: Zinc works with manganese and magnesium to promote the same enzyme functions. Zinc cooperates with other elements to help form chlorophyll as well as prevent its demise. It is an essential catalyst for most plants' enzymes and auxins, and it is crucial for stem growth. Zinc plays a vital part in sugar and protein production. It is fairly common to find zinc-deficient plants. Deficiencies are most common in soils with a pH of 7 or more.

Deficiency: Zinc is the most common micronutrient found deficient. First, younger leaves exhibit interveinal chlorosis, and new leaves and growing tips develop small, thin blades that contort and wrinkle. The leaf tips, and later the margins, discolor and burn. Burned spots on the leaves could grow progressively larger. These symptoms are often confused with a lack of manganese or iron, but when zinc deficiency is severe, new leaf blades contort and dry out. Flowers can also contort into odd shapes, turn crispy dry, and are often hard. A lack of zinc stunts all new growth.

Progression of zinc deficiency symptoms at a glance:
Interveinal chlorosis of young leaves.
New leaves develop as thin, wispy leaves.
Leaf tips discolor, turn dark, and die back.
New growth contorts horizontally.
New bud and leaf growth stops.

Treat deficiency by flushing the growing medium with a diluted mix of a complete fertilizer containing chelated trace elements including zinc, iron, and manganese. Or add a quality-brand hydroponic micronutrient mix containing chelated trace elements.

Toxicity: Zinc is extremely toxic in excess. Severely toxic plants die quickly. Excess zinc interferes with iron's ability to function properly and causes an iron deficiency.

Manganese (Mn) – immobile

Practical information: Manganese deficiency is relatively common indoors.

Technical information: Manganese is engaged in the oxidation-reduction process associated with photosynthetic electron transport. This element activates many enzymes and plays a fundamental part in the chloroplast membrane system. Manganese assists in nitrogen utilization along with iron in chlorophyll production.

Deficiency: Young leaves show symptoms first. They become yellow between veins (interveinal chlorosis), and the veins remain green. Symptoms spread from younger to older leaves as the deficiency progresses. Necrotic (dead) spots develop on severely affected leaves which become pale and fall off; overall plant growth is stunted, and maturation may be prolonged. Severe deficiency looks like a severe lack of magnesium.

Treat deficiency: Lower the pH, leach the soil, and add a complete, chelated micronutrient formula.

Progression of manganese deficiency symptoms at a glance:

Interveinal chlorosis of young leaves.
Interveinal chlorosis of progressively older leaves.
Dead spots develop on acutely affected leaves.

Beginning of manganese deficiency.

Toxicity: Young and newer growth develop chlorotic, dark orange to dark rusty-brown mottling on the leaves. Tissue damage shows on young leaves before progressing to older leaves. Growth is slower, and overall vigor is lost. Toxicity is compounded by low humidity. The additional transpiration causes more manganese to be drawn into the foliage. A low pH can cause toxic intake of manganese. An excess of manganese causes a deficiency of iron and zinc.

Iron (Fe) – immobile

Practical information: Iron is available in a soluble chelated form that is immediately available for absorption by the roots. Deficiency indoors is common in alkaline soils.

Technical information: Iron is fundamental to enzyme systems and to the transport of electrons during photosynthesis, respiration, and chlorophyll production. Iron permits plants to use the energy provided by sugar. A catalyst for chlorophyll production, iron is necessary for nitrate and sulfate reduction and assimilation. Iron colors the earth from brown to red, according to concentration. Plants have a difficult time absorbing iron. Acidic soils normally contain adequate iron for plant growth.

Progression of manganese deficiency.

Deficiency: Iron deficiencies are common when the pH is above 6.5 and uncommon when the pH is below 6.5. Symptoms may appear during rapid growth or stressful times and disappear by themselves. Young leaves are unable to draw immobile iron from older leaves, even though it is present in the soil. The first symptoms appear on smaller leaves as veins remain green and areas between veins turn yellow. Interveinal

Later stage of manganese deficiency.

Beginning of iron deficiency.

Progression of iron deficiency.

Later stage of iron deficiency.

chlorosis starts at the opposite end of the leaf tip: the apex of the leaves attached by the petiole. Leaf edges can turn upward as the deficiency progresses. Leaves fall off in severe cases. Iron deficiency is sometimes traced to an excess of copper. See "Copper."

Progression of iron deficiency symptoms at a glance:

Younger leaves and growing shoots turn pale green and progress to yellow between veins starting at the petiole, but veins remain green.

More and more leaves turn yellow and develop interveinal chlorosis.

Larger leaves finally yellow and develop interveinal chlorosis.

In acute cases, leaves develop necrosis and drop.

Treat deficiency by lowering the soil pH to 6.5 or less. Avoid fertilizers that contain excessive amounts of manganese, zinc, and copper, which inhibit iron uptake. High levels of phosphorus compete with the uptake of iron. Improve drainage; excessively wet soil holds little oxygen to spur iron uptake. Damaged or rotten roots also lower iron uptake. Increase root-zone temperature. Apply chelated iron in liquid form to root zone. Chelates are decomposed by light and must be thoroughly mixed with the growing medium to be effective. Exposing the nutrient solution to light causes depleted iron. Sterilizing the nutrient solution with UV light causes iron to precipitate. Leaves should green up in four or five days. Complete, balanced hydroponic nutrients contain iron, and deficiencies are seldom a problem. Organic sources of iron, as well as chelates, include cow, horse, and chicken manure. Use only well-rotted manures to avoid burning plants.

Toxicity: Excess of iron is rare. High levels of iron do not damage most plants but can interfere with phosphorus uptake. An excess of iron causes leaves to turn bronze accompanied by small, dark-brown leaf spots. If iron chelate is overapplied, it will kill the plant in a few days.

Treat toxicity by leaching plants heavily.

The following group of micronutrients is seldom found deficient. Avoid deficiencies by using a high-quality hydroponic fertilizer that contains chelated micronutrients.

Boron (B) – immobile

Practical information: Boron usually causes no problems but must be available during the entire life of a plant.

Technical information: Boron deficiencies seldom occur indoors. Boron is still somewhat of a biochemical mystery, but we do know that boron helps with calcium uptake and numerous plant functions. Scientists have collected evidence to suggest boron helps with synthesis, a base for the formation of nucleic acid (RNA uracil) formation. Strong evidence also supports boron's role in cell division, differentiation, maturation, and respiration as well as a link to pollen germination.

Deficiency: Stem tip and root tip grow abnormally. Root tips often swell, discolor, and stop elongating. Growing shoots look burned and may be confused with a burn from being too close to the HID light. First leaves thicken and become brittle, top shoots contort and/or turn dark, which is later followed by progressively lower-growing shoots. When severe, growing tips die, and leaf margins discolor and die back in places. Necrotic spots develop between leaf veins. Root steles (insides) often become mushy—perfect hosts for rot and disease. Deficient leaves become thick, distorted, and wilted with chlorotic and necrotic spotting.

Treat deficiency with one teaspoon of boric acid per gallon of water. Apply this solution as a soil drench to be taken up by roots, or apply hydroponic micronutrients containing boron. Hydroponic gardeners should keep boron dosage below 20 parts per million (ppm) because boron quickly becomes toxic if it is concentrated in the solution.

Toxicity: Leaf tips yellow first, and as toxic conditions progress, leaf margins become necrotic toward the center of the leaf. After the leaves yellow, they fall off. Avoid using excessive amounts of boric acid–based insecticides.

Chlorine (Chloride) (Cl) – immobile

Practical information: Chloride is found in many municipal water systems. Most plants tolerate low levels of chlorine. It is not usually a component of fertilizers and is almost never deficient in gardens.

Technical information: Chlorine, in the form of chloride, is fundamental to photosynthesis and cell division in roots and foliage. It also increases osmotic pressure in the cells, which opens and closes the stomata to regulate moisture flow within plant tissue.

Deficiency: Chlorine deficiency is uncommon. Young leaves pale and wilt, and roots become stubby. As the deficiency progresses, leaves become chlorotic and develop a characteristic bronze color. Roots develop thick tips and become stunted. NOTE: Both severe deficiency and excess of chloride have the same symptoms: bronze-colored leaves.

Treat deficiency by adding chlorinated water.

Toxicity: Young leaves develop burned leaf tips and margins. Very young seedlings and cuttings are most susceptible to damage. Later, symptoms progress throughout the plant. Characteristic yellowish-bronze leaves are smaller and slower to develop.

Treat toxicity by letting heavily chlorinated water sit out overnight, stirring occasionally. Chlorine will volatilize and disappear into the atmosphere. Use this water to mix the nutrient solution or to irrigate the garden.

Cobalt (Co) – immobile

Practical information: This nutrient is seldom mentioned as necessary for plant growth, and most fertilizer labels do not include cobalt. Cobalt is virtually never deficient in indoor gardens.

Technical information: Cobalt is necessary for countless beneficial bacteria to grow and flourish. It is also vital for nitrogen absorption. Scientific evidence suggests this element is linked to enzymes needed to form aromatic compounds.

Deficiency: When cobalt is deficient, problems with nitrogen availability occur.

Toxicity: Quick wilting and death of plant.

Copper (Cu) – immobile

Practical information: Copper is concentrated in roots. It is also used as a fungicide.

Technical information: Copper is a component of numerous enzymes and proteins. Necessary in minute amounts, copper helps with carbohydrate metabolism, nitrogen fixation, and the process of oxygen reduction. It also helps with the making of proteins and sugars.

Deficiency: Copper deficiencies are not rare. Young leaves and growing shoots wilt; leaf tips and margins develop necrosis and turn a dark copper-gray. Occasionally, an entire copper-deficient plant wilts, drooping even when adequately watered. Growth is slow and the yield decreases. A small deficiency can cause new shoots to die back.

Treat deficiency by applying a copper-based fungicide such as copper sulfate. To avoid burning foliage, do not apply if the temperature is above 75°F (24°C). Apply a complete hydroponic nutrient that contains copper. Indoor plants seldom develop a copper deficiency.

Toxicity: Copper, although essential, is extremely toxic to plants even in minor excess. Toxic levels slow overall plant growth. As toxic level climbs, symptoms include interveinal iron chlorosis (deficiency) and stunted growth. Fewer branches grow, and roots become dark, thick, and slow growing. Toxic conditions accelerate quickly in acidic soils. Hydroponic gardeners must carefully monitor their solution to avoid copper excess.

Treat toxicity by flushing the soil or the growing medium to help expel the excess copper. Do not use copper-based fungicides.

Molybdenum (Mb) – immobile

Practical information: Molybdenum is seldom deficient.

Technical information: Molybdenum is a part of two major enzyme systems that convert nitrate to ammonium. This essential element is used by plants in very small quantities. It is most active in roots and seeds.

Deficiency: This micronutrient is almost never found deficient in indoor gardens. Deficiency promotes nitrogen shortage. First, the older and middle-aged leaves yellow, and some develop interveinal chlorosis; then the leaves continue to yellow and develop cupped or rolled-up margins as the deficiency progresses. Acute symptoms cause the leaves to become severely twisted, die, and drop. Overall growth is stunted. Deficiencies are worst in acidic soils.

Toxicity: Excess is uncommon in indoor gardens. An excess of molybdenum causes a deficiency of copper and iron.

Silicon (Si) – immobile

Practical information: Silicon is readily available in most soils and water. As far as I know, it does not cause most indoor plants any complications due to deficiencies or excesses.

Technical information: Silicon is absorbed by plants as silicic acid. Silicon assists in keeping iron and manganese levels consistent. It is found mainly in epidermal cell walls where it collects in the form of hydrated amorphous silica. It also accumulates in the walls of other cells. Adequate and soluble silicon guarantees stronger cell walls that resist pest attacks and increase heat and drought tolerance.

Deficiency: A lack of silicon has been proven to decrease yields of some fruits and cause new leaves to deform.

Toxicity: Never heard of a problem.

NOTE: Pests and diseases have a difficult time penetrating plants that are sprayed with a silicon-based repellent/insecticide.

Nickel (Ni)

Enzymes require nickel to break down and use nitrogen from urea. It is also essential to iron absorption. Nickel is seldom deficient, often subtly mixed with other nutrient deficiencies, most commonly nitrogen.

Sodium (Na)

This is one of the problem elements. A little bit will go a long way! Sodium is taken up by the roots very quickly and in small amounts (50 ppm). It can block enough other nutrients causing severe deficiencies to result. When mixed with chlorine, it turns into table salt, which is the worst possible salt to put on the plants. Be very careful to measure your input water to ensure that it contains less than 50 ppm sodium. The less sodium in the solution, the better.

Fluoride (F)

Some water systems are abundant with fluoride. If concentrated, fluoride can become toxic. I have yet to see fluoride toxicity or deficiency cause problems in an indoor garden.

Other Elements

Other elements are needed in very small quantities by some plants. These include selenium, vanadium, iodine, fluorine, tellurium, and rubidium. Plants usually need sub-microgram quantities which are found as impurities in ordinary plant fertilizers in sufficient quantities. Excesses are deadly.

Fertilizers

The goal of fertilizing is to supply plants with the proper amounts of nutrients for vigorous growth, without creating toxic conditions by overfertilizing. A two-gallon (8 L) container full of rich, fertile potting soil will supply all necessary nutrients for the first month of growth, but development might be slow. After roots have absorbed most of the available nutrients, more must be added to sustain vigorous growth. Unless fortified, soilless mixes require fertilization from the start. I like to begin fertilizing fortified soilless mixes after the first week or two of growth. Most commercial soilless mixes are fortified with trace elements.

A plant's metabolism changes as it grows and so do its fertilizer needs. During germination and seedling growth, phosphorus intake is high. The vegetative growth stage requires larger amounts of nitrogen for green-leaf growth, and phosphorus and potassium are also necessary in substantial levels. During this leafy vegetative growth stage, use a general purpose or a grow fertilizer with high nitrogen content. In the flowering stage, nitrogen takes a backseat to potassium, phosphorus, and calcium intake. Using a super-bloom fertilizer with less nitrogen and more potassium, phosphorus, and calcium promotes sturdy flowers and fat vegetables. Plants need some nitrogen during flowering, but very little. With no nitrogen, flowers do not develop to their full potential.

Now we come to the confusing part about the guaranteed analysis of commercial fertilizer mixes. Federal and state laws require nutrient concentrations to appear prominently on the face of fertilizer packages, even though the accuracy of the values is dubious.

Do you think the N-P-K numbers on the label give the percentages of nitrogen, phosphorus, and potassium? Well, yes and no. Nutrients are measured with different scales. Nitrogen is listed as total combined elemental. Most hydroponic fertilizers break nitrogen into slow-acting nitrate (NO_3) and ammonium (NH_4). Phosphoric anhydride (P_2O_5) is listed as the form of phosphorus, but this figure understates phosphorus content by 44 percent. It gets worse! The balance (56 percent) of the phosphorus molecule is comprised of oxygen. Twenty percent P_2O_5 is 8.8 percent actual phosphorus. Potassium (K) is listed in the potash form of potassium oxide (K_2O) of which 83 percent of the stated value is actually elemental potassium.

The rest of the mineral nutrients are listed in their elemental form that represents the actual content. Most often, mineral elements used in fertilizer formulas are listed in chemical compounds on the label. Look at the fertilizer label to ensure that the elements, especially trace elements, are chelated and readily available for root absorption. Also, be careful about having too much sodium in your water/nutrient solution. The sodium will block potassium and several other nutrients, causing deficiencies and slow growth.

In the USA, nutrients are measured in parts-per-million (ppm) even though they are expressed as a percentage concentration on the label. The ppm scale is simple and finite—almost. The basics are simple: one part per million is one part of 1,000,000, so divide by one million to find parts per million. To convert percentages into ppm, multiply by 10,000 and move the decimal four (4) spaces to the right. For example: two percent equals 20,000 ppm. For more information on ppm and Electrical Conductivity, see Chapter Ten, "Hydroponic Gardening."

Fertilizers are either water-soluble or partially soluble (gradual-release). Both soluble and gradual-release fertilizers can be organic or chemical.

These are the suggested soluble-salts fertilizer recommendations for fast-growing annuals. The values are expressed in parts per million.

Chemical Fertilizers

The diversity of hydroponic fertilizers is amazing. Local shop owners know which ones work best in the local climate and water. Store owners know a lot about the local water and gardeners' needs. They are in a perfect position to develop their own nutrient solution or adapt one that works well with their water. A few manufacturers do not do their homework and make bad nutrients. Most manufacturers are conscientious and manufacture excellent fertilizers. As always, read the entire fertilizer label and follow the directions.

Soluble-chemical fertilizers are an excellent choice for indoor container cultivation. Soluble fertilizers dissolve in water and are easy to control. They can be added or washed (leached) out of the growing medium. Control the exacting amounts of nutrients available to plants in an available form with water-soluble fertilizers.

Element	Limits	Average
Nitrogen	150 – 1000	250
Calcium	100 – 150	200
Magnesium	50 – 100	75
Phosphorus	50 – 100	80
Potassium	100 – 400	300
Sulfur	200 – 1000	400
Copper	0.1 – 0.5	0.5
Boron	0.5 – 5.0	1.0
Iron	2.0 – 10	5.0
Manganese	0.5 – 5.0	2.0
Molybdenum	0.01 – 0.05	0.02
Zinc	0.5 – 1.0	0.5

The soluble fertilizer may be applied in a water solution onto the soil. In general, high-quality hydroponic fertilizers that use completely soluble food-grade nutrients are the best value. Avoid low-quality fertilizers that do not list all necessary micronutrients on the label.

Chemical granular fertilizers work well but can easily be overapplied, creating toxic soil. They are almost impossible to leach out fast enough to save the plant.

Osmocote™ chemical fertilizers are time-release and are used by many nurseries because they are easy to apply and only require one application every few months. Using this type of fertilizer may be convenient, but exacting control is lost. They are best suited for ornamental, containerized plants for which labor costs and uniform growth are the main concerns.

Organic Fertilizers

Organically grown vegetables have a sweeter taste, but implementing an organic indoor garden requires horticultural know-how. The limited soil, space, and the necessity for sanitation must be considered when growing organically. Outdoors, organic gardening is easy because all of the forces of nature are there for you to seek out and harness. Indoors, few of the natural phenomena are free and easy. Remember, you are Mother Nature and must create everything! The nature of gardening indoors does not lend itself to long-term organic gardens, but some organic techniques have been practiced with amazing success.

Most indoor organic gardens use potting soil high in worm castings, peat, sand, manure, leaf mold, compost, and fine dolomite lime. In a container, there is little space to build the soil by mixing all kinds of neat composts and organic nutrients to cook down. Even if it were possible to build the soil in a container, it would take months of valuable growing time and it could foster bad insects, fungi, etc. It is easier and safer to throw old, depleted soil outdoors and start new plants with fresh organic soil.

Organic nutrients, manure, worm castings, blood and bone meal, etc., all work very well to increase the soil nutrient content, but nutrients are released and available at different rates. The nutrient availability may be tricky to calculate, but it is somewhat difficult to overapply organic fertilizers. Organic nutrients seem to be more consistently available when used in combination with one another. Many gardeners use a mix of about 20 percent worm castings with other organic agents to get a strong, readily available nitrogen base. They fertilize with bat guano, the organic super bloom, during flowering.

An indoor garden using raised beds allows true organic methods. Raised beds have enough soil to hold nutrients, pro-

The number of fertilizers available commercially is staggering. There are so many brands ranging from organic to chemical and combinations in between that it is difficult to make a recommendation.

mote organic activity, and when managed properly, ensure a constant supply of nutrients. Raised beds must have enough soil mass to promote heat and fundamental organic activity.

Outdoor organic gardens are easy to implement and maintain. Using compost tea, manures, bulky compost, and other big, smelly things is much easier outdoors.

Organic Teas

This compost tea-maker also utilizes live worms in the process. You can see them crawling around inside the hopper.

This commercial-sized compost tea-maker is in use at the Garden Spout, in Willits, CA.

Nature's Solution offers a compost tea mix boxed and ready to use.

Compost teas not only contain soluble organic nutrients diluted in water, but they support a potent elixir that is loaded with beneficial microbes that fight off pests and diseases. For example, a quarter-teaspoon of a well-made compost tea holds more than a billion bacteria and at least 15 feet of fungi strands! A good compost tea also contains thousands of different species of protozoa, nematodes, and mycorrhizal fungi.

Disease-causing organisms are unable to compete with beneficial bacteria and fungi. Beneficial bacteria also work to break down plant residues and toxic materials, plus they improve soil structure and water-holding ability.

The best teas are made from well-rotted compost because it contains a complex collection of microbes and nutrients. Just make sure the compost pile has heated to 135°F (52°C) for at least three days to ensure it is free of most diseases. You can usually buy quality compost at the local nursery. If using manure, make sure it has been well-composted.

You can brew the tea in a five-gallon (19 L) bucket. Add about a gallon (3.8 L) of rotted compost or manure to four gallons (15 L) of water. Stir well, and let the mix sit for several days. You can also put sifted compost into a nylon stocking, and submerge it in the bucket. To stir, simply bounce the stocking around in the water. Stir the mixture gently several times a day to integrate oxygen and remove microbes from the compost. Adequate oxygen keeps the brew fresh. If it starts to smell foul, anaerobic bacteria are present. Add fresh water and stir more often. The good aerobic bacteria re-establish as soon as they have an ample supply of oxygen.

Dilute the tea at the rate of one to five with water. Add more water to the same bucket, and continue to brew three to four more batches before starting a new batch.

To make "super tea," gently agitate and oxygenate the soup. This will supercharge the tea and add 10 to 100 times more microbes than regular compost tea. *The Compost Tea Brewing Manual* by Dr. Elaine R. Ingham of Soil Foodweb, Inc., compares some commercial tea-makers, including a bio-blender used in a five-gallon bucket or 100- and 500-gallon brewers. The book includes recipes for high-bacterial, high-fungal, and high-mycorrhizal teas. Take a look at the super-compost tea-makers at www.soilsoup.com.

Fill a nylon stocking with sifted, well-rotted compost and soak in a bucket for a few days to make a potent fertilizer and plant elixir.

Mixing Fertilizers

Always read the entire label, and follow the directions. To mix, dissolve the powder and the crystals into a little warm water, and make sure it is totally dissolved before adding the balance of the tepid water. This will ensure that the fertilizer and the water mix evenly. Liquid fertilizers can be mixed directly with water.

Containers have very little growing medium in which to hold nutrients, and toxic salt buildup may become a problem. Follow dosage instructions to the letter. Adding too much fertilizer will not make plants grow faster. It could change the chemical balance of the soil, supply too much of a nutrient, or lock in other nutrients making them unavailable to the plants.

Fertilizer Application

Some varieties can take high doses of nutrients, and other varieties grow best with a minimum of supplemental fertilizer. Many fertilizer programs are augmented with different additives that expedite nutrient uptake.

Determine if plants need to be fertilized: make a visual inspection, take an N-P-K soil test, or experiment on test plants. No matter which method is used, remember that plants in small containers use available nutrients quickly and need frequent fertilizing, while plants in large planters have more soil, supply more nutrients, and can go longer between fertilizer applications.

Visual Inspection: If plants are growing well and have deep-green, healthy leaves, they are probably getting all necessary nutrients. The moment growth slows or leaves begin to turn pale green, it is time to fertilize. Do not confuse yellow leaves caused by a lack of light with yellow leaves caused by a nutrient deficiency.

Taking an N-P-K soil test will reveal exactly how much of each major nutrient is available to the plant. The test kits mix a soil sample with a chemical. After the soil settles, a color reading is taken from the liquid and matched to a color chart. The appropriate percent of fertilizer is then added. This method is exact but more trouble than it is worth.

Experimenting on two or three test plants is the best way to gain experience and develop horticultural skills. Cuttings are perfect for this type of experiment. Give the test plants some fertilizer, and see if they green up and grow faster. You should notice a change within three to four days. If it is good for one, it should be good for all.

Now, it has been determined that the plants need fertilizer. How much? The answer is simple. Mix the fertilizer as per the instructions and water as normal, or dilute the fertilizer and apply it more often. Many liquid fertilizers are diluted already. Consider using more-concentrated

Organic Nutrients Chart

Alfalfa meal has two and one-half percent nitrogen, five percent phosphorus, and about two percent potash. Outdoor gardeners use pelletized animal feed as a slow-release fertilizer.

Blood and bone meal are wonderful organic fertilizers but could transport Mad Cow Disease and other maladies. I can't recommend these with a clear conscience.

Blood (dried or meal) is collected at slaughterhouses, dried, and ground into a powder or meal. It's packed with fast-acting soluble nitrogen (12 to 15 percent by weight), about 1.2 percent phosphorus, and under one percent potash. Apply carefully because it's easy to burn foliage. We advise avoiding use of any dried blood or blood meal that could carry Mad Cow Disease.

Bone meal is rich in phosphorus and nitrogen. The age and type of bone determine the nutrient content of this pulverized slaughterhouse product. Older bones have higher phosphorus content than young bones. Use bone meal in conjunction with other organic fertilizers for best results. Its lime content helps reduce soil acidity and acts fast in well-aerated soil. We advise avoiding any bone meal that could carry Mad Cow Disease.

Raw, unsteamed bone meal contains two to four percent nitrogen and 15 to 25 percent phosphorus. Fatty acids in raw bone meal retard decomposition. We advise avoiding any bone meal that could carry Mad Cow Disease.

Gardening Indoors

Steamed or cooked bone meal is made from fresh animal bones that have been boiled or steamed under pressure to render out fats. The pressure treatment causes a little nitrogen loss and an increase in phosphorus. Steamed bones are easier to grind into a fine powder, and the process helps nutrients become available sooner. It contains up to 30 percent phosphorus and about one and one-half percent nitrogen. The finer the bone meal is ground, the faster it becomes available to plants.

Cottonseed meal is the leftover by-product of oil extraction. According to the manufacturer, virtually all chemical residues from commercial cotton production are dissolved in the oil and not found in the meal. This acidic fertilizer contains about seven percent nitrogen, two and one-half percent phosphorus, and one and one-half percent potash. It should be combined with steamed bone meal and seaweed to form a balanced fertilizer blend.

Chicken manure is rich in available nitrogen, phosphorus, potassium, and trace elements. Indoor gardeners most often prefer to purchase dry, composted chicken manure in a bag. Use it as a topdressing or mix it with the soil before planting. Often chicken manure collected from farms is packed with feathers, which contain as much as 17 percent nitrogen; this is an added bonus. The average nutrient content of wet chicken manure is as follows: N – 1.5%, P – 1.5%, K – 0.5%; and dry chicken manure, N – 4%, P – 4%, K – 1.5%. Both have a full range of trace elements.

Coffee grounds are acidic and encourage acetic bacteria in the soil. Drip-coffee grounds are the richest, containing about two percent nitrogen and traces of other nutrients. Add this to the compost pile or scatter and cultivate it in. Use it as topdressing, but in moderation, because it is very acidic.

Compost tea is used by many organic gardeners as the only source of fertilizer. Comfrey is packed with nutrients, and many gardeners grow it just to make compost tea.

Cow manure is sold as steer manure, but it is often collected from dairy herds. Gardeners have used cow manure for centuries, and this has led to the belief that it is a good fertilizer as well as a soil amendment.

Steer manure is most valuable as mulch and a soil amendment. It holds water well and maintains fertility for a long time. The nutrient value is low, and it should not be relied upon for the main source of nitrogen. The average nutrient content of cow manure is N – 0.6%, P – 0.3%, K – 0.3%, and a full range of trace elements. Apply at the rate of 25 to 30 pounds per square yard.

Diatomaceous earth, the fossilized skeletal remains of fresh and saltwater diatoms, contains a full range of trace elements, and it is a good insecticide. Apply it to the soil when cultivating or as a topdressing.

Dolomite lime adjusts and balances the pH and makes phosphates more available. Generally applied to sweeten or deacidify the soil. It consists of calcium and magnesium, and is sometimes listed as a primary nutrient, though it is generally referred to as a secondary nutrient.

Feathers and feather meal contain from 12 to 15 percent nitrogen that is released slowly. Feathers included in barnyard chicken manure or obtained from slaughterhouses are an excellent addition to the compost pile or as a fertilizer. Feathers are steamed under pressure, dried, and ground into a powdery feather meal. Feather meal contains about 12.5 percent slow-release nitrogen.

Fish meal is made from dried fish ground into a meal. It is rich in nitrogen (about eight percent) and contains around seven percent phosphoric acid and many trace elements. It has an unpleasant odor causing it to be avoided by most indoor gardeners. It is a great compost activator. Apply it to the soil as a fast-acting topdressing. To help control odor, cultivate it into the soil or cover it with mulch after applying. Always store it in an airtight container so it will not attract cats, dogs, or flies. Fish meal and fish emulsion can contain up to ten percent nitrogen. The liquid generally contains less nitrogen than the meal. Even when deodorized, the liquid form has an unpleasant odor.

Fish emulsion, an inexpensive soluble liquid, is high in organic nitrogen, trace elements, and some phosphorus and potassium. This natural fertilizer is difficult to overapply, and it is immediately available to the plants. Even deodorized fish emulsion smells like dead fish. Inorganic potash is added to the fish emulsion by some manufacturers and is semi-organic.

Goat manure is much like horse manure but more potent. Compost this manure and treat it as you would horse manure.

Granite dust or granite stone meal contains up to five percent potash and several trace elements. Releasing nutrients slowly over several years, granite dust is an inexpensive source of potash and does not affect soil pH. Not recommended indoors because it is too slow acting.

Greensand (glaucomite) is an iron-potassium silicate that gives the minerals in which it occurs a green tint. It is mined from ancient New Jersey seabed deposits of shells and organic material rich in iron, phosphorus, potash (five to seven percent), and numerous micronutrients. Some organic gardeners do not use Greensand because it is such a limited resource. Greensand slowly releases its treasures in about four years. This is too slow acting for indoor gardens.

Guano (bat) consists of the droppings and remains of bats. It is rich in soluble nitrogen, phosphorus, and trace elements. The limited supply of this fertilizer—known as the soluble organic super bloom—makes it somewhat expensive. Mined in sheltered caves, guano dries with minimal decomposition. Bat guano can be thousands of years old. Newer deposits contain high levels of nitrogen and can burn foliage if applied too heavily. Older deposits are high in phosphorus and make an excellent flowering fertilizer. Bat guano is usually powdery and is used any time of year as topdressing or diluted in a tea. Do not breathe the dust when handling it, because it can cause nausea and irritation.

Guano (sea bird) is high in nitrogen and other nutrients. The Humboldt Current, along the coast of Peru and northern Chile, keeps the rain from falling, and decomposition of the guano is minimal. South American guano is the world's best guano. The guano is scraped off rocks of arid sea islands. Guano is also collected from many coastlines around the world, so its nutrient content varies.

Gypsum (hydrated calcium sulfate) is used to lower the soil pH, and it improves drainage and aeration. It is also used to hold or slow the rapid decomposition of nitrogen. This is seldom used indoors.

Hoof and horn meal is an excellent source of slow-release nitrogen. Fine-ground horn meal makes nitrogen available quicker and has few problems with fly maggots. Soil bacteria must break it down before it is available to roots. Apply it two to three weeks before planting. It remains in the soil for six months or longer. Hoof and horn meal contains from six to fifteen percent nitrogen and about two percent phosphoric acid. We advise avoiding use of any dried blood or bone meal that could carry Mad Cow Disease.

Horse manure is readily available from horse stables and racetracks. Use horse manure that has straw or peat for bedding, since wood shavings could be a source of plant disease. Compost horse manure for two months or longer before adding it to the garden. The composting process kills weed seeds, and it will make better use of the nutrients. Straw bedding often uses up much of the available nitrogen. Nutrient content is N – 0.6%, P – 0.6%, K – 0.4%, and a full range of trace elements.

Kelp is the Cedilla of trace minerals. Kelp should be deep-green, fresh, and smell like the ocean. Seaweed contains 60 to 70 trace minerals that are already chelated (existing in a form that's water soluble and mobile in the soil). Check the label to ensure all elements are not cooked out. See "Seaweed" below.

Oyster shells are ground and normally used as a calcium source for poultry. They contain up to 55 percent calcium and traces of many other nutrients that release slowly. Not practical to use indoors because they break down too slowly.

Paper ash contains about five percent phosphorus and over two percent potash. It is an excellent water-soluble fertilizer, but do not apply in large doses, because the pH is quite high. Paper ash can be full of toxic inks.

Pigeon manure has a very high concentration of nitrogen but is difficult to find. It can be used in the same fashion as chicken manure.

Rabbit manure is also excellent fertilizer but can be difficult to find in large quantities. Use rabbit manure as you would chicken or pigeon manure. According to some experts, rabbit poop is the best. Bunnies rule!

Potash rock supplies up to eight percent potassium and may contain many trace elements. It releases too slowly to be practical indoors.

Rock phosphate (hard) is a calcium or lime-based phosphate rock that is finely ground to the consistency of talcum powder. The rock powder contains over 30 percent phosphate and a menagerie of trace elements, but it is available very, very slowly.

Colloidal phosphate (powdered or soft phosphate) is a natural clay phosphate deposit that contains just over 20 percent phosphorus (P_2O_5), calcium, and many trace elements. It yields only two percent phosphate by weight the first few months.

Seaweed meal and/or kelp meal is harvested from the ocean or picked up along the beaches, cleansed of salty water, dried, and ground into a powdery meal. It is packed with potassium (potash), numerous trace elements, vitamins, amino acids, and plant hormones. The nutrient content varies according to the type of kelp and growing conditions. Seaweed meal is easily assimilated by plants, and contributes to soil life, structure, and nitrogen fixation. It may help plants resist many diseases and withstand light frosts. Kelp meal also eases transplant shock.

Seaweed (liquid) contains nitrogen, phosphorus, potash, and all necessary trace elements in a chelated form, as well as plant hormones. Apply diluted solution to soil for a quick cure of nutrient deficiencies. Liquid seaweed is also great for soaking seeds and dipping cuttings and bare roots before planting.

Sheep manure is high in nutrients and makes a wonderful tea. The average nutrient content is: N – 0.8%, P – 0.5%, K – 0.4%, and a full range of trace elements. Sheep manures contain little water and lots of air. They heat up readily in a compost pile. Cow and pig manures are cold because they hold a lot of water and can be compacted easily, squeezing out the air.

Shrimp and crab wastes contain relatively high levels of phosphorus.

Sulfate of potash is normally produced by chemically treating rock powders with sulfuric acid, but one company, Great Salt Lake Minerals and Chemicals Company, produces a concentrated natural form. The sulfate of potash is extracted from the Great Salt Lake.

Swine manure has a high nutrient content but is slower acting and wetter (more anaerobic) than cow and horse manure. The average nutrient content of pig manure is: N – 0.6%, P – 0.6%, K – 0.4%, and a full range of trace elements.

Wood ashes (hardwood) supply up to ten percent potash, and softwood ashes contain about five percent. Potash leaches rapidly. Collect the ash soon after burning, and store in a dry place. Apply in a mix with other fertilizers at the rate of one-quarter cup per 3-gallon (25 cl per 11 L) pot. Potash washes out of the wood ash quickly and can cause compacted, sticky soil. Avoid using alkaline wood ashes in soil with a pH above 6.5.

Worm castings are excreted, digested humus and other (decomposing) organic matter that contains varying amounts of nitrogen as well as many other elements. They are an excellent source of nonburning soluble nitrogen and an excellent soil amendment that promotes fertility and structure. Mix with potting soil to form a rich, fertile blend. Pure worm castings look like coarse graphite powder and are heavy and dense. Do not add more than 20 percent worm castings to any mix. They are so heavy that root growth can be impaired. Worm castings are very popular and easier to obtain at commercial nurseries.

Note: The nutrients in organic fertilizers may vary greatly depending upon source, age, erosion, climate, etc. For exact nutrient content, consult the vendor's specifications.

fertilizers whenever possible. Remember, small plants use much less fertilizer than large ones. Fertilize early in the day so plants have all day to absorb and process the fertilizer.

It is hard to explain how often to apply all fertilizers in a few sentences. We know that large plants use more nutrients than small plants. The more often the fertilizer is applied, the less concentrated it should be. Frequency of fertilization and dosage are two of the most widely disagreed upon subjects among gardeners. Indoor containerized plants can be pushed to incredible lengths. Some varieties will absorb amazing amounts of fertilizer and grow well. Many gardeners add as much as one tablespoon per gallon (15 ml per 4 L) of Peters™ (20-20-20) with each watering. This works best with growing mediums that drain readily and are easy to leach. Other gardeners use only rich, organic potting soil. No supplemental fertilizer is applied until a super bloom formula is needed for flowering.

Fertilizing plants in the ground is much easier than fertilizing containerized plants. In the soil outdoors, roots can find many nutrients, and fertilization is not as critical. There are several ways to apply chemical fertilizer. You can top-dress a garden bed by applying the fertilizer evenly over the entire area. You can side-dress plants by applying fertilizer around the bases of the plants. You can foliar-feed plants by spraying a liquid fertilizer solution on the foliage. The method you choose will depend upon the kind of fertilizer, the needs of the plants, and the convenience of a chosen method.

When using synthetic fertilizers, it is extremely important to read the label carefully, and follow the directions. The initials "WSN" and "WIN" that you may see on the label stand for water-soluble nitrogen and water-insoluble nitrogen. WSN dissolves readily, and it is considered a fast-release nitrogen source. WIN does not dissolve easily. It is often an organic form of nitrogen and is considered a slow-release nitrogen source.

Use a siphon applicator—found at most nurseries—to mix soluble fertilizers with water. The applicator is simply attached to the faucet with the siphon submerged in the concentrated fertilizer solution with the hose attached to the other end. Often, applicators are set at a ratio of one to fifteen. This means that for every one unit of liquid concentrate fertilizer, fifteen units of water will be mixed with it. Sufficient water flow is necessary for the suction to work properly. Misting nozzles restrict this flow. When the water is turned on, fertilizer is siphoned into the system and flows out the hose. The fertilizer is generally applied with each watering, since a small percentage of fertilizer is metered in.

A garbage can (with a garden-hose fitting attached at the bottom) that is set three to four feet (90–120 cm) off the floor will act as a gravity-flow source for the fertilizer solution. The container is filled with water and fertilizer.

When it comes to fertilization, experience with specific varieties and growing systems will tell gardeners more than anything else. There are hundreds of N-P-K mixes, and they all work! When choosing a fertilizer, make sure to read the entire label and know what the fertilizer claims it can do. Do not be afraid to ask the retail clerk questions or to contact the manufacturer with questions.

Once you have an idea of how often to fertilize, put the garden on a regular feeding schedule. A schedule usually works very well, but it must be combined with a vigilant, caring eye that looks for overfertilization and signs of nutrient deficiency.

Leach soil with one to two gallons (4–8 liters) of mild nutrient solution per gallon of soil every month. This is the best form of preventive maintenance against toxic salt buildup in the soil.

overdo. High levels of nutrients in the foliage stop the roots from taking in more; this is confusing for the plant. Foliar sprays can accumulate and build up in the foliage. Be wary of spraying more than once every ten days, and keep the spray concentration to less than 500 ppm or with an EC of less than 1.0.

Earth Juice Wetting Agent

Foliar Feeding

Foliar feeding means to spray nutrients or bio-stimulants onto foliage to augment available nutrients, vitamins, hormones, etc. Timing is key to achieving the best coverage and absorption.

The waxy (cuticle) surface coating (cystolith hairs and resin) on some plants' foliage makes them very poor water absorbers. This barrier wards off pest and disease attacks, but it also slows the penetration of sprays.

Young leaves are more permeable than older leaves. Nutrients and additives penetrate immature leaves faster than tougher, older leaves, making young leaves easier to damage with strong sprays.

Foliar feed indoor plants only when specific deficiency symptoms manifest. Foliar feeding is a quick fix only and is easy to

Spray foliage from underneath so the spray is able to penetrate stomata located on leaf undersides.

Spreader-Stickers

Smart gardeners use a surfactant, a surface-active substance (adjuvant), which enhances the effectiveness of foliar fertilization.

Gardening Indoors

Spreaders (wetting agents) reduce the surface tension of sprays and keep them from beading up and rolling off the foliage. Big, bulbous drops on the leaves mean you need to use a spreader. Flat drops that slide off the foliage mean there is too much spreader. There are nonionic, antionic, and cationic spreaders. The nonionic spreaders that do not ionize in water are the most common, and they do not react with most pesticides. Antionic and cationic spreaders are not used often.

Stickers help spray adhere to the leaf after spraying, so it does not wash off when it rains or when dew forms. Stickers not only increase adhesion, they slow evaporation, and impart a waterproof coating. Some stickers are spreaders, too. Spreader-stickers allow the stomata on the leaves to be penetrated.

Extenders (stabilizing agents) protect applied sprays against the UV radiation and heat that degrade the sprays.

Liquid and powder soaps and detergents act as surfactants, too, but they are not nearly as effective as horticultural surfactants. Biodegradable surfactants disappear the fastest. Silicone surfactants are also mild insecticides that work to impair pest functions.

Foliar spray concentration is cumulative. Nutrients delivered via foliage can cause a buildup of salts in and around the leaves. This is similar to the way salts accumulate in soil.

Overfertilizing can become one of the biggest problems for indoor gardeners. Too much fertilizer causes a buildup of nutrients (salts) to toxic levels, and it changes the soil chemistry. When overfertilized, growth is rapid and lush until toxic levels are reached. At this point, things become complicated.

Chance of overfertilization is greater in a small amount of soil that can hold only a small amount of nutrients. A large pot or planter can safely hold much more soil and nutrients, but it will take longer to flush if overdone. It is very easy to add too much fertilizer to a small container. Large containers have good nutrient-holding ability.

To treat severely overfertilized plants, leach the soil with two gallons (8 L) of diluted nutrient solution per gallon (4 L) of soil to wash out all excess nutrients. The plant should start new growth and look better in one week. If the problem is severe and the leaves are curled, the soil may need to be leached several times. After the plant appears to have leveled off to normal growth, apply the diluted fertilizer solution.

Use a spreader-sticker to keep spray droplets from bouncing off foliage.

Additives

Numerous additives or growth supplements have hit the market over the last few years. Generally, additives contain a cocktail of some of the elements listed below. Most additives came from the greenhouse industry or were developed for organic gardeners. Many of these additives do what they say they will do and work quickly; however, when growing a short eight-to-ten–week crop, some of these additives do not have time to work properly if added near the end of the flowering cycle.

The following list will give you an idea of what specific additives are and how they are used.

Abscisic Acid (ABA)

Abscisic acid is a naturally occurring

Without a spreader-sticker, the surfactant sprays often bead up and roll off the foliage, rendering them ineffective.

hormone that assists plants in adapting to environmental stresses such as drought or cold temperatures. During winter, ABA converts leaves into stiff bud scales which cover the meristem, protecting it from cold damage or dehydration. In case of an early spring, ABA will also prolong dormancy, preventing premature sprouts which could be damaged by frost.

Used in the garden, ABA may help plants resist drought and unseasonable conditions and improve productivity, strength, and performance.

Ascorbic Acid (Vitamin C)

Vitamin C is thought to build bigger flowers and act as an antioxidant. It is often combined with fructose, molasses, or sugar and added to the nutrient solution during the last two weeks before harvest. However, some botanists believe that although vitamin C is very important in fighting the free radical byproducts of photosynthesis, plants make their own vitamin C and are unlikely to realize any benefit from its addition to the nutrient mix.

Aspirin

Salicylic acid is a naturally occurring plant hormone associated with the Willow. It is effective in preventing pathogens by speeding up the natural "systemic acquired resistance (SAR)," thereby reducing the need for pesticides. Salicylic acid (SA) will block abscisic acid (ABA) allowing the plant to return to normal after a period of stress—something to consider if ABA is being used to strengthen plants.

Aspirin can be used as a spray, a soak, or added to compost and rooting compounds. A 1:10,000 solution used as a spray will stimulate the SAR response, and the effects will last weeks to months. "Willow water" also makes a popular rooting bath.

Auxins

Auxins represent a group of plant hormones that regulate growth and phototropism. They are associated with elongation of plant cells causing the branches to grow vertically while inhibiting lateral growth. "Pinching off" branch tips will reduce the auxin level and encourage bushy lateral growth as well as inducing new root formation.

Synthetic auxins are more stable and last longer than natural solutions. They can be used as an herbicide against broadleaf weeds like dandelions, but are most often used to encourage root growth and promote flowering.

Bacteria

Bacteria such as mycorrhizal fungi and rhizobacteria are extremely beneficial in organic gardening. The presence of these organisms in the growing medium produces stronger, healthier plants that require less chemical intervention.

Actino-Iron is a commercial soil additive that contains the *streptomyces lydicus* microbe. Applied to the soil, the bacterium grows around the root system, protecting it from harmful pathogens while producing anti-fungals. Actino-Iron also contains fulvic acid and iron, which feed the plant. For perennials, the effects last one growing season; for annuals, the life of the plant.

B-9 Folic Acid

There is little literature on the effects of B_9 on plants. It appears to serve in energy transfer within the plant and inhibits the enzyme that makes gibberellic acid result-

ing in a bushier, dwarf-type plant without pruning.

B_9 can be applied as a spray or as a soil drench.

Cellulase

Cellulase is a group of enzymes that act in the root zone to break down organic material which may rot and cause disease. Dead materials are converted into glucose and returned to the substrate to be absorbed by the plant.

It can be used in water gardens to clean up organic sludge.

Cytokinins

Cytokinins are plant hormones derivative of the purine, adenine, the most common cytokinin being Zeatin. They are synthesized in the roots promoting cell division, chloroplast development, leaf development, and leaf senescence. As an additive, cytokinins are most often derived from the seaweed *Ascophyllum nodosum*.

Added to soil or sprayed on plants, cytokinins help plants make more efficient use of existing nutrients and water even in drought conditions. The result is a healthier plant and increased crop. Care must be given to application of cytokinins along with other plant hormones. Many commercial formulas contain a hormone cocktail which includes hormones such as auxins and cytokinins that work against one another.

Enzymes

Enzymes are biological protein catalysts that were first crystallized and isolated in 1926. Enzymes accelerate rates of reactions but do not change themselves as a result of this action. Enzymes are added to fertilizers and growth additives to accelerate biological activity and speed nutrient uptake by roots.

Most enzymatic reactions happen within a temperature range of 85–105°F (30–40°C), and each enzyme has an optimal range of pH for activity. Most enzymes react with only a small group of closely related chemical compounds.

More than 1500 different enzymes have been identified. Enzymes are grouped into six main classes and many subclasses.

Ethylene Gas

Ethylene gas is a growth regulator hormone that activates the aging and ripening of flowers, prevents the development of new growth, and retards plant growth. It is most often used by vegetable gardeners who force the ripening of produce heading to market. It may also be used to trigger flowering in plants.

Flower Saver Plus

Flower Saver Plus is a commercial product that contains the mycorrhizae fungus which enters into a symbiotic relationship with the plant by attaching itself to the root system. Mycorrhizal threads enter into root tissue then grow out into the substrate reaching more water and nutrients than the plant could find on its own. In return, the mycorrhizae receive a protected environment and the sugars they need to thrive.

Use of mycorrhizae improves root depth, speeds maturation, and helps create resistance to drought and disease. Larger, more robust root systems also improve the soil structure promoting better air and water movement.

Flower Saver Plus should be used at planting time either as a root bath or worked into the top 2-4 inches (6-12 cm)

of soil. Look for a product that has at least 50 to 100 spores per square foot.

Seek medical attention if ingested. Avoid breathing the dust or spray, and keep out of reach of children.

Fulvic Acid

Fulvic acid is a naturally occurring organic substance resulting from microbial action on decomposing plants. Absorbed into a plant, fulvic acid will remain in the tissues and serve as a powerful antioxidant as well as providing nutrients and acting as a bio-stimulant. Fulvic acid is an excellent source of nutrition for mycorrhizae.

Gardeners can create fulvic acid by composting, or purchase the product from a retailer. It is available in forms suitable for soil or hydroponics mediums.

Gibberellins

Gibberellic acid (GA) is a natural plant growth hormone that acts with auxins to break dormancy, stimulate seed germination, and grow long stems.

Gibberellic acid can be purchased as a commercial product like Mega-Grow and is used to extend the growing season and force larger blooms. For best effect, use GA in complement with fertilizer and mixed into the water supply. Results can be seen in as little as a few weeks.

According to the Material Safety Data Sheet (MSDS), GA is very hazardous to humans. I do not advise using it; however, retail advertisements claim the product is safe.

Humic Acid

Humic acids are carbons formed by the decomposition of organic substances, primarily that of vegetation. Applied to sub-

How to get the most out of your spray

1) Spray the bottoms of leaves. Spray with a fine mist, and do not create droplets on the leaves. Fine mist is electrically attracted by the foliage. Even some young plants have waxy hairs that impair liquid penetration.

2) Do not spray plants that are hot or when the atmosphere is too dry. Spray in low light, either before the lights go off or just as they are coming on. If spraying in hot conditions, first spray everything with plain water until the temperatures of the room and foliage drop, before applying the real spray. Spraying when the plant foliage is hot causes the spray to crystallize on the surface, and it stops the penetration. Spraying with water ten minutes afterward often increases the penetration. Mobile nutrients move freely within a plant. Immobile nutrients move slowly, but once deposited, they stay.

3) Apply mobile nutrients sparingly. Immobile nutrients—sulfur, boron, copper, iron, manganese, molybdenum, sulfur, and zinc—often require two or three applications. Calcium and boron are poor candidates for foliar feeding because they translocate poorly. But urea nitrogen applied as a spray in high humidity penetrates almost instantly into leaves. Be careful when spraying urea-based fertilizers, and keep them diluted. Urea also carries other nutrients into the plant and works well for a base to the mix. Foliar feeding should turn the plant around in less than a week. A second spray could be necessary at week's end to ensure the cure sticks.

4) Boron, calcium, and iron move slowly during flowering. A supplemental foliar dose often speeds the growth when it slows. A foliar spray of potassium can also help flowering, especially if the temperatures dip below 50°F (10°C) or above 80°F (25°C).

5) Always spray new growth. The thin, waxy layer allows for good penetration.

6) Measure the pH of the spray, and keep it between 7 and 8.5. Potassium phosphate (K_2HPO_4) becomes phytotoxic below pH 4 and above 8.5. Stomata are signaled to close within these pH ranges.

7) Use a surfactant with all sprays, and apply these per instructions on the label.

8) Add the proper amount of surfactant so droplets do not form on leaves. Once formed, droplets roll off foliage, rendering it ineffective.

9) Stop the application before droplets form on leaves. Make a test spray on a mirror to ensure the spray is even and does not form droplets that roll off the mirror.

10) Spray with as fine a mist as possible to minimize the size of the drop.

strate, it encourages strong tissue growth and helps in nutrient transport. Plants grow thicker foliage and are more resistant to drought and disease.

Poor soils can be improved by humic acid, which enhances the water-holding capability and aeration in sandy soils and frees up nutrients bound in clay. It can be used as a root dip or sprayed directly onto the soil.

Humic acids are extracted from humic substances found in soil. Colors range from yellow (fulvic acid) to brown (humic acid) and black (humin).

Fulvic acid is the fraction of humic substances that is water soluble under all pH conditions. Fulvic acid stays in solution after humic acid dissipates due to acidification.

Humin is the fraction of the soil's organic matter that is not dissolved when the soil is treated with dilute alkali.

Hydrogen Peroxide

Hydrogen peroxide (H_2O_2) is similar to water but carries an extra, unstable oxygen molecule which can break down into a reactive atom and either attach itself to another oxygen atom or attack an organic molecule.

Used in horticulture, hydrogen peroxide provides a host of benefits by cleansing water of harmful substances such as spores, dead organic material, and disease-causing organisms while preventing new infections from occurring. It removes the methane and organic sulfates often found in well water and removes chlorine from tap water.

Hydrogen peroxide is especially useful in hydroponics, where overwatering can be a problem. It prevents oxygen depletion in the water around roots, leading to better root growth. A solution of hydrogen peroxide can be used to sterilize seeds, resulting in better germination rates.

Hydrogen peroxide is dangerous at high concentrations (35%) and will damage skin, clothing, and most anything it contacts. Lower concentrations like those found at the drug store (3%) will still need to be diluted before use, though they are not as toxic to the gardener.

Indole 3 Butyric Acid (IBA)

Indole 3 butyric acid is one of the auxin growth hormones. It is most often used as an effective rooting hormone. Application of IBA helps generate roots, build a larger root mass, and improve plant growth and yield.

Many commercial formulas are available in the form of water-soluble salts. Cuttings can be dipped or immersed before planting. Roots can be dipped or sprayed or the soil drenched during transplanting. Once established, plants should be treated at three- to five-week intervals during the growing season. After harvest, IBA can be used to encourage flower regeneration.

IBA is hazardous to humans and animals. It can cause moderate eye injury and is harmful if inhaled or absorbed through the skin.

Isopentyl Adenine (IPA)

Isopentyl adenine is a naturally occurring cytokinin which is synthetically manufactured as benzylaminopurine (BAP) for use in commercial bio-stimulants such as Rush Foliar, XCell Veg, and Xcell Bloom.

Xcell Veg acts in the plant's growth stage by improving nutrient transport. Glycine betaine in the solution provides a barrier to environmental stress. The product is used as part of an established feeding program. It can be sprayed on plants just before turning off the lights or used as a soak in the growing medium.

Xcell Bloom has antistress properties, too, and improves nutrient transport. It stimulates flowering, reduces plant growth time, and increases cell division and lateral root growth. Flowers are larger, heavier, and have enhanced color.

Both products can be used in hydroponic or soil mediums.

Rhizobium

Rhizobium is the genus name given to any of a group of bacteria which infect the roots of legumes and create nodules that act in symbiosis with the plant. Rhizobia are host-specific and will not work with all crops. With the proper host, however, rhizobia improve nitrogen fixation while simultaneously providing an additional source of nitrogen.

Rhizobia are most effective when added to irrigation but can be added to a drip or directly to the soil. Benefits will depend on proper crop/rhizobia match. Re-inoculation is recommended every three to five years.

Spray-N-Grow

Spray-N-Grow is a brand name vitamin and nutrient solution that includes barium and zinc. It is sprayed on plants to provide micronutrients through the foliage, a technique said to be more effective than root nutrition. Plants will grow faster, bloom earlier and more prolifically, have larger roots, and have a higher vitamin, mineral, and sugar content.

Because it is absorbed through the leaves, Spray-N-Grow works quickly, in as little as seven to thirty days. Tender plants realize benefits faster than woody plants. Spray-N-Grow can be used in any type of growing medium as a complement to the established feeding regimen. It is non-chemical and is safe for people and pets.

Sugar

Molasses, honey, and other sugars are said to increase soil microbials, enhance regrowth, and make the plant's use of nitrogen more effective. Molasses will raise the plant's energy level and act as a mild, natural fungicide. Molasses is the "secret ingredient" in many organic fertilizers.

Trichoderma (002/003)

Trichoderma are fungi that colonize in the root zone, crowding out negative fungi and microorganisms while stimulating root development and resistance to environmental stress. The result is a stronger, more vibrant plant.

There is a commercial product that functions as a growth-promoter, which contains *Trichoderma* fungi. Colorado State University studies indicate that Promot Plus, a product containing *Trichoderma*, is effective in suppressing pathogenic fungi that cause rot in seeds, roots, and stems.

The product can be applied to seeds, used during transplanting, mixed with liquid fertilizer or via drip irrigation and/or watered in. Promot Plus contains living organisms that will reproduce after application, so a small amount will do a lot. It is nontoxic and environmentally safe.

Zeatin

Zeatin is one of the cytokinin growth hormones. Upon germination, zeatin moves from the endosperm to the root tip where it stimulates mitosis.

Outdoor hydroponic setup in Queensland, Australia, filled with baby lettuce.

Introduction

Hydroponics is the science of growing plants without soil, most often in a soilless mix. In fact, many gardeners are already cultivating hydroponically. Cultivating cuttings in rockwool, peat moss, and coconut fiber is growing hydroponically. Growing mature plants in soilless Sunshine Mix or Terra-Lite, even when watered by hand, is hydroponic gardening. With hydroponics, nutrient uptake and grow medium oxygen content can be controlled easily. Manage these two factors, along with a few other requirements, to grow a bumper crop with every harvest.

The inert soilless hydroponic medium contains essentially no nutrients. All the nutrients are supplied via the nutrient solution—fertilizer diluted in water. This solution passes over or floods around roots at regular intervals, later draining off. The extra oxygen trapped in the soilless medium and around the roots speeds nutrient uptake by tiny root hairs. Plants grow fast hydroponically because they are able to take in food as fast as it can be used. In soil, as in hydroponics, the roots absorb nutrients and water. Even the best soil rarely has as much oxygen in it as a soilless hydroponic medium.

Contrary to popular belief, hydroponic gardens often require more care than soil gardens. If growing hydroponically, expect to spend more time in the garden. Extra maintenance is necessary because plants grow faster, there are more things to check, and more can go wrong. In fact, some gardeners do not like hydroponic gardening, because it requires too much additional care.

Hydroponic gardening is productive, but exacting—not as forgiving as soil gardening. Soil works as a buffer for nutrients and holds them longer than inert hydroponic growing mediums. In fact, advanced aeroponic systems do not use a soilless mix; they use nothing at all!

In hydroponics, the nutrient solution can be controlled, so plants grow less leafy foliage and more profuse flower buds. The stepped-up nutrient control makes plants flower faster and be ready for harvest a few days earlier than soil-grown plants.

Small flowering plants grow well in small hydroponic containers and horizontal tubes. Large plants grow longer and are best suited to a large bucket system, which allows room for root development. The plant's root system is easily contained in the bucket. For example mother plants used for cuttings must have a huge root system to take in lots of nutrients to keep up with the heavy growth and cutting production schedule.

Most indoor gardens have two limiting factors: the number of plants in the garden and the electrical consumption expressed in watts. The flowering room could be illuminated with two 600-watt HP sodium lamps. A 40-watt fluorescent fixture could be used to root cuttings, and a 175-watt metal halide will keep vegetative plants growing. This is a total of 1415 watts that cost about $35 to $60 monthly. That's a bargain, considering the indoor garden's bountiful yields!

Hydroponic Systems

Hydroponic systems are distinguished by the way the nutrient solution is applied. The first distinction is whether nutrient solution is applied in an "active" or "passive" manner.

Passive systems rely on capillary action to transfer the nutrient solution from the reservoir to the growing medium. Nutrient solution is passively absorbed by a wick or growing medium and transported to the roots. Absorbent growing mediums such as vermiculite, sawdust, peat moss, etc., are ideal for passive systems. The growing medium can stay very wet in passive systems, and substrate selection is important. Soggy substrates hold less air and deprive roots of rapid nutrient uptake. Although passive gardens are not considered "high performance," the Dutch have managed to perfect them and achieve amazing results. Wick systems have no moving parts. Seldom does anything break or malfunction. Low initial cost and low maintenance enhance wick systems' popularity.

days. No nutrient solution is drained off; it is all absorbed by plants!

One Spanish gardener uses passive irrigation to water his garden. He drives a delivery truck and is away from home five days a week. He keeps his indoor garden under a 400-watt HPS lamp. The plants are in a rich potting soil, and the pots are in a large tray with four-inch (12 cm) sides. Every Monday morning he fills the tray with mild nutrient solution. When he returns on Friday, the plants are strong and happy!

Classic wick gardens use cloth wicks that absorb nutrient solution and transport it to the growing medium.

This cutaway of a top-feed bucket system shows how roots dangle in a 100 percent humid environment before growing into the nutrient solution. Remember to screen the drain in the reservoir so roots do not block it.

Dutch gardeners line the floor of a room with heavy plastic or pond liner. They fill three-gallon (3 L) pots with an absorbent soilless mix that holds plenty of air. They flood the garden with two to three inches (6–9 cm) of nutrient solution. Roots absorb the nutrient solution in two to five

Active hydroponic systems "actively" move the nutrient solution. Examples of active systems are: flood and drain, and top feed. Fast-growing plants are very well suited to active hydroponic systems.

Active hydroponic gardens are considered a "recovery" system if the nutrient solution is recovered and reused after irrigation. A "non-recovery" system applies the nutrient solution once, and then it runs to waste. The solution is not reused. Non-recovery systems have few complications but are not practical for most indoor hydroponic gardens. The commercial gardeners' "run-to-waste" systems are avoided, because they pollute ground water with high levels of nitrates, phosphates, and other elements. Indoor gardeners seldom use non-recovery systems, because they require disposing of so much nutrient solution into the local sewer system.

Active recovery hydroponic systems such as the flood and drain (ebb and flow), top feed, and nutrient film technique (NFT) are the most popular and productive available today. All three systems cycle reused nutrient solution into contact with roots. Recovering and reusing the nutrient solution makes management more complex, but with the proper nutrient solution, schedule, and a little experience, it is easy to manage. Active recovery systems use growing mediums that drain rapidly and hold plenty of air, including: expanded clay, pea gravel, pumice rock, crushed brick, rockwool, and coconut coir.

Ebb and Flow Gardens

Ebb and flow (flood and drain) hydroponic systems are popular because they have proven track records as low maintenance, easy-to-use gardens. Ebb and flow systems are versatile, simple by design, and very efficient. Individual plants in pots or rockwool cubes are set on a special table. The table is a growing bed that can hold one to four inches (3–10 cm) of nutrient solution. Nutrient solution is pumped into the table or growing bed. The rockwool blocks or containers are flooded from the bottom, which pushes the oxygen-poor air out. Once the nutrient solu-

tion reaches a set level, an overflow pipe drains the excess to the reservoir. When the pump is turned off and the growing medium drains, it draws new oxygen-rich air into contact with the roots. A maze of drainage gulleys in the bottom of the table directs runoff solution back to the catchment tank or reservoir. This cycle is repeated several times a day.

Nutrient solution is pumped up into the bed via the short flood fixture on the left. The overflow fitting on the right guarantees the nutrient solution will not spill over the top of the table.

Self-leveling legs, similar to those of a washing machine, support this ebb and flow garden bed and ensure all plants receive a level dose of nutrient solution and that it all drains back into the reservoir below.

Build Your Own Ebb & Flow System

1. First, take an inventory of all the parts.

2. Different size containers fit in the ebb and flow table.

3. Nursery flat before drilling two holes near the center.

4. Use a hole drill bit to cut a hole in the bottom of the nursery flat.

5. Once holes are drilled, set nursery flat over the top of the reservoir. Mark a bull's-eye in the middle of each hole. These marks will serve as the center of the holes in the reservoir lid.

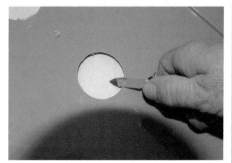

6. Make the holes in the reservoir lid big enough for the bottom of the fill/drain and overflow fittings to fit through.

7. Overflow fitting on the left and fill/drain fitting on the right.

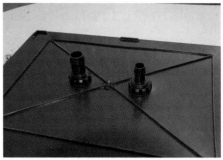

8. Overflow fitting on the left and fill/drain fitting on the right as viewed from the bottom of the nursery flat.

9. Overflow fitting on the left and fill/drain fitting on the right.

10. View from the bottom of the reservoir lid of fill/drain fitting on the left and overflow fitting on the right.

11. View from under reservoir lid of overflow fitting on left and on the right, a pump attached to fill/drain fitting with green supply tubing.

12. Ebb and flow reservoir on bottom covered with a blue reservoir lid. A nursery flat is used as a fill and drain table. Near the center of the table, an overflow fitting on the left and a fill/drain fitting on the right can be seen. Different sized containers fill the growing table.

Flood the table to half to three-quarters the height of the container to ensure even nutrient solution distribution. Avoid light-weight mediums such as perlite that may cause containers to float and fall over.

A large volume of water is necessary to fill the entire table. Make sure the reservoir has enough solution to flood the reservoir and still retain a minimum of 25 percent extra to allow for daily evaporation. Replenish reservoir daily if necessary. Do not let nutrient solution stand in the table for more than a half hour. Submerged roots drown in the depleted-oxygen environment.

Nutrient solution floods the growing bed and drains back into a reservoir in an ebb and flow garden.

Flood the table when the medium is about half-full of moisture. Remember, rockwool holds a lot of moisture. Irrigation regimens will need to change substantially when temperatures cool and light is lacking.

Ebb and flow tables or growing beds are designed to let excess water flow freely away from the growing medium and roots. When flooded with an inch (3 cm) or more of nutrient solution, the growing medium

wicks up the solution into the freshly aerated medium.

Air Tables

The simple air table design makes them low maintenance. Air is pumped into a reservoir filled with nutrient solution. The air pressure forces the solution up into the growing bed.

Air Table garden by Terraponics is operated with a solar-powered 12-volt pump and was left unattended for 30 days.

Air tables are simple, easy-to-use hydroponic gardens. Seasoned gardeners and novices love their simplicity and low maintenance. The unique operating principle is simple, effective, and nearly fail-safe. The nutrient solution is forced up to the growing bed with air pressure generated by an external air pump. The pump can run on ordinary household electrical current or a solar-powered 12-volt system. Once flooded, the nutrient solution stays in the

Various emitters are available to apply nutrient solution. A single application point is common when growing in absorbent growing mediums such as rockwool and coco coir. Expanded clay works best when nutrient solution is applied via a large round emitter, several single emitters, or a spray emitter.

Always use a filter when using emitters. The filter will remove foreign objects that plug emitters.

Circular emitters apply nutrient solution all the way around the plant, so all roots receive adequate moisture.

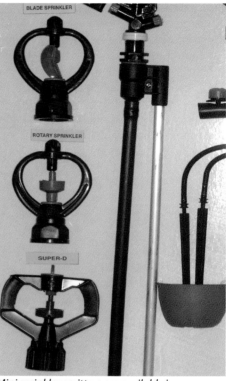

Pressure regulated drip emitters control solution flow.

This emitter sprays nutrient solution over the top of the growing medium to aerate and disperse it evenly.

Mini sprinkler emitters are available in many sizes and outputs.

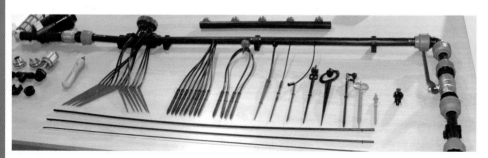

An array of different emitters connected to a main manifold shows the many different kinds of emitters available to hydroponic gardeners. Across the bottom are three different diameters of spaghetti tubes that dispense three different volumes of nutrient solution to plants.

growing bed for a few minutes before it drains back to the reservoir. Constant air pressure during flooding also aerates the growing medium. The sealed, airtight reservoir limits evaporation, which in turn prevents algae growth and keeps the nutrient fresh. The external pump reduces the overall cost of the system and helps prevent electrical accidents. You can use rockwool, coco coir, peat, or a composite growing medium with excellent results.

Deep Water Culture (DWC)

Growing in deep water culture is simple, easy, and productive.

If growing outdoors in a DWC garden, a simple overflow drainage hole can be cut in the side of the reservoir to prevent rainwater from causing it to overflow.

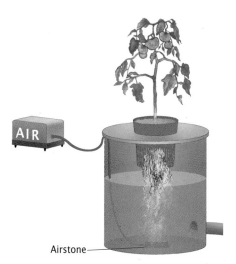

Airstone

Cutaway of the inside of a DWC garden.

Seedlings and cuttings are held in net pots full of expanded clay pellets, rockwool or other growing medium. The net pots are nestled in holes in a lid that covers the reservoir. The roots of seedlings and cuttings dangle down into the nutrient solution. A submersible pump lifts nutrient solution to the top of a discharge tube where it splashes into the access lid. Nutrient solution cascades down, wetting roots and splashing into the self-contained reservoir below, which in turn increases dissolved oxygen in the solution. Roots easily absorb nutrients and water from the solution in the oxygenated environment. Many gardens also keep an air stone bubbling new air into the reservoir to supply more oxygen.

These gardens are simple by design and require no timer because the pumps are on 24 hours a day. This low-maintenance garden is perfect for casual gardeners as well as hydroponics enthusiasts.

Top-feed Systems

Top-feed hydroponic systems are very productive, easy to control, precise, easy to maintain, and efficient. The nutrient solution is metered out in specific doses and delivered via spaghetti tubing or an emitter placed at the base of individual plants. Aerated nutrient solution flows into the growing medium and is taken up by roots. The runoff nutrient solution is directed back to the reservoir as soon as it drains from the growing medium. Rockwool, gravel, coconut coir, and expanded clay are the most common growing mediums found in top-feed systems. Versatile top-feed systems can be used with individual containers or slabs in individual beds or lined up on tables.

Top-feed systems come in many configurations. Systems with several gallons of growing medium are best for growing large plants that may require support. Small containers are perfect for smaller plants.

Top-feed Buckets

solution in the system, aerating the solution and irrigating the plant. Roots grow down into the nutrient solution to form a mass on the bottom. Irrigation from the top circulates aerated nutrient solution and flushes out old oxygen-poor solution. Some systems contain a one-inch (3 cm) pipe to draw air directly down to the root zone. There are many different variations of this system, and they all work!

This top-feed bucket has a reservoir below the grow medium. The semi-translucent blue drain tube also serves to measure nutrient solution level.

Containers are irrigated with spaghetti tubes attached to a manifold that runs between the rows. Excess nutrient solution drains out the bottom and is directed back to the reservoir via a drain tube.

Self-contained top-feed buckets consist of a growing container nested inside a reservoir containing a pump. Individual buckets make culling and replacing a sick plant quick and easy. Self-contained top-feed bucket systems are also perfect for growing large mother plants.

The container can be moved anywhere easily. Some containers have a net pot suspended in the lid of a five-gallon (19 L) bucket/reservoir. The roots hang down into the reservoir. An air stone in the bottom of the reservoir aerates the nutrient solution. A separate pump cycles the irrigation to the container. Other self-contained top-feed buckets use a large growing container filled with expanded clay pellets. A pump constantly cycles nutrient

These top-feed buckets filled with hydroclay are all set up and ready to be planted. More hydroclay will be added when cuttings are transplanted.

Multiple Bucket Top-feed

Other top-feed bucket systems employ multiple buckets that are connected to a main reservoir. A flexible drain hose is attached near the bottom of the bucket/reservoir. The hose is connected to a drainage manifold that shuttles runoff nutrient solution back to a central reservoir.

This battery-powered pump delivers water to several plants quietly and efficiently.

Each reservoir below the growing container holds an inch or two (3–6 cm) of water. It is important to regularly cycle irrigation in these gardens, so the solution in the bottom of the buckets does not stagnate.

Top-feed buckets can also be lined up on a drainage table. Square containers make most efficient use of space. Plants are fed with irrigation tubing attached to a manifold. Once delivered, the nutrient solution flows and percolates through the growing medium. Roots take in the aerated nutrient solution before it drains onto the tray and back to the reservoir.

Individual containers in top-feed bucket systems are easy to arrange to fit into the allotted garden space. Plants can also be transplanted or removed from pots and cared for individually.

The cutaway drawing above shows how nutrient delivery is simple and easy with a top-feed bat system. Aerated nutrient solution is metered via emitter onto a grow cube. Aerated solution percolates down through the medium. Channels in the bottom of the tray speed drainage back to the reservoir.

Top-feed Slabs

Top-feed slab systems are popular among small and large indoor and greenhouse gardeners. Rockwool or coco slabs covered in plastic serve as growing containers. The nutrient solution is delivered via spaghetti tubes from the top of the slab. An emitter attached to the spaghetti tube doses a specific measure of nutrient solution to each plant. The nutrient solution is aerated as it is applied, before being absorbed by the growing medium and draining back to the reservoir.

A simple nutrient solution delivery manifold consists of emitters connected to spaghetti delivery tubes. The tubes are attached to a short manifold that is fed by a pump submerged in a reservoir.

Vertical gardens like this "Cage" from B.C., Canada, save horizontal space.

This new vertical garden uses rockwool as a growing medium and compact fluorescent lamps.

Emitters are designed to be anchored in growing medium and to emit a measured dose of nutrient solution.

Slabs in Individual Trays

Some systems use individual trays to contain slabs. Nutrient solution is pumped from the reservoir and delivered to plants via spaghetti tubes attached to emitters. Individual trays are easy to configure for different size gardens.

Tables of Slabs

You can also set up a drainage table and place slabs on top. The nutrient solution is pumped from the reservoir below the table and delivered to individual plants via spaghetti tubes attached to emitters. The solution flows into the growing medium where it comes into contact with roots. Excess nutrient solution drains from pots onto the table and is carried back to the reservoir. Make sure the table is set up on an incline so it drains evenly. Pockets of standing water on the table contain less oxygen and promote rot.

Individual Blocks

Individual blocks in this rockwool system allow gardeners the possibility of removing or changing plants if necessary. Nutrient solution is pumped via spaghetti tubes from the reservoir below and distributed via emitters pressed into rockwool cubes.

Vertical Top-feed Systems

Vertical hydroponic systems save space, but require more maintenance. These systems can also be tricky to fine-tune so they operate at peak capacity.

Vertical gardens can increase overall yield more than ten-fold over a flat garden. Substrate bags, tubes, or slabs are positioned vertically around an HID. Short plants are placed in the medium and fed individually with a drip emitter. The runoff drains through the growing medium and back to the reservoir. The solution is re-circulated once it returns to the reservoir. Use rockwool or coco mixed with light-weight vermiculite as a growing medium to lessen weight when substrate is wet. Irrigate constantly to keep roots supplied with water and nutrients from a well-aer-ated solution.

The capillary matting is being rolled out in this Nutrient Film Technique garden.

Nutrient Film Technique (NFT)

NFT hydroponic systems are high performance gardens that perform well when fine-tuned. This relatively new form of hydroponics supplies aerated nutrient solution to roots located in gulleys. Seedlings or cuttings with a strong root system are placed on capillary matting located on the bottom in a covered channel. The capillary matting stabilizes nutrient solution flow and holds roots in place. Constantly aerated nutrient solution flows down the channel, or gulley, over and around the roots, and back to the reservoir. Irrigation is most often constant, 24 hours a day. Roots receive plenty of oxygen and are able to absorb a maximum of nutrient solution. Proper gulley incline, volume, and flow of nutrient solution are key elements in NFT gardens.

Gulleys or channels are covered to keep humidity high in the root zone and light from shining on roots. Root hairs responsible for most water and nutrient uptake cover the growing tips of advancing roots. These roots are submerged in turbulently flowing nutrient solution and the plant tops are intermittently in humid air. The nutrient solution is constantly aerated as it

NFT garden from General Hydroponics.

Small net pots are preferred for most NFT systems. Larger net pots are used in NFT systems as well as top-feed hydroponic systems.

flows down the inclined gulley. The slope of the gulley is adequate to prevent water from stagnating. Often a filter is necessary to prevent debris from blocking gulleys and pump.

Although high performance, NFT systems offer practically no buffering ability. In the absence of a growing medium, roots must be kept perfectly moist by the nutrient solution at all times. If a pump fails, roots dry and die. If the system dries out for a day or longer, small feeder roots will die and grave consequences will result. The system is very easy to clean and lay out after each crop. Only gardeners with several years experience should try an NFT system if working alone. With help, they are easier to master.

Double reinforced bottoms make gulleys durable and rigid when supporting large plants, root systems, and large volumes of nutrient solution. Some NFT gulleys have ribs below to provide support and prevent warping and movement. The ribs also function as drainage channels and direct nutrient solution evenly along the bottom of the gulley.

Many NFT systems are hybrids. For example, the nutrient solution in some hybrid NFT systems is delivered via spaghetti tubing to each plant. More irrigation sites help each plant receive proper irrigation. The nutrient solution flows through a small basket of growing medium before it runs down the gulley, over the roots, and back to the reservoir. Yet another hybrid NFT system employs spray nozzles inside the gulley. The nozzles spray nutrient solution on and around roots to keep the root zone environment at 100 percent humidity. The nutrient solution flows down a PVC pipe, over roots, and back to the reservoir.

Too often, these hybrid systems are poorly planned and designed. Many times they are constructed from white four-inch PVC pipe. The thin white walls of the PVC pipe allow enough light to illuminate roots that they turn green or rot more easily. I have also seen systems with nozzles inside the PVC pipe. If a nozzle plugged inside the pipe, there was no easy way to access the nozzle for maintenance.

Gulleys with rounded corners are very popular in Australia. Growers who use them say the nutrient solution flows more smoothly.

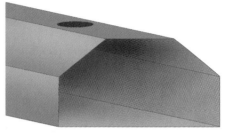

Many gulleys are flat on the bottom. Capillary matting is placed on the bottom under the growing cubes. The capillary matting anchors roots and helps direct nutrient solution evenly over roots.

Nutrient solution is pumped from the reservoir into gulleys via a manifold and tubing at the upper end. The table is set up on an incline so the nutrient solution flows quickly over roots to create an environment packed with air and available nutrients. A catchment drain directs the nutrient back into the nutrient reservoir.

Bioponic Culture

Bioponic culture recreates the chemistry found in organic soil and preserves the benefits of hydroponic culture. Bonafide organic fertilizer must be natural and contain no refined mineral salts. These mineral elements must be in the form of complex organic molecules, which are not immediately absorbed by plants. First they require biological decomposition before transforming into ions, when they can be absorbed.

In soil, bacteria and fungus contained in humus divide the organic molecules into two parts: carbon, providing nutrients, and the minerals that can be used by the plant in the presence of water.

In hydroponic culture, only purified, dissolved and easily absorbable mineral salts are added.

Bioponic culture reproduces the same decomposition that naturally occurs in the soil when using a fertilizer with a specific mix of bacteria and fungus to facilitate digestion. These micro-organisms separate the carbon and feed on it, like soil cultures, freeing the minerals that are immediately dissolved in the water in the form of absorbable ions. In bare root aeroponic and aero-hydroponic cultures, they live in an organic filter that provides oxygen and the appropriate substrate for reproduction. In a substrate like coir fiber, they live right in the root zone. This new patented technology covers the use of microorganisms and the formulation of fertilizer required to operate the system.

A bioponic system contains microorganisms that give microbial life and participate in the carbon cycle, humic or fulvic acid, available in liquid form from many suppliers. And silicium and all of the metals and trace elements contained in the soil (like GHE's Mineral Magic).

For bioponics you need:

1. Bioponic soluble liquid fertilizer with no large particles that decompose slowly.

2. Living organisms that foster healthy living substrate. Keep them in an airy location away from nutrient solution turbulence. They must stay humid because if they dry out, they die.

3. A pump filter is imperative, especially if bare roots are directly in the nutrient solution. The larger particles contained in the fertilizer must be filtered as they could asphyxiate the roots, particularly at high temperatures.

Managing a bioponic garden is more difficult and requires more monitoring because it is teeming with life. Electrical conductivity and pH are less important than in conventional hydroponic systems and results are often different. Similar to soil regarding crop yield, bioponic culture harvests pack a higher sugar content and active ingredients.

Water and fertilizer consumption are lower than in other types of culture. In addition, the green mass (stems and leaves) is lower and proportionate fruit production higher.

pH in bioponic gardens is more difficult to stabilize because the best buffers are not on the list of certified organic products. The pH always tends to drift upward, but it can climb to 7.5 with no ill affects. Most growers start readjusting the pH when it hits 6. It could take a few days to adjust. For best results use an organic pH rectifier. Do not use hydrochloric acid and acetic acid (vinegar, etc.).

Microorganisms need oxygen and humidity. A significant decrease in pH is a warning signal of the death of a significant number of organisms.

Organic molecules do not contain an electric charge and cannot be read by the conductivity reader. When bioponic fertil-

The modular bioponic test garden from General Hydroponics Europe, on the left, was fertilized bioponically. The two on the right were not.

Tomato roots grow profusely bioponically.

izer dissolves in water, a very small portion is immediately transformed into ions, providing slight conductivity. With a dose of 4 to 5 ml per liter (1 tsp per qt) of fertilizer and the normal conductivity of water is about 0.65 (from 0.6 to 0.7), this very low conductivity is usually sufficient. Add fertilizer when conductivity falls below 0.65. As some elements are freed, others are absorbed. Conductivity tends to balance out close to these values. When the organic substance reserves are not sufficient, it decreases and it is time to add fertilizer. For optimum results, you must anticipate the drop in conductivity and make sure a constant supply of organic matter is available. But it is easy to add too much, because microorganism activity varies significantly depending on temperature. For example, too much organic matter in the system coupled with an increase in temperature could push the conductivity high enough to kill plants. It takes a bit of experience to manage properly.

Aeroponics

Aeroponic systems use no growing medium and offer the highest performance possible. Roots are suspended in a dark growth chamber without growing medium where they are misted with oxygen-rich nutrient solution at regular intervals. The humidity in the chamber remains at or near 100 percent 24 hours a day. Roots have the maximum potential to absorb nutrients in the presence of air.

Humid air and nutrient solution are all that fill the growth chamber. Plants are most often grown in net pots full of growing medium and suspended from the top of the system.

Aeroponic systems require greater attention to detail. There is no growing medium to act as a water/nutrient bank, which makes the system delicate and touchy to use. If the pump fails, roots soon dry, and plants suffer. Systems that use delicate spray nozzles must be kept free of debris. Imbalanced nutrient solution and pH can also cause problems quickly. This is why it is important to purchase quality components or a ready-made system from a qualified supplier.

The RainForest (www.general hydroponics.com) is very popular. Nutrient solution is actually atomized into the air creating 100 percent humidity. Nutrient solution is dripped onto a spinning plate. The solution atomizes, mixing with the air as it spins off the plate. The spinning plate is located above the water in the reservoir.

Growing Mediums

Soilless growing mediums provide support for the root system, as well as hold and make available oxygen, water, and nutrients. Three factors contribute to plant roots' ability to grow in a substrate: texture, pH, and nutrient content, which is measured in EC, electrical conductivity.

The texture of any substrate is governed by the size and physical structure of the particles that constitute it. Proper texture promotes strong root penetration, oxygen retention, nutrient uptake, and drainage. Growing mediums that consist of large particles permit good aeration and drainage. Increased irrigation frequency is necessary to compensate for low water retention. Water- and air-holding ability and root penetration are a function of texture. The smaller the particles, the closer they pack together and the slower they drain. Larger particles drain faster and retain more air.

Irregular shaped substrates such as perlite and some expanded clays have more surface area and hold more water than round soilless mediums. Avoid crushed gravel with sharp edges that cut into roots if the plant falls or is jostled around. Round

Long root systems develop quickly on cuttings in this RainForest aeroponic system.

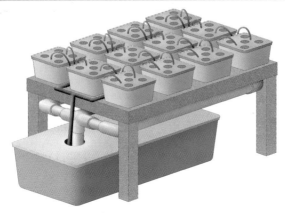

Top-feed buckets are irrigated via spaghetti tubes attached to the black manifold tube. The large white PVC pipe drains nutrient solution into the reservoir. Single or multiple plants can be grown in each bucket.

Coconut fiber is also available in bags.

pea gravel; smooth, washed gravel; and lava rocks are excellent mediums to grow fast-growing annuals in an active recovery system. Thoroughly wash clay and rock growing mediums to get out all the dust that will turn to sediment in your system.

Fibrous materials like vermiculite, peat moss, rockwool, and coconut coir retain large amounts of moisture within their cells. Such substrates are ideal for passive hydroponic systems that operate via capillary action.

Expanded clay holds moisture and nutrients along with lots of oxygen.

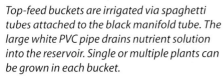

Coco is compressed into slabs and packaged in plastic. Add water to expand coco to full size.

Mineral growing mediums are inert and do not react with living organisms or chemicals to change the integrity of the nutrient solution. Coconut coir and peat moss are also inert.

Artificial foam slabs are used by some growers. To date they are still gaining popularity.

Pumice is a good growing medium. It can also be used as mulch or as an inert soil amendment.

Soilless grow medium.

Peat moss mixed with perlite is one of the all-time favorite growing mediums. It is also an excellent soil amendment.

Vermiculite holds a lot of nutrient solution.

Perlite is sand or volcanic glass expanded by heat.

Non-inert growing mediums cause unforeseen problems. For example, gravel from a limestone quarry is full of calcium carbonate, and old concrete is full of lime. When mixed with water, calcium carbonate will raise the pH, and it is very difficult to make it go down. Growing mediums made from reconstituted concrete bleed out so much lime, they soon kill the garden.

Avoid substrates found within a few miles of the ocean or large bodies of salt water. Most likely, such mediums are packed with toxic salts. Rather than washing and leaching salts from the medium, it is easier and more economical to find another source of substrate.

Air is a great medium when it is filled with 100 percent humidity 24 hours a day.

Coconut fiber is an excellent hydroponic medium. See "Coconut Fiber" under soil amendments.

Rockwool cubes hold plenty of air and nutrient solution within their fiber; plus, they are clean and easy to use.

This chart shows the porosity and airspace available in different substrates.

Substrate	Porosity	Airspace
Coconut fiber	90%	10%
Peat:/Vermiculite	88%	9%
Peat:/Perlite	78%	15%
Peat:/Rockwool	88%	14%
Peat moss	90%	15%
Perlite	68%	30%
Rockwool	90%	20%
Sand	38%	3%
Vermiculite	80%	10%

Expanded clay, also called hydroclay or hydrocorn, is made by many different manufacturers. The clay pellets are cooked at high temperatures in a kiln until they expand. Many little catacomb-like pockets form inside each pellet, which hold air and nutrient solution. It is an excellent medium to mix with Peat-Lite and to grow plants in large containers. I like the way it drains so well and still retains nutrient solution while holding lots of oxygen. Examples of expanded clay include commercially available Hydroton, Leca, Grorox, and Geolite.

Grow Rocks

Some clay pellets will float.

Expanded clay can be reused again and again. Once used, pour expanded clay pellets into a container and soak in a sterilizing solution of ten milliliters hydrogen peroxide per four liters of water. Soak for 20–30 minutes. Remove expanded clay and place on a screen of hardware cloth. Wash and separate clay pellets from dead roots and dust. Let dry and reuse.

Expanded mica is similar to expanded clay. For lots of exacting information on how and why this stuff works so well, check out www.hydroponics.com for more details.

Foam is somewhat popular. It lasts a long time, lends itself to easy sterilization, and holds a lot of water and air.

Gravel is one of the original hydroponic mediums. Although heavy, gravel is inert, holds plenty of air, drains well, and is inexpensive. Still popular today, gravel is difficult to overwater. It holds moisture, nutrient, and oxygen on its outer surfaces. Use pea gravel or washed river gravel with round edges that do not cut roots when jostled about. Gravel should be 0.125–0.375-inches (3–10 mm) in diameter, with more than half of the medium about 0.25-inch (6 mm) across. Crushed rock can be packed with many salts. Pre-soak and adjust its pH before use. Gravel has low water retention and low buffering ability.

Pumice is a naturally occurring, porous, lightweight volcanic rock that holds moisture and air in catacomb-like surfaces. Light and easy to work with, some lava rock is so light it floats. Be careful that sharp edges on the rocks do not damage roots. Lava rock is still a good medium and acts similarly to expanded clay. See "Pumice" under "Soil Amendments."

Peat moss is partially decomposed vegetation. Decomposition has been slow in the northern regions where it is found in bogs. There are three common kinds of peat moss: sphagnum, hypnum, and reed/sedge. Sphagnum peat is about 75 percent fiber with a pH of 3 to 4. Hypnum peat is about 50 percent fiber with a pH of about 6. Reed/sedge peat is about 35 percent fiber with a pH of six or more. For more information see "Soil Amendments" in Chapter Eight.

Perlite drains fast, but it's very light and tends to float when flooded with water. Perlite has no buffering capacity and is best used to aerate soil or soilless mix. See "Soil Amendments" in Chapter Eight.

Rockwool is an exceptional growing medium and a favorite of many indoor gardeners. It is an inert, sterile, porous, non-degradable growing medium that provides firm root support. Rockwool has the ability to hold water and air for the roots. The roots are able to draw in most of the water stored in the rockwool, but it has no buffering capacity and a high pH. Rockwool is probably the most popular hydroponic growing medium in the world. Popular brand names include Grodan, HydroGro, and Vacrok.

Sand is heavy and has no buffering ability. Some sand has a high pH. Make sure to use sharp river sand. Do not use ocean or salty beach sand. Sand drains quickly but still retains moisture. Sand is best used as a soil amendment in volumes of less than ten percent.

Sawdust holds too much water for most plants' growth and is usually too acidic. Be wary of soils with too much wood matter. Such mediums use available nitrogen to decompose the leglin in the wood.

Vermiculite holds a lot of water and is best suited for rooting cuttings when it is mixed with sand or perlite. With excellent buffering qualities, vermiculite holds lots of water and has traces of magnesium (Mg), phosphorus (P), aluminum (Al), and silicon (Si). Do not use construction grade vermiculite which is treated with phytotoxic chemicals. See "Soil Amendments" in Chapter Eight for more information.

Water alone is a poor medium, because it cannot hold enough oxygen to support plant life. When aerated, water becomes a good growing medium.

How to remove roots from the growing medium:

1. Manually remove the mat of roots that are entwined near the bottom of the bed, and shake loose any attached growing medium. It may be easier to add more medium than to pick it from between the matted roots

2. Pour growing mediums such as expanded clay and gravel through a screen placed over a large bucket. Most of the roots will stay on the screen.

3. Lay growing medium out on the floor, and train an oscillating fan on it to dry out remaining roots.

Sterilizing

To reuse a growing medium, it must be sterilized to remove destructive pests and diseases. Sterilizing is less expensive and often easier than replacing the growing medium. Sterilizing works best on rigid growing mediums that do not lose their shape such as gravel, expanded clay, and mica. Avoid sterilizing and reusing substrates that compact and lose structure such as rockwool, coconut coir, peat moss, perlite, and vermiculite. Avoid problems caused by compaction and dead roots by replacing used growing mediums. Once sterilized, the medium is free of harmful microorganisms including bacteria and fungi, plus pests and their eggs.

Remove roots from the growing medium before sterilizing. A three- to four-month-old plant has a root mass about the size of an old desk telephone. Separate the medium by shaking and pulling roots away. Bounce the medium on a screen so roots come to the top. Scoop up and remove roots by hand. Fewer decaying roots cause fewer pest and disease problems, and decrease incidence of clogged feeder tubes.

Substrate can also be washed in a large container such as a barrel or bathtub. Washing works best with lighter substrates such as expanded clay or mica. Roots float to the top and are readily skimmed off with a screen or by hand.

Once roots are removed, soak the substrate in a sterilant such as a five percent laundry bleach (calcium or sodium hypochlorite) solution for at least an hour. Or mix hydrochloric acid, the kind used in hot tubs and swimming pools. Pour, drain, or pump off the sterilant, and flush the medium with plenty of fresh water. A bathtub and a shower nozzle on a hose are perfect for washing substrate. Place the substrate in the bathtub, set a screen over the drain, and use the showerhead or a hose to wash down the medium. It may be necessary to fill the tub with fresh water and drain it a couple of times to rinse any residual sterilants from the substrate.

Remove harvested plant root balls from the growing medium, and remove roots and stems.

If you decide to use rockwool or coco a second time, you may have problems with pests and diseases. In general, I recommend reusing a medium only if it does not deteriorate or compact. Examples include: pea gravel, expanded clay, lava rock, sand, etc. Once used indoors, reuse rockwool and biodegradable coco in the outdoor garden.

Buy pH Up and pH Down rather than making your own from concentrated acids. Commercial mixes are buffered and safe to use.

Adjust nutrient solution pH level up with:
pH Up
Potassium hydroxide
Do not use dangerous and caustic sodium hydroxide to raise pH.

Adjust nutrient solution pH level down with:
pH Down
Nitric acid
Phosphoric acid
Citric acid
Vinegar

pH Up and pH Down can be purchased in liquid or dry forms.

To sterilize a hydroponic garden, remove the nutrient solution from the reservoir. Pump the solution into the outdoor garden. Avoid pumping it down household drains, and definitely do not pump it into a septic tank. The nutrients will disrupt the chemistry!

Wash substrate with plenty of fresh water to remove built-up salts and dead roots

Flood the growing medium with the sterilizing solution for at least one-half hour, let drain, and flush again. Pump the bleach solution out of the system and down the drain. Do not dump sterilants outdoors; they will defoliate plants where they are dumped. Use lots of fresh water to leach and flush the entire system including beds, connecting hoses, drains, and reservoir. Make sure all residues are gone by flushing entire system twice for a half hour. Remove all solution from the tank, and scrub away any visible signs of salt buildup with a big soapy sponge. Have a bucket of clean water handy to rinse the sponge.

An alternate sterilization method is to "solarize" the rockwool. In a sunny location, set dry slabs of rockwool outside on a sheet of black plastic, and cover with black plastic. Let the sun bake the layer of slabs, or flock, for several days. The temperatures in the rockwool will climb to 140°F (60°C)

or more, enough to sterilize for most all harmful diseases and pests.

pH

The pH of the nutrient solution controls the availability of ions that plants need to assimilate. Fast-growing annuals grow well hydroponically within a pH range of 5.5–6.5, with 5.8–6.0 being ideal. The pH in hydroponic gardens requires a somewhat vigilant eye. In hydroponics, the nutrients are in solution and more available than when in soil. The pH of the solution can fluctuate a half point and not cause any problems.

Roots take in nutrients at different rates, which causes the ratios of nutrients in solution to change the pH. When the pH is above 7 or below 5.5, some nutrients are not absorbed as fast as possible. Check the pH every day or two to make sure it is at or near the perfect level.

Deviations in pH levels often affect element solubility. Values change slightly with different plants, grow mediums, and hydroponic systems. Overall, hydroponic gardens require lower pH levels than that of soil. The best pH range for hydroponic gardens is from 5.5 to 6.5. Different mediums perform best at different pH levels. Follow manufacturer's guidelines for pH level, and correct the pH using the manufacturer's suggested chemicals, because they will react best with their fertilizer.

The pH can easily fluctuate up and down one full point in hydroponic systems and cause little or no problem with nutrient uptake.

Follow the directions on the container, and remember to mix adjusters into the reservoir slowly and completely. Fertilizers are normally acidic and lower the pH of the nutrient solution. But nutrient solution is still taken in by plants, and water transpires and evaporates into the air, which causes the pH to climb.

Stabilize the pH of the water before adding fertilizer.

Make a correction if readings vary ± one-half point.

This controller monitors and controls the pH in the reservoir by dispersing pH Up or pH Down. The separate thermometer/hygrometer on top of the controller in the photo monitors ambient temperature and humidity.

EC, TDS, DS, CF, PPM
EC Meters

Pure distilled water has no resistance and conducts no electrical current. When impurities are added to pure distilled water in the form of fertilizer salts, it conducts electricity. A water analysis will indicate the impurities or dissolved solids found in household tap water. These impurities conduct electricity.

Nutrient (salt) concentrations are measured by their ability to conduct electricity

1. Hanna 1 mS/cm = 500 ppm
2. Eutech 1 mS/cm = 640 ppm
3. New Zealand Hydro. 1 mS/cm = 700 ppm

Parts per million recommendations are inaccurate and confusing. To help you through this confusion, an Australian friend compiled the following easy reference conversion chart.

1 mS/cm = 10 CF e.g., 0.7 EC = 7 CF

Conversion Scale from ppm to CF and EC

EC mS/cm	Hanna 0.5ppm	Eutech 0.64ppm	Truncheon 0.70ppm	CF 0
0.1	50	64	70	01
0.2	100	128	140	02
0.3	150	192	210	03
0.4	200	56	280	04
0.5	250	320	350	05
0.6	300	384	420	06
0.7	350	448	490	07
0.8	400	512	560	08
0.9	450	576	630	09
1.0	500	640	700	10
1.1	550	704	770	11
1.2	600	768	840	12
1.3	650	832	910	13
1.4	700	896	980	14
1.5	750	960	1050	15
1.6	800	1024	1120	16
1.7	850	1088	1190	17
1.8	900	1152	1260	18
1.9	950	1260	1330	19
2.0	1000	1280	1400	20
2.1	1050	1344	1470	21
2.2	1100	1408	1540	22
2.3	1150	1472	1610	23
2.4	1200	1536	1680	24
2.5	1250	1600	1750	25
2.6	1300	1664	1820	26
2.7	1350	1728	1890	27
2.8	1400	1792	1960	28
2.9	1450	1856	2030	29
3.0	1500	1920	2100	30
3.1	1550	1984	2170	31
3.2	1600	2048	2240	32

> EC = Electrical Conductivity
>
> CF = Conductivity Factor
>
> PPM = Parts Per Million
>
> TDS = Total Dissolved Solids
>
> DS = Dissolved Solids

through a solution. Dissolved ionic salts create electrical current in solution. The main constituent of hydroponic solutions is ionic salts. Several scales are currently used to measure how much electricity is conducted by nutrients including: Electrical Conductivity (EC), Conductivity Factor (CF), Parts Per Million (ppm), Total Dissolved Solids (TDS), and Dissolved Solids (DS). Most American gardeners use ppm to measure overall fertilizer concentration. European, Australian, and New Zealand gardeners use EC, however they still use CF in parts of Australia and New Zealand. Parts per million is not as accurate or consistent as EC to measure nutrient solution strength.

The difference between EC, CF, ppm, TDS, and DS is more complex than originally meets the eye. Different measurement systems all use the same base, but interpret the information differently. Let's start with EC, the most accurate and consistent scale.

Electrical conductivity is measured in milliSiemens per centimeter (mS/cm) or microSiemens per centimeter (μS/cm). One microSiemen/cm = 1000 milliSiemens/cm.

Parts per million testers actually measure in EC and convert to ppm. Unfortunately, the two scales (EC and ppm) are not directly related. Each nutrient or salt gives a different electronic discharge reading. To overcome this obstacle, an arbitrary stan-

dard was implemented which assumes "a specific EC equates to a specific amount of nutrient solution." Consequently, the ppm reading is not precise; it is only an approximation, a ballpark figure! It gets more complex! Manufacturers of nutrient testers use different standards to convert from EC to the ppm reading.

Every salt in a multi-element solution has a different conductivity factor. Pure water will not conduct electrical current, but when elemental salts/metals are added, electrical conductivity increases proportionately. Simple electronic meters measure this value and interpret it as total dissolved solids (TDS). Nutrient solutions used to grow fast-growing annuals generally range between 500 and 2000 ppm. If the solution concentration is too high, the internal osmotic systems can reverse and actually dehydrate the plant. In general, try to maintain a moderate value of approximately 800 to 1200 ppm.

RIGHT: This quick-dip Thruegeon measures EC quickly and efficiently. It was one of the first accurate, economical EC meters that was easy to use.

Nutrient solution concentration levels are affected by nutrient absorption by roots and by water evaporation. The solution weakens as plants use nutrients, but water also evaporates from the solution, which increases the

ABOVE LEFT: The probe of this meter is submerged in the nutrient solution to monitor pH 24 hours a day.
ABOVE RIGHT: Constant-readout, temperature-compensated EC/ppm meters with a probe immersed in the nutrient tank provide round-the-clock intelligence.

nutrient concentration. Adjust the concentration of the solution by adding fertilizer or diluting with more water.

Many factors can alter the EC balance of a solution. For example, if underwatered or allowed to dry completely, the EC reading will rise. In fact, the EC may increase to two or three times as high as the input solution when too little water is applied to rockwool. This increase in slab EC causes some nutrients to build up faster than others. When the EC doubles, the amount of sodium can increase as much as four- to six-fold under the right conditions! There should not be any sodium present in your garden unless it is in the water supply, and it should not be in excess of 50 ppm.

Let 10–20 percent of the nutrient solution drain from the growing medium after each irrigation cycle to help maintain EC stability. The runoff carries away any excess fertilizer salt buildup in the growing medium.

If the EC level of a solution is too high, increase the amount of runoff you create with each flush. Instead of a 10–20 percent runoff, flush so 20–30 percent of the solution runs off. To raise the EC, add more fertilizer to the solution, or change the nutrient solution.

A dissolved solids (DS) measurement indicates how many parts per million (ppm) of dissolved solids exist in a solution. A reading of 1800 ppm means there are 1800 parts of nutrient in one million parts solution, or 1800/1,000,000.

An EC meter measures the overall volume or strength of elements in water or solution. A digital LCD screen displays the reading or the EC of the electrical current flowing between the two electrodes. Pure rainwater has an EC close to zero. Check the pH and EC of rainwater to find out if it is acidic (acid rain) before using it.

Distilled bottled water from the grocery store often registers a small amount of electrical resistance, because it is not perfectly pure. Pure water with no resistance is very difficult to obtain and not necessary for a hydroponic nutrient solution.

Electrical conductivity measurement is temperature-sensitive and must be factored into the EC reading to retain accuracy. High-quality meters have automatic and manual temperature adjustments. Calibrating an EC meter is similar to calibrating a pH meter. Simply follow manufacturer's instructions. For an accurate reading, make sure your nutrient solution and stock solution are the same temperature.

Inexpensive meters last for about a year, and expensive meters can last for many years. However, the life of most EC me-

Parts per million meters measure the overall level of dissolved solids or fertilizer salts. Each fertilizer salt conducts different quantities of electricity. Use a calibrating solution that imitates the fertilizer in the nutrient solution to calibrate ppm or EC meters. Using such a solution ensures the meter readings will be as accurate as possible. For example, 90 percent of ammonium nitrate dissolved in water is measured, and a mere 40 percent of the magnesium is measured! Do not use sodium-based calibration solutions. They are intended for other applications than gardening. Purchase calibrating solution from the manufacturer or retailer when you buy the meter. Ask for a stable calibrating solution that mimics your fertilizer. Calibrate EC and ppm meters regularly. A good combination ppm, EC, pH meter that compensates for temperature costs about $200 and is well worth the money. Batteries last a long time, too.

ters, regardless of cost, is contingent upon regular maintenance. The probes must be kept moist and clean at all times. This is the most important part of keeping the meter in good repair. Read instructions on care and maintenance. Watch for corrosion buildup on the probes of your meter. When the probes are corroded, readings will not be accurate.

To check the EC of the nutrient solution, collect samples from both the reservoir and the growing medium. Save time and effort; collect EC and pH samples simultaneously. Collect samples with a syringe or baster inserted at least two inches deep into the rockwool and coco. Collect separate sample from the reservoir. Place each sample in a clean jar. Use calibrated EC meter to measure the samples. Under normal conditions, the EC in the slab should be a little higher than the nutrient solution in the reservoir. If the EC of the solution drawn from the growing medium is substantially higher than the one from the reservoir, there is a salt buildup in the substrate. Correct the imbalance by flushing substrate thoroughly with diluted nutrient solution, and replace with new solution. Regularly check the EC of your water, slab, and runoff.

Hydroponic Nutrients

High-quality hydroponic formulations are soluble, contain all the necessary nutrients, and leave no impure residues in the bottom of the reservoir. Always use the best hydroponic fertilizer you can find. There are many excellent commercial hydroponic fertilizers that contain all the nutrients in a balanced form to grow great plants. Quality hydroponic fertilizers packed in one-, two-, or three-part formulas have all the necessary macronutrients and micronutrients for rapid nutrient assimilation and growth. Cheap fertilizers contain low-quality, impure components that leave residue and sediments. These impurities build up readily and cause extra maintenance. High-quality, soluble hydroponic nutrients properly applied are immediately available for uptake. Exact control is much easier when using pure high-grade nutrients. Many companies use food-grade nutrients to manufacture their fertilizer formulations.

Nutrients are necessary for plants to grow and flourish. These nutrients must be broken down chemically within the plant, regardless of origin.

The nutrients could be derived from a natural organic base which was not heated or processed to change form, or they could be simple chemical elements and compounds. When properly applied, each type of fertilizer, organic or chemical, theoretically produces the same results.

For a complete background on nutrients and fertilizers, see Chapter Nine, "Water and Nutrients." Many of the same principles that apply to soil apply to the hydroponic medium.

Here are some of the many popular brands of liquid hydroponic fertilizer.

Nutrient Solutions

To avoid nutrient problems, change the nutrient solution in the reservoir every week. Change nutrient solution every two weeks in systems with a large reservoir. Change the nutrient solution more often when plants are in the last stages of flowering, because they use more nutrients. You can wait to change the nutrient solution, but imbalances are more common. Plants absorb nutrients at different rates, and some of them run out before others, which can cause more complex problems.

The best form of preventive maintenance is to change the solution often. Skimping on fertilizer can cause stunted growth. Nutrient imbalances also cause the pH to fluctuate, usually to drop. Nutrients used at different rates create an imbalanced formulation. Avert problems by using pure nutrients and thoroughly flushing the soilless medium with fresh tepid water between nutrient solutions.

Hydroponics gives the means to supply the maximum amount of nutrients a plant needs, but it can also starve them to death or rapidly overfertilize them. Remember, hydroponic systems are designed for high performance. If one thing malfunctions, say the electricity goes off, the pump breaks, the drain gets clogged with roots, or there is a rapid fluctuation in the pH, major problems could result in the garden. A mistake could kill or stunt plants so seriously that they do not have time to recover before harvest.

Solution Maintenance

Plants use so much water that nutrient solutions need to be replenished regularly. Water is used at a much faster rate than nutrients. Casually "topping off" the reservoir with pH-balanced water will keep the solution relatively balanced for a week or two. Some gardeners top off the nutrient solution with 500–700 ppm-strength nutrient solution every two to three days. Never let the nutrient solution go for more than four weeks before draining it and adding fresh solution. Smart gardeners leach the entire system with weak nutrient solution for an hour or more when changing the reservoir. Wipe down the entire system with the solution.

Do not flush with plain water. Flushing with mild (quarter-strength) nutrient solution will actually remove more excess fertilizer than plain water.

Check EC of reservoir, growing medium, and runoff nutrient solution at the same time every day.

Use an electronic EC pen to monitor the level of dissolved solids in the solution. Occasionally you will need to add more fertilizer concentrate to maintain the EC level in the reservoir during the "topping off" times. Keep the reservoir full at all times. The smaller the reservoir, the more-rapid the depletion and the more critical it is to keep it full. Smaller reservoirs should be refilled daily.

Hydro-organic

Hydro-organic is a means of growing plants in an inert soilless medium and feeding with a soluble organic nutrient solution. Organic fertilizers are most often defined as containing substances with a carbon molecule or a natural unaltered substance such as ground-up rocks.

Dedicated gardeners spend the time and trouble it takes to grow hydro-organically, because the natural nutrients bring out a sweet organic taste in vegetables. Indoor and outdoor crops grown in less than 90 days do not have time to wait for organic nutrients to be broken down. Organic nutrients must be soluble and readily available for fast-growing annuals to benefit.

An exact balance of organic nutrients can be achieved with constant experimentation and attention to details. Even when you buy ready-mixed commercial fertilizers like BioCanna, Earth Juice, or Fox Farm, you will need to try different feeding amounts and schedules to get the exact combination to grow top-quality organic produce.

Taking an accurate EC reading or mixing the exact amount of a specific nutrient is very difficult in organic hydroponics. Chemical fertilizers are easy to measure out and apply. It is easy to give plants the specific amount of fertilizer they need in each stage of growth.

Organic nutrients have a complex structure, and measuring content is difficult. Organics are difficult to keep stable, too. Some manufacturers, including BioCanna, Earth Juice, and Fox Farm, have managed to stabilize their fertilizers. When buying organic nutrients, always buy from the same supplier, and find out as much as possible about the source from which the fertilizers were derived.

Combine premixed soluble organic fertilizers with other organic ingredients to make your own blend. Indoor gardeners experiment to find the perfect mix for their system and the varieties they are growing. Adding too much fertilizer can toxify soil and bind up nutrients, making them unavailable. Foliage and roots burn when the condition is severe.

Soluble organic fertilizers are fairly easy to flush from the growing medium. Like chemical fertilizers, organic fertilizers build to toxic levels easily. Look for the same symptoms as in soil—burned leaf tips, discolored misshapen leaves, brittle leaves, etc. Organic nutrients require heavier flushing. Rinse medium with three gallons of water for every gallon of medium. Some indoor gardeners flush with plain water the last two weeks of flowering to get all fertilizer taste out of their vegetables.

Mix seaweed with macronutrients and secondary nutrients to make a hydro-organic fertilizer. The amount of primary and secondary nutrients is not as important as the menagerie of trace elements that are in an available form in the seaweed. Major nutrients can be applied via soluble fish emulsion for nitrogen; phosphorus and potassium are supplied by bat guano, bone meal, and manures. More and more organic gardeners are adding growth stimulators such as humic acid, *Trichoderma* bacteria, and hormones.

Reservoirs

Nutrient solution reservoirs should be as big as possible and have a lid to lessen evaporation. Gardens use from 5–25 percent of the nutrient solution every day. A big volume of nutrient solution will minimize nutrient imbalances. When the water is used, the concentration of elements in the solution increases; there is less water in the solution and nearly the same amount of nutrients. Add water as soon as the solution level drops. The reservoir should contain at least 25 percent more nutrient solution than it takes to fill the beds to compensate for daily use and evaporation. The greater the volume of nutrient solution, the more forgiving the system and the easier it is to control. Forgetting to replenish the water supply and/or nutrient solution could result in crop failure.

Check the level of the reservoir daily, and replenish if necessary. A reservoir that loses more than 20 percent of its volume daily can be topped off with pure or low (500 ppm) EC water. Sophisticated systems have a float valve that controls the level of water in the reservoir.

If your reservoir does not have graduated measurements to denote liquid volume, use an indelible marker to make a "full" line and mark the number of gallons or liters contained at that point on the inside of the reservoir tank. Use this volume measure when mixing nutrients.

Nutrient Solution Composition

The chart below is a guideline of satisfactory nutrient limits expressed in ppm. Do not deviate too far from these ranges to avert nutrient deficiencies and excesses.

ELEMENT	Limits	Average
Nitrogen	150–1000	250
Calcium	100–500	200
Magnesium	50–100	75
Phosphorus	50–100	80
Potassium	100–400	300
Sulfur	200–1000	400
Copper	0.1–0.5	0.05
Boron	0.5–5.0	1.0
Iron	2.0–10	5.0
Manganese	0.5–5.0	2.0
Molybdenum	0.01–0.05	0.02
Zinc	0.5–1.0	0.5

The pump should be set up to lift the solution out of the reservoir. Set reservoirs high enough so spent nutrient solution can be siphoned or can gravity-flow into a drain or the outdoor garden.

Reservoir Temperature

The temperature of the nutrient solution should stay between 60°F and 75°F (15–24°C). However, nutrient solution will hold much more oxygen at 60°F (15°C) than it will at 75°F (24°C). Never let the nutrient solution temperature climb above 85°F (29°C). Above 85°F (29°C), the solution holds little oxygen. Roots are easily damaged by temperatures 85°F (29°C) and above. Heat-damaged roots are very susceptible to rot, wilts, and fungus gnat attacks.

Large non-submersible pumps quickly and efficiently move considerable volumes of nutrient solution.

When air is cooler than water, moisture rapidly evaporates into the air; the greater the temperature differential, the higher the relative humidity. Maintaining the nutrient solution temperature around 60°F (15°C) will help control transpiration and humidity. It will also promote the uptake of nutrients.

An air pump submerged in the reservoir not only aerates the solution, it will help level out the temperature differential between ambient air and reservoir.

To save energy and money, heat the nutrient solution instead of the air in a room. Heat the nutrient solution with a submersible aquarium heater or grounded propagation heating cables. The heaters might take a day or longer to raise the temperature of a large volume of solution. Do not leave heaters in an empty reservoir. They will soon overheat and burn out. Aquarium heaters seldom have ground wires, a seemingly obvious oversight. But I have yet to learn of an electrocution by aquarium heater. Avoid submersible heaters that give off harmful residues.

Irrigation

Irrigation is a science unto itself. Irrigation cycles depend on plant size, climate conditions, and the type of medium used. Large, round, smooth particles of substrate drain rapidly and need to be irrigated more often—four to twelve times daily for five- to thirty-minute cycles.

Fibrous mediums with irregular surfaces, such as vermiculite, drain slowly and require less frequent watering, often just once per day. The water comes to within one-half inch (1.5 cm) of the top of the gravel and should completely drain out of the medium after each watering.

Soluble Salts Range Chart
Electrical conductivity (EC) as milliSiemen (mS) and total dissolved solids (TDS) as parts per million (ppm)

RANGE DESIRABLE	PERMISSIBLE	PROBABLE SALT DAMAGE (but potential for concern)
EC as mS		
0.75 to 2.0	2.0 to 3.0	3.0 and up TDS as ppm
500 to 1300	1300 to 2000	2000 and up

For nutrient solutions' determinations, one (1) mS (milliSiemen) or one mMho/cm^2 is equivalent to approximately 650 ppm total dissolved solids.

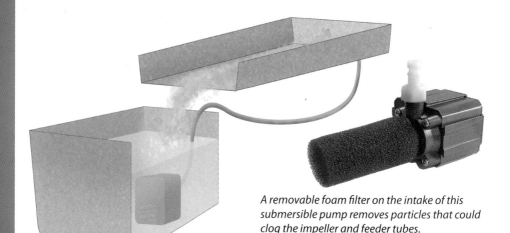

A removable foam filter on the intake of this submersible pump removes particles that could clog the impeller and feeder tubes.

Reservoirs should be as big as possible. Letting nutrient solution fall into the reservoir will help keep it well aerated.

Top-feed systems cycle for about five minutes or longer and should be irrigated at least three times daily. Often gardeners cycle the nutrient solution 24 hours a day, especially when growing in fast-draining expanded clay or similar mediums.

A handle and stand on this pump make it easy to move and mount into a fixed position.

In fast-draining mediums, overhead irrigation is continual. Drip irrigation in coco coir is four or five times daily. Flood and drain irrigation cycles are five to ten times daily.

During and soon after irrigation, the nutrient content of the bed and the reservoir are the same concentration. As time passes between irrigations, the EC and the pH gradually change. If enough time passes between irrigations, the nutrient concentration might change so much that the plant is not able to draw it in.

There are many variations on how often to water. Experimentation will tell you more than anything else.

Nutrient Disorders

When the hydroponic garden is on a regular maintenance schedule and the gardener knows the crop well, nutrient problems are usually averted. If nutrient deficiency or excess affects more than a few plants, check the irrigation fittings to ensure nutrient-challenged plants are receiving a full dose of nutrient solution. Next, check the substrate around affected plants to ensure nutrient solution is penetrating entire medium and all roots are wet. Check the root zone to ensure roots have not plugged drainage conduits and are not standing in stagnant solution.

This innovative reservoir was made by lining a large galvanized pipe with heavy-duty plastic.

A two-part nutrient solution is mixed before application. Each reservoir holds one part of the solution.

Cover reservoirs to avoid extra evaporation, and to prevent contamination and algae growth.

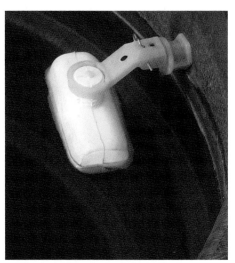

Attach a recirculating pipe with an on/off valve to the pump outlet pipe. This is a convenient and easy-to-control method of aerating the nutrient solution.

A float valve will turn water on to fill the reservoir when the level drops.

Reservoir temperature range.

Reservoir

75°   24°
65°   18°

Use an aquarium heater to warm cold reservoirs. Do not let the reservoir dry out when the heater is on or it will burn out.

Change the nutrient solution if there is a good flow of nutrient solution through the root zone, but plants still appear sickly. Make sure the pH of the water is within the acceptable 5.5–6.5 range before adding new nutrients.

If changing solution does not solve the problem, changing to a new brand of fertilizer may do the trick. Check out the color drawings of specific nutrient deficiencies and excesses in Chapter Nine to determine the exact problem, and add 10 to 20 percent more of the deficient nutrient in a chelated form until the disorder has disappeared. Leach growing medium with dilute nutrient solution to solve simple overdose nutrient problems.

Hydroponic gardens have no soil to buffer the uptake of nutrients. This causes nutrient disorders to manifest as discolored foliage, slow growth, spotting, etc., at a rapid rate. Novice gardeners must learn how to recognize nutrient problems in their early stages to avoid serious problems that cost valuable time for plants to recoup. Treatment for a nutrient deficiency or excess must be rapid and certain. But once treated, plants take several days to respond to the remedy. For a fast fix, foliar feed plants. See "Foliar Feeding" in Chapter Nine.

Nutrient deficiency or excess diagnosis becomes difficult when two or more elements are deficient or in excess at the same time. Symptoms might not point directly at the cause. Solve mind-bending nutrient deficiency syndromes by changing the nutrient solution. Plants do not always need an accurate diagnosis when the nutrient solution is changed.

Overfertilization, once diagnosed, is easy to remedy. Drain the nutrient solution. Flush the system at least twice with fresh, dilute (5–10 percent) nutrient solution to remove any lingering sediment and salt buildup in the reservoir. Replace with properly mixed solution.

Nutrient disorders most often affect a plant variety at the same time it is receiving the nutrient solution. Different varieties may react differently to the same nutrient solution. Do not confuse other problems—windburn, lack of light, temperature stress, fungi and pest damage—with nutrient deficiencies. Such problems usually appear on individual plants that are most affected. For example, foliage next to a heat vent might show signs of heat scorch, while the rest of the garden looks healthy. Or a plant on the edge of the garden would be small and leggy because it receives less light.

Here are some watering guidelines:

1. Water when plants are half-empty of water; weigh pots to tell.

2. Water soil gardens when soil is dry one-half inch (1.5 cm) below the surface.

3. Water soil gardens with a mild nutrient solution and let 10–20 percent drain off at each watering.

4. Do not let soil dry out to the point that plants wilt.

This air-powered windmill in San Francisco's Golden Gate Park has been pumping water to the gardens here for almost a century, without the use of any fossil fuels. Air has many uses!

Introduction

Fresh air is essential in all gardens. Indoors, it could be the difference between success and failure. Outdoor air is abundant and packed with carbon dioxide (CO_2) necessary for plant life. For example, the level of CO_2 in the air over a field of rapidly growing annuals could be only a third of normal on a very still day. Wind blows in fresh CO_2-rich air. Rain washes air and plants of dust and pollutants. The outdoor environment is often harsh and unpredictable, but there is always fresh air. Indoor gardens must be meticulously controlled to replicate the outdoor atmosphere.

Smoke is immediately sucked out of the room when using this in-line fan. The fan demonstration took place at a trade show in Germany.

Carbon dioxide and oxygen provide basic building blocks for plant life. Oxygen is used for respiration—burning carbohydrates and other foods to provide energy. Carbon dioxide must be present during photosynthesis. Without CO_2 a plant will die. Carbon dioxide combines light energy with water to produce sugars. These sugars fuel the growth and metabolism of the plant. With reduced levels of CO_2 growth

slows to a crawl. Except during darkness, a plant releases more oxygen than is used and uses much more carbon dioxide than it releases.

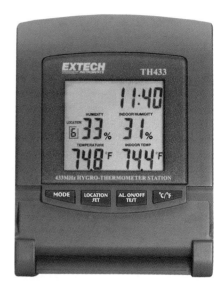

Monitor temperature and humidity regularly. This multi-station setup allows you to monitor several areas at once.

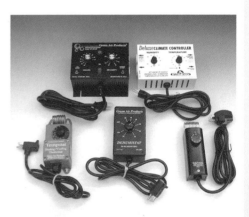

An assortment of temperature and humidity controllers are commercially available.

At least one good circulation fan and an extraction fan are necessary in indoor gardens.

Roots use air, too. Oxygen must be present along with water and nutrients for the roots to be able to absorb nutrients. Compacted, water-saturated soil allows roots little or no air, causing nutrient uptake to stall.

Air Movement

Air ventilation and circulation are essential to a healthy indoor harvest. Indoors, fresh air is one of the most overlooked factors contributing to a healthy garden and a bountiful harvest. Fresh air is the least expensive essential component required to produce a bumper crop. Experienced indoor gardeners understand the importance of fresh air and take the time to set up an adequate ventilation system. Three factors affect air movement: stomata, ventilation, and circulation.

Stomata

Stomata are microscopic pores on leaf undersides that are similar to an animal's nostrils. Animals regulate the amount of oxygen inhaled and carbon dioxide and other elements exhaled through the nostrils via the lungs. In plants, oxygen and carbon dioxide flows are regulated by the stomata. The larger the plant, the more stomata it has to take in carbon dioxide and release oxygen. The greater the volume of plants, the more fresh CO_2-rich air they will need to grow quickly. Dirty, clogged stomata do not work properly and restrict airflow. Stomata are easily clogged by dirt from polluted air and sprays that leave filmy residues. Keep foliage clean. To avoid clogging stomata, spray foliage with tepid water a day or two after spraying with pesticides, fungicides, or nutrient solution.

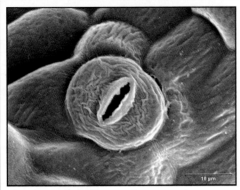

This photo of a half-opened stomata, the mouth-like opening on leaf underside, was magnified 2500 times.

Circulation

Plants use all CO_2 around the leaf within a few minutes. When no new CO_2-rich air replaces the used CO_2-depleted air, a dead air zone forms around the leaf. This stifles stomata and virtually stops growth. If it is not actively moved, the air around leaves stratifies. Warm air stays near the ceiling, and cool air settles near the floor. Air circulation breaks up these air masses, mixing them together. Avoid these would-be problems by opening a door or window and/or installing an oscillating circulation fan. Air circulation also helps prevent harmful pest and fungus attacks. Omnipresent mold spores do not land and grow as readily when air is stirred by a fan. Insects and spider mites find it difficult to live in an environment that is constantly bombarded by air currents.

Ventilation

Fresh air is easy to obtain and inexpensive to maintain—as simple as hooking up and placing the proper-sized exhaust fan in the most efficient location. An intake vent may be necessary to create a flow of fresh air in the room.

A 10-foot square (0.92 m²) garden will use from 10 to 50 gallons (38 to 190 L) or more of water every week. Plants transpire (similar to evaporation) most of this water

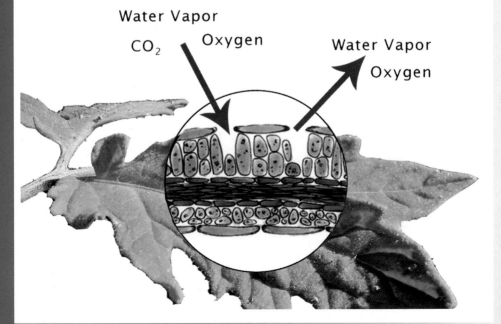

Water Vapor

CO_2 Oxygen

Water Vapor

Oxygen

Hot air flows upward naturally. Always design indoor gardens and greenhouses to take advantage of this principle.

CO_2 around leaves is used quickly and must be replaced every few minutes.

Here is an example of a heavy-duty extractor fan from a Dutch garden.

Place circulation fans far enough away from plants to prevent too much airflow on any one portion of the garden.

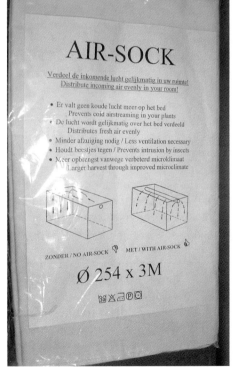

A Dutch innovation is the Air-Sock, a simple, inexpensive method of distribuiting fresh air throughout your indoor garden. Hang the Air-Sock from an intake vent powered by a blower and the air is spread evenly through the holes along the length of the sock.

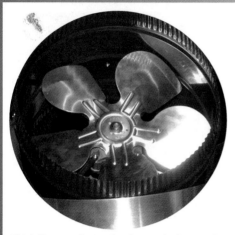

This inline ventilation fan fits inside ductwork.

This blower is at the end of intake air ducting. The main fan is at the other end.

into the air. Every day and night, rapidly growing plants transpire more moisture into the air. If this moisture is left in the indoor garden, humidity increases to 100 percent, which stifles stomata and causes growth to screech to a halt. It also opens the door for pest and disease attacks. Replace moist air with fresh, dry air, and transpiration increases, stomata function properly, and growth rebounds. A vent fan that extracts air from the indoor garden is the perfect solution to remove this humid, stale air. Fresh air flows in through an intake vent or with the help of an intake fan.

Ventilation is as important as water, light, heat, and fertilizer. In many cases, fresh air is even more important. Greenhouses use large ventilation fans. Indoor gardens are very similar to greenhouses and should follow their example. Most indoor gardens have an easy-to-use opening, such as a window, in which to mount a fan, but room location may render it unusable. If no vent opening is available, one will have to be created.

All grow rooms require ventilation. This system could be as simple as an open door

or window that supplies and circulates fresh air throughout the room, but open doors and windows can be inconvenient and problematic. Most gardeners elect to install a vent fan. Some gardeners need to install an entire ventilation system including ductwork and several fans.

A vent fan *pulls* air out of a room four times more efficiently than a fan is able to push it out. Vent fans are rated by the amount of air, measured in cubic feet-per minute (CFM) or (square meters per hour [m^2/h]), that they can move. The fan should be able to replace the air volume (length × width × height = total volume in cubic feet) of the indoor garden in less than five minutes. Once evacuated, new air is immediately drawn in through an intake vent or with the help of an intake fan. (Covering the intake vent with fine mesh silk screen will help exclude pests.) An intake fan might be necessary to bring an adequate volume of fresh air into the room quickly. Some rooms have so many little cracks for air to drift in that they do not need an intake vent.

Do not set up a circulation fan in the room and expect it to vent the area by pushing air out a distant vent. The circulation fan must be very large to adequately increase air pressure and push enough air out a vent to create an exchange of air.

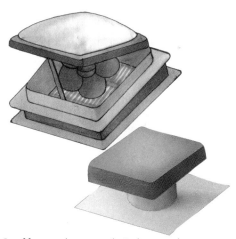

Roof fans and vents make indoor garden ventilation easy and inconspicuous.

A vent fan, on the other hand, is able to change the pressure and exchange the air quickly and efficiently.

Squirrel cage blowers are efficient at moving air but are very loud. Blowers with a balanced well-oiled wheel run most quietly. Felt or rubber grommets below each increase air pressure and push enough air out a vent to create an exchange of air. A vent fan, on the other hand, is able to change the pressure and exchange the air quickly and efficiently.

Squirrel cage blowers are efficient at moving air but are very loud. Blowers with a balanced, well-oiled wheel run most quietly. Felt or rubber grommets below each foot of the fan will reduce noise caused by vibrations. Run motor at a low RPM to lessen noise.

Inline fans are designed to fit into a duct pipe. The propellers are mounted to increase the airflow quickly, effortlessly, and as quietly as possible. Inline fans are available in quiet, high-quality models that run smoothly.

Propeller or muffin fans with large fan blades expel air through a large opening,

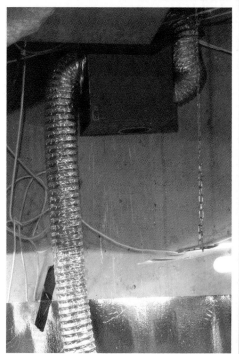

A booster fan in the gray box pushes intake air down the duct to the bottom of the garden.

and are most efficient and quiet when operated at low RPM. A slow-moving propeller fan on the ceiling of an indoor garden will quietly and efficiently move the air.

Hot air rises. Adept gardeners locate air exit vents in the hottest peak of the room for passive, silent air venting. The larger the diameter of the exhaust ducts, the more air that can travel through them. By installing a big, slow-moving vent fan in this vent, hot stale air is quietly and efficiently evacuated. A fan running at 50 RPM is quieter than one running at 200 RPM. Smart gardeners install 12-inch ducting and inline fans.

Most often, the vent fan is attached to ducting that directs air out of the indoor garden. Flexible ducting is easier to use than rigid ducting. To install, run the duct

Straight with no bend is the most efficient

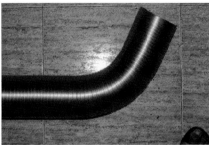

Thirty-degree curve cuts up to 20 percent of air transmission.

Forty-five–degree curve cuts up to 40 percent of air transmission.

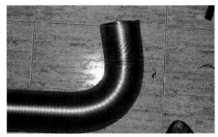

Ninety-degree curve cuts up to 60 percent of air transmission.

the shortest possible distance, and keep curves to a minimum. When turned at more than 30°, much of the air that enters a duct will not exit the other end. Keep the ducting straight and short.

Intake Air

Many rooms have enough fresh air coming in via cracks and holes. But other indoor gardens are tightly sealed and require fresh air to be ushered in with the help of an intake fan. An intake fan is the same as an exhaust fan, except it blows fresh air into the room. The ratio of one to four (100 CFM [m³/h] incoming and 400 CFM [m³/h] outgoing) should give the room a little negative pressure. Delivering fresh air to plants ensures they will have adequate CO_2 to continue rapid growth. One of the best ways to deliver air directly to plants is

to pipe it in via flexible ducting. Ingenious gardeners cut holes in the intake ducting to direct air where it is needed. The air is dispersed evenly throughout the room.

Always make sure fresh air is neither too hot nor too cold. For example, one friend who lives in a hot, arid climate brings cool, fresh air in from under the house, where the air is a few degrees cooler than ambient air.

Place one end of the duct outdoors. It should be high enough, preferably over 12 feet (3.6 m) , so that air flows away freely. One of the best vents is the chimney. The vent fan is then placed near the ceiling so it vents hot, humid air. See below: "Setting Up the Vent Fan."

Greenhouse fans are equipped with louvers (flaps or baffles) to prevent backdrafts. During cold and hot weather, undesirable backdrafts could alter the climate in the room and usher in a menagerie of pests and diseases. Installing a vent fan with louvers eliminates backdrafts.

Temperature

An accurate thermometer is essential to measure temperature in all indoor gardens. Mercury or liquid thermometers are typically more accurate than spring or dial types but are ecologically unsound. An inexpensive thermometer will collect basic information, but the ideal thermometer is a day/night or maximum/minimum type that measures how low the temperature drops at night and how high it reaches during the day. The maximum and minimum temperatures in an indoor garden are important for the reasons explained below.

Under normal conditions, the ideal temperature range for indoor growth is 72–76°F (22–24°C). At night, the temperature can drop 5–10°F (2–5°C) with little noticeable effect on growth rate. The temperature should not drop more than 15°F (8°C), or excessive humidity and mold might

Squirrel cage blower moves a lot of air, but it is noisy! This blower has been necked down to force more air through the ducting.

For indoor rooms, inline fans are one of gardeners' favorites. These fans are quiet and efficiently move large volumes of air.

This fan is suspended by bungee cords to shunt noisy vibrations. Always keep your fans well lubricated so they run smoothly and quietly.

Fresh air in this room is piped in directly where plants need it.

become problems. Daytime temperatures above 85°F (29°C) or below 60°F (15°C) will slow growth. Maintaining the proper, constant temperature in the indoor garden promotes strong, even, healthy growth. Make sure plants are not too close to a heat source such as a ballast or heat vent, or they may dry out, maybe even get heat scorch. Cold intake air will also stunt plant growth.

Plants regulate oxygen uptake in relation to the ambient air temperature rather than the amount of available oxygen. Plants use a lot of oxygen; in fact, a plant cell uses as much oxygen as a human cell. The air must contain at least 20 percent oxygen for plants to thrive. Leaves are not able to make oxygen at night, but roots still need oxygen to grow. A plant's respi-

ration rate approximately doubles every 20°F (10°C). Root respiration increases as the roots warm up, which is why fresh air is important both day and night.

Temperatures above 85°F (29°C) are not recommended even when using CO_2 enrichment. Under the proper conditions, which are very demanding to maintain, higher temperatures step up metabolic activity and speed growth. The warmer it is, the more water the air is able to hold. This moist air often restrains plant functions and decelerates growth rather than speeding it. Other complications and problems result from excess humidity and moisture condensation when the temperature drops at night.

Heat buildup during warm weather can catch gardeners off guard and cause serious problems. Ideal indoor gardens are located underground in a basement, taking advantage of the insulating qualities of Mother Earth. With the added heat of the HID and hot, humid weather outdoors, a room can heat up rapidly. More than a few American gardeners have lost their crops to heatstroke during the Fourth of July weekend, since it is the first big holiday of the summer and everybody in the city wants to get away to enjoy it. There are always some gardeners who forget or are too paranoid to maintain good ventilation in the indoor garden while on vacation. Temperatures can easily climb to 100°F (38°C) or more in indoor gardens that are poorly insulated and vented. The hotter it is, the more ventilation and water that are necessary.

The cold of winter is the other temperature extreme. In Montreal, Quebec, Canada, gardeners will remember the year of the big ice storm. Electricity went out all over the city and surrounding ar-

A thermometer that measures in Fahrenheit and Celsius will come in very handy.

Thermometer Hygrometer

eas. Water pipes froze, and heating systems failed. Residents were driven from their homes until electricity was restored some days later. Many gardeners returned to find their beautiful gardens wilted, stricken with the deepest, most disgusting green only a freeze can bring. Broken water pipes, ice everywhere! It is difficult to combat such acts of God, but if possible, always keep the indoor garden above 40°F (5°C) and definitely above freezing, 32°F (0°C). If the temperature dips below this mark, the freeze will rupture plant cells, and foliage will die back or, at best, grow slowly. Growth slows when the temperature dips below 50°F (10°C). Stressing plants with cold-weather conditions is not recommended; it will reduce plants' overall productivity.

A thermostat measures the temperature and controls it by turning on or off a device that regulates heating or cooling, keeping the temperature within a predetermined range. A thermostat can be attached to an electric or combustion heater. In fact, many homes are already set up with electric baseboard heat and a thermostat in each room.

Thermostats

A thermostat can be used to control cooling vent fans in all but the coldest indoor gardens. When it gets too hot in a room, the thermostat turns on the vent fan, which evacuates the hot, stale air. The vent fan remains on until the desired temperature is reached, then the thermostat turns off the fan. A thermostat-controlled vent fan offers adequate temperature and humidity control for many indoor gardens. A refrigerated air conditioner can be installed if heat and humidity are a major problem. Just remember, air conditioners

To control the air temperature, hang the thermostat near the canopy of the garden.

Check the temperature and humidity in several places in the indoor garden. Lights really heat a room!

This combination thermometer/ hygrometer is fairly accurate and easy to mount.

Knowing Celsius and Fahrenheit equivalents makes garden calculations more precise.

Fill barrels with water and let the sun heat them several days. Water stays warm all night to heat the greenhouse!

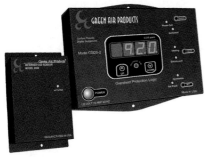

This simple humidistat/thermostat controller is just one of many different time/controllers found at www.greenair.com. It is very easy to use and foolproof.

draw a lot of electricity. If excessive heat is a problem, but humidity is not a concern, use a swamp cooler. These evaporative coolers are inexpensive to operate and keep rooms cool in arid climates.

Common thermostats include single-stage and two-stage. The single-stage thermostat controls a device that keeps the temperature the same both day and night. A two-stage thermostat is more expensive but can be set to maintain different daytime and nighttime temperatures. This convenience can save money on heating, since room temperature can drop 5–10°F (2–5°C) at night with little effect on growth.

Many new indoor garden controllers have been developed in the last ten years. These controllers can operate and integrate every appliance in the indoor garden. More sophisticated controllers integrate the operation of CO_2 equipment, vent, and intake fans. Relatively inexpensive computerized controllers are also available for indoor gardens. If temperature and humidity regulation are causing cultural problems in the indoor garden, consider purchasing a controller.

Uninsulated indoor gardens, or indoor gardens that experience significant temperature fluctuations, require special consideration and care. Before growing in such a location, make sure it is the only choice. If forced to use a sun-baked attic that cools at night, make sure maximum insulation is in place to help balance temperature instability. Enclose the room to control heating and cooling.

When CO_2 is enriched to 0.12–0.15 percent (1200–1500 ppm), a temperature of 85°F (29°C) promotes more rapid exchange of gases. Photosynthesis and chlorophyll synthesis are able to take place at a more rapid rate causing plants to grow faster. Remember, this higher temperature increases water, nutrient, and space consumption, so be prepared! Carbon dioxide-enriched plants still need ventilation to remove stale, humid air and promote plant health.

The temperature in the indoor garden tends to stay the same, top to bottom, when the air is circulated with an oscillating fan(s). In an enclosed indoor garden, HID lamps and ballasts keep the area warm. A remote ballast placed near the floor on a shelf or a stand also helps break up air stratification by radiating heat upward. Indoor gardens in cool climates stay warm during the day when the outdoor temperature peaks, but often cool off too much at night when cold temperatures set in. To compensate, gardeners turn on the lamp at night to help heat the room, but leave it off during the day.

This air conditioner lowers indoor garden temperature and humidity. The hot radiator is outside, about 10 feet (3 m) away.

Sometimes it is too cold for the lamp and ballast to maintain satisfactory room temperatures. Indoor gardens located in homes are usually equipped with a central heating and/or air conditioning vent. The vent is usually controlled by a central thermostat that regulates the temperature of the home. By adjusting the thermostat to 72°F (22°C) and opening the door to the indoor garden, it can stay a cozy 72°F (22°C). However, using so much power is expensive. Keeping the thermostat between 60 and 65°F (15–18°C), coupled with the heat from the HID system, should be enough to sustain 75°F (24°C) temperatures.

A simple electric heater may be necessary to warm the room after lights go out.

Other supplemental heat sources such as inefficient incandescent lightbulbs and electric heaters are expensive and draw extra electricity, but they provide instant heat that is easy to regulate. Propane and natural gas heaters increase temperatures and burn oxygen from the air, creating CO_2 and water vapor as by-products. This dual advantage makes using a CO_2 generator economical and practical.

Kerosene heaters also work to generate heat and CO_2. Look for a heater that burns its fuel efficiently and completely with no telltale odor of the fuel in the room. Do not use old kerosene heaters or fuel-oil heaters if they burn fuel inefficiently. A blue flame is burning all the fuel cleanly. A red flame indicates only part of the fuel is being burned. I'm not a big fan of kerosene heaters and do not recommend using them. The room must be vented regularly to avoid buildup of toxic carbon monoxide, also a by-product of combustion.

Diesel oil is a common source of indoor heat. Many furnaces use this dirty, polluting fuel. Wood heat is not the cleanest either, but works well as a heat source. A vent fan is extremely important to exhaust polluted air and draw fresh air into a room heated by an oil furnace or wood stove.

Insect populations and fungi are also affected by temperature. In general, the cooler it is, the slower the insects and fungi reproduce and develop. Temperature control is effectively integrated into many insect and fungus control programs. Check recommendations in Chapter 12, "Pests and Diseases."

Humidity

Humidity is relative; that is, air holds different quantities of water at different temperatures. Relative humidity is the ratio between the amount of moisture in the air and the greatest amount of moisture the air could hold at the same temperature. In other words, the hotter it is, the more moisture air can hold; the cooler it is, the less moisture air can hold. When temperature in an indoor garden drops, humidity climbs and moisture condenses. For example, an 800 cubic foot ($10 \times 10 \times 8$ feet) (21.5 m^2) indoor garden will hold about 14 ounces (414 ml) of water when the temperature is 70°F (21°C) and relative humidity is at 100 percent. When the temperature is increased to 100°F (38°C), the same room will hold 56 ounces (1.65 L) of moisture at 100 percent relative humidity. That is four times more moisture! Where does this water go when the temperature drops? It condenses, onto the surface of plants and garden walls, just as dew condenses outdoors.

Relative humidity increases when the temperature drops at night. The greater the temperature variation, the greater the relative humidity variation will be. Supplemental heat or extra ventilation is often necessary at night if temperatures fluctuate more than 15°F (8°C).

Seedlings and vegetative plants grow best when the relative humidity is from 65 to 70 percent. Flowering plants grow best in a relative humidity range from 55 to 60 percent. The lower humidity discourages diseases and pests. As with temperature, consistent humidity promotes healthy, even growth. Relative humidity level affects transpiration rate of the stomata. When humidity is high, water evaporates slowly. The stomata close, transpiration slows, and so does plant growth. Water evaporates quickly into drier air causing stomata to open, increasing transpiration, fluid flow, and growth. Transpiration in arid conditions will be rapid only if there is enough water available for roots to draw in. If water is inadequate, stomata will close to protect the plant from dehydration, causing growth to slow.

When relative humidity climbs beyond 70 percent, pressure outside the leaf is too high and inside too low. This causes stomata to close, which slows growth. For example, a 40-inch (1 m) tall plant can easily transpire a gallon (4 L) per day when the humidity is below 50 percent. However, the same plant will transpire about a half-pint (0.5 L) on a cool, humid day.

Measuring Relative Humidity

Relative humidity control is an integral part of insect and fungus prevention and control. Humidity above 80 percent discourages spider mites but promotes fungus as well as root and stem rot. Humidity levels below 60 percent reduce the chance of fungus and rot.

Measure relative humidity with a hygrometer. This extremely important instrument will save you and your garden much frustration and fungi. By knowing the air's exact moisture content, humidity may be adjusted to a safe 55 to 60 percent level that encourages transpiration and discourages fungus growth.

There are two common types of hygrometers. The spring type is accurate within five to ten percent. This hygrometer is inexpensive and adequate for most hobby gardeners whose main concern is to keep the humidity near 55 to 60 percent. The second type, a psychrometer, is more expensive but very accurate. A psychrometer that measures relative humidity with a wet and dry bulb is an excellent way to keep an accurate vigil on relative humidity. Today there are many exceptionally accurate high-tech gadgets, plus they are equipped with memory!

A humidistat is similar to a thermostat, but regulates humidity instead of temperature. Humidistats are wonderful and make controlling the environment very easy. Humidistats cost less than $100 and are well worth purchasing. A humidistat and thermostat can be wired "inline" to control a vent fan. Each can operate the fan independently. As soon as the humidity (or temperature) exceeds the acceptable range, the fan turns on to vent the humid (or hot) air outdoors.

The HID lamp and ballast radiate heat, which lowers humidity. Heat from the HID system and a vent fan on a thermostat/humidistat are all the humidity control necessary for most indoor gardens. Other dry heat sources, such as hot air vented from a furnace or wood stove, dry the air and lower the humidity. Be careful. Do not let piped-in, warm, dry air blow directly on foliage. It will rapidly dehydrate plants.

Increase humidity by misting the air with water or setting out a bucket of water to evaporate into the air. A humidifier is convenient and relatively inexpensive. Humidifiers evaporate water into the air to increase humidity. Just set the dial to a specific humidity, and presto! The humidity changes to the desired level as soon as

A 10 × 10 × 8-foot (800 cubic feet) (21.5 m³) indoor garden can hold:

4 oz (118 ml) of water at 32°F (0°C).
7 oz (207 ml) of water at 50°F (10°C).
14 oz (414 ml) of water at 70°F (21°C).
18 oz (532 ml) of water at 80°F (26°C).
28 oz (828 ml) of water at 90°F (32°C).
56 oz (1.65 L) of water at 100°F (38°C).

The moisture-holding capacity of air doubles with every 20°F (10°C) increase in temperature.

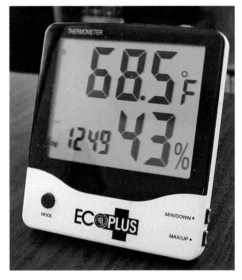

A maximum/minimum digital hygrometer registers the high and low humidity as well as current humidity.

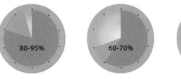

CUTTINGS 80-95% **VEGETATIVE** 60-70% **FLOWERING** 40-60%

This is the best relative humidity range for cuttings, as well as vegetative and flowering plants.

This air intake ducting has small holes that disperse fresh air throughout the garden.

easy to remove and catch ten ounces (0.3 L) of water in a 10 × 10 × 8-foot (21.5 m²) room when the temperature drops just 10°F (5°C).

A dehumidifier can be used anytime to help guard against fungus. Just set the dial to the desired percent humidity and presto, perfect humidity. Dehumidifiers are more complex, use more electricity than humidifiers, and cost more, but to gardeners with extreme humidity problems not yet cured by a vent fan, they are worth the added expense. The best prices on dehumidifiers have been found at Home Depot, Home Base, and other discount stores. Check the rental companies in the Yellow Pages for large dehumidifiers if only needed for a short time. Air conditioners also function as dehumidifiers but use a lot of electricity. The water collected from a dehumidifier or air conditioner has a very low EC and can be used to water plants.

Rooting cuttings thrive when the humidity is from 70 to 100 percent. Under arid conditions, the undeveloped root system is not able to supply water fast enough to keep cuttings alive. See "Taking Cuttings" for more specific information on humidity levels during different stages of propagation via cuttings.

the humidifier is able to evaporate enough water into the air. A humidifier is not necessary unless there is an extreme problem with the indoor garden drying out. Problems seldom occur that can be remedied by a humidifier. All too often, there is too much humidity in the air as a result of irrigation and transpiration. If a ventilation system is unable to remove enough air to lower humidity, a dehumidifier could be just the ticket!

A dehumidifier removes moisture in a room by condensing it from the air. Once the water is separated from the air, it is captured in a removable container. This container should be emptied daily. It is

CO_2 Enrichment

Carbon dioxide (CO_2) is a colorless, odorless, nonflammable gas that is around us all the time. The air we breathe contains 0.03–0.04 percent CO_2. Rapidly growing plants can use all of the available CO_2 in an enclosed indoor garden within a few hours. Photosynthesis and growth slow to a crawl when the CO_2 level falls below 0.02 percent.

Carbon dioxide enrichment has been used in commercial greenhouses for more than 35 years. Adding more CO_2 to indoor garden air stimulates growth. Indoor gardens have similar cultivation conditions to those in a greenhouse, and indoor gardeners apply the same principles. Plants can use more CO_2 than the 0.03–0.04 percent (300–400 ppm) that naturally occurs in the air. By increasing the amount of CO_2 to 0.12–0.15 percent (1200–1500 ppm)—the optimum amount widely agreed upon by professional gardeners—plants can grow up to 30 percent faster, providing that light, water, and nutrients are not limiting. Carbon dioxide enrichment has little or no affect on plants grown under fluorescent lights. Fluorescent tubes do not supply enough light for the plant to process the extra available CO_2.

Carbon dioxide can make people woozy when it rises above 5000 ppm and can become toxic at super high levels. When CO_2 rises to such high levels, there is always a lack of oxygen!

Carbon dioxide enrichment does not make plants produce stronger flavors or essential oils; it causes more foliage to grow in less time.

Carbon dioxide-enriched plants demand a higher level of maintenance than normal plants. Carbon dioxide-enriched plants use nutrients, water, and space faster than non-enriched plants. A higher temperature, from 75 to 80°F (24 to 26°C) will help stimulate more rapid metabolism within the super-enriched plants. When temperatures climb beyond 85°F (29°C), CO_2 enrichment becomes ineffective, and

at 90°F (32°C) growth stops.

Carbon dioxide-enriched plants use more water. Water rises from plant roots and is released into the air by the same stomata the plant uses to absorb CO_2 during transpiration. Carbon dioxide enrichment affects transpiration by causing the plants' stomata to partially close. This slows down the loss of water vapor into the air. Foliage on CO_2-enriched plants is measurably thicker, more turgid, and slower to wilt than leaves on non-enriched plants.

Carbon dioxide affects plant morphology. In an enriched growing environment, stems and branches grow faster, and the cells of these plant parts are more densely packed. Flower stems carry more weight without bending. Because of the increased rate of branching, plants have more flower initiation sites. Plants that sometimes do not bear from the first flower set are more likely to set flowers early if CO_2 enrichment is used.

With CO_2-enriched air, plants that do not have the support of the other critical elements for life will not benefit at all, and the CO_2 is wasted. The plant can be limited by just one of the critical factors. For example, the plants use water and nutrients a lot faster, and if they are not supplied, the plants will not grow. They might even be stunted.

To be most effective, the CO_2 level must be maintained at 1000 to 1500 ppm everywhere in the room. To accomplish this, the indoor garden must be completely enclosed. Cracks in and around the walls should be sealed off to prevent CO_2 from escaping. Enclosing the room makes it easier to control the CO_2 content of the air within. The room must also have a vent fan with flaps or a baffle. The vent fan will

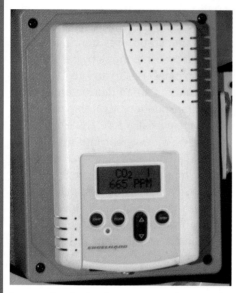

Inexpensive electronic components have made it possible for manufacturers to lower the price on CO_2 monitors.

change in the cylinder where the active ingredient reacts with the CO_2 in the air drawn through the cylinder. These kits are reliable to within 40 ppm.

Electrochemical sensing systems measure electrical conductivity of an air sample in either an alkali solution or distilled or deionized water. These systems are relatively inexpensive, but they have drawbacks: limited accuracy and sensitivity to temperature and air pollutants.

Infrared monitoring systems are more accurate and versatile. They correctly measure CO_2 and can be synchronized with controllers that operate heat, ventilation, and CO_2 generators. Even though the initial cost for a monitor is high, they can solve many CO_2 problems before they occur and can ensure optimum growing conditions. Specialty indoor garden stores sell the monitors for less than $1000.

Gardeners who do not want to spend the time and energy required to monitor CO_2 can use a set of scales and simple mathematics to determine the approximate amount of CO_2 in the air, but this calculation does not account for ventilation, air leaks, and other things that could skew the measurement. It is easier to measure the amount of CO_2 produced rather than to measure the amount of CO_2 in the indoor garden's atmosphere.

To measure the amount of fuel used, simply weigh the tank before it is turned on, use it for an hour, and then weigh it again. The difference in weight is the amount of gas or fuel used. See the calculations below for more information on calculating the amount of CO_2 in the room.

remove the stale air that will be replaced with CO_2-enriched air. The flaps or baffle will help contain the CO_2 in the enclosed indoor garden. Venting requirements will change with each type of CO_2-enrichment system and are discussed below.

Measuring CO_2

Measuring and monitoring CO_2 levels in the air is rather expensive and often unnecessary for small gardeners. Monitoring CO_2 levels in indoor gardens with ten or more lights really helps keep the levels consistent.

Disposable comparative colorimetry CO_2 test kits are easy to use, accurate, and inexpensive. The test kits contain a syringe and test tubes and sell for about $30. To use the kit, break off each end tip of the test tube, and insert one end into the closed syringe. Pull 100 cubic centimeters into the syringe, and note the blue color

Producing CO_2

There are many ways to raise the CO_2 content of an enclosed indoor garden. The two most popular ways are to disperse it from a tank or by burning a fuel to manufacture it. Carbon dioxide is one of the by-products of combustion. Gardeners can burn any fossil (carbon-based) fuel to produce CO_2 except for those containing sulfur dioxide and ethylene, which are harmful to plants.

Carbon dioxide gas is a by-product of fermentation and organic decomposition. The CO_2 level near the ground of a rain forest covered with decaying organic matter could be two to three times as high as normal, but bringing a compost pile inside to cook down is not practical.

Dry ice is made from frozen CO_2. The CO_2 is released when dry ice comes in contact with the atmosphere. It can get expensive and be a lot of trouble to keep a large room constantly supplied with dry ice. It is difficult to calculate how much CO_2 is released into the air by fermentation, decomposition, or dry ice without purchasing expensive equipment.

CO_2 Emitter Systems

Compressed CO_2 systems are virtually risk-free, producing no toxic gases, heat, or water. These systems are also precise, metering an exact amount of CO_2 into the room. Carbon dioxide is metered out of a cylinder of the compressed gas using a regulator, flow meter, a solenoid valve, and a short-range timer. Two types of systems are: continuous flow and short range.

Metal carbon dioxide cylinders that hold the gas under 1000 to 2200 pounds of pressure per square inch (psi) (depending upon temperature) can be purchased from welding or beverage supply stores. The cylinders are often available at hydroponics stores.

In North America, cylinders come in three sizes: 20, 35, and 50 pounds (9, 16,

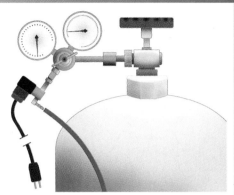

When open, the red on/off valve on top supplies compressed CO_2 via the regulator and flow meter. An electric solenoid valve controls the timed bursts of CO_2 gas.

and 23 kg) and average between $100 and $200, with refills costing about $30.

Tanks must be inspected annually and registered with a nationwide safety agency. Welding suppliers and beverage suppliers often require identification such as a driver's license. Most suppliers exchange tanks and refill them. Fire extinguisher companies and beverage supply companies normally fill CO_2 tanks on the spot. If you purchase a lighter and stronger aluminum tank, make sure to request an aluminum tank exchange. Remember, the tank you buy is not necessarily the one you keep.

To experiment before purchasing equipment, rent a 50-pound (23 kg) tank. A large 50-pound (23 kg) cylinder is heavier but saves you the time of returning to the store to have it refilled. When full, a 50-pound steel tank weighs 170 pounds (77 kg). A full 20-pound (9 kg) steel tank weighs 70 pounds (32 kg) and might be too heavy to carry up and down stairs. A full 20-pound (9 kg) aluminum tank weighs about 50 pounds (23 kg), and a full 35-pound (16 kg) tank weighs 75 pounds (34 kg).

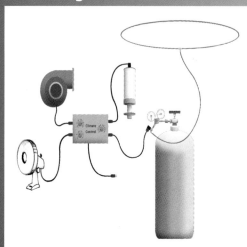

A setup consists of a tank of CO_2 gas, regulator, solenoid valve, and a flow meter.

Make sure CO_2 tanks have a protective collar on top to shield the valve. If the valve is knocked off by an accidental fall, there is enough pressure to send the top (regulator, flow meter, valve, etc.) straight through a parked car.

Buying a complete CO_2 emitter system at a hydroponics store is the best option for most small-scale indoor gardeners. These systems offer a good value. You can make your own system as described below, but such systems often cost more than the pre-manufactured models.

Welding suppliers also carry regulators, and flow meters. Flow meters reduce and control the cubic feet per hour (cfh). The regulator controls the psi. Models with smaller flow rates, 10 to 60 cfh, are preferable for gardening purposes. Buy a quality regulator-flow meter. Buy all components at the same time, and make sure they are compatible.

Carbon dioxide is very cold when released from a bottle where it has been kept under pressure. Even a quick blast can do damage to skin or eyes. If the flow rate is above 20 cfh, your regulator might freeze.

A regulator and flow valve are essential, but the solenoid valve and timer are optional. However, gardeners who do not use a solenoid valve and timer waste CO_2.

The solenoid valve and timer regulate the flow of CO_2. A solenoid valve is electrically operated and is used to start and stop the gas flow from the regulator and flow meter.

The least expensive timer is plastic and is commonly used for automatic sprinkler systems, but 240-, 115-, 24- and 12-volt systems are available. They cost about the same, but the lower voltages offer added safety from electrical shock. To automate the system, you need a short-range digital timer to open the solenoid valve for brief periods several times a day.

Control the exact amount of CO_2 released into the garden room by altering the flow and duration of CO_2. To determine how long the valve should remain open, divide the number of cubic feet of gas required by the flow rate. If the flow meter is set at 10 cfh, the valve will need to be open for 0.1 hours (1 divided by 10) or six minutes (0.1 hour $\times$ 60 minutes) to bring the room up to 1500 ppm. Remember, CO_2 leaks out of the indoor garden. On average, the CO_2 level of the room returns to 300 ppm in about three hours due to plant usage and room leakage. To maintain a steady level of CO_2, split the amount of CO_2 released per hour into two or four smaller increments dispersed more frequently.

Distribute the CO_2 from the tank to the indoor garden by using a tube or fan. Suspend lightweight perforated plastic from the ceiling to disperse the CO_2. The tubing carries CO_2 from the supply tank to the center of the indoor garden. The main supply line is attached to several smaller branches that extend throughout the garden. CO_2 is heavier and cooler than air and cascades onto the plants below.

To make sure CO_2 is evenly dispersed from the tubing, submerge lightweight plastic tubing in water and punch the emission holes under water while the CO_2 is being piped into the line. This way you know the proper diameter holes to punch and where to punch them to create the ideal CO_2 flow over the garden.

Overhead fans help distribute CO_2 evenly throughout the room. The CO_2 is released directly below the fan into its airflow. This evenly mixes the CO_2 throughout the air and keeps it recirculating across the plants.

Compressed CO_2 is expensive, especially in large indoor gardens. At roughly $0.50 per pound (450 gm), compressed gas is much more expensive than fuels used in generators. Cost of equipment and fuel make compressed CO_2 enrichment systems less economical than generators.

CO_2 Generator Systems

CO_2 generators are used by commercial flower, vegetable, and ornamental plant growers. Green Air Products has introduced a complete line of reasonably priced CO_2 generators that burn natural gas or LP (propane) to produce CO_2. However, heat and water are by-products of the combustion process. Generators use a pilot light with a flow meter and burner. The inside of the generator is similar to a gas stove burner with a pilot light enclosed in a protective housing. The generator must have a cover over the open flame. You can operate the generators manually or synchronize them with a

CO_2 generators produce carbon dioxide by burning LP or propane gas. They also generate heat and water vapor as by-products.

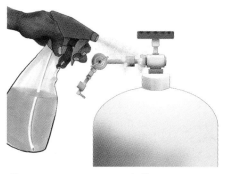

Spray soapy water around all propane gas connections to check for bubbles (leaks).

timer to operate with other indoor garden equipment such as ventilation fans.

CO_2 generators produce hot exhaust gases (CO_2 + H_2O). Even though CO_2 is heavier than air, it is hotter when generated and therefore less dense and rises in a garden room. You must have good air circulation for even distribution of CO_2.

Carbon dioxide generators can burn any fossil fuel—kerosene, propane, or natural gas. Low grades of kerosene can have sulfur content as high as 0.01 of 1 percent, enough to cause sulfur dioxide pollution. Use only high-quality kerosene

---

1 pound of CO_2 displaces 8.7 cubic feet (246 cm³) of CO_2.
0.3 pound (0.135 kg) of fuel produces 1 pound (454 gm) of CO_2.

Divide the total amount of CO_2 needed by 8.7 and multiply by 0.33 to determine the amount of fuel needed. If we need 1 cubic foot of CO_2 for an 800 cubic foot garden room:

$L \times W \times H$ = room volume (cubic feet)
$12 \times 14 \times 8 = 1344$ cubic feet (38 m³)

Desired CO_2 level is 1200 ppm (0.0012 ppm)*
Multiply room volume by 0.0012 = desired CO_2 level
1344 cubic feet (38 m³) $\times$ 0.0012 = 1.613 cubic feet (46 cm³) CO_2

1 pound (0.45 kg) of fuel burned = three pounds (1.35 kg) of CO_2 gas
0.33 pound (0.148 kg) fuel burned = one pound CO_2 gas

$0.33 \times 1.613 = 0.56$ pounds of CO_2 fuel to bring the CO_2 level to 1200 ppm.

Three times this amount ($0.53 \times 3 = 1.59$ pounds) of fuel will create enough CO_2 for the room for 12–18 hours.

Convert this into ounces by multiplying by 16 (there are 16 ounces in a pound).
$.037 \times 16 = 0.59$ ounces of fuel are needed for every injection.

Check out www.onlineconversion.com to convert to or from the English and Metric Systems.

---

even though it is expensive. Always use grade "1-K" kerosene. Maintenance costs for kerosene generators are high because they use electrodes, pumps, and fuel filters. For most indoor gardens, propane or natural gas burners are the best choice.

When filling a new propane tank, first empty it of the inert gas which is used to protect it from rust. Never completely fill a propane tank. Propane expands and contracts with temperature change and could release flammable gas from the pressure vent if too full.

Generators burn either propane or natu-ral gas, but must be set up for one or the other. They are inexpensive to maintain and do not use filters or pumps. Hobby CO_2 generators range from $300 to $500, depending on size.

The initial cost of a generator is slightly higher than a CO_2 emitter system that uses small, compressed-gas cylinders. Nonetheless, gardeners prefer propane and natural gas generators because they are about four times less expensive to operate than bottled CO_2 generators. One gallon of propane, which costs about $2, contains 36 cubic feet of gas and over 100 cubic feet of CO_2 (every cubic foot of propane gas produces three cubic feet of CO_2). For example, if a garden used one gallon of propane every day, the cost would be about $60 per month. In contrast, bottled CO_2 for the same room would cost more than $200 per month!

CO_2 generators are less expensive to maintain and less cumbersome, but they have disadvantages, too. One pound of fuel produces one and one-half pounds of water and 21,800 Btu's of heat. For indoor gardens less than 400 cubic feet, this makes generators unusable. Even for larger garden rooms, the added heat and humidity must be carefully monitored and controlled so as not to affect plants. Gardeners in warm climates do not use generators because they produce too much heat and humidity.

The Excellofizz puck is a low-cost product that releases CO_2 when it is bathed in water.

If fuel does not burn completely or cleanly, CO_2 generators can release toxic gases—including carbon monoxide (CO)—into the indoor garden. Nitrous oxide, also a by-product of burning propane, can grow to toxic levels, too. Well-made CO_2 generators have a pilot and timer. If leaks or problems are detected, the pilot and timer will turn off.

A CO_2 monitor is necessary if you are sensitive to high levels of the gas. Digital alarm units or color change plates (used in aircraft) are an economical alternative. Carbon monoxide is a deadly gas and can be detected with a carbon monoxide alarm available at most hardware and building supply stores.

Check homemade generators frequently, including kerosene or gas heaters. Propane and natural gas produce a blue flame when burning efficiently. A yellow flame indicates unburned gas (which creates carbon monoxide) and needs more oxygen to burn cleanly. Leaks in a system can be detected by applying a solution of equal parts water and concentrated dish soap to all connections. If bubbles appear, gas is leaking. Never use a leaky system.

Oxygen is also burned. As it becomes deficient in the room, the oxygen/fuel mixture changes. The flame burns too rich and yellows. This is why fresh air is essential.

Turn off CO_2 generators at night. They create excess heat and humidity in the indoor garden, and they need oxygen to operate. At night, roots need the extra oxygen in the room for continued growth.

If you are using CO_2 and the yield does not increase, check to make sure the entire indoor garden is running properly and that plants have the proper light and nutrient levels, as well as the correct temperature, humidity, grow-medium moisture, and pH. Make sure roots receive enough oxygen both day and night.

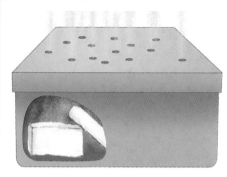

Put dry ice in a plastic container with holes to slow evaporation of CO_2 gas.

Other Ways to Make CO_2

There are many ways to make CO_2. You can enrich small areas by burning ethyl or methyl alcohol in a kerosene lamp. Norwegian scientists are studying charcoal burners as a source of CO_2. When refined, the system will combine the advantages of generators and compressed gas. Charcoal is much less expensive than bottled CO_2 and is less risky than generators in terms of toxic by-products. Others are studying the use of new technology to extract or filter CO_2 from the air.

A little inexpensive puck called Excellofizz (www.fearlessgardener.com) releases CO_2 into the atmosphere. It is simple to use; just add a few ounces of water and a puck or two to cause a chemical reaction that will disperse enough CO_2 to augment the air in a 10-foot-square (9 m²) room to about 1000 ppm all day. It also releases a eucalyptus fragrance. Make sure to keep the fizz contained, and if using an ozone generator, keep the lamp clean.

Compost and Organic Growing Mediums

Decomposing organic materials like wood chips, hay, leaves, and manures re-lease large amounts of CO_2. You can capture CO_2 from this decomposition, but it is most often impractical for indoor gardeners. Piping indoors the CO_2 and fumes from a compost pile is complicated, expensive, and more work than it is worth.

Fermentation

Some small-scale gardeners use fermentation to produce CO_2. Combine water, sugar, and yeast to produce CO_2. The yeast eats the sugar and releases CO_2 and alcohol as by-products. Gardeners who brew beer at home can use a small-scale system to increase the CO_2 levels in a room. Non-brewers can mix one cup of sugar, a packet of brewer's yeast, and three quarts of warm water in a gallon jug to make CO_2. You will have to experiment a little with the water temperature to get it right. Yeast dies in hot water and does not activate in cold water. Once the yeast is activated, CO_2 is released into the air in bursts. Punch a small hole in the cap of the jug, and place it in a warm spot (80–95°F [26–34°C]) in your indoor garden. Many gardeners buy a fermentation lock (available for under $10 at beer-brewing stores). Such locks prevent contaminants from entering the jug, and they bubble CO_2 through water so the rate of production can be observed. The hitch is that you must change the concoction up to three times a day. Pour out half the solution, and add one and one-half quarts (1.4 L) of water and another cup (24 cl) of sugar. As long as the yeast continues to grow and bubble, the mixture can last indefinitely. When the yeast starts to die, add another packet. This basic formula can be adapted to make smaller or larger-scale fermenters. Several jugs scattered around the garden room have a significant impact on CO_2 levels.

Fermentation is an inexpensive alternative to produce CO_2. It releases no heat, toxic gases, or water and uses no electricity. But because it stinks, it is unlikely that a gardener could tolerate a large-scale fermentation process. In addition, it is difficult to measure CO_2 production from this system, making it difficult to maintain uniform levels throughout the day.

Dry Ice

Dry ice gets very expensive with prolonged use. Two pounds of dry ice will raise the CO_2 level in a 10×10-foot ($3\ m^2$) indoor garden to about 2000 ppm for a 24-hour period. One chagrined gardener remarked, "I can't believe that stuff melts so fast."

Gardeners have long used large, insulated tanks filled with dry ice to add CO_2. Dry ice is carbon dioxide that has been chilled and compressed. As it melts, it changes from solid to gas. Gaseous CO_2 can be mixed into the air with fans that circulate it among the plants. Dry ice works well on a smaller scale without a tank and converter. It is readily available (check out the Yellow Pages) and inexpensive. Because CO_2 has no liquid stage, the transformation from solid to gas as the ice melts is clean and tidy. It's also easy to approximate the amount of CO_2 being released. A pound of dry ice is equal to a pound of liquid CO_2. Determining the thawing period for a particular size of dry ice will allow you to estimate how much CO_2 is released during a particular time period. To prolong the thawing process, put dry ice in insulating containers such as foam ice coolers, and cut holes in the top and sides to release the CO_2. The size and number of holes allow you to control the rate at which the block melts and releases CO_2.

Although a bit of a trick to keep going all the time, pouring vinegar on baking soda is a fair source of CO_2.

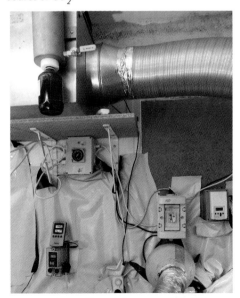

Some gardeners like to inject essential oils into their gardens. Such products are available in liquid, gel, and spray forms.

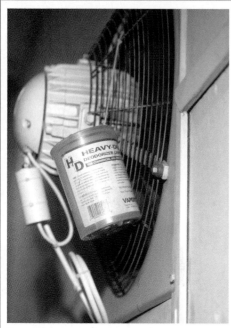

You can disperse pleasant-smelling essential oils into the garden with a fan.

Dry ice is economical and risk free; it releases no toxic gases, heat, or water. Although dry ice is easier to handle than compressed CO_2 tanks, it is difficult to store. The melting can be slowed through insulation, but it cannot be stopped. Because it is extremely cold, dry ice can also cause tissue damage or burn the skin after prolonged contact.

Baking Soda and Vinegar

Consider using vinegar and baking soda to produce CO_2 in a small indoor garden. This method eliminates excess heat and water-vapor production and requires only household items. Create a system that drips vinegar (acetic acid) into a bed of baking soda. The main disadvantage of this system is the erratic level of CO_2 produced. It takes a considerable amount of time for the CO_2 to build up to a level where it helps plants. However, once it reaches an optimal level, it can continue to rise until it reaches levels detrimental to plants. If you have time to experiment, it is possible to set up a drip system operated by a solenoid valve and a short-term timer. With such a system, CO_2 could be released periodically in small increments and coordinated with ventilation schedules.

Note: Some recipes replace vinegar with muriatic (hydrochloric) acid. I advise using vinegar, because hydrochloric acid is very dangerous. It can burn flesh, eyes, and respiratory system; it can even burn through concrete.

Negative Ion Generators

Negative ion generators are small and somewhat efficient to keep the garden fresh and control smoke, airborne pollen, mold, dust, and static electricity. They pump negative ions into the atmosphere. The negative ions are attracted to positive ions containing airborne pollutants. The negative ions attach to positive ions, and the pollutant becomes neutralized. The particles fall to the floor and create a fine

Ozone generators are rated by the number of cubic feet (m^3) they are able to treat.

covering of dust on the ground, walls, and objects in the room. These devices work fairly well for small indoor gardens with minimal odor problems. The generator uses very little electricity and plugs into a regular 115-volt current. Visually check the filter every few days, and make sure to keep it clean.

Ozone Generators

Ozone has many applications including food and water sterilization and removing pollutants from the air at the molecular level. Some gardeners even use high levels of ozone to exterminate indoor garden pests.

Ozone generators neutralize odors by converting oxygen (O_2) into ozone (O_3) by exposing the stinky air to ultraviolet (UV) light. The extra molecule is always a

The Air Tiger is a very popular ozone generator that is designed to fit inside ductwork.

positively charged ion that is predisposed to attach to a negatively charged ion (cation). Pollutants are negatively charged cations. When the extra oxygen ion attaches to the cation, they neutralize one another. Once the extra molecule is shed,

Mixing ozone-treated air for a minute or more allows O_3 to shed a molecule and become O_2.

O_3 is converted back into O_2. The chemistry takes a minute or longer to occur, so treated air must be held in a chamber to be converted effectively.

Ozone has an unusual odor similar to the smell of the air after a good rain. Anybody who has ever smelled the air in a room recently treated with ozone knows the smell and will never forget it. Make sure not to produce too much ozone, and give it enough time to mix with smelly air to neutralize odors.

There are many ozone generators available. When shopping for an ozone generator, look for one that has been on the market for a few years and has an established track record. Watch for important features such as self-cleaning (or easy to clean) and easy, safe bulb replacement. When UV light encounters moisture in the air, nitric acid is produced as a by-product. This white, powdery nitric acid collects around the lamps at connection points. This is an unpleasant, very corrosive acid that will severely burn skin and eyes. Verify that the ozone generator has proper safety features built in, such as a switch that turns off the lamp for maintenance, making it impossible to look at the retina-searing UV rays. Legal exposure for humans is about 0.1 ppm for a maximum of eight hours. Most indoor garden ozone generators produce about 0.05 ppm at timed intervals. See below for plant symptoms of ozone overdose.

UV light is very dangerous. In a flash, intense UV light can burn your skin and the retinas in your eyes beyond repair. Never, under any circumstances, look at the UV lamp in an ozone generator. Sneaking a peek at a UV lamp in an ozone generator has cost more than one aspiring gardener their eyesight! Ozone is also capable of burning your lungs. At low levels, there is no damage, but at higher levels, danger is imminent. Never, never use too much!

The Air Tiger™, manufactured by Rambridge, www.rambridge.com, is an excellent value for gardeners. It is one of the safest available and easy to maintain. A dead man's switch makes direct eye contact with the 10-inch-long UV light tube impossible. Highly corrosive ozone stays away from interior wiring, and little moisture can penetrate the outer shell to combine with O_3 to form powdery nitric acid.

Ozone generators are rated by the number of cubic feet (m^3) they are able to treat. (To figure cubic feet or meters, multiply the length × width × height of the room.) Some gardeners set up the ozone generator in the indoor garden and let it treat all the air in the room. They add a timer so the ozone generator intermittently disperses ozone into the room to maintain a relatively constant level. Once generated, ozone has a life of about 30 minutes. It takes a minute or two for the O_3 molecules to combine with oxygen to neutralize odors.

Ozone Damage

For best results, keep the ozone generator in another room or isolated from the growing plants. Ozone causes chlorotic spots on leaves. The mottled spots that

Ozone can severely damage foliage, as shown above.

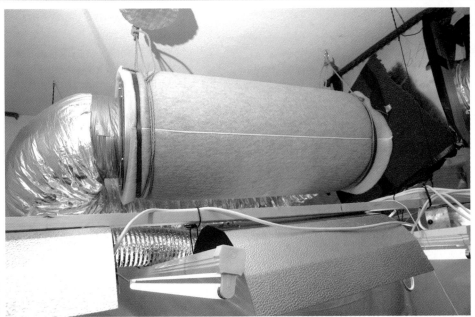

Charcoal filters remove fragrance and pollen from the air. The model shown above has a half-inch outer filter that encases porous ducting surrounded by activated charcoal. These filters are efficient until humidity climbs beyond 60 percent, at which point moisture-filled charcoal fails to absorb.

appear at first to be a Mg deficiency, increase in size and turn dark in the process. Most often, the symptoms are found on foliage near the generator. Leaves wither and drop, and overall plant growth slows to a crawl.

Activated Carbon Filters

Activated charcoal filters are fantastic, and they work! The charcoal is "activated" with oxygen, which opens millions of pores in the carbon. The activated charcoal absorbs pollutants in the air. The mechanics are simple, and there are three important things to remember when using a charcoal filter. First, keep room humidity below 55 percent. At about 65 to 70 percent relative humidity, the charcoal absorbs moisture and clogs. At 80 percent humidity, it stops removing odors. Second, air must move slowly through charcoal filters to

extract pollution. The fan on professional units lets just enough air through the filter so the pollutants have enough (dwell) time to be absorbed by the carbon filter. Third, use a pre-filter. The pre-filter catches most of the dust and airborne pollutants before they foul the carbon filter. Change the pre-filter regularly—every 60 days, or more often if the room is dusty. Carbon lasts about a year. Many gardeners prefer activated carbon made from coco. Do not use activated carbon that is "crushed." It is less efficient than charcoal pellets.

Install an intake screen that filters out large particles of dust to prolong the life of the activated charcoal filter. Whether the intake is passive or brought in by a fan, use a filter for incoming air to minimize pollutants in the indoor garden.

Check with filter manufacturers or retailers about venting specifications for your

Setting Up the Vent Fan – Step-by-Step

Step One: Figure the total volume of the indoor garden. Length × width × height = total volume. For example, an indoor garden that is 10 × 10 × 8 feet (21.5 m²) has a total volume of 800 cubic feet (10 × 10 × 8 feet = 800 cubic feet (21.5 m²). A room measuring 4 × 5 × 2 meters has a total volume of 40 cubic meters.

Step Two: Use a vent fan that will remove the total volume of air in the room in less than five minutes. Buy a fan that can easily be mounted on the wall or inline in a duct pipe. Quality inline fans move much air and make very little noise. It's worth spending the extra money on an inline fan. Small rooms can use a fan that can be attached to a flexible four-inch (12 cm) dryer hose. Many stores sell special ducting to connect high-speed squirrel cage fans with the four-inch (12 cm) ducting.

Step Three: Place the fan high on a wall or near the ceiling of the indoor garden so it vents off hot, humid air.

Step Four: If possible, cut a hole in the wall and secure the fan in place over the hole. Most locations require special installation. See: Steps five through nine.

Step Five: To place a fan in a window, cut a half-inch (1.5 mm) piece of plywood to fit the windowsill. Cover window with a lightproof, dark-colored paint or similar covering. Mount the fan near the top of the plywood so

Can carbon filters are available in many sizes and are a popular brand.

garden area. A more powerful exhaust fan will be necessary to draw an adequate volume of air through the activated charcoal filter. An adequate airflow is imperative to keep a high CO_2 content in the indoor garden air.

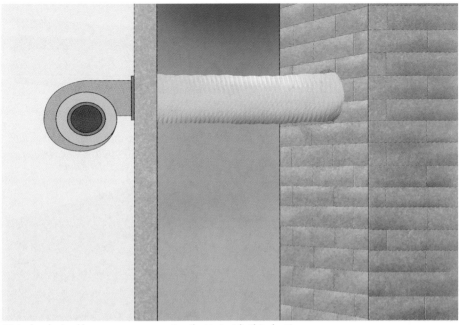

Air is deodorized by an ozone generator that is inside this ducting.

it vents air out the indoor garden. Secure the plywood and fan in the windowsill with sheetrock screws. Open the window from the bottom.

Step Six: Another option to make a lightproof vent is to use 4-inch (12 cm) flexible dryer ducting. Vent the hose outdoors and attach a small squirrel cage fan to the other end of the ducting. Make sure there is an airtight connection between the fan and hose by using a large hose clamp or duct tape. Stretch the flexible ducting so it is as smooth as possible inside. Irregular interior surfaces cause air turbulence and seriously diminish airflow.

Step Seven: Another option is to vent the air up the chimney or into the attic where light leakage and odor are seldom a problem. If using the chimney for a vent, first clean out the excess ash and creosote. Tie a chain to a rope. Lower the chain down the chimney, banging and knock-

ing all debris inside to the bottom. There should be a door at the bottom to remove the debris. This door is also used as the exhaust vent.

Step Eight: Attach the fan to a thermostat/humidistat or other temperature/humidity monitor/control device to vent hot, humid air outside. Set the temperature on 75°F (24°C) and the humidity on 55 percent in flowering rooms and 60 to 65 percent in vegetative rooms. Most control devices have wiring instructions. More sophisticated controllers have built-in electrical outlets, and the peripherals are simply plugged into them.

Step Nine: Or attach the vent fan to a timer and run it for a specific length of time. This is the method used with CO_2 enrichment. Set the fan to turn on and vent out used CO_2-depleted air just before new CO_2-rich air is injected.

Here is a charcoal filter without the outer dust filter. The inline fan adds extra suction to pull and push air through flexible ducting before it meets the extraction fan at the end of the duct.

This grower uses insulated ducting to dampen noise and vibrations caused by moving air.

A small fan placed in a window box removes smelly air 24 hours a day.

Turning air around a corner keeps indoor garden light from signaling passersby.

Aphids are big enough to see with the naked eye.
These frolicking bugs are what you'll get if you don't keep your garden clean.

Introduction

Insects, mites, and maggots slither into indoor gardens eating, reproducing, and wasting your beautiful plants. Outdoors, they live everywhere they can. Indoors, they live anywhere you let them. Fungi are present in the air at all times. They may be introduced by an infected plant or from air containing fungus spores. Fungi will settle down and grow if climatic conditions are right. Pests, fungi, and diseases can be prevented, but if allowed to grow unchecked, extreme control measures are often necessary to eradicate them.

Prevention

Cleanliness is the key to insect and fungus prevention. The indoor garden should be totally enclosed so the environment can be controlled easily. Keep the floor clean. Keep all debris off soil surface. Do not use mulch indoors. Insects and fungi like nice hideaway homes found in dirty, dank corners and under decaying leaves or rotting mulch.

Gardeners and their tools often transport microscopic pests, diseases, and fungi that could ultimately destroy the garden. This does not mean gardeners and their tools have to be hospital-clean every time they enter an indoor garden, even though that would be nice. It does mean normal and regular sanitary precautions must be taken. Gardeners who wear clean clothes and use clean tools reduce problems considerably. A separate set of indoor tools is easy to keep clean. Pests, diseases, and fungi habitually ride from plant to plant on dirty tools. Disinfect tools by dipping in rubbing alcohol or washing with soap and hot water after using them on each diseased plant. Another quick way to sterilize

pruners is with a hand-held torch. A quick heating with the torch will sterilize metal tools immediately.

Simple hygiene in the indoor garden keeps pests and diseases in check.

Dirty indoor gardens contribute to pest and disease problems.

Sweep the indoor garden floor every few days to avoid problems with pests and diseases.

Personal cleanliness is fundamental to preventing pests and diseases. Wash your hands before touching foliage and after handling diseased plants. Smart gardeners do not walk around the buggy outdoor garden and then visit the indoor garden. They do it vice versa. Think before entering the indoor garden and possibly contaminating it. Did you walk across a lawn covered with rust fungi or pet the dog that just came in from the garden outside? Did you just fondle your spider mite-infested split-leaf philodendron in the living room? Avoid such problems by washing your hands and changing shirt, pants, and shoes before entering an indoor garden.

Once a crop has been grown in potting soil or soilless mix, throw out the grow medium. Some gardeners brag about using the same old potting soil over and over, unaware that this savings is repaid with a diminished harvest. Used soil may harbor harmful pests and diseases that have developed immunity to sprays. Starting a new crop in new potting soil will cost more up front but will eliminate many potential problems. Used soil makes excellent outdoor garden soil.

Once potting soil is used, it loses much of the fluff in the texture, and compaction becomes a problem. Roots penetrate compacted soil slowly, and there is little room for oxygen, which restricts nutrient uptake. Used potting soil is depleted of nutrients. A plant with a slow start is a perfect target for disease, and, worst of all, it will yield less!

Companion planting helps discourage insects outdoors. Pests have nowhere to go indoors, so companion planting is not viable in indoor gardens.

Plant insect- and fungus-resistant varieties of fast-growing annuals and ornamental plants. If buying seeds from one of the many seed companies, always check for disease resistance. Choose healthy plants that you know are resistant to pests and diseases.

Keep plants healthy and growing fast at all times. Disease attacks sick plants first. Strong plants tend to grow faster than pests and diseases can spread.

Forced air circulation makes life miserable for pests and diseases. Pests hate wind because holding on to plants is difficult, and flight paths are haphazard. Fungal spores have little time to settle in a breeze and grow poorly on wind-dried soil, stems, and leaves.

Ventilation changes the humidity of a room quickly. In fact, a vent fan attached to a humidistat is often the most effective form of humidity control. Mold was a big problem in one indoor garden I visited. The room did not have a vent fan. Upon entering the enclosed room, the humid air was overpowering. It was terrible! The environment was so humid that roots grew from plant stems. The gardener installed a vent fan to suck out moist, stale air. The humidity dropped from nearly 100 percent to around 50 percent. The mold problem disappeared, and harvest volume increased.

Indoor horticulturists who practice all the preventative measures have fewer problems with pests and diseases. It is much easier to prevent the start of a disease than it is to wipe out an infestation. If pests and diseases are left unchecked, they can devastate the garden in a few short weeks.

Control

Sometimes, even when all preventative measures are taken, pests and diseases

Logical Progression of Insect Control

1. Prevention	2. Manual Removal
a. Cleanliness	a. Fingers
b. Use new soil	b. Sponge
c. One indoor set of tools	
d. Disease-resistant plants	3. Organic Sprays
e. Healthy plants	
f. Climate control	4. Natural Predators
g. No animals	
h. Companion planting	5. Chemicals

a few weeks. For example, if 100 microscopic munchers each lay 1000 eggs during their two weeks of life, and these eggs grow into adults, two weeks later 100,000 young adults would lay 100 eggs each. By the end of the month, there would be 100,000,000 pests attacking the infested garden. Imagine how many there would be in another two weeks!

Sprays often kill adults only. In general, sprays should be applied soon after eggs hatch so young adults are caught in their weakest stage of life. Very lightweight (low viscosity) horticultural oil spray works well alone or as an additive to help kill larvae and eggs.

The availability of some sprays can be seasonal, especially in areas that are more rural. Garden sections of stores are changed for the winter, but extra stock is sometimes kept in a storage room. Look for bargains on sprays at season-end sales. Today, there are many indoor gardening stores that carry pest and disease controls all year round.

still slink in and set up housekeeping. First, they establish a base on a weak, susceptible plant. Once set up, they launch an all-out assault on the rest of the garden. They move out in all directions from the infested base, taking over more and more space, until they have conquered the entire garden. An infestation can happen in a matter of days. Most insects lay thousands of eggs in short periods. These eggs hatch and grow into mature adults within

Common chemicals with their trade names and the insects they control:

Note: Do not apply these substances to edible plants

Generic Name	Purpose	Enter System
Griseofulvin	fungicide	systemic
Streptomycin	bactericide	systemic
Carbaryl	fungicide	systemic
Tetracycline	bactericide	semisynthetic (Terramycin®)
Nitrates	foliar fertilizers	systemic
Avid	insecticide	not truly systemic, actually translaminar
Pentac	miticide	systemic
Temik	insecticide	systemic
Neem	insecticide	systemic
Funginex	fungicide	systemic
Vitavax	fungicide	systemic
Orthene	insecticide	systemic

NOTE: This list is not all-inclusive. The basic rule is not to use systemic products.

EPA pesticide acute toxicity classification:

Class	LD50 to kill Rat Oral (mg kg-1)	LD50 to kill Rat Dermal (mg kg-1)	LD50 to kill Rat Inhaled (mg kg-1)	Eye Effects	Skin Effects
I	50 or less	200 or less	0.2 or less	corrosive opacity not reversible	corrosive
II	50–500	200–2000	0.2–2.0	corneal opacity reversible within 7 days, irritation persists for 7 days	severe irritation at 72 hours
III	500–5000	2000–20,000	2.0–20	no corneal opacity, irritation reversible within 7 days	moderate irritation at 72 hours
IV	> 5000	> 20, 000	> 20	no irritation	mild irritation

Natural Remedy Chart

Generic name Active ingredient	Form	Trade name	Toxicity precautions EPA Class
Bacillus species	G, D, WP	Bt, DiPel, M-Trak, Mattch, Javelin, etc.	IV
Copper sulfate	D, WP	Brsicop	III
Copper sulfate/lime	D, WP	Bordeaux mixture	III
Diatomaceous earth	D	Celite	IV
Neem	O, EL	Neem, Bioneem	IV
Nicotine sulfate	L, D	Black Leaf 40	II
Oil, dormant horticultural	O	Sunspray	IV
Pyrethrins	A, L, WP	Many trade names	III, IV
Quassia	WP	Bitterwood	IV
Rotenone	D, WP, EC	Derris, Cubé	II, III
Ryania	D, WP	Dyan 50	IV
Sabadilla	D	Red Devil	IV
Soap, insecticidal	L	M-Pede, Safer's	IV
Sodium bicarbonate	P	Baking soda	IV
Sodium hypochlorite	L	Bleach	II, III
Sulfur	D, WP	Cosan	V

Legend

A - Aerosol
D - Dust
EL - Emulsifiable Liquid

L - Liquid
WP - Wettable Powder
O - Oil
G - Glandular

Insect Control

Indoor gardeners have many options to control insects and fungi. Prevention and cleanliness are at the top of the control list. A logical progression to pest and disease control is outlined in the chart on this page. (Note that it begins with cleanliness!)

Manual removal is just what the name implies—smashing all pests and their eggs in sight between the thumb and forefinger or between two sponges.

I like natural/organic sprays such as pyrethrum and neem. I use harsh chemicals only as a last resort. Any spray, no matter how benign, always seems to slow plant growth a little. Stomata become clogged when foliage is sprayed and covered with a filmy residue. Stomata stay plugged up until the spray wears off or is washed off. Stronger sprays are often more phytotoxic, burning foliage. Spray plants as little as possible and avoid spraying for two weeks before harvest. Read all labels thoroughly before use.

Use only contact sprays approved for edible plants. Avoid spraying seedlings and tender, unrooted cuttings. Wait until cuttings are rooted and seedlings are at least a month old before spraying.

Sprays and Traps
Chemical Fungicides, Insecticides, and Miticides

I do not recommend using chemical fungicides, fungistats, insecticides, or miticides on plants destined for human consumption. Most contact sprays that do not enter the plant system are approved for edible fruits and vegetables. However, there are numerous ways to control fungi, diseases, and pests without resorting to chemicals. On the previous page is a chart of common chemicals with their trade names and the insects they control.

Spreader-Sticker for Pesticides

Spreader-stickers improve and promote wetting and increase sticking and absorption through foliage. Spreader-sticker products increase effectiveness of fertilizers, fungicides, insecticides, etc. They are especially important to use when plants develop a waxy coating. Spreader-stickers also impair insects' respiration mechanisms and function as pesticides. One of my favorite spreader-stickers is Coco-Wet from Spray-N-Grow.

Abamectin

Ingredients: Abamectin derivatives include emamectin and milbemectin. Does not bioaccumulate. Used extensively on hops. Abamectin is not truly systemic. It is absorbed from the exterior of foliage to other leaf parts, especially young leaves, in the process of translaminar activity.

Controls: Russet and spider mites, fire ants, leaf miners, and nematodes.

Mixing: Dilute in water. Mix one-fourth teaspoon (0.125 cl) per gallon (3.8 L). Use a wetting agent.

Application: Spray. Works best when temperature is above 70°F (21°C). Repeat applications every seven to ten days.

Persistence: One day.

Forms: Liquid.

Toxicity: Toxic to mammals, fish, and honeybees in high concentrations. Sucking insects are subject to control, while beneficials are not hurt.

Safety: Wear gloves, mask, and safety glasses.

Bacillus thuringiensis (Bt) and other *Bacillus* species

Ingredients: *Bacillus thuringiensis* (Bt) is the best known of several bacteria that are fatal to caterpillars, larvae, and maggots.

Caterpillars, larvae, and maggots all eat Bt bacteria, which can be applied as a spray, dust, or granules. Inject liquid Bt into stalks to kill borers. Shortly after they ingest it, their appetite is ruined, and they stop eating. Within a few days, they shrivel up and die; cabbage loopers, cabbageworms, corn earworms, cutworms, gypsy moth larvae, and hornworms are controlled. Commercial Bt products do not reproduce within insect bodies, so several applications may be necessary to control an infestation. Microbial Bt bacteria are nontoxic to animals (humans), beneficial insects, and plants; however, some people do develop an allergic reaction. Commercial Bt products do not contain living Bt bacteria, but the Bt toxin is extremely perishable. Keep within prescribed temperature range, and apply according to the directions. Most effective on young caterpillars, larvae, and maggots, so apply as soon as they are spotted.

Get the most out of Bt applications by adding a UV inhibitor, spreader-sticker, and a feeding stimulant such as Entice®, Konsume®, or Pheast®. Bt is completely broken down by UV light in one to three days.

B. thuringiensis var. *kurstaki* (Btk)—introduced on the market in the early 1960s—is the most popular Bt. Toxic to many moth and caterpillar larvae including most of the species that feed on flowers and vegetables. Sold under many trade names DiPel®, Bio-Bit®, Javelin®, etc., Btk is also available in a microencapsulated form, M-Trak®, Mattch®, etc. The encapsulation extends the effective life on foliage to more than a week.

B. thuringiensis var. *aizawai* (Bta) is effective against hard-to-kill budworms, borers, armyworms, and pests that have built up a resistance to Btk.

B. thuringiensis var. *israelensis* (Bt-i) is effective against the larvae of mosquitoes, blackflies, and fungus gnats. Look for Gnatrol®, Vectobac®, and Bacrimos®. All are lethal to larvae. Adults do not feed on plants and are not affected. Fungus gnats can cause root problems including rot. Use Bt-i to get rid of them as soon as they are identified.

B. thuringiensis var. *morrisoni* is a new strain of Bt under development for insect larvae with a high pH in their guts.

B. thuringiensis var. *san diego* (Btsd) targets the larvae of Colorado potato beetles and elm beetle adults and other leaf beetles.

B. thuringiensis var. *tenebrionis* (Btt) is lethal to Colorado potato beetle larvae.

B. cereus helps control damping-off and root-knot fungus. It flourishes in water-saturated mediums and promotes beneficial fungus that attacks the diseases.

B. subtilis is a soil-dwelling bacterium that curbs *Fusarium*, *Pythium*, and *Rhizoctonia* that cause damping-off. It is commercially available under the brand names Epic®, Kodiac®, Rhizo-Plus®, Serenade®, etc. Soak seeds and apply as a soil-drench.

B. popilliae colonize larvae and grub bodies that consume it, causing them to turn milky-white before dying. It is often called milky spore disease. It is most effective against Japanese beetle grubs.

Baking Soda

Ingredients: Sodium bicarbonate.

Controls: Powdery mildew.

Caution: Baking soda kills fungus by changing the pH of foliage surface. It functions as a fungistat—not as a fungicide—that eradicates the organisms.

Mixing: Saturate in water.

Application: Spray or dust foliage.

Persistence: One to three days.

Forms: Powder.

Toxicity: None to mammals, fish, or beneficials.

Safety: Wear a mask to avoid inhaling dust.

Bleach, laundry

Ingredients: Sodium hypochlorite.

Controls: Numerous bacteria and fungi.

Caution: Avoid skin contact and inhalation. Concentrate burns skin and stains clothes.

Mixing: Dilute five- or ten-percent solution with water.

Application: Use as a disinfectant on containers, walls, tools, etc.

Persistence: Evaporates with little residual in a couple of days.

Forms: Liquid.

Toxicity: Toxic to fish, beneficials, and humans if swallowed or gets in eyes.

Safety: Wear a mask and gloves when handling concentrate. Avoid skin contact and respiration.

Bordeaux mixture

Ingredients: Water, sulfur, copper (copper sulfate) and lime (calcium hydroxide).

Controls: Most often used as a foliar fungicide. Also, controls bacteria and fends off other insects.

Caution: Phytotoxic when applied to tender seedlings or foliage in cool and humid conditions.

Mixing: Apply immediately after preparing.

Application: Agitate the mixture often while spraying so ingredients do not settle out.

Persistence: Until it is washed from foliage.

Forms: Powder and liquid.

Toxicity: Not toxic to humans and animals, but somewhat toxic to honeybees and very toxic to fish.

Safety: Wear a mask, gloves, and long sleeves.

Boric acid

Ingredients: Available in the form of borax hand soap and dust.

Controls: Lethal as a contact or stomach poison. Kills earwigs, roaches, crickets, and ants.

Caution: Phytotoxic when applied to foliage.

Mixing: Mix borax soap in equal parts with powdered sugar to make toxic bait.

Application: Set bait out on soil near base of plants.

Persistence: Avoid getting bait wet, as it disperses rapidly.

Forms: Powder.

Toxicity: Not toxic to honeybees or birds.

Safety: Avoid breathing dust.

Bug Bombs

Ingredients: Often bug bombs are packed with very strong insecticides and miticides, including synthetic pyrethrins that exterminate every pest in the room. They were developed to kill fleas, roaches, and their eggs that hide in furniture and in carpets.

Controls: According to most bug bomb labels, they kill everything in the room!

Caution: Use only as a last resort and follow the label's instructions to the letter.

Mixing: None.

Application: Place the bug bomb in the empty room. Turn it on and then leave the room.

Persistence: Low residual. Persistence is limited to a day or two.

Forms: Aerosol.

Toxicity: Read label for details.

Safety: Wear a mask and gloves. Cover exposed skin and hair. Leave the room.

Copper

Ingredients: The compounds—copper sulfate, copper oxychloride, cupric hydroxide, and cuprous oxide—are common forms of fixed copper used as a fungicide and are less phytotoxic than unfixed (pure) copper.

Controls: Gray mold, foliar fungus, anthracnose, blights, mildews, and a number of bacterial diseases.

Caution: Easy to overapply and burn foliage or create a copper excess in plant.

Mixing: Apply immediately after preparing.

Application: Agitate the mixture often while spraying, so ingredients do not settle out. Preferred temperature range for application is 65–85°F (18–29°C).

Persistence: Lasts two weeks or longer indoors, if not washed off.

Forms: Powder and liquid.

Toxicity: Toxic to fish. Not toxic to birds, bees, or mammals.

Safety: Wear a mask and gloves. Cover exposed skin and hair.

Diatomaceous Earth (DE)

Ingredients: Naturally occurring DE includes fossilized silica shell, remains of the tiny one-celled or colonial creatures called diatoms. It also contains 14 trace minerals in a chelated (available) form.

Controls: Although not registered as a pesticide or fungicide, DE abrades the waxy coating on pest shells and skin, including aphids and slugs, causing body fluids to leak out. Once ingested, the razor-sharp particles in DE rip tiny holes in the pest's guts, causing death.

Caution: Do not use swimming pool diatomaceous earth. Chemically treated and heated, it contains crystalline silica that is very hazardous if inhaled. The body is unable to dissolve the crystalline form of silica that causes chronic irritation.

Mixing: No mixing required when used as a dust. Mixing required when used as spray. Apply as a powder or encircle slug-damaged plants and use as a barrier.

Application: Apply this spray to infestations caused by pest insects.

Persistence: Stays on foliage for a few days or until washed off.

Forms: Powder.

Toxicity: Earthworms, animals, humans, and birds can digest diatomaceous earth with no ill effects. Avoid contact with skin and eyes.

Safety: Wear a protective mask and goggles when handling this fine powder to guard against respiratory and eye irritations.

Homemade Pest and Disease Sprays

Ingredients: A strong hot taste, smelly odor, and a desiccating powder or liquid are the main ingredients in home-pesticide and fungicide potions. See the chart on next page.

Controls: Homemade sprays discourage and control pests including aphids, thrips, spider mites, scale, and many others.

Gardening Indoors

Recipes and Controls Chart

Ingredients:

Alcohol: Use isopropyl (rubbing). Add to sprays to dry out pests.

Bleach: Use a five-percent solution as a general disinfectant.

Cinnamon: Dilute cinnamon oil with water. Use just a few drops per pint as pesticide.

Citrus: Citrus oils make great ingredients that kill insects dead.

Garlic: Use a garlic press to squeeze garlic juice into mix. Use liberal amounts.

Horseradish: Stinky stuff! Add as you would garlic. Best to use fresh root.

Hot pepper: Dilute Tabasco® or any store-bought concentrate in water.

Hydrated lime: Saturate in water to form a fungicide.

Mint: Mint oil drives insects away. Dilute in water, measure several drops per pint.

Oil, vegetable: is comprised mainly of fatty acids and glycerides. Mix with rubbing alcohol to emulsify in water. Great stuff!

Oregano: Grind up fresh herb and use as a repellent. Mix with water.

Soap: I like Ivory® or Castille® soap. Use as an insecticide and wetting agent. Mix with water.

Tobacco: Mix tobacco with hot water to extract the poisonous alkaloid. Do not boil. Dilute concentrate with water.

Precautions:

Cooking or heating preparations can destroy active ingredients. To draw out (extract) ingredients, mince plant and soak in mineral oil for a couple of days. Add this oil to the water including a little detergent or soap to emulsify the oil droplets in water. Biodegradable detergents and soaps are good wetting-sticking agents for these preparations. Soap dissolves best if a teaspoon (0.75 cl) of alcohol is also added to each quart (0.9 L) of mix.

Chrysanthemum, marigold, and nasturtium blossoms; pennyroyal; garlic; chive; onion; hot pepper; insect juice (target insects mixed in a blender); horseradish; mint; oregano; tomato; and tobacco residues all will repel many insects including aphids, caterpillars, mites, and whiteflies.

Spray made from pests ground up in a blender and emulsified in water will reputedly repel related pests. Best used on large pests! The insecticidal qualities in the dead bug parts will degrade quickly if combined with other things; do not include insects mixed in a blender with other ingredients besides water. Mixes that include tobacco may kill these pests if it is strong enough. These mixes can vary in proportions, but always filter the blended slurry before mixing with water for the final spray. Straining avoids clogging spray nozzles and plumbing.

Recipe 1. Mix three tablespoons (4.5 cl) each of isopropyl alcohol, lemon juice, garlic juice, horseradish juice, Ivory liquid, and a few drops of Tabasco®, mint, and cinnamon oil. Mix all of the ingredients in a small bowl into a slurry. Dilute the slurry at the rate of one teaspoon (0.5 cl per 47 cl) per pint of water and mix in a blender. Potent mix!

Recipe 2. Place one teaspoon (0.5 cl) of hot pepper or Tabasco® sauce and four cloves of garlic in a blender with a pint of water and liquefy, then strain through a nylon stocking or cheesecloth before using in the sprayer.

Recipe 3. A mix of one-eighth to one-quarter cup (3-6 cl) of hydrated lime combined with a quart (0.9 L) of water makes an effective insect and mite spray. Mix a non-detergent soap with lime. The soap acts as both a sticking agent and insecticide. Lime can be phytotoxic to plants in large doses. Always try the spray on a test plant and wait a few days to check for adverse effects to the plant before applying to similar plants.

Recipe 4. Liquid laundry bleach—sodium hypochlorite—is a good fungicide for non-plant surfaces. Mix as a 5- or 10-percent solution. It is an eye and skin irritant, so wear gloves and goggles when using it. Mix 1 part bleach to 9 parts water for a 5-percent solution. Mix one part to four parts water for a 10-percent solution. Use this solution as a general disinfectant for indoor garden equipment, tools, and plant wounds. The bleach solution breaks down rapidly and has little, if any, residual effect.

Caution: Be careful when testing a new spray. Apply it to a single plant and wait for a few days to learn the outcome before applying to all plants.

Mixing: Make spray concentrates by mixing repellent substances with a little water in a blender. Strain the resulting slurry concentrate through a nylon stocking or fine cheesecloth before being diluted with water for application.

Application: Spray foliage until it drips from both sides of leaves.

Persistence: A few days.

Forms: Liquid.

Toxicity: Usually not toxic to humans in dosages lethal to pests.

Safety: Wear a mask and gloves. Cover skin and hair. Avoid contact with eyes, nose, lips, and ears.

Neem

Ingredients: Relatively new in the USA, neem has been used for medicine and pest control for more than four centuries in India and Southeast Asia. Extracted from the Indian neem tree, *Azadirachta indica*, or the chinaberry tree, *Melia azedarach*, neem is an antifeedant and disrupts insect life cycles. The trees are known as the "village pharmacy" because they supply cures for humans and animals as well as safely control countless pests and fungi. Neem powder is made from leaves. The active ingredient, azadirachtin, confuses growth hormones, and pests never mature into adults to produce more young. It is most effective against young insects and is available in various concentrations. It also contains N-P-K and trace elements.

Controls: Most effective against caterpillars and other immature insects including larvae of whiteflies, fungus gnats, mealybugs, and leaf miners.

Caution: Neem is not as effective against spider mites as neem oil.

Mixing: Often mixed with vegetable (canola) oil. Mix just before using in water with a pH below 7, and use a spreader-sticker. Agitate constantly while using to keep emulsified. Throw out excess.

Homemade sprays can be made by blending water, lemon, vegetable oil, and garlic.

Application: Use as a soil-drench or add to the nutrient solution. This allows neem to enter into the plant's tissue and become systemic. Used as a spray, neem becomes a contact spray and an antifeedant when eaten by pests. Performs best in rooms with 60 percent plus humidity.

Persistence: Contact neem stays on foliage for up to a month or until it is washed off. Stays in plant system up to a month when absorbed via roots.

Forms: Emulsifiable concentrate.

Toxicity: Not toxic to honeybees, fish, and earthworms. Not toxic to beneficial insects in normal concentrations that kill target insects.

Safety: Irritates eyes; wear a mask and gloves.

Neem Oil

Ingredients: Purified extract from neem seeds. Do not use heat-processed neem oil. Buy only cold-pressed oil that is stronger and contains all the natural ingredients. Cold-pressed oil also contains azadirachtin, the active ingredient in neem. Brand names include Neemguard®, Triact®, and Einstein Oil®. NOTE: Einstein Oil works the best of all brands tested.

Controls: Effective against spider mites, fungus gnats, and aphids. It is also a fungistat against powdery mildew and rust.

Caution: Neem oil is very effective against spider mites.

Mixing: Mix just before using in water with a pH below 7, and use a spreader-sticker. Agitate constantly while using to keep emulsified. Throw out excess.

Application: Spray on foliage, especially under leaves, where mites live. Apply every few days so hatching larvae will eat it immediately. Spray heavily so mites have little choice but to eat it. Avoid spraying the last few days before harvest. Some gardeners report a foul taste in produce when applied just before harvest.

Persistence: Contact neem stays on foliage for up to a month or until it is washed off. Stays in plant system up to a month when absorbed via roots.

Forms: Emulsifiable concentrate.

Toxicity: Toxicity to beneficial insects has been reported. Not toxic to humans.

Safety: Irritates eyes; wear a mask and gloves.

Neem products have numerous other applications. For more information check out the Neem Foundation (www.neemfoundation.org), and www.einsteinoil.com, or *Neem: India's Miraculous Healing Plant*, by Ellen Norten, ISBN: 0-89281-837-9.

Nicotine and Tobacco Sprays

Ingredients: Nicotine is a nonpersistent pesticide derived from tobacco, *Nicotiana tabacum*. It is a stomach poison, contact poison, and respiratory poison. This very poisonous compound affects the neuromuscular system, causing pests to go into convulsions and die. Nicotine sulfate is the most common form.

Caution: Do not swallow any of this vile poison, and avoid skin contact. Do not use around nightshade family—eggplants, tomatoes, peppers and potatoes—because they may contract Tobacco Mosaic Virus (TMV) from exposure to tobacco-based substances.

Controls: Sucking and chewing insects.

Mixing: Use a spreader-sticker.

Application: Seldom phytotoxic when used as directed. Combine with insecticidal soap to increase killing ability.

Persistence: One week to ten days.

Forms: Liquid.

Toxicity: Although naturally derived, nico-

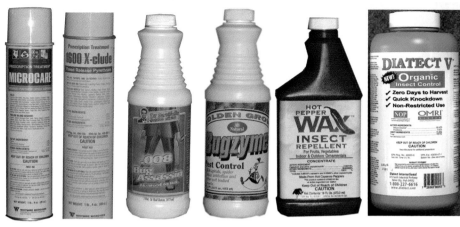

Here are some of the most popular miticides and insecticides available. One of my favorites is X-clude because it is so effective against spider mites.

tine is very toxic to most insects (including beneficials), honeybees, fish, and humans. If concentrate is ingested or built up over years, humans may develop lung cancer and other cancers.

Safety: Wear a mask and gloves; avoid skin and eye contact.

Oil, horticultural

Ingredients: Often underrated and overlooked as an insecticide and miticide, horticultural oil is very popular in greenhouses and is regaining popularity among indoor gardeners. Similar to medicinal mineral oil, horticultural oils are made from animal (fish) oils, plant seed oils, and petroleum oils refined by removing most of the portion that is toxic to plants. Lighter weight oil (viscosity 60–70) is less phytotoxic. Vegetable oil is also horticultural oil.

Controls: Virtually invisible horticultural oil kills slow moving and immobile sucking insects, spider mites, and their eggs by smothering, as well as generally impairing their life cycle.

Caution: Do not use lubricating oils such as 3-in-1 or motor oil!

Mixing: Mix three-fourths of a teaspoon (0.75 cl) of oil spray—no more than a one percent solution—per quart (0.9 L) of water. More than a few drops could burn tender, growing shoots.

Application: Spray foliage entirely, including under the surface of the leaves. Apply oil sprays until two weeks before harvest. Repeat applications as needed. Usually three applications—one every five to ten days—will put insects and mites in check. Lightweight-oil residue evaporates into the air in a short time.

Persistence: Disappears in one to three days, under normal growing conditions.

Forms: Liquid.

Toxicity: Safe, nonpoisonous, and nonpolluting insecticide. Can become phytotoxic if too heavy (viscosity), if applied too heavily, or when temperatures are below 70°F (21°C) or very humid; this slows evaporation, increasing phytotoxicity.

Safety: Wear a mask and gloves.

Oil, vegetable

Ingredients: Fatty acids and glycerides.

Controls: Lightweight vegetable oil kills slow-moving and immobile sucking insects, spider mites, and their eggs by smothering as well as generally interrupting their life cycles.

Caution: Vegetable oil does not kill as well as horticultural oil.

Mixing: Mix two drops of oil spray—no more than a one-percent solution—per quart of water.

Application: Spray foliage entirely, including under surface of leaves. Stop spraying two weeks before harvest.

Persistence: Several days.

Forms: Liquid.

Toxicity: Not toxic to mammals or fish.

Safety: Wear a mask and gloves.

Pyrethrum

Ingredients: Pyrethrum, the best-known botanical pesticide, is extracted from the flowers of the pyrethrum chrysanthemum, *Chrysanthemum coccineum* and *C. cinerariifoliu*. Pyrethrins—pyrethrins, cinerins, and jasmolins—are the active ingredients in natural pyrethrum and kill insects on contact. Pyrethrum is often combined with rotenone or ryania to ensure effectiveness. Aerosol forms contain synergists. (See "Application" below.)

Controls: A broad-spectrum contact pesticide, pyrethrum kills aphids, whiteflies, spider mites, and insects, including beneficials. It is very effective to control flying insects, but they must receive a killing knockdown dose, or they may revive and buzz off.

Caution: Do not mix with sulfur, lime, copper, or soaps. The high pH of these substances renders it ineffective. Wash these substances off foliage with plain water (pH below 7) before applying pyrethrum.

Mixing: Mix in water with a pH below 7 and use a spreader-sticker.

Application: Spot-spray infested plants. Aerosol sprays are most effective, especially on spider mites. This can burn foliage—spray is ice-cold when it exits the nozzle—if applied closer than one foot. Aerosol sprays contains a synergist, piperonyl butoxide (PBO) or MGK 264. Both are toxic to people. Pyrethrum dissipates within a few hours in the presence of air, HID light, and sunlight. Overcome this limitation by applying just before turning off the lights, air circulation, and vent fans for the night. One manufacturer, Whitmire®, offers encapsulated pyrethrum in aerosol form called X-clude®. As the spray fogs out of the nozzle, a bubble forms around each droplet of pyrethrum mist. The outside coating keeps the pyrethrum intact and extends its life for several days. When a pest prances by touching the bubble, it bursts, releasing the pyrethrum. Liquid and wettable pyrethrum applied with a pump-type sprayer are difficult to apply under leaves where spider mites live.

Persistence: Effective several hours after application when the lights are on, longer when applied after lights are out and the fan is turned off.

Forms: Wettable powder, dust, liquid,

granular bait, and aerosol.

Toxicity: Not toxic to animals and humans when eaten but becomes toxic to people when inhaled. It is toxic to fish and beneficials.

Safety: Wear a mask and protective clothing when applying spray or breathing in any form of pyrethrum, especially aerosols. Aerosols contain toxic PBO and MGK 464—possible carcinogens—which are easily inhaled.

Synthetic Pyrethroids

Ingredients: Synthetic pyrethroids such as permethrin and cypermethrin act as broad-spectrum, nonselective contact insecticides and miticides. There are more than 30 synthetic pyrethroids available in different formulations. Deltamethrin is available as a sticky paint that is used as a trap when applied to stems and colored objects. Other pyrethroids include Allethrin, cyflutrin, fenpropathin, phenothrin, sumithrin, resmitherin, and tefluthrin.

Controls: Aphids, whiteflies, thrips, beetles, cockroaches, caterpillars, and spider mites. NOTE: Many insects and mites are resistant to pyrethroids.

Caution: Nonselective pyrethroids kill all insects and mites including beneficials and bees.

Mixing: Follow directions on container.

Application: Follow directions on container. (See "Application" under "Pyrethrum" above.)

Persistence: Breaks down in one to three days. Newer pyrethroids such as Permethrin stay active the longest.

Forms: Powder, liquid, aerosol.

Toxicity: Toxic to all insects. It is somewhat toxic to mammals.

Safety: Wear a mask and protective clothing when applying sprays or breathing in any form of pyrethrum, especially aerosols. Aerosols contain toxic PBO and MGK 464—possible carcinogens—which are easily inhaled.

Quassia

Ingredients: Quassia is made from a subtropical South American tree, *Quassia amara*, and the tree-of-heaven, *Ailanthus altissima*.

Controls: Soft-bodied insects including aphids, leaf miners, and some caterpillars.

Mixing: Available in the form of bark, wood chips and shavings. Soak six ounces (18 cl) of chips per gallon (0.9 L) of water for 24 hours. Afterward, boil for two hours. Add a potassium-based soap to increase effectiveness. Strain and cool before spraying.

Application: Spray on foliage until saturated.

Persistence: Two to five days on the surface of plants.

Forms: Bark, wood chips and shavings.

Toxicity: Safe for mammals and (possibly) beneficials.

Safety: Wear a mask and gloves.

Rotenone

Ingredients: Rotenone is an extract of roots of several plants including *Derris* species, *Lonchocarpus* species, and *Tephrosia* species. This poison is a nonselective con-

tact insecticide, stomach poison, and slow-acting nerve poison.

Controls: Nonselective control of beetles, caterpillars, flies, mosquitoes, thrips, weevils, and beneficial insects, but death is slow.

Caution: Kills beneficials. New evidence indicates rotenone may be toxic to people and may cause Parkinson's disease. Use only as a last resort!

Mixing: Follow directions on the package.

Application: Follow directions on the package.

Persistence: Breaks down in three to ten days.

Forms: Powder, wettable powder, liquid.

Toxicity: The effect on mammals is undetermined. Chronic exposure may cause Parkinson's. It is toxic to birds, fish, and beneficials.

Safety: Wear a mask and gloves. Cover exposed skin and hair. Avoid skin contact.

Ryania

Ingredients: This contact-alkaloid stomach poison is made from stems and roots of the tropical shrub, *Ryania speciosa*.

Controls: Toxic to aphids, thrips, European corn borers, hemp borers, flea beetles, leaf rollers, and many caterpillars. Once pests consume ryania, they stop feeding immediately and die within 24 hours.

Caution: Somewhat toxic to beneficials and mammals!

Mixing: Follow directions on package.

Application: Follow directions on package. Apply as dust.

Persistence: Two weeks or longer.

Forms: Powder, wettable powder.

Toxicity: Toxic to mammals, birds, fish, and beneficials.

Safety: Wear a mask, gloves, and safety glasses. Cover exposed skin and hair. Avoid skin contact.

Sabadilla

Ingredients: This alkaloid pesticide is made from the seeds of a tropical lily, *Schoenocaulon officinale*, native to Central and South America, and a European hellebore, *Veratrum album*.

Controls: A contact and stomach poison, this centuries-old poison controls aphids, beetles, cabbage loopers, chinch bugs, grasshoppers, and squash bugs.

Caution: Very toxic to honeybees and moderately toxic to mammals!

Mixing: Follow directions on package.

Application: Most potent when applied at 75–80°F. Follow directions on package.

Persistence: Two or three days.

Forms: Powder, liquid.

Toxicity: Somewhat toxic to mammals; toxic to honeybees.

Safety: Wear a mask, gloves, and safety glasses. Cover exposed skin and hair. Avoid skin, eye, ear, and nose contact. Irritates eyes and nose.

Seaweed

Ingredients: Numerous elements including nutrients, bacteria, and hormones.

Controls: Suspended particles in seaweed

impair and even kill insects and spider mites by causing lesions. The particles cut and penetrate the soft-bodied pest insects and mites causing their body fluids to leak out.

Mixing: Dilute as per instructions for soil application.

Application: Spray on foliage, especially under leaves where mites live.

Persistence: Up to two weeks when spreader-sticker is used.

Forms: Powder and liquid.

Toxicity: Not toxic to mammals, birds, or fish. Nonselective; kills beneficials.

Safety: Wear a mask and gloves.

Soap, insecticidal

Ingredients: Mild contact insecticides made from fatty acids of animals and plants. A variety of soaps are available in potassium salt-based liquid concentrates. Soft soaps such as Ivory liquid dish soap, Castille soap, and Murphy's Oil soap are biodegradable and kill insects in a similar manner to commercial insecticidal soaps, but they are not as potent or effective.

Controls: Controls soft-bodied insects such as aphids and mealybugs, spider mites, thrips, and whiteflies by penetrating and clogging body membranes.

Caution: Do not use detergent soaps; they may be caustic.

Mixing: Add a few capfuls of soap to a quart of water to make a spray. Ivory or Castille soap can also be used as a spreader-sticker to mix with other sprays. The soaps help the spray stick to the foliage better.

Application: Spray at the first appearance of insect pests. Follow directions on commercial preparations. Spray homemade mixes every four to five days.

Persistence: Soft soaps will last only for

about a day before dissipating.

Forms: Liquid.

Toxicity: These soaps are safe for bees, animals, and humans.

Safety: Wear a mask and gloves.

Sulfur

Ingredients: Sulfur. Mixed with lime, sulfur is more toxic to insects but more phytotoxic to plants.

Controls: Centuries-old fungicide is effective against rusts and powdery mildew.

Caution: Do not apply in temperatures above 90°F (32°C) and less than 50 percent humidity. It will burn foliage.

Mixing: Follow directions on package.

Application: Apply in light concentration. It is phytotoxic during hot, 90°F, arid weather.

Persistence: It stays on foliage until washed off.

Forms: Powder.

Toxicity: Not toxic to honeybees, birds, and fish.

Safety: Wear a mask, gloves, and safety goggles. Cover exposed skin and hair. Avoid skin, eye, ear, and nose contact. Irritates eyes, lungs, and skin.

Traps

Ingredients: Sticky traps, such as Tanglefoot resins, can be smeared on attractive yellow or red cards to simulate ripe fruit. When the pests land on the fruit, they are

edges of pots, base of stems, and at the end of drying lines to form an impenetrable barrier-trap against mites and insects. This simple precaution helps keep mites isolated. However, resourceful spider mites can spin a web above the barrier. The marauding mites also ride the air currents created by fans from plant to plant!

Persistence: It is persistent until it is wiped off or completely fouled with insect bodies.

Forms: Sticky, thick paint.

Toxicity: Not toxic to mammals or insects. Trapped insects and mites starve to death.

Safety: Wear gloves.

Water

Ingredients: A cold jet of water—preferably with a pH between 6 and 7—blasts insects, spider mites, and their eggs off leaves and often kills them. Hot water vapor and steam also work as a sterilant.

Controls: A cold jet of water is an excellent first wave of attack against spider mites, aphids, and other sucking insects. Steam controls spider mites, insects, and diseases on pots, growing medium, and other indoor garden surfaces.

Caution: Avoid spraying fully formed flowers with water. Standing water in or on flowers promotes gray mold. Do not apply hot steam to foliage.

Mixing: None.

Application: Spray leaf undersides with a jet of cold water to knock off sucking spider mites and aphids. Apply water as a mist or spray when predatory mites are present. The extra-humid conditions impair the pest mite life cycles and promote predatory mite health. Rent a wallpaper steamer. Get it cooking, and direct a jet

stuck forever!

Controls: Helps contain spider mites and nonflying insects within the bounds of the barriers. Monitors fungus gnat populations and helps control thrips. Other insects get stuck haphazardly to the sticky stuff.

Blacklight traps catch egg-laying moths and other flying insects, most of which are not plant pests. Light and fan traps attract many insects including beneficials, and their use may do more harm than good.

Sex-lure traps exude specific insect pheromones, sexual scents, of females that are ready to mate. These traps are most effective to monitor insect populations for large farms.

Caution: Do not touch sticky substance. It is difficult to remove!

Mixing: Follow directions on container. Smear on desired objects.

Application: Smear Tanglefoot around the

of steam at all indoor garden cracks and surfaces.

Persistence: None.

Forms: Liquid, steam vapor.

Toxicity: Not toxic to mammals, fish, or beneficials.

Safety: Do not spray strong jet of water in eyes, up nose, or into other body orifices.

Biological Controls
Predators and Parasites

Predator and parasite availability and supply have changed substantially over the last ten years. Today, many more predators and parasites are available to home gardeners than ever before. Shipping, care, cost, and application of each predator or parasite are very specific and should be provided in detail by the supplier. Make sure the supplier answers the following questions:

1) Latin name of the predator so there is no confusion as to identity.

2) Specific pests attacked.

3) Life cycle.

4) Preferred climate including temperature and humidity range.

5) Application rate and mode of application.

For more information about predators check out the following web sites:

www.naturescontrol.com

www.koppert.nl/

www.entomology.wisc.edu/mbcn/mbcn.html

By definition, a predator must eat more than one victim before adulthood. Predators, such as ladybugs (ladybird beetles) and praying mantises, have chewing mouthparts. Other predators, such as lacewing larvae, have piercing-sucking

Progressive Control Measures
for Spider Mites

Cleanliness - Clean room daily, disinfect tools, do not introduce new pests into the garden on clothes, no animal visits, etc.

Create hostile environment - Humidity, temperature, water spray.

Create barriers - Smear Tanglefoot™ around pot lips, stems, drying lines.

Dip cuttings and vegetative plants - Dip small plants in pyrethrum, horticultural oil, neem oil.

Remove damaged foliage - Remove foliage more than 50 percent damaged.

Introduce predatory mites - Release predators before infestations grow out of hand.

Spray - Apply pyrethrum or neem oil; use strong miticides only if necessary. Rotate sprays so mites do not develop immunity.

Frolicking ladybugs reproducing gleefully indoors. These bugs are good predators and eat lots of bad bugs.

mouthparts. Chewing predators eat their prey whole. The piercing-sucking type suck the fluids from their prey's body.

Parasites consume a single individual host before adulthood. Adult parasitoids typically place a single egg into many hosts. The egg hatches into larvae that eat the host insect from the inside out. They save the vital organs for dessert! Most often, the larvae pupate inside the host's body and emerge as adults.

Parasites, unlike predators, hunt until the prey is almost eliminated. Predators choose to be surrounded by prey. When prey population starts to diminish a little, predators move on to find a nice, fat infestation. They never truly eradicate the pests. This is why predators work best for preventative control but are slow to stop an infestation.

The rate at which the predators and parasites keep the infestation in check is directly proportionate to the amount of predators. The more predators and parasites, the sooner they will get infestations into check. Predators and parasites outbreed their victims, reproducing faster than pests are able to keep up with.

One of the best places in the country to buy predatory and parasitoid insects is Nature's Control, Medford, Oregon. This supplier gives advice and supplies specific care and release instructions. Nature's Control has a good predator and parasite supply and can ship year round. Predators and parasites are shipped special delivery and may arrive after the daily-mail delivery. Make sure to pick them up as soon as they arrive. Do not let predators sit inside a mailbox in the hot sun. It could easily reach 120°F (49°C) or more!

When predators and parasites are introduced into a garden, special precautions must be taken to ensure their well-being.

Chemical Insecticides and Miticides

Chemical	Trade Name*	Notes
abamectin	Avid®	Produced by soil fungi, *Streptomyces* species
dienochlor	Pentac®	Slow-acting but selective against mites
aldicarb	Temik®	Systemic miticide DO NOT USE
methomyl	Subdue®	Systemic insecticide DO NOT USE
dicofol	Kelthane®	Selective miticide, DDT relative, DO NOT USE
acephate	Orthene®	Systemic miticide/ insecticide, DO NOT USE

*All trade names are not included. Check insecticides and miticides for chemical name.

Stop spraying all toxic chemicals at least two weeks before introducing the predators. Pyrethrum and insecticidal soaps can be applied up to a few days before, providing any residue is washed off with fresh water. Do not spray after releasing predators and parasites.

Predators and parasites survive best in gardens that are not sterilized between crops. Gardens with perpetual harvests are ideal for predators.

Most of the predators and parasites that do well in an indoor HID garden cannot fly. Insects that can fly often head straight for the lamp. Ladybugs are the best example. If 500 ladybugs are released on Monday, by Friday, only a few diehards will be left. The rest will have popped off the lamp. If using flying predators or parasitoids, release when it is dark. They will live longer.

Predators are most often very small and must be introduced to each plant separately. Introducing predators to a garden and plants takes a little time and patience. Predators also have very specific climatic requirements. Pay attention to the predators' needs and maintain them for best results.

Spider Mites and Insects

Here is one of the best web sites I have found that describes insects. They have excellent photos of all pests and predators that attack annual flowers and vegetables: http://vegipm.tamu.edu/.

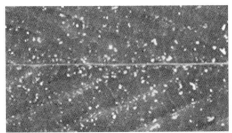

Spider mites cause stippling, small spots, on the top of leaves.

Spider Mites

Identify: The spider mite is the most common pest found on indoor plants and causes the most problems. Spider mites have eight legs and are classified as spiders rather than insects, which have six legs. Find microscopic spider mites on leaf undersides sucking away life-giving fluids. To an untrained naked eye, they are hard to spot. Spider mites appear as tiny specks on leaf undersides; however, their telltale signs of feeding—yellowish-white spots, stippling—on the tops of leaves are easy to see. Careful inspection reveals tiny spider webs—easily seen when misted with water—on stems and under leaves as infestations progress. A magnifying glass or low-power microscope (10–30X) helps to identify the yellow-white, two-spotted brown or red mites and their translucent eggs. Indoors, the most common is the two-spotted spider mite. After a single mating, females are fertilized for life and reproduce about 75 percent female and 25 percent male eggs. Females lay about 100 eggs.

Damage: Mites suck life-giving sap from plants, causing overall vigor loss and stunting. Leaves are pocked with suck-hole marks and yellow from failure to produce chlorophyll. They lose partial to full function, and leaves turn yellow and drop. Once a plant is overrun with spider mites, the infestation progresses rapidly. Severe cases cause plant death.

Controls: Cleanliness! This is the all-important first step to spider mite control. Keep the indoor garden and tools spotless and disinfected. Older plants often have spider mites. Spray susceptible plants regularly with miticides, including once three days before taking cuttings. Once mite infestations get out of control and miticides work poorly, the entire indoor garden will have to be cleaned out and disinfected with a pesticide and five-percent bleach solution. Steam disinfection is also possible but too difficult in most situations.

Cultural and Physical Control: Spider mites thrive in a dry, 70–80°F (21–27°C) climate and reproduce every five days in temperatures above 80°F (27°C). Create a hostile environment by lowering the temperature to 60°F (16°C) and spray foliage, especially under leaves, with a jet of cold water. Spraying literally blasts them off the leaves as well as increases humidity. Their reproductive cycle will be slowed, and you will have a chance to kill them before they do much damage. Manual removal works for small populations. Smash all mites in sight between the thumb and index finger, or wash leaves individually in between two sponges. Avoid infecting other plants with contaminated hands or sponges.

Remove and safely dispose of leaves with more than 50 percent damage, making sure insects and eggs do not reenter the garden. If mites have attacked only one or two plants, isolate the infected plants and treat them separately. When removing foliage, take care not to spread mites to other plants. Severely damaged plants should be carefully removed from the garden and destroyed.

Keep relative humidity below 50 percent to discourage spider mites.

If plants are infested with spider mites, lower the temperature to 60-70°F (10-21°C). This temperature range will slow their reproduction.

Smear a layer of Tanglefoot™ around the lips of containers and at the base of stems to create barriers spider mites cannot cross. This will help isolate them to spe-cific plants. Note: to contain spider mites, smear a layer of Tanglefoot™ at each end of drying lines when hanging herbs to dry. Once foliage is dead, mites try to migrate down drying lines to find live foliage with fresh, flowing sap.

Biological: *Neoseiulus (Amblyseius) californicus* and *Mesoseiulus (phytoseiulus) longipes*, are the two most common and effective predators. *Phytoseiulus persimilis, Neoseiulus (Amblyseius) fallacius, Galendromus (Metaseiulus) occidentalis*, and *Galendromus (Typhlodromus) pyri* predators are also available commercially.

When properly applied and reared, predatory spider mites work very well. There are many things to consider when using the predators. First, predators can eat only a limited number of mites a day; the average predator can eat 20 eggs or five adults daily. As soon as the predators' source of food is gone, some mites die of starvation while others survive on other insects or pollen. Check with suppliers for release instructions of specific species. A general dosage of 20 predators per plant is a good place to start. Predatory mites have a difficult time traveling from plant to plant, so setting them out on each plant is necessary. Temperature and humidity must be at the proper levels to give predators the best possible chance to thrive. When spider mites have infested a garden, the predatory mites cannot eat them fast enough to solve the problem. Predatory mites work best when there are only a few spider mites. Introduce predators as soon as spider mites are seen on vegetative growth, and release them every month thereafter. This gives predators a chance to keep up with mites. Before releasing predators, rinse all plants thoroughly to ensure all toxic spray residues from insecticides and fungicides are gone.

The fungus, *Hirsutella thompsonii*, trade name Mycar®, kills spider mites.

Sprays: Homemade sprays often lack the strength to kill infestations but work as a deterrent by repelling mites. Popular homemade sprays include Dr. Bonner's Soap, garlic, hot pepper, citrus oil, and liquid seaweed combinations. If these sprays do not deter spider mites after four to five applications, switch to a stronger spray: neem oil, pyrethrum, horticultural oil, or nicotine sulfate cinnamaldehyde.

Insecticidal soap does a fair job of controlling mites. Usually two or three applications at five- to ten-day intervals will do the trick.

Horticultural oil smothers eggs and can be mixed with pyrethrum and homemade sprays to improve extermination.

Pyrethrum (aerosol) is the best natural miticide! Spider mites should be gone after two or three applications at five- to ten-day intervals, providing sanitary preventative conditions are maintained. Eggs hatch in five to ten days. The second spraying will kill the newly hatched eggs and the remaining adults. The third and subsequent applications will kill any new spider mites, but mites soon develop a resistance to synthetic pyrethrum.

Neem oil works great!

Heavy-duty chemical miticides are available but are not recommended on plants that will be consumed by humans. If using any chemical miticide, be sure it is a contact poison and not systemic. Use StirrupM®, described below, to improve the spider mite kill rate. Cinnamaldehyde extracted from *Cinnamonum zeylanicum* kills mites. The synthetic hormone—sold under the brand name StirrupM®—attracts spider mites and is used very successfully to enhance miticides.

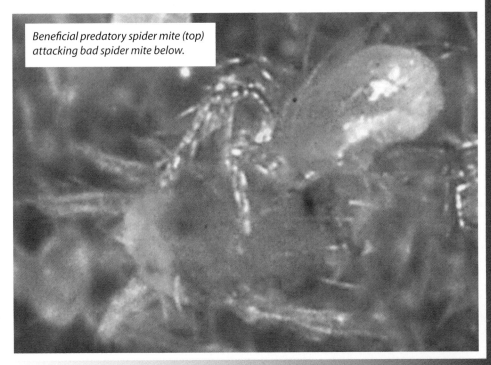

Beneficial predatory spider mite (top) attacking bad spider mite below.

Aphids

Identify: Aphids, also called plant lice, are about the size of a pinhead. They are easy to spot with the naked eye, but use a 10X magnifying glass for positive identification. Aphids are found in all climates. Normally grayish to black, aphids can be green to pink—in any color, aphids attack plants. Most aphids have no wings, but those that do have wings about four times the size of their bodies. Aphids give birth to mainly live female larvae without mating and can pump out three to 100 hungry larvae every day. Each female reproduces between 40 and 100 offspring that start reproducing soon after birth. Aphids are most common indoors when they are plentiful outdoors. Install yellow sticky traps near base of several plants and near the tops of other plants to monitor invasions of winged aphids, often the first to enter the garden. As they feed, aphids exude sticky honeydew that attracts ants that feed on it. Ants like honeydew so much that they take the aphids hostage and make them produce honeydew. Look for columns of ants marching around plants, and you will find aphids.

Damage: Aphids suck the life-giving sap from foliage causing leaves to wilt and yellow. When infestation mounts, you may notice sticky honeydew excreted by aphids. They prefer to attack weak, stressed plants. Some species prefer succulent, new growth, and other aphids like older foliage or even flower buds. Look for them under leaves, huddled around branch nodes, and growing tips. This pest transports (vectors) bacterium, fungi, and viruses. Aphids vector more viruses than any other source. Destructive sooty mold also grows on honeydew. Any aphid control must also control ants, if they are present.

Controls: Manually remove small numbers. Spot-spray small infestations, and control ants. Introduce predators if problem is persistent.

Cultural and Physical Control: Manual removal is easy and works well to kill aphids. When affixed to foliage—sucking out fluid—aphids are unable to move and easy to crush with fingers or sponges dipped in an insecticidal solution.

Biological: Lacewings, *Chrysoperla* species, are the most effective and available predators for aphids. Release one to 20 lacewings per plant, depending on infestation level, as soon as aphids appear. Repeat every month. Eggs take a few days to hatch into larvae that exterminate aphids. Gall-midge, *Aphidoletes aphidimyz*, is available under the trade name Aphidend. Parasitic wasp, *Aphidius matricaria*, is available commercially as Aphidpar.

Ladybugs also work well to exterminate aphids. Adults are easily obtained at many retail nurseries during the summer months. The only drawback to ladybugs is their attraction to the HID lamp—release about 50 ladybugs per plant, and at least half of them will fly directly into the HID, hit the hot bulb, and buzz to their death. Within one or two weeks, all the ladybugs will fall victim to the lamp, requiring frequent replenishment.

Verticillium lecanii (fungus), available under the trade name Vertalec®, is aphid-specific and very effective.

Control ants by mixing borax hand soap or borax powder with powdered sugar. Ants eat the sweet mix and borax kills them. They excrete sweet borax mix in the nest where other ants eat the feces and die.

Sprays: Homemade and insecticidal soap sprays are very effective. Apply two or three times at five- to ten-day intervals. Pyrethrum (aerosol) applied two to three times at five- to ten-day intervals.

Bees and Wasps

Identify: Bees and wasps that sting are usually from one-half inch (1.5 cm) to more than an inch (3 cm) long. Most have yellow stripes around their bodies, but others have none. They are especially attracted to indoor gardens when weather cools outdoors—they move right in.

Damage: They cause no damage to plants but can become a nuisance in indoor gardens and hurt like hell when they sting.

Controls: Occasionally a problem indoors, bees and wasps are most efficiently controlled with sprays.

Cultural and Physical Control: Bees enter indoor gardens through vents and cracks, attracted by the growing plants, a valuable commodity in the middle of a cold winter! Screen all entrances to the room. Install more circulation fans to make flying difficult. Wasp traps, sweet flypaper, and Tanglefoot impair these pests. Bees and wasps are also attracted to the hot HID and fly into it and die.

Biological: Unnecessary.

Sprays: Pyrethrum is recommended. Stuff small nests into a wide-mouthed jar—do it at night when the wasps are quiet—and place the jar in a freezer for a few hours. Use Sevin, Carbaryl, only if there is a problem with a wasp nest.

Beetle Borers

Identify: Larvae from several boring beetles tunnel or bore into stems and roots. Look for their entry hole and dead growth on either side of the entry hole along the main stem, often discolored and accompanied by sawdust. Borers are more common outdoors than indoors.

Small handheld sprayers are convenient and economical.

Damage: Tunnels inside the stem and roots, curtailing fluid flow and causing plant parts to wilt. If borers damage the main stem severely, fluid flow to the entire plant could stop, causing death.

Controls: Seldom a problem indoors. Borers often cause so much damage on a particular stem that it has to be removed and destroyed.

Cultural and Physical Control: Handpick all beetle grubs.

Biological: Several mixes of beneficial nematodes control these borers in soil.

Sprays: *Bacillus popilliae* is specific to beetles or rotenone individually injected into stems.

Distinguish loopers by their two sets of feet and curious arched movement.

Caterpillars and Loopers

Caterpillars and loopers leave plenty of droppings on the plant. The droppings accumulate in foliage and fall out when the foliage is removed; inspect below to find the droppings.

Identify: From half-inch to four inches long, (1.5–10 cm), caterpillars and loopers are cylindrical with feet. They are often green but can be virtually any color from white to black. Caterpillars have sets of feet the entire length of the body, while loopers have two sets of feet at either end of the body. Loopers place their front feet forward, arch their body upward in the middle, and pull their rear sets of legs forward. Some have stripes, spots, and other designs. Seldom a problem indoors, caterpillars and loopers are in a life stage—between a larva and a flying moth or butterfly—and are most common when prevalent outdoors. One way to check for caterpillars and loopers is to spray one plant with pyrethrum aerosol spray and shake the plant afterward. The spray has a quick knockout effect, and most caterpillars will fall from the plant.

Damage: These munching critters chew and eat pieces of foliage and leave telltale bites in leaves. Some caterpillars will roll themselves inside leaves. An infestation of caterpillars or leafhoppers will damage foliage and slow growth, eventually defoliating, stunting, and killing a plant.

Cultural and Physical Control: Manually remove.

Biological: *Trichogramma* wasps, spined soldier bug (*Podisus maculiventris* Podibug®).

Sprays: Homemade spray/repellent, hot pepper and garlic. Bt, pyrethrum, and rotenone.

Leafhoppers

Identify: Leafhoppers include many small, 0.125 inch (3 mm) long, wedge-shaped insects that are usually green, white, or yellow. Many species have minute stripes on wings and bodies. Their wings peak like roof rafters when not in use. Leafhoppers suck plant sap for food and exude sticky honeydew as a by-product. Spittlebug and leafhopper larvae wrap themselves in foliage and envelop themselves in a saliva-like liquid plant sap.

Damage: Stippling (spotting) similar to that caused by spider mites and thrips on foliage. Leaves and plant lose vigor, and in severe cases, death could result.

Cultural and Physical Control: Cleanliness! Blacklight traps are attractive to potato beetles.

Biological: The fungus, *Metarhizium anisopliae*, is commercially available under the trade name Metaquino®.

Sprays: Pyrethrum, rotenone, sabadilla.

Leaf Miner

Identify: Adult leaf miner flies lay eggs that hatch into eighth-inch (0.25 mm) long green or black maggots. You seldom see the maggots before you see the leaf damage they create when they tunnel through leaf tissue. Leaf miners are more common in greenhouses and outdoors than indoors.

Damage: The tiny maggots burrow between leaf surfaces, leaving a telltale whitish-tunnel outline. The damage usually occurs on or in young supple growth. It is seldom fatal unless left unchecked. Damage causes plant growth to slow, and if left unchecked, flowering is prolonged and fruit is small. In rare cases, the damage is fatal. Wound damage encourages disease.

Controls: These pests cause little problem to indoor crops. The most efficient and effective control is to remove and dispose of damaged foliage, which includes the rogue maggot, or to use the cultural and physical control listed below.

Cultural and Physical Control: Smash the little maggot trapped within the leaf with your fingers. If the infestation is severe, smash all larvae possible and remove severely infested leaves. Compost or burn infested leaves. Install yellow sticky traps to capture adults.

Larger pump-up sprayers are efficient for larger gardens.

Biological: Branchid Wasp (*Dacnusa sibirica*), chalcid wasp (*Diglyphus isaea*), parasitic wasp (*Opius pallipes*).

Sprays: Repel with neem oil and pyrethrum sprays. Maggots are protected within tunnels, and sprays are often ineffective. Water plants with a 0.5 percent solution of neem; this solution works fast and stays on plants for four weeks after application.

Fungus Gnat

Identify: Maggots, larvae, grow to four or five millimeters long and have translucent bodies with black heads. Winged adult gnats are gray to black, two to four millimeters long, with long legs. Look for them around the base of plants in soil and soilless gardens. They love the moist, dank environment in rockwool and the environment created in NFT-type hydroponic gardens. Adult females lay about 200 eggs every week to ten days.

Damage: Infests growing medium and roots near the surface. They eat fine root

Microscopic fungus gnats appear as small black specs on roots.

Controls: The easiest way to control these pests is with Vectobac®, Gnatrol®, and Bactimos®, all contain *Bacillus thuringiensis* var. *israelensis* (Bt-i). This strain of Bt controls the maggots; unfortunately, it is available only in large one-gallon (3.8 L) containers. Difficult to find at garden centers, check hydroponics stores.

Cultural and Physical Control: Do not overwater, and keep ambient humidity low. Do not let growing medium remain soggy. Cover growing medium so green algae won't grow. Yellow sticky traps placed horizontally one to two inches (3–6 cm) over growing medium catch adults.

Biological: The aforementioned Bt-i works best. Alternatives include the predatory soil mite (*Hypoaspis* (Geolaelapumites) and the nematode (*Steinernema feltiae*).

Sprays: Apply neem or insecticidal soap as a soil-drench.

Mealybugs and Scales

Mealybugs

hairs and scar larger roots, causing plants to lose vigor and foliage to pale. Root wounds invite wilt fungi such as *Fusarium* or *Pythium* especially if plants are nutrient-stressed and growing in soggy conditions. Maggots prefer to consume dead or decaying, soggy plant material; they also eat green algae growing in soggy conditions. Adults and larvae can get out of control quickly, especially in hydroponic systems with very moist growing mediums. A fun trick is to hold a yellow sticky trap above infested grow medium and watch them stick to it!

Identify: Somewhat common indoors, these 0.08–0.2 inch (2–7 mm) oblong, waxy-white insects move very little, mature slowly, and live in colonies that are usually located at stem joints. Like aphids, mealybugs excrete sticky honeydew.

Close up look at scale.

As uncommon indoors as mealybugs, scale looks and acts similar to mealybugs but is usually more round than oblong. Scales may be white, yellow, brown, gray, or black. Their hard protective shell is 0.08–0.15 inch (2–4 mm) across. Mealybugs rarely or never move. Check for them around stem joints where they live in colonies. Scales sometimes excrete sticky honeydew.

Damage: These pests suck sap from plants, causing growth to slow. They also exude sticky honeydew as a by-product of their diet of plant sap, which encourages sooty mold and draws ants that eat the honeydew.

Controls: These pests present little problem to indoor gardeners. The easiest and most efficient control is listed under "Cultural and Physical Control" below.

Cultural and Physical Control: Manual removal is somewhat tedious but very effective. Wet a Q-Tip in rubbing alcohol and wash scale away. A small knife, fingernails, or tweezers may also be necessary to scrape and pluck the tightly affixed mealybugs and scales after they are Q-Tipped with alcohol.

Biological: There are numerous species of mealybugs and scales. Each has natural predators including species of ladybeetles (ladybugs) and parasitic and predatory wasps. There are so many species of each that it would be exhaustive to list them here.

Sprays: Homemade sprays that contain rubbing alcohol, nicotine, and soaps all kill these pests. Insecticidal soap, pyrethrum, and neem oil are all recommended.

Nematodes

Identify: Of the hundreds and thousands of species of microscopic nematodes—big ones are sometimes called eelworms—a few are destructive to plants. Most often nematodes attack roots and are found in the soil; however, a few nematodes attack stems and foliage. Root nematodes can be seen in and around roots with the help of a 30X microscope. Gardeners often diagnose from damage caused by destructive nematodes rather than actually seeing them.

Damage: Slow growth, leaf chlorosis, wilting several hours during daylight period from lack of fluid flow—symptoms can be difficult to discern from nitrogen deficiency. Root damage is often severe by the time they are examined. Root-knot nematodes are some of the worst. They cause roots to swell with galls. Other nematodes scrape and cut roots, compounded by fungal attacks. Roots turn soft and mushy.

Cultural and Physical Control: Cleanliness! Use new, sterilized potting soil or soilless mix to exclude nematodes. Nematodes rarely cause problems in clean indoor gardens.

Biological: French marigolds, *Tagetes patula*, repel soil nematodes. Fungus (*Myrothecium verrucaria*, trade name DeTera ES®)

Sprays: Neem used as a soil-drench.

Logical Progression of Fungus Control
Prevention
Cleanliness
Low humidity
Ventilation
Removal
Copper, lime sulfur sprays
Specific fungicide

Root Maggot

Identify: Both the seed corn maggot and the cabbage maggot attack plant roots. The seed corn maggot is one and one-half to two inches (5–6 cm) long. The seed corn maggot converts into a fly and is a bit smaller than a common housefly. Cabbage maggots are 0.3 inch (1 cm) long, and the adult fly is bigger than a housefly. These pests winter over in the soil and live in unclean soil. In the spring, they emerge as adult flies and soon lay eggs in the soil at the base of young plants. The squirmy, whitish larvae hatch several days later with a ravenous appetite.

Damage: Root maggots chew and burrow into stems and roots. The seed corn maggot attacks seeds and seedling roots. Cabbage maggots attack roots, leaving hollowed out channels and holes in larger roots. Both maggots destroy small hairlike feeder roots. Wounds made by the root maggots also foster soft rot and fungal diseases.

Cultural and Physical Control: Cleanliness! Use fresh, new, store-bought soil when planting in containers. Cover seedlings with Agronet® to exclude flies, and plant late in the year to avoid most adult flies. Place an 18-inch (45 cm) collar of foam rubber around the base of the plant to exclude flies.

Biological: Control with parasitic nematodes, *Steinernema feltiae* or *Heterorhabditis bacteriophora*.

Sprays: Kill root maggots with neem and horticultural oil used as a soil-drench.

Slugs and Snails

Identify: Slugs and snails are soft; slimy white, dark, or yellow; and occasionally striped. They are one-fourth to three inches (1–9 cm) long. Snails live in a circular shell; slugs do not. They hide by day and feed at night. Slugs and snails leave a slimy, silvery trail of mucus in their wake. They lay translucent eggs that hatch in about a month. They reproduce prolifically, and the young mollusks often eat relatively more than adults.

Damage: They make holes in leaves often with a weblike appearance. They will eat almost any vegetation, roots included. These creatures winter over in warm, damp locations in most climates. Slugs and snails especially like tender seedlings. They will migrate to adjacent gardens in quest of food.

Cultural and Physical Control: A clean, dry perimeter around the garden will make it difficult for them to pass. Spotlight and handpick at night. A thin layer of lime, diatomaceous earth, or salty beach sand two to six (6–15 cm) inches wide around individual plants, beds, or the entire garden will present an impassable barrier. The lime is not thick enough to alter the pH and will repel or dissolve pests. To trap, attach short one-inch (3 cm) feet on a wide board and leave it in the garden. The pests will seek refuge under the board. Pick up the board every day or two, shake the slugs off, and step on them.

Poisonous baits usually have metaldahyde as a base. Confine the bait to a slug hotel. Cut a 1 × 2-inch slot in a covered plastic container to make a slug and snail hotel. Place slug and snail bait inside the hotel. The hotel must keep the bait dry and off the soil. In a slug hotel, none of the poison bait touches the soil, and the bait is inaccessible to children, pets, and birds. Place slug and snail hotels in out of the way places. Natural baits include a mix of jam and water and beer. If using beer, it must be deep enough to drown mollusks.

Biological: The predatory snail, *Ruminia decollata*—available commercially—is yet another way to combat plant-eating slugs and snails.

Sprays: Young slugs and snails are not attracted to bait. Spray for young at night or early morning with a 50-percent ammonia-water solution.

Thrips

Identify: More common in greenhouses than indoors, these tiny, winged, fast-moving little critters are hard to see but not hard to spot. From 0.04–0.05 inch (1–1.5 mm) long, thrips can be different colors, including white, gray, and dark colors, often with petite stripes. Check for them under leaves by shaking parts of the plant. If there are many thrips present, they choose to jump and run rather than fly to safety. But often you will see them as a herd of specks thundering across foliage. Females make holes in soft plant tissue where they deposit eggs that are virtually invisible to the naked eye. Winged thrips easily migrate from infested plants to the entire garden.

Damage: Thrips scrape tissue from leaves and stems, afterward sucking out the plant juices for food. Stipples, whitish-yellowish specks, appear on tops of leaves; chlorophyll production diminishes and leaves become brittle. You will also see black specks of thrip feces and little thrips. Many times thrips feed inside flower buds or wrap and distort leaves.

Cultural and Physical Control: Cleanliness! Use blue or pink sticky traps, and mist plants with water to impair travel. Manual removal works okay if only a few thrips are present, but they are hard to catch. Thrips can be very vexing to control once they get established.

Biological: Predatory mites (*Ambly-*

One of the many slug solutions available on the market.

seius cucumeris and *Amblyseius barkeri, Neoseiulus cucumeris, Iphiseius degenerans, Neoseiulus barkeri, Euseius hibisci*); parasitic wasps (*Thripobis semiluteus, Ceranisus menes, Goetheana shakespearei*); pirate bugs (*Orius* species); and *Verticillium lecanii* fungus is effective.

Sprays: Homemade sprays such as tobacco-nicotine base; commercial pyrethrum; synthetic pyrethrum; and insecticidal soap. Apply two to four times at five- to ten-day intervals.

Whiteflies

Whiteflies flutter from foliage when it is shaken.

Identify: The easiest way to check for the little buggers is to grab a limb and shake it. If there are any whiteflies, they will fly from under leaves. Whiteflies look like a small, white moth about 0.04-inch (1 mm) long. Adult whiteflies have wings. They usually appear near the top of the weakest plant first. They will move downward on the plant or fly off to infest another plant. Eggs are found on leaf undersides, where they are connected with a small hook.

Damage: Whiteflies, like mites, may cause white speckles, stipples, on the tops of leaves. Loss of chlorophyll production. Plant vigor diminishes as infestation progresses.

Cultural and Physical Control: Mites are difficult to remove manually because they fly. Adults are attracted to the color yellow. To build a whitefly trap similar to flypaper, cover a bright, yellow object with a sticky substance like Tanglefoot. Place traps on the tops of pots among the plants. Traps work very well. When they are full of insects, toss them out.

Biological: The wasp, *Encarsia formosa*, is the most effective whitefly parasite. The small wasps only attack whiteflies; they do not sting people! All toxic sprays must be washed off completely before introducing parasites and predators. Since the *Encarsia formosa* is a parasite about 0.125 inch (3 mm) long, smaller than the whitefly, it takes them much longer to control or even keep the whitefly population in check. The parasitic wasp lays an egg in the whitefly larva that later hatches and eats the larva alive, from the inside out—death is slow. If you use them, set them out at the rate of two or more parasites per plant as soon as the first whitefly is detected. Repeat every two to four weeks throughout the life of the plants.

The fungus *Verticillium lecanii*, aka *Cephalosporium lecanii*, trade name Mycatal®, is also very effective in whitefly control.

Sprays: Easily eradicated with natural sprays. Before spraying, remove any leaves that have been over 50 percent damaged and either cure with heat or burn infested foliage. Homemade sprays applied at five- to ten-day intervals work well. Insecticidal soap applied at five- to ten-day intervals. Pyrethrum (aerosol) applied at five- to ten-day intervals.

Fungi and Diseases

Fungi are primitive plants and do not produce chlorophyll, the substance that gives higher plants their green color. Fungi reproduce by spreading tiny microscopic spores rather than seeds. Countless fungal spores are present in the air at all times. When these microscopic airborne spores find the proper conditions, they will settle, take hold, and start growing. Some fungi, such as gray mold (*Botrytis*) are so prolific that they can spread through an entire crop in a matter of days! In fact, one indoor garden was located near a swamp and *Botrytis* spores were omnipresent in the environment. Flowers and stems contracted gray mold quickly and were often reduced to a wisp-of-powdery-foliage in short order. The gardener lost four consecutive crops. Finally, the gardener moved to greener pastures and had no trouble with mold.

Unsterile, soggy soil coupled with humid, stagnant air provides the environment most fungi need to thrive. Although there are many different types of fungi, they are usually prevented with similar methods.

Prevention

Prevention is the first step and the true key to fungi control. The section, "Setting up the Indoor Garden," instructs gardeners to remove anything—cloth curtains, clothes, and other debris—that might attract, harbor, and spread fungi. Cover the carpet with white Visqueen® plastic. If mold should surface on the walls, spray with fungicide. Wash walls with a five-percent bleach solution or Pinesol® (made from natural pine oil) and apply paint that contains a fungus-inhibiting agent. Specially designed paints for damp conditions contain a fungicide and are attracted by moisture. When applied to a damp, cracked basement wall, the paint is drawn into the moist crack. Remove all mold from the walls by washing it with a

Stem rot: Causes leaf destruction with brownish yellow halo. Stems weaken and fruit often spots. Remove and destroy affected plants. Prevent by growing in sterile substrate.

bleach solution before painting with fungus-resistant paint. Cleanliness and climate control are the keys to preventing fungi. Few clean, well-ventilated indoor gardens have problems with fungi. In contrast, every dingy, dank, ill-kept indoor garden I have seen had fungal problems and yielded a substandard harvest.

Install a vent fan(s) large enough to remove moist air quickly and keep humidity at 50 percent or less. A vent fan is the easiest and least expensive humidity control device available. CO_2 generators produce humidity-increasing water vapor as a by-product. Dehumidifiers are relatively inexpensive, readily available at discount stores, and do a good job of keeping humidity under control in enclosed indoor gardens. Dehumidifiers draw extra electricity, and the condensed water must be removed daily. Wood, coal, and electric heat all dry and dehumidify the air. Most air conditioners can be set to a specific humidity level. If the indoor garden(s) have a central heating/air-conditioning vent, the vent can be opened to control temperature and lower humidity.

Control

Prevent fungus by controlling all the factors contributing to its growth: remove hiding places, keep room clean, lower humidity to 50 percent, and keep the air well circulated. If prevention proves inadequate and fungi appear, advanced control measures are necessary. Carefully remove and destroy dead leaves. Wash your hands after handling diseased foliage. If the problem attacks one or a few plants, isolate and treat them separately. Remember, fungi can spread like wildfire if the conditions are right. If they get a good start even after all preventive measures are taken, do not hesitate to take extreme control methods including spraying the entire garden with the proper fungicide.

Gray Mold (*Botrytis*)

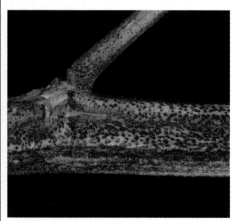

Gray Mold (Botrytis).

Identify: Gray mold is the most common fungus that attacks indoor plants and flourishes in moist temperate climates common to many indoor gardens.

Botrytis damage is compounded by humid climates (above 50 percent). It starts within the flower buds and is difficult to see at the onset—grayish-whitish to bluish-green in color—*Botrytis* appears hairlike and similar to laundry lint in moist climates. As the disease progresses, the foliage turns somewhat slimy. Damage can also appear as dark, brownish spots on flowers and foliage in less humid environments. Dry to the touch, *Botrytis*-affected area often crumbles if rubbed.

Gray mold attacks countless crops, and airborne spores are present virtually everywhere. While most commonly found attacking dense and swelling flower buds, it also attacks stems, leaves, and seeds, causes damping-off, and decomposes dry, stored plant material, such as herbs. It is also transmitted via seeds.

Damage: Watch for single leaves that mysteriously dry out. They could be the telltale signs of a *Botrytis* attack inside flower buds. Constant observation, especially during the last two weeks before harvest, is necessary to keep this disease out of the garden. Flower buds are quickly reduced to slime in cool, humid conditions or powder in warm, dry rooms. *Botrytis* can destroy an entire crop in seven to ten days if left unchecked. Stem damage—*Botrytis* starts on stems and not flowers—is less common indoors. First, stems turn yellow and cankerous growths develop. The damage causes growth above the wound to wilt and can cause stems to fold over. Transported by air, contaminated hands, and tools, gray mold spreads very quickly indoors, infecting an entire indoor garden in less than a week when conditions are right.

Control: Minimize *Botrytis* attack incidence with low humidity (50 percent or less), ample air circulation, and ventilation. Cool (below 70°F [21°C]), moist climates with humidity above 50 percent are perfect for rampant gray mold growth. Remove dead leaf stems, petioles, from stalks when removing damaged leaves to avoid *Botrytis* outbreaks, which are often harbored by dead, rotting foliage. Increase ventilation and keep humidity below 60 percent, and keep the indoor garden clean! Use fresh, sterile growing medium for each crop.

Cultural and Physical Control: As soon as *Botrytis* symptoms appear, use alcohol-sterilized pruners to remove *Botrytis*-infected flower buds at least one inch (3 cm) below the infected area. Some gardeners amputate two to four inches (5–10 cm) below damage to ensure removal. Do not let the flower or anything that touches it contaminate other flowers and foliage. Remove from the garden and destroy. Wash your hands and tools after removing. Increase temperature to 80°F (26°C) and lower humidity to below 50 percent.

Excessive nitrogen and phosphorus levels make foliage tender, so *Botrytis* can get a foothold. Make sure pH is around 6 to facilitate calcium uptake. Low light levels also encourage weak growth and gray mold attack. Avoid heavy crowding of plants and keep the light levels bright. *Botrytis* needs UV light to complete its life cycle; without UV light it cannot live. Some plant varieties seldom fall victim to gray mold. Many crosses are more resistant to gray mold than pure varieties.

Biological: Spray plants with *Gliocladium roseum* and *Trichoderma* species. Prevent damping-off with a soil application of *Gliocladium* and *Trichoderma* species. Try experimenting with the yeasts *Pichia guilliermondii* and *Candida oleophila* or the bacterium *Pseudomonas syringae*.

Sprays: Bordeaux mixture keeps early stages of *Botrytis* in check as long as it is present on the foliage. Preventive spraying is advised if in a high-risk area, but spraying near harvesttime is not advised. Seeds are protected from *Botrytis* with a coating of Captan. Check with your local nursery for product recommendations.

Damping-off

Damping-off rots stems at the soil line.

Identify: This fungal condition, sometimes called *Pythium* wilt, is often found in soil and growing mediums. It prevents newly sprouted seeds from emerging; attacks seedlings, causing them to rot at the soil line; yellows foliage; and rots older plants at soil line. It occasionally attacks rooting cuttings at the soil line, too. It is caused by different fungal species, including *Botrytis*, *Pythium*, and *Fusarium*. Once initiated,

Troubleshooting Chart for Pests & Diseases

Growth Stage	Cause	Quick Fix
Seeds and Seedlings		
Seeds do not germinate	Damping-off	Buy new seed, start over
	Bad seed	Get your money back!
	Root maggots	Drench soil with neem or horticultural oil
Seed germinates, seedling has signs of pests eating/sucking foliage	Spider mites (stippled leaves)	Spray neem oil, pyrethrum
	Aphids (exude honeydew)	Spray pyrethrum, insecticidal soap, or nicotine sulfate
Seedling stem at base has dark or sickly growth, suddenly falls over or suddenly wilts	Damping-off	Drench soil with metalaxyl or buy new seeds
	Damping-off or a wilt disease	Uncommon in cuttings
	Too much or too little moisture	Correct accordingly
Seedling leaves have yellow, gray, black, and/or dark green (fungus-like) spots	Blight or anthracnose	Remove growing plants and growing medium
Cuttings		
Wilt and die	Lack of moisture	Add humidity dome, mist 4–6 times daily
Wilt and die	Medium too wet	Drain medium, do not water, no standing water in tray
Won't root	Medium too dry or too wet	See "Wilt and die" see above
	Inconsistent rooting hormone	Change to liquid or gel rooting hormone
Vegetative stage		
Leggy, weak plants	Lack of light	Add lamp, change reflector, move lamp closer to plants
Leggy, weak plants	Lack of ventilation,	Add vent fan
	Soil too wet	Irrigate less
	Soil too dry	Irrigate more
	Toxic nutrient buildup	Leach grow medium* Change nutrient solution
Stunted, stubby plants	Insect damage	Spray pyrethrum**
	Rotten roots	Irrigate less
	Toxic nutrient buildup	Leach grow medium*
Burned leaf tips	Toxic nutrient buildup	Leach medium* weekly
Purple stems & burned leaf spots	Could be one of many different nutrients	Lower nutrient dose & leach medium* weekly

Leaf spots, margins burned, discolored leaves, pale leaves	Nutrient toxicity	Leach medium* Change nutrient solution Change fertilizer Refer to specific nutrient problems
Small, whitish spots on leaves	Spider mite damage	Spray pyrethrum**, neem oil
Insect damage—chewed leaves, insects/eggs visible on plants— check under leaves with 20X loop.	Whiteflies, aphids, scale, caterpillars, larva, etc.	Spray pyrethrum** or neem oil
Fungus or mold on foliage or soil	High humidity (above 60%) High temperature (above 80°F)	Add vent fan Add vent fan Spray soil with 5%-bleach solution and wash off next day. Spray foliage with 10%-baking soda solution.
Severe, sudden wilting of plant	*Fusarium* or *Verticillium* wilt Lack of water	Remove plant & growing medium and destroy Irrigate plant, submerge roots in water
Flowering Slow growth and small flowers	Overfertilized, water/light/air-stressed, cooked or rotten roots	Leach* grow medium Add big/more vent fans Keep grow medium evenly moist. The closer to harvest, the less that can be done. Must remedy three to six weeks before harvest for results.
Older leaf discoloration and dieback	Nitrogen, potassium, phosphorus, or zinc deficiency	See specific nutrient for solution
New leaf discoloration and dieback	One of the secondary or trace elements	See specific nutrient for solution
Dead grayish spots in flowers	Flower bud mold (*Botrytis*)	Remove entire flower. Drop the humidity
Pungent odors from indoor garden		Install ozone generator in large rooms. Use "Ona" or "Odor Killer" in small rooms

*Leach or flush growing medium with mild (quarter-strength) nutrient solution. Flush with at least three times the volume of nutrient solution per gallon of medium.
**Spray at five-day intervals for 15 days. Use aerosol pyrethrum, and spray under leaves. If problem persists, switch to neem oil and alternate with pyrethrum.

damping-off is fatal. At the onset of damping-off, the stem looses girth at the soil line, weakens, then grows dark, and finally fluid circulation is cut, killing the seedling or cutting.

Control: Damping-off is caused by a combination of the following: (1) Fungi are already present in an unsterile rooting medium; (2) Overwatering and maintaining a soggy growing medium; (3) Excessive humidity. The disease can be avoided by controlling soil moisture. Overwatering is the biggest cause of damping-off and the key to its prevention. Careful daily scrutiny of soil will ensure the proper amount of moisture is available to seeds or cuttings.

Start seeds and root cuttings in a fast-draining, sterile coarse sand, rockwool, Oasis™, or Jiffy™ cubes, which are difficult to overwater. Do not place a humidity tent over sprouted seedlings—a tent can lead to excessive humidity and damping-off. Cuttings are less susceptible to damping-off and love a humidity tent to promote rooting. Keep germination temperatures between 70 and 85°F (21–29°C). Damping-off is inhibited by bright light; grow seedlings under the HID rather than fluorescent bulbs. Keep fertilization to a minimum during the first couple weeks of growth. Germinate seeds between clean, fresh paper towels and move seeds to soil once sprouted. Do not plant seeds too deeply; cover with soil the depth of the seed. Use fresh, sterile growing medium and clean pots to guard against harmful fungus in the soil.

Biological: Apply Polygangron® (*Pythium oligandrum*) granules to soil and seed. Bak Pak® or Intercept® are applied to the soil and Deny® or Dagger®—forms of the bacterium *Burkholderia cepacia*—are put on the seeds. Epic®, Kodiac®, Quantum 4000®, Rhizo-Plus®, System 3®, and Seranade® also suppress many causes of damping-off.

Chemical: Dust the seeds with Captan®. Avoid benomyl fungicide soil-drench because it kills beneficial organisms.

Downy Mildew

Identify: Sometimes called *false mildew*, downy mildew affects vegetative and flowering plants. Young, succulent foliage is a favorite starting place. Powdery mildew develops in temperatures below 76°F (26°C).

It appears as whitish-yellow spots on top of leaves creating pale patches. Grayish mycelium spawn is on leaf undersides, opposite the pale patches. Downy mildew can spread very quickly, causing a lack of vigor and slow growth; leaves yellow, die back, and drop. The disease is in the plant system and grows outward. It is often fatal, spreads quickly, and can wipe out a crop. Avoid promoting this disease by not crowding plants. Keep temperatures above 76°F (26°C) and the humidity below 50 percent.

Control: Cleanliness! Use sterile growing medium. Remove and destroy affected plants, not just foliage.

Biological: Apply Serenade® (*Bacillus subtilis*). Bordeaux mixture is also somewhat effective.

Blight

Identify: Blight is a general term that describes many plant diseases that are caused by fungus, most often a few weeks before harvest. Signs of blight include dark, blotchy spots on foliage, slow growth, sudden yellowing, wilting, and plant death. Most blights spread quickly through large areas of plants.

Control: Cleanliness! Use fresh, sterile growing medium. Avoid excess nitrogen fertilization. Avoid blights by keeping plants healthy with the proper nutrient balance and good drainage to prevent nutrient buildup.

Biological: Use Serenade® (*Bacillus subtilis*) against Brown Blight. Use Binab®, Bio-Fungus®, RootShield®, Supresivit®, Trichopel®, (*Trichoderma harzianum*) or SoilGuard® (*Trichoderma virens*). Use a Bordeaux mixture to stop fungal blights. Stopping blights in advanced stages is difficult; the best solution is to remove diseased plants and destroy them.

Foliar Spots and Fungi

Identify: Leaf and stem fungi, including leaf spot, attack foliage. Brown, gray, black, or yellow-to-white spots or blotches develop on leaves and stems. Leaves and stems discolor and develop spots that impair plant fluid flow and other life processes. Spots expand over leaves causing them to yellow and drop. Growth is slowed, harvest prolonged, and in severe cases death results. Leaf spot is the symptomatic name given to many diseases. These diseases may be caused by bacteria, fungus, and nematodes. Spots or lesions caused by fungi often develop different colors as fruiting bodies grow. Leaf spots are often caused by cold water that was sprayed on plants under a hot HID. Temperature stress can cause the spots that often develop into a disease.

Control: Cleanliness! Use fresh, sterile growing medium with each crop. Move HIDs away from the garden canopy about 30 minutes before spraying so plants won't be too hot. Do not spray within four hours of turning the lights off as excess moisture sits on the foliage and fosters fungal growth. Do not wet foliage when watering, avoid overwatering, and lower indoor garden humidity to 50 percent or less. Check the humidity both day and night. Employ dry heat to raise the nighttime temperature 5–10°F (3–6°C) below the daytime levels, and keep humidity more constant. Allow adequate spacing between plants to provide air circulation. Remove damaged foliage. Avoid excessive nitrogen application.

Biological: Bordeaux mixture may help keep leaf spots in check, but it is often phytotoxic when applied regularly indoors.

Sprays: Bordeaux mixture.

Fusarium Wilt

Identify: *Fusarium* wilt is most common in warm indoor gardens and greenhouses. Recirculating nutrient solutions above 75°F (24°C) creates perfect conditions for *Fusarium*. The water and nutrient solution carries this disease with it when contaminated. *Fusarium* starts as small spots on older, lower leaves. Interveinal leaf chlorosis appears swiftly. Leaf tips may curl before wilting and suddenly drying to a crisp. Portions of the plant or the entire plant will wilt. The whole process happens so fast that yellow, dead leaves dangle from branches. This disease starts in the plant's xylem, the base of the fluid transport system. Plants wilt when fungi plug the fluid flow in plant tissue. Cut one of the main stems in two, and look for the telltale reddish-brown color.

Control: Cleanliness! Use fresh, clean growing medium. Avoid nitrogen overfertilization.

Preventive action is necessary. Keep nutrient solution below 75°F (24°C). Hydrogen peroxide infusions will also arrest *Fusarium*. Always remove and destroy infested plants.

Biological: Mycostop® (*Streptomyces griseoviridis*), or Deny®, or Dagger® (*Burkholderia cepacia*) and *Trichoderma*.

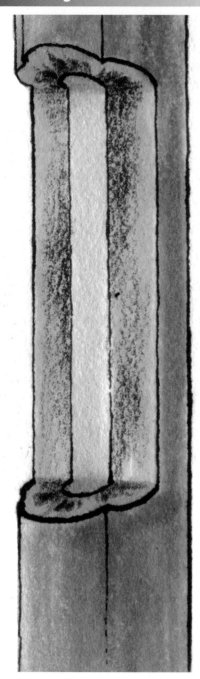

Fusarium *Wilt*

Sprays: Treat seeds with chemical fungicides to eradicate the seed-borne infection. Chemical fungicides are not effective on foliage.

Green Algae

Identify: Slimy green algae need nutrients, light, and a moist surface on which to grow. These algae are found growing on moist rockwool and other growing mediums exposed to light. They cause little damage but attract fungus gnats and other critters that damage roots. Once roots have lesions and abrasions, diseases enter easily.

Control: Cover the moist rockwool and growing mediums to exclude light. Run an algaecide in the nutrient solution or water with an algaecide.

Powdery Mildew

Identify: First indication of infection is small spots on the tops of leaves. At this point, the disease has been inside the plant a week or more. Spots progress to a fine, pale, gray-white powdery coating on growing shoots, leaves, and stems. Powdery mildew is not always limited to the upper surface of foliage. Growth slows, leaves yellow, and plants die as the disease advances. Occasionally fatal indoors, this disease is at its worst when roots dry out and foliage is moist. Plants are infected for weeks before they show the first symptoms.

Control: Cleanliness! Prevent this mildew by avoiding cool, damp, humid, dim indoor garden conditions, as well as fluctuating temperatures and humidity. Low light levels and stale air affect this disease. Increase air circulation and ventilation, and make sure light intensity is high. Space containers far enough apart so air freely flows between plants. Allow foliage to dry before turning off lights. Remove and destroy foliage more than 50 percent infected. Avoid excess nitrogen. Copper and sulfur-lime sprays are a good prophylactic.

Biological: Apply Serenade® (*Bacillus subtilis*) or spray with a saturation mix of baking soda and water.

Sprays: Bordeaux mixture may keep this mold in check. A saturation of baking soda spray dries to a fine powder on the leaf; the baking soda changes the surface pH of the leaf to 7, and powdery mildew cannot grow.

Root Rot

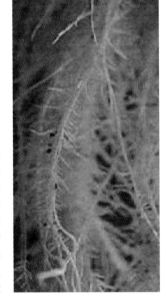

Right: Root rot causes roots to turn brown and slimy.

Identify: Root rot fungi cause roots to turn from a healthy white to light brown. As the rot progresses, roots turn darker and darker brown. Leaf chlorosis is followed by wilting of the older leaves on the entire plant, and its growth slows. When severe, rot progresses up to the base of the plant stock, turning it dark.

Root rot is most common when roots are deprived of oxygen and stand in un-aerated water. Soil pests that cut, suck, and chew roots create openings for rotting diseases to enter. Inspect roots with a 10X magnifying glass for signs of pest damage.

Control: Cleanliness! Use fresh, sterile growing medium. Make sure calcium levels are adequate, and do not overfertilize with nitrogen. Keep pH above 6.5 in soil and about 6.0 in hydroponic mediums to lower disease occurrence. Control any insects, fungi, bacteria, etc., that eat roots.

Biological: Binab®, Bio-Fungus®, Root-Shield®, Supresivit®, Trichopel® (*Trichoderma harzianum*), or SoilGuard® (*Trichoderma virens*).

Sprays: Sprays are not effective.

Pythium Wilt/Rot

Identify: (See "Damping-off" above.)

Sooty Mold

Identify: Black sooty mold is a surface fungus that grows on sticky honeydew excreted by aphids, mealybugs, scale, whiteflies, etc. Sooty mold is only a problem on indoor plants when honeydew is present. Sooty mold restricts plant development, slows growth, and diminishes harvest.

Control: Remove insects that excrete honeydew. Once honeydew is controlled, mold dies. Wash away honeydew and mold with a biodegradable soapy solution. Rinse away soapy water a few hours after applying.

Verticillium Wilt

Identify: Lower leaves develop chlorotic yellowing on margins and between veins before turning dingy brown. Plants wilt

Verticillium wit is less common than
Pythium *wilt, but the symptoms are similar.*
Cut a stem and look for discolored xylem.

during the day and recoup when the light
goes off. Wilt soon overcomes parts of the
plant or the entire plant. Cut the stem in
two and look for the telltale brownish xylem tissue. The fungus blocks the flow of
plant fluids, causing wilting.

Control: Cleanliness! Use fresh, sterile
soil with good drainage. Use ammoniacal
nitrogen as a source of nitrogen. Do not
overfertilize.

Biological: Bio-Fungus® (*Trichoderma* species), Rhizo-Plus® (*Bacillus subtilis*).

Sprays: No chemical spray is effective.

Viruses

Cucumber mosaic virus: Causes yellow and dark
mottled patches on leaves. Leaf surfaces swell
and distort. Destroy affected leaves, wash hands
and tools. Prevent by keeping garden clean and
insect free.

Identify: Viruses are still a mystery. They
act like living organisms in some instanc-
es and nonliving chemicals in other cases.
They must enter plants via wounds. Once
a virus takes over plant cells, it is able to
multiply. Viruses are spread by insects,
mites, plants, animals, and human vectors. Aphids and whiteflies are the worst.
Infected tools also transport viruses from
one plant to another. Typical symptoms of
viral infection are: sickly growth, leaf and
stem spots, yellowing, and low yields. Viral

diseases move into the plant's fluid distribution system and destroy it, which often causes leaf spots and mottling. A virus can completely take over a plant in a few days. Once a plant gets a virus, there's little you can do.

Control: Cleanliness! Always use fresh, sterile growing medium. Disinfect tools before cutting foliage on different plants. Destroy all plants infected with virus.

Biological: None.

Sprays: No chemical sprays are effective against viruses.

Above: Dark spots multiply as anthracnose blight progresses.

Below: Anthracnose *blight first shows a few ugly spots on leaves.*

At Right - Blight: Often devastating to outdoor crops in wet weather. Brown patches on leaf fringes that spread inward. No treatment. Prevent with low humidity and good ventilation.

Above: Leaf mold: Purplish brown patches appear on leaf undersides while top of leaf turns yellowish. Remove affected leaves. Prevent with good ventilation both day and night.

Tomato Problem Images

Greenback tomato: The stem and top of tomato remain green. Caused by lack of light and potash. Prevent with regular fertilization.

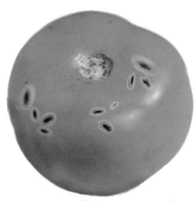

Ghost spot: Grey mold spots on fruit. Distinguish by small "halo" around spots. Prevent with good ventilation and cleanliness.

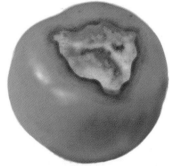

Tomato moth: Big brown or green caterpillars burrow into fruit and stems. Destroy fruit. Prevent by spraying with pyrethrum or rotenone bait at first sign of caterpillars.

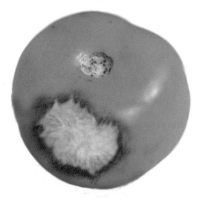

Sun scald: Papery pale brown depression where sun hits fruit. Prevent by shading fruit.

Blossom end rot: Tough dark-colored patch on bottom of fruit. Prevent by keeping growing medium from drying out after fruit sets.

Split fruit: Caused by excessive irrigation after growing medium has dried out. Prevent by keeping soil evenly moist.

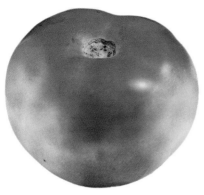

Blossom drop: flowers wither and often stem breaks. Flowers not pollinated. Caused by low humidity and dry substrate. Prevent with regular irrigation; shake plants to pollinate.

Uneven ripening: Fruit ripens unevenly , caused by excessive heat or lack of potash. Prevent with even temperatures and regular irrigation.

Excess heat and dry conditions cause many problems with the plant and fruit in general. See specific examples of fruit.

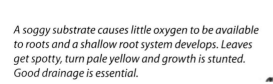

A soggy substrate causes little oxygen to be available to roots and a shallow root system develops. Leaves get spotty, turn pale yellow and growth is stunted. Good drainage is essential.

Spraying

Use only contact sprays approved for edible fruits and vegetables.

Warning: Do not use TOXIC SYSTEMIC CHEMICALS! Read the entire label on all sprays. The toxic or active life of the spray is listed on the label. Wait twice as long as the label recommends, and thoroughly wash any foliage before ingesting it. Toxic life is many times longer indoors, because sunlight and other natural forces are not able to break down chemicals.

Sprays are beneficial if not overdone. Every time a plant is sprayed, the stomata are clogged and growth slows. At 24–28 hours after spraying, rinse leaves on both sides with plain water until it drips from leaves. Avoid sprays that leave a residual during the weeks before harvest. Spraying increases chances of gray mold once flower buds form.

Phytotoxicity is the injury to plants caused by sprays. Symptoms include burned leaves, slow growth, or sudden wilt. Spray a test plant and wait a few days to see if spray is phytotoxic. Water plants before spraying. Phytotoxicity is diminished when more liquid is in foliage.

Temperatures above 68°F (20°C) make virtually all sprays, even organic ones, phytotoxic and damaging to foliage.

Intense light causes leaves to take in the chemicals too quickly and will often cause leaf damage.

Spray early in the day so ingredients are absorbed and foliage dries. Spraying two hours or less before lights-out can cause foliar fungus when water sits on leaves too long.

Do not mix two products. It could change the characteristics of both.

Warm temperatures mean spraying twice as often, because the bugs breed twice as fast.

Use a clean, accurate measuring cup or spoon. Measure quantities carefully!

Mix pesticides and fungicides just before using them, and safely dispose of unused spray. Mix fertilizer and use for several weeks.

Mix wettable powders and soluble crystals in a little hot water to make sure they dissolve before adding the balance of the tepid water.

Use chemical sprays with extreme care, if at all, in enclosed areas; they are more concentrated indoors than outdoors in the open air.

Use a face mask when spraying, especially if using an aerosol fogger.

Spray entire plants, both sides of the leaves, stems, soil, and pot. Be careful with new, tender-growing shoots; they are easily burned by harsh sprays.

A one-quart (0.9–1.8 L) or two-quart pump-up spray bottle with a removable nozzle that is easy to clean is ideal. Keep a paper clip handy to ream out clogged debris in nozzle.

A 1–2 gallon (3.8–7.6 L) sprayer costs less than $50 and works well for large gardens. An application wand and nozzle attached to a flexible hose makes spraying under leaves where insects live easy. Plastic is recommended; it does not corrode or rust.

Electric foggers work well for large jobs. The spray is metered out a nozzle under high pressure, which creates a fine penetrating fog.

Wash the sprayer and the nozzle thoroughly after each use. Using the same bottle for fertilizers and insecticides is okay. Do not mix insecticides and fungicides together or with anything else. Mixing chemicals could cause a reaction that lessens their effectiveness.

Raise HID lamp out of the way so mist from spray will not touch the bulb; temperature stress, resulting from the relatively cold water hitting the hot bulb, may cause it to shatter. This could not only scare the hell out of you, it could burn eyes and skin. If the bulb breaks, turn off the system immediately and unplug!

Beautify your environment with a window box like the one here. Above are Potato Vine, two types of Coleus, and some Licorice plant.

Plant Selection Guide
Ornamentals

African violets (*Saintpaulia*) are the most popular flowering perennial houseplants. With proper care, they bloom almost continuously. Most are hybrids developed from several East African natives. Leaves form rosettes of velvet green leaves that are roundish or pointed. Blossoms of original species range from pale blue to lavender and purple. Hybrid flowers range in color: blue, purple, white, many shades of pink, and burgundy. Yellow flowers are available, but they change back to pink or purple after blooming several times. A few hybrids have bands of colors. Flowers can be single, semi-double, or double, and can have ruffled petals.

These plants grow best in a fast-draining, moisture-retentive potting soil. A popular mix is three parts peat moss or coco peat, one part well-rotted compost, and one part perlite. Use small pots. Crowded roots make African violets bloom best.

African violets require low levels of light and grow very well under fluorescents and compact fluorescent bulbs. Place close to fluorescents—two to six inches (5–10 cm) and in a dim area of the indoor garden lit with HID light. Give parent plants and cuttings of this short-day plant 18 hours of light a day at a level of 6000 (milliwatts per square meter) mWm^2. Flowering is induced with a short 12- to 14-hour photoperiod.

A temperature range of 60–70°F (16–21°C) and high humidity, above 70 percent, are best. In low humidity conditions, place a saucer filled with expanded clay or gravel below the container. Keep the plate wet to increase humidity around plants. Apply water from below or above, but be careful to not let water sit on leaves or stand around rosette center, which will cause leaves to rot. Irrigate with tepid water to avoid shocking plants. Water until soil is soaked, and do not water again until soil is dry to touch. Fertilize only when soil is moist. Use a slightly acidic fertilizer once every two to four weeks. Plant seeds, or propagate via leaf cuttings or plant division. Common pests include aphids, mites, thrips, and mealybugs.

Begonia

Begonias (Begoniaceae) need filtered sunlight and can be placed under the HID in low-light areas of the garden room. These perennials grow textured, multicolored foliage with colorful flowers. Flowers are edible, with a subtle citrus flavor. They are native to numerous subtropical and tropical regions around the globe. They grow very well in hanging baskets around the indoor garden, in greenhouses or lath houses, and can be moved outdoors into filtered shade. They need nutrient-rich, fast-draining soil and bloom best when they receive consistent, light feeding. Keep the soil moist but not soggy. Humidity should be at or in excess of 40 percent but less than 80 percent for best results. In dry areas, fill trays below pots with expanded clay, and keep water in the trays. Begonias are easy to propagate asexually by leaf, stem, or rhizome cuttings.

Supplemental lighting promotes cuttings for the varieties 'Rieger', 'Elatior', and 'Lorraine' when natural light is lacking. A light level of 6000 mWm^2 is the norm. Use 6000 mWm^2 for 18 hours a day to nurture young seedlings and to speed flowering. Rooting in begonia cuttings is stimulated by artificial light.

There are many different kinds of begonias including cane-type, hardy, *Hiemalis*, *Multiflora*, *Rex*, *Rhizomatous*, *Semperflorens*, shrub-like, trailing, climbing, and tuberous. There is one to fit your needs. Check your local nursery for available varieties.

Impatiens (Balsaminaceae) are native to regions from the Himalayas to New Guinea. They are one of the most popular blooming shade plants found in gardens today. Most are annuals or tender perennials that are grown as annuals.

Impatiens are revered for their long blooming season outdoors in summer. Indoors under lights, the blooming season can be extended. Foliage ranges in shape from pointed to somewhat round leaves and height from less than a foot to more than eight feet (2 m) tall and ten feet (2.5 m) wide. Impatiens are easy to grow. They grow best in moist, relatively fast-draining soil mix, moderate temperatures 60–80°F (15–22°C), and humidity that ranges from 40–80 percent. Grow in hanging baskets or around the indoor garden where they receive less intense HID light.

Impatiens

Of the hundreds of impatiens species, only the following are found in most gardens: *I. balforii, I. balsamina, I. glandulifera, I. roylei, I. holstii, I. walleriana,* and the relatively new *I. New Guinea* hybrids. The New Guinea hybrids can be upright or spreading and grow from one to two feet (25–50 cm) tall or taller and about the same width. Large, pointed leaves are often variegated with creamy or reddish spots. Large 2.5-inch–wide (10–15 cm) flowers on stems above foliage range

in colors from lavender, purple, pink, orange, red, and white. Check with your local nursery for the varieties of the above species that grow best in your area.

The **cactus** (Cactaceae) family includes many succulents. Most often leafless, cactus and succulents have stems that are adapted into barrel-like cylinders, pads, and joints that bank water during drought. Their thick skin decreases evaporation. Most species of cactus have spines to protect them against animal pests. Flowers are often brightly colored and large. Fruit is generally colorful and may be edible.

Virtually all cacti are native to the Americas. They can be from a few inches tall to as much as 50 feet (12 m). Smaller cacti are popular for indoor and greenhouse gardens. Most are very easy to grow and require fast-draining soil.

Give newly planted cacti and succulents very little water to avoid root rot until roots start strong active growth in four to six weeks. Once roots start active growth, drench soil and wait until soil is dry before watering again. Reduce watering in autumn to promote dormancy. Feed monthly during active growth.

One of my friends who lived in a rainy climate always dominated cactus competitions because his plants were grown under HID lights. Cacti and succulents—jade; miniature crassulas; Christmas, Easter, and Thanksgiving cacti, etc.—are some of the easiest to care for under lights. They require minimal care and infrequent watering but need lots of bright light.

In winter when the days are short, cacti greatly benefit from intense supplemental light. A lighting level of 9000 mWm^2 for 18 hours a day will produce phenomenal results in seedlings, cuttings, and adult cacti. Some varieties of cactus respond more favorably to 24 hours of light.

Calceolaria (Scrophulariaceae) are native from Chile to Mexico. Flowers form in loose clusters and are small and pouch-like. Flowers are most often yellow but can be bronze, red, and orange-brown. Numerous branches support dark green, wrinkled leaves. The *C. Herbeohybrida* Group and *C. integrifolia* are the most

popular varieties of this soft perennial and are normally grown as annuals.

Early flowering is achieved by applying supplemental lighting (3000 mWm^2) for 24 hours a day from flower bud induction until flowering. Maintain the temperature between 60°F and 65°F for maximum productivity.

Carnations are in the **Dianthus** (Caryophyllaceae) family. More than 300 species and numerous hybrids are available. Flowers are single, semi-double, and double in white or different shades of orange, pink, red, and yellow, many of which are quite fragrant. The highly prized carnation is a very popular cut flower.

Members of the Dianthus family thrive in light, fast-draining soil. Some, such as carnations, Sweet William, and cottage pinks need rich soil. Do not overwater. Carnations and Sweet William are prone to rust and *Fusarium* wilt.

Carnations are propagated very successfully from cuttings and by using supplemental light. Side shoots from cut flowers make excellent cuttings. Cuttings are taken, then given 16 hours of light (6000 mWm^2). Excessive flowering may occur if more than 16 hours of light per day is permitted. The carnation is a long-day plant. It is possible to light it 24 hours a day to grow more and more profuse flowers. However, after 18 hours of light a day, the extra light produces minimal growth.

Chrysanthemums (Compositae) are annuals and perennials that are mostly native to China, Europe, and Japan. A few are native to the Americas. They are very easy to grow and grow best in a moist, relatively fast-draining soil mix, moderate temperatures from 60–80°F (15–22° C) and humidity that ranges from 40–70 percent.

Chrysanthemums are some of the most responsive flowers to supplemental light in all stages of life. In winter, parent plants are given 9000 mWm^2, 20 hours a day. Supplemental lighting during the first month of vegetative growth increases flower bud count and foliage production. Being a short-day plant, the chrysanthemum requires 20 hours of light per day during the first month of vegetative growth and 12 hours of light (4500 mWm^2) plus 12 hours of uninterrupted darkness to flower properly.

Cyclamen (Primulaceae) are native to Asia and Europe. The attractive flowers are on spikes above a clump of basal leaves. Colors range from white to shades of pink and red. They grow and flower best in cool temperatures (12°C) and often lose all their leaves when they go dormant in warm weather.

Cyclamen

These popular container-grown plants grow well outdoors or in cool indoor gardens and greenhouses. They require fairly humus-rich soil with good drainage. The large tuberous root grows best when lightly fertilized with a complete fertilizer. Do not cultivate soil surface or around roots. Plants purchased at the nursery are most popular because seeds take from 15–18 months to grow and bloom.

Seedlings given supplemental lighting (6000 mWm^2) have more uniform growth and less damping off. Give young plants 18 hours of light a day.

Geranium (Geraniaceae) is the common name generally used for Pelargoniums. They can endure soft frosts, and most varieties are native to South Africa. Flower clusters come in many colors, of which shades of pink, red, and white are the most popular. Most types bloom over a long period. Roundish to ruffled leaves can be solid colors or variegated. The leaves of scented geraniums (*Pelargonium graveolens*) have a light lemon to mint fragrance that disperses when foliage is handled.

Geranium

These flowering plants need good, fast-draining soil with plenty of organic matter. Feed regularly to encourage and prolong blooming. Pelargoniums grow in a wide variety of climates and do very well indoors under lights. They bloom most profusely when somewhat potbound.

Most common pests include aphids, spider mites, and whiteflies.

Geraniums can be propagated by seed or from cuttings, and greatly benefit from supplemental light. Parent plants are given 18 hours of light at a level of 6000 mWm² to increase cutting production. The cuttings are given less light but for the same 18 hours a day. Geraniums are a short-day plant and flower with shorter days or colder temperatures.

F1 hybrid seed-propagated geraniums can be given 24 hours of light a day at a level of 6000 mWm² from the beginning of life. These F1 hybrids do not need short days for flower induction.

Gloxinias (Gesneriaceae) are native to Brazil. This squat plant is packed with large, oval, slightly pointed leaves and grows to one foot (30 cm) tall and wide. The showy bell-shaped four-inch-wide (12 cm) flowers form in clusters near the top of plants. Colors include blue, pink, red, white, and various shades of purple. Some flowers are speckled with dark spots or have contrasting bands of color at fringes.

Gloxinias thrive when kept warm, 70–75°F (21–22°C) during the day and no less than 65°F (18°C) at night. They love a soil mix of even parts peat moss, perlite, and compost. Water seeds lightly until leaves appear, and increase water volume gradually until a strong root system is in place. To avoid rot, do not water leaves. Water soil only or let water absorb from a saucer below. Fertilize with half-strength complete fertilizer every two weeks. Once blooming period is completed, withhold gradually until soil dries. Store plants in warm, 60°F (16°C), room and keep foliage lightly moist to avoid wilting. Repot when new growth appears in midwinter.

Give gloxinias a light level of 6000 mWm² 18 hours a day to enhance growth and development of seedlings and young plants. Give potted gloxinias a light level of 4500 mWm^2 to promote large healthy flowers.

Kalanchoe (Crassulaceae) is a popular houseplant that grows well indoors under lights. The thick triangular to lace-shaped leaves are four to eight inches(12–24 cm) long or longer and half as wide. Flowers come in a variety of colors including orange, salmon, purple, and yellow. Kalanchoes are very easy to grow and require average potting soil and a warm, nonfreezing climate.

Kalanchoe

Give parent plants 18 hours of light per day to prevent flowering of this short-day plant. Kalanchoes are most often propagated vegetatively. Cuttings are given 18 to 24 hours of light at a level of 6000 mWm^2. Induce flowering by giving plants 12 hours of light and 12 hours of darkness.

Snapdragons (Scrophulariaceae) are a favorite fall and early spring flower. There are two genetically different types of snapdragons: short-day, referred to as Group I or II or "winter flowering;" and long-day, referred to as Group III or IV or

"summer flowering." When setting this plant out for early spring blooms, give seedlings supplementary lighting at a level of 9000 mWm^2 so that a daylength of 16 hours is reached. This will speed flowering by about four weeks. Even better results can be achieved by giving long-day plants 24 hours of light (4500 mWm^2) throughout their life. After they are about two months old, short-day snapdragons should receive short 12-hour days for maximum blooming potential.

Snapdragons

Orchids

The blooms and overall growth of many orchid varieties grown in greenhouses are greatly enhanced by supplemental lighting during the winter. Orchids also grow very well indoors under lights when the proper temperature, humidity, and lighting regimens are followed. Rather than explain all the details of orchid growth here, I have listed the temperature and light requirements for the different groups of orchids.

Light requirements for orchids fall into three categories.

High: 3000 foot-candles or more, which is equivalent to the amount of light available to plants growing in the middle of a sunny field.

good example of this type of orchid. The *Phalaenopsis* genus, on the other hand, prefers low light and warm air.

All orchids may be divided into two groups: species and hybrid. Hybridization often eliminates many of the natural limitations imposed by the original climatic requirements of an orchid. For example, if you breed a high-light, warm-air species with a medium-light, medium-temperature species, the result is a hybrid that grows well in either category.

Vegetables

Cucumbers, lettuce, eggplants, peppers, and tomatoes are favorite indoor vegetables that flourish under HID light.

Cucurbitaceae Family

Cucurbits, or the Cucurbitaceae family, include cucumbers, melons, and squashes. They all love warm weather and sandy soil. They grow poorly in cool, damp climates and are sensitive to frost. Cucurbits, in descending order of frost tolerance, are squash, pumpkin, cucumber, cantaloupe, and watermelon.

Cucurbits develop separate male and female flowers. Male flowers develop first and are easily distinguished as a plain flower on a long stem having only stamens. The female flower forms large ovaries that look like small fruit. After the first female flowers are pollinated, the vines develop both male and female flowers.

Some melons, many squashes, and all cucumbers cross-pollinate with one another. When cultivating a seed crop, grow only one variety of each type. Hand-pollinate by removing a male flower and shaking it inside a female flower on another plant to ensure vigorous seed.

Medium: 1500–3000 foot-candles, which is similar to the amount of light received by lightly shaded plants.

Low: under 1500 foot-candles, for plants that grow deep beneath the canopy of the forest.

Temperature requirements are divided into three groups:

Warm: (70–75°F [21–24°C]) day; (60–65°F [15–18°C]) night; similar to the climate of a seacoast or swampy lowland.

Medium: (65–70°F [18–21°C]) day; (55–60°F [13–15°C]) night; similar to rolling forests and fields.

Cool: (60–65°F [15–18°C]) day; (50–55°F [10–13°C]) night; similar to high mountainous regions.

Orchids can be referred to as being high-light, cool-air plants. The cymbidium is a

To prevent further pollination, close the female bloom with a piece of string, or twist-tie for a few days.

Cucumber *(Cucumis sativus)*

This warm-weather vine or bush crop is a favorite in salads, fresh from the vine, or when preserved as pickles. A native to southern Asia, cucumbers come in all shapes and sizes. Pickling "cukes" are short and stubby; slicers are long and slender; apple or lemon cucumbers are spherical and yellow. Popular greenhouse cucumbers are long, green, and smooth.

Greenhouse varieties, often referred to as English cucumbers, grow well indoors and must avoid pollination by bees in order to retain their form and flavor. One of my favorites is 'Sweet Success', a mild, seedless variety. This is a female variety, but flowers require no pollination. Armenian cucumbers are really long, slender melons that grow up to three feet in length. Asian varieties and Armenian cucumbers are increasingly popular.

Each type of cucumber has its own distinctive flavor. The short pickling varieties are bitter when eaten fresh, and when used to make pickles should be picked when only a few inches long. Some slicing varieties possess a tough, bitter skin that is peeled before eating the sweet, creamy flesh within. Since cucumbers are mostly water, many commercial gardeners cover them with a thin layer of wax after harvesting to retain moisture. To enjoy the peak flavor of cucumbers, they should be eaten within a few hours of harvest.

Available in compact bush and larger trailing varieties, cucumbers are easy to grow, but novice gardeners still have problems. Bush varieties can stand on their own, but trailing varieties climb and need a trellis. I like the large leaves and grow cucumbers as a "notification" crop because the leaves show nutrient deficiencies quickly, usually before other crops.

Basic Facts: Germination time: 6–10 days. Soil temperature for germination: minimum: 60°F (16°C), optimum: 95°F (35°C), maximum: 100°F (40°C). Approximate seeds per ounce: 175. Yield per 20-liters: 20–30 fruit. Yield per meter square raised bed: 100–200 fruit; must have a trellis. Life expectancy of stored seed: 5–6 years. Estimated time between sowing and first picking: 48–60 days (pickling), 52–72 (slicing). Effort to cultivate: easy in warm climates, requires protection from cold weather for an early outdoor or greenhouse crop in cool climates.

Seed Saving: best to hand-pollinate. See "Cucurbits" above.

Climate: Annual in all zones. Needs full sun and warm weather, above 70°F (21°C).

Cold temperatures slow vine growth and stop flowering and fruit set.

Soil: Use soilless mix or quality potting soil. Incorporate well-rotted compost and manure if desired. Add dolomite lime to neutralize the pH to 7.0 and keep cucumbers from "bubbling" and turning pithy on one end. Add a complete organic fertilizer. Soil should hold moisture and drain well.

Seed Sowing and Planting Do not plant in soil where cucumbers, melons or squash grew.

Plant seeds one-half inch (1.5 cm) deep in small containers, and keep evenly moist in a relatively fast-draining soil mix. Give moderate temperatures 60–80°F (15–22°C) and humidity that ranges from 40–80 percent. The soil temperature must be at least 60°F (16°C) for germination and strong growth. Transplant to mounds or rows after all danger of frost has passed. Pollinate varieties with a small artists' paintbrush by carefully dipping the brush into male flowers (they are the first to form near the base of plants) and touching the pollen-laden brush on larger female flowers. Keep irrigation regimens regular so cucumbers receive a constant supply of water to avoid misshapen and bitter fruit.

Build mounds of soil outdoors on flat beds to warm sooner. Mound soil at least 12 inches high and 12–24 inches across.

The best way to build a mound is similar to the "no-till" raised bed. Pile compost about four feet high, incorporating manure. Place a three to six-inch layer of topsoil on the top of the mound. Now the mound is ready to plant.

A clear plastic container makes an excellent cloche to protect seedlings from cold. But do not set out until nights are above 45°F (7°C).

In mounds: Sow four to six seeds one and one-half inches deep. Drench the mound with water and do not water again until after sprouting. In rows: Sow seeds one and one-half inches deep, one to two inches apart. Thin to six inches apart when seedlings are four to six inches tall.

Pickling Varieties: Plant several dozen plants, so that many become ripe at the same time, and an entire batch can be processed at once. Build a trellis or support for vine types. This saves precious garden space and keeps the fruit off the ground, which discourages insects and rot. The fruit develops straight and makes them easier to spot when picking. Trellised fruit, when shaded by leaves, is protected from sunburn, which causes bitterness. Replant seeds if the first sowing does not germinate rapidly or is slowed by spring rains. Grow about one to four slicing plants and four to six pickling plants per person.

Crop Care: Keep seedlings moist enough to avoid wilting, but be careful not to overwater, which promotes damping-off.

Mulch outdoor crops with dark, heat-absorbing mulch or black plastic to retain heat after soil is well warmed. Deep-water as needed to encourage a long taproot. The crop consumes more water when fruit sets, and surface watering is necessary. Fruit is over 90 percent water and must have adequate irrigation to form large fruit. Water stress will cause deformed cucumbers and a smaller crop. Add a complete low-nitrogen soluble fertilizer as soon as flowers set and twice a month thereafter until the end of season. Removing side or lateral shoots will send all the nutrients to remaining fruit, which makes fruit grow larger and mature faster.

Pinch off the end of vines about two weeks before the first frost so all fruit that has set will mature.

Harvesting: For maximum production, harvest cucumbers as soon as they become ripe. When left too long on the vine, they yellow, become sour, and slow the ripening of other fruit. Pickling varieties should be harvested when they are three to six inches long. When longer, they preserve poorly and become mushy. Slicing varieties are picked when they are from six to ten inches long. If slicers get too long or start to yellow, they become bitter and pithy. Apple or lemon cucumbers should be picked when they are the size of a small lemon.

Seedlings grow exceptionally well under HID lights. Give young seedlings a light level of 4500 mWm^2 for the first ten days of growth for 24 hours a day. After this, shorten the photoperiod to 16 hours per day and increase the light level to 6000 mWm^2.

Lettuce (Asteraceae/Compositae) is botanically classified as *Lactuca sativa*. There are four main types of lettuce: crisphead, butterhead or Boston, loose-leaf, and romaine.

Lettuce (*Lactuca sativa*) is one crop all gardeners can grow with very little effort. The onset of hot weather turns cool-weather lettuce varieties bitter and induces bolting, but there are several heat-tolerant varieties. The challenge to growing lettuce is maintaining a constant supply. This requires successive sowing. Lettuce is a light feeder, requires little direct light, and is fast growing. There are varieties for all tastes and climates. Lettuce can be nurtured indoors and grows well under glass in an insulated cold frame or in a plastic tunnel.

Basic Facts: Germination time: three to seven days. Soil temperature for germination: minimum: 35°F (2°C), optimum: 75°F (24°C), maximum: 85°F (29°C). Approximate seeds per gram: 700. Yield per 20-liter: one to two kilograms. Yield per ten-foot row: five to ten kilograms. Yield per 4 × 4-foot raised bed: five to ten kilograms. Life expectancy of stored seed: two years. Estimated time between sowing and first picking: 45–75 days. Effort to cultivate: easy, requires moderate temperatures.

Seed Saving: isolate seed crops 200 feet from other varieties. Harvest seed stocks when dry.

Climate: This annual needs medium to intense light. It starts to bolt when temperatures climb beyond 85°F (29°C) unless bolt-free varieties are grown.

Soil: Ideal soil for lettuce cultivation is a fertile, well-drained loam with a pH range of 5.8–6.8. Incorporate plenty of compost and well-rotted manure into the soil before planting.

Seed Sowing and Planting: Sow seed one-fourth-inch (1 cm) deep, two to four seeds per inch (3 cm). Sow two or three different types to mature at different rates to ensure a longer harvest.

Broadcast seed on soil surface, then gently cover seed with fine soil. Or, cover

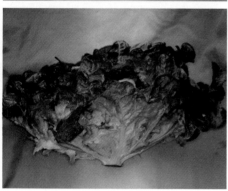

Indoor crops can also be grown in containers if the weather outdoors is too cold. Move plants outdoors under a cold frame or transplant into the garden. A cold frame will extend the lettuce season over a month both in spring and fall.

Transplant seedlings at the same depth as they were in their seedling containers. Planting too deeply may cause rot at the base of plants.

Grow about six to eight plants (Crisphead), 15–20 (leaf) plants per person.

Crop Care: Thin seedlings when they are two to four inches tall. Water small plants the day before thinning or transplanting. Water regularly to keep the shallow surface root system moist.

Fertilize with a soluble high-nitrogen mix every two to four weeks after seedlings are three to four inches tall or if the leaves begin to yellow.

If growing in a greenhouse, shade in hot weather with other taller plants, shade cloth, or lattice.

Harvesting: Harvest larger outer leaves of maturing loose-leaf and romaine varieties. Remove two to four outer leaves from each plant.

Harvest entire crisp head plants when head is well formed.

Harvest all plants that start to bolt. Symptoms of bolting include sudden growth from the center of the plant (heart) and bitterness.

Varieties: Lettuce is available in butterhead, loose-leaf, crisphead or iceberg, and romaine or cos varieties.

Give all lettuce varieties a level of 6000 mWm^2 during its entire life. If given a higher level of light, lettuce might bolt.

Eggplant (*Solanum melongena*) also known as Aubergine, is native to Asia and Africa. It needs daytime temperatures of 60–95°F (16–35°C) and minimum

seed with a quarter-inch (1 cm) layer of peat moss or sifted compost. Or, cover with a layer of newspaper, which will hold moisture until the seeds sprout in a few days. Remove the newspaper as soon as the first seeds germinate.

In hot weather, ensure germination by wrapping seed in a moist paper towel and storing in the refrigerator for about five days. The ideal temperature range for growth is 65–70°F (19–21°C) and can dip to 45°F (7°C) at night with no ill effects.

nighttime temperatures of 65°F (19°C) to yield fruit. If the temperature dips below this point, they will not grow or produce fruit. For early outdoor production in northern climates, grow seedlings indoors and transplant them into a cold frame or under plastic tunnels until the temperature has warmed.

The oblong (egg-shaped) purple fruit is most common, but varieties are available in green, yellow, white, and striped that can be oblong, round, or cylindrical in form.

Basic Facts: Germination time from four to ten days. Soil temperature for germination: minimum: 60°F (16°C), optimum: 85°F (29°C), maximum: 95°F (35°C). Approximate seeds per gram: 200. Yield per 20-liter container: 10–20 fruit. Yield per 4 × 4-foot bed: 40–80 fruit. Life expectancy of stored seed: five years.

Estimated time between sowing and first picking: 52–75 days.

Effort to cultivate: somewhat difficult. It must have warm weather and adequate water to bear fruit.

Seed Saving: self-pollinated. Harvest seed from fruit that has overripened and has a tough skin.

Climate: Annual in all climates when days and nights are above 60°F (16°C) for over 90 consecutive days. Must have daytime temperatures from 60–95°F (16–35°C), and nighttime temperatures must stay above 65°F (19°C) to set and grow fruit. Needs a lot of light.

Soil: Eggplants love rich soil with plenty of compost, manure, and a complete organic fertilizer. The pH should be in the 5.6–6.8 range.

Seed Sowing and Planting: Indoors, plant seeds one-half inch (1.5 cm) deep in small containers of fine potting soil.

Harden-off gradually, preferably under a cold frame. Transplant outdoors into a cold frame or under plastic tunnels.

The temperature must be at least 60°F (16°C) for germination and 65–90°F (19–32°C) for strong, rapid growth.

In pots or beds, space seedlings on 12–18-inch centers, or sow seed on 4-inch centers and thin to 12–18-inch centers.

Make another sowing if the first sowing does not germinate rapidly or is slowed by cold temperatures.

Grow about one to four plants per person.

Crop Care: Keep seedlings moist enough to avoid wilting. Be careful not to overwater. Roots love warm soil. Do not let plants wilt. Water stress causes deformed fruit and lower yield.

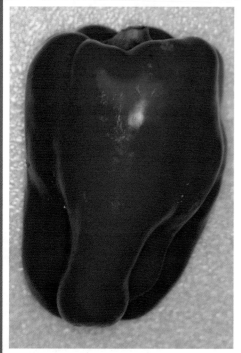

Apply a fertilizer tea as soon as flowers set and twice a month thereafter until the end of the growing season.

Harvesting: Harvest when the fruit has stopped expanding, while the skin is still glossy and thin. This is just before peak maturity when eggplants are succulent and the most flavorful.

Use pruners to cut each fruit from the plant as it matures. Keep fruit picked; letting fruit overdevelop will retard the ripening of other fruit.

If light diminishes and temperatures cool, fruit development virtually stops.

Varieties: Eggplant is available in standard purple as well as long green or white varieties.

The more light eggplants are given, the bigger they grow and the more fruit they produce. Give plants 9000 mWm² as soon as the first true leaves appear, and maintain the light level throughout their entire life.

Pepper (*Capsicum annuum*) is a Mediterranean native and a member of the Solanum family. Peppers require ample heat to grow and set fruit. Nighttime temperatures below 50°F (10°C) will stunt seedling peppers so badly that they may never recover. Grow indoors all year long or set outdoors into a cold frame that provides young plants cold protection in the spring and early summer. This added warmth allows peppers to develop and bear much earlier and heavier. Choose smaller sweet peppers for growing in cool, short-season climates. Just about any pepper will grow in warm indoor gardens and greenhouses, including heat-loving bell and all the hot varieties.

Basic Facts: Germination time: 8–25 days. Soil temperature for germination: minimum: 60°F (16°C), optimum: 85°F (29°C, maximum: 95°F (35°C). Approximate seeds per gram: 140. Yield per 20-liter container: 10–30 (large peppers), 40–60 (small peppers). Yield per 4 × 4-foot bed: 60–200 (large peppers), 180–400 (small peppers).

Life expectancy of stored seed: two years. Estimated time between sowing and first picking: 65–80 days. Effort to cultivate: fairly easy. They must have a temperature range from 50–90°F (10–32°C) for best production.

Seed Saving: Separate different varieties by at least 100 feet to prevent cross-pollination by insects. Seeds are scraped out of fruit and dried slowly.

Climate: Annual outdoors, but can be grown as a perennial indoors and where no freezing temperatures are experienced. Seedlings must have a minimum of 50°F (10°C) to grow. Mature peppers are more tolerant of cooler temperatures (below 50°F [10°C]). The variety 'Sweet Banana' is a standout, producing until first frost.

The ideal temperature range for growth is 70°F (21°C) at night and 80°F (27°C) during the day. Flowers will drop and fruit develops very slowly if temperatures deviate beyond this ideal range.

Day and night temperatures are the most important factors in growing peppers.

Soil: Peppers prefer warm, humus-rich, well-drained, fertile ground with a pH range of 6.0–6.8.

Seed Sowing and Planting: Sow seed indoors in flats or small containers. Sow seeds one-fourth inch (1 cm) deep, and keep evenly moist until they sprout. Seedlings must have full, bright HID light, and will grow spindly if starved of light. Raising seedlings indoors or purchasing them from a nursery will give your crop a big jump on the season in both warm and cool climates. Growing plants indoors will make year-round harvests possible.

Bell peppers grow best in a 60–80°F (16–27°C) temperature range.

Peppers respond well to transplanting and suffer little or no shock if handled gently, given plenty of water, and shaded for the first few days after transplanting. The soil temperature must be at least 60°F (16°C) to transplant seedlings without inhibiting growth.

Transplant seedlings into a cold frame outdoors if temperatures are below 50°F (10°C). If temperatures fall below 50°F (10°C), seedlings may be stunted for several months. Plant peppers so that they are shaded from the midday sun in climates with temperatures that regularly climb beyond 80°F (27°C). Give bright HID light. Many peppers produce poorly in hot weather.

Grow about two to four plants (bell) and/or two to ten plants (hot) per person.

Crop Care: Keep indoor soil warm and use a black plastic mulch to help raise soil temperature in cool weather and boost production.

Daily watering is necessary in dry and hot weather. Do not let soil dry out. Daily watering leaches nutrients from the soil, and additional fertilizer will be necessary.

Fertilize every two to four weeks. Peppers are heavy nitrogen, potassium, calcium, and magnesium feeders. Feeding is most important just before and during fruit set.

Give a super bloom mix that has less nitrogen to promote fruit development.

Harvesting: For highest production, pick the first few peppers that set when they are about half-size. This will cause more fruit to set. Use scissors or pruners to snip the ripe fruit from the stem.

Numerous bell and hot pepper varieties grow thicker, juicier walls and become sweeter as they ripen, changing color from green to yellow or red. If possible, leave fruit on the vine to turn color and grow sweeter. Leaving them on the vine stops new peppers from developing.

Near the end of the season, uproot the entire plant of hot, thin-walled varieties such as cayenne and red chili before rains or a sudden cold snap destroy ripening fruit. Hang the plants upside down so the fruit can dry slowly and keep for the winter.

Varieties: Peppers are available in sweet and hot varieties.

Tomato (*Lycopersicon lycopersicum*) is a must grow in all indoor gardens. A special satisfaction comes from picking that first vine-ripened fruit, slicing it open, and enjoying the zesty-sweet taste and refined fleshy texture. Homegrown tomatoes are allowed to ripen on the vine, developing sweet, rich pulp and a tender skin. Variety selection is very important to achieve the best flavor and to get a tomato to produce well in your climate. You can choose from numerous varieties such as yellow pear, bicolored, or Beefsteak types that are impossible to find in the grocery store. Pasta tomatoes are also becoming very popular in home gardens.

As a member of the Solanum family, this South American native needs warm weather to grow and produce fruit; tomato blossoms fall off below 50°F (10°C).

Basic Facts: Germination time: 6–14 days. Soil temperature for germination: minimum: 50°F (10°C), optimum: 85°F (29°C), maximum: 95°F (35°C). Approximate seeds per gram: 300. Yield per 20-liter container: five to ten kilograms. Yield per 4 × 4-foot bed: 15–30 kilograms; must be trellised. Life expectancy of stored seed: three to four years. Estimated time between sowing and first picking: 55–110 days. Effort to cultivate: easy; may require a trellis and some pruning.

Seed Saving: Let open-pollinated tomatoes self-pollinate. Pick fruit when fully ripe. Set fruit in a jar for three to five days to ferment; stir daily. Keep seeds that sink to the bottom of the jar. Let seeds dry on a paper towel.

Climate: Tomatoes require temperature range of 50–90°F (10–33°C) in order to set flowers and form fruit. Tomatoes stop flowering and fruiting outside this temperature range.

Tomatoes need all the HID light they can get. In short-season cold climates, grow in containers that can be moved indoors on cold nights.

Soil: Heavy feeders, tomatoes need deep, fertile soil. Plant in large (20-liter minimum) containers. Soil pH should be 6.0–6.8.

Seed Sowing and Planting: Seeds can be started indoors from six to eight weeks before setting the seedlings outdoors when nighttime temperatures warm to above 40°F (5°C). Sow seed in flats or small containers; keep warm and moist.

Do not transplant seedlings outdoors without protection early in the year if temperatures are apt to dip below 40°F (5°C). Protect tender outdoor seedlings with a plastic tunnel or greenhouse. Some gardeners use a white five-gallon plastic bucket with the bottom removed. The lid is secured on the bucket at night and removed in the morning.

Transplant seedlings several inches deeper than they were growing in their seedling container so new roots will sprout along the stem. Pinch off the cotyledons and one or two sets of true leaves before transplanting the seedlings deep in the hole.

Grow about two to three plants per person.

Crop Care: Water regularly, and do not let soil dry out. Tomatoes use much water, especially in hot weather and when developing fruit. If they suffer a drought followed by heavy watering, the fruit will split or resemble a boxing glove.

Fertilize every two to four weeks after plants are about two feet tall. Supplemental fertilizer should include a complete mix that includes calcium if dolomite was not added when planting. Be careful about adding too much nitrogen-rich fertilizer after flowers form. Nitrogen stimulates leafy growth at the expense of fruit production.

Trellis indeterminate tomatoes to encourage a high yield and to keep the fruit from touching the floor and rotting.

Most tomato baskets available at garden centers are perfect for determinate varieties.

Pruning indeterminate varieties to just one or two main shoots is a very productive cultivation technique used by many gardeners. This allows HID light to shine on fruit and speed ripening. Pruning also permits air to circulate through the bush, helping to prevent fungus and insect infestations.

Thin fruit if it sets too heavily on the vine. After you get an idea of how much the plant can produce, pick off the smaller or remove a few fruit from clusters if they are developing slowly.

Harvesting: Remove fruit from vines by hand. Simply snap the fruit from the vine, taking care to leave the vine intact.

Keep ripe fruit picked, daily if necessary, to encourage more fruit to ripen. The lowest clusters of tomatoes will ripen first.

Fruit ripens best in cool climates when exposed to HID light or sunlight. Sunlight exposure must be gradual to prevent fruit from suffering sunburn. Removing leaves that shade fruit will speed ripening when sunlight intensity diminishes at the end of the season outdoors.

Pinch out the growing tip from each branch about a month before the first expected freeze (about mid-September in warm climates) and remove small fruit that is not likely to ripen.

Once cold weather slows growth to a standstill, the ripening green tomatoes can be harvested. Pick all fruit before frost. If fruit is starting to turn red, set on a shelf

at room temperature to ripen. Do not set in a sunny windowsill, they will overheat.

Green tomatoes can still be harvested both early and late in the year. They can be wrapped in paper to speed ripening.

Varieties: A determinate tomato produces flower buds on the end of trusses and tends to bear heavily for about a month, and then stop. But some varieties, such as 'Oregon Spring', bear fruit over a long season, only slowing production when cold or hot weather sets in. The compact bushes that are common to determinate tomatoes grow well in tomato cages and are an excellent choice for low-maintenance gardens.

Indeterminate tomatoes yield flowers from lateral branches and main stems; the tips continue to vine upward. These types produce over a long season, requiring staking, training, and, in many cases, pruning for the best yields.

Tomato seed is available in cherry, early, mid-season, late, pasta, greenhouse, and novelty varieties.

Conversion Charts and Tables

Carbon Dioxide Facts and Figures
molecular weight = 44 grams/mole
sublimes (solid to gas) at 78.5°C at 1 atmosphere - air density = 1.2928 grams/liter (i.e., at equal temperatures and pressures carbon dioxide is heavier than air, and CO_2 will fall to the bottom of an air/ CO_2 mixture.

psi = 1 atmosphere

Physical properties of Propane:

specific gravity of gas (air = 1)	1.50
pounds per gallon of liquid @ 60°F (15°C)	4.23
gallons per pound of liquid @ 60°F (15°C)	0.236
Btu per cubic foot of gas @ 60°F (15°C)	2488
Btu per pound of gas	21548
Btu per gallon of gas @ 60°F	90502
cubic feet of gas per gallon of liquid	36.38
octane number	100+

Combustion Data:

cubic feet of air to burn 1 gallon of propane	873.6
cubic feet of CO_2 per gallon of propane burned	109.2
cubic feet of nitrogen per gallon of propane burned	688
pounds of CO_2 per gallon of propane burned	12.7
pounds of nitrogen per gallon of propane burned	51.2
pounds of water vapor per gallon of propane burned	6.8
1 pound of propane produces in kWh	6.3
Btu's per kW hour	3412

1 Therm	100,000 Btu	Specific gravity of liquid	0.509
1 cubic foot natural gas	1000 Btu	Vapor pressure (psig) 00F	23.5
1 pound steam	970 Btu	Vapor pressure (psig) 700 F	109
1 kilowatt	3413 Btu	Vapor pressure (psig) 1000 F	172

Calculations for Metric Users

1 cubic meter = 1 m × 1 m × 1 m = 1000 liters
fans are rated at liters per minute or liters per second

cubic feet = L × W × H
cubic meters = L × W × H

Buy a fan that will clear the indoor garden volume of air in one to five minutes. Run the fan for twice the time to theoretically clear the indoor garden of air.

Work out the amount of CO_2 gas to add:
For example, if you want 1500 ppm and ambient CO_2 is 350 ppm, you will need to add: 1500 ppm minus 350 ppm = 1150 ppm CO_2.

A poorly sealed indoor garden can have 20 percent leakage which should be added to the amount of CO_2 required.

For example, to get the desired 1500 ppm of CO_2 for an indoor garden with 21.6 cubic meters, add: 21.4 × 1150 = 24.61 liters × 1.2 = 29.53 liters.

This information tells you to set the flow meter to 6 liters per minute and run the gas for 5 minutes.

Leave the gas-enriched air for 20 minutes and exhaust the air from the garden room.

Metric Conversion Chart - Approximations

When You Know	Multiply by	To Find
Length		
millimeters	0.04	inches
centimeters	0.39	inches
meters	3.28	feet
kilometers	0.62	miles
inches	25.40	millimeters
inches	2.54	centimeters
feet	30.48	centimeters
yards	0.91	meters
miles	1.16	kilometers
Area		
sq. centimeters	0.16	square inches
square meters	1.20	square yards
square kilometers	0.39	square miles
hectares	2.47	acres
square inches	6.45	sq. centimeters
square feet	0.09	square meters
square yards	0.84	square meters
square miles	2.60	sq. kilometers
acres	0.40	hectares
Volume		
milliliters	0.20	teaspoons
milliliters	0.60	tablespoons
milliliters	0.03	fluid ounces
liters	4.23	cups
liters	2.12	pints
liters	1.06	quarts
liters	0.26	gallons
cubic meters	35.32	cubic feet
cubic meters	1.35	cubic yards
teaspoons	4.93	milliliters
tablespoons	14.78	milliliters
fluid ounces	29.57	milliliters
cups	0.24	liters
pints	0.47	liters
quarts	0.95	liters
gallons	3.790	liters

Mass and Weight
1 gram = 0.035 ounces
1 kilogram = 2.21 pounds
1 ounce = 28.35 grams
1 pound = 0.45 kilograms

Area
1 inch (in) = 25.4 millimeters (mm)
1 foot (12 in) = 0.3048 meters (m)
1 yard (3 ft) = 0.9144 meters
1 mile = 1.60937 kilometers
1 square inch = 645.16 square millimeters
1 square foot = 0.0929 square meters
1 square yard = 0.8361 square meters
1 square mile = 2.59 square kilometers

Liquid Measure Conversion
1 pint (UK) = 0.56826 liters
1 pint dry (USA) = 0.55059 liters
1 pint liquid (USA) = 0.47318 liters
1 gallon (UK) (8 pints) = 4.5459 liters
1 gallon dry (USA) = 4.4047 liters
1 gallon liquid (USA) = 3.7853 liters

1 ounce = 28.3495 grams
1 pound (16 ounces) = 0.453592 kilograms

1 gram = 15.4325 grains
1 kilogram = 2.2046223 pounds

1 millimeter = 0.03937014 inches (UK)
1 millimeter = 0.03937 inches (USA)
1 centimeter = 0.3937014 inches (UK)
1 centimeter = 0.3937 inches (USA)
1 meter = 3.280845 feet (UK)
1 meter = 3.280833 feet (USA)
1 kilometer = 0.6213722 miles
1 cm = 0.001 meter
mm = 0.0001 meter
nm = 0.000 000 001 meter

gm = grams
sq = squared
EC = electrical conductivity
ppm = parts per million
Celsius to Fahrenheit
Celsius temperature = (°F - 32) × 0.55
Fahrenheit temperature = (°C × 1.8) + 32

Light Conversion
1 foot-candle = 10.76 = lux
1 lux = 0.09293
lux = 1 lumen/square meters
lumens per square foot = lumens per meter squared

cfm (cubic feet per minute) = liters per hour
inches of rain = liters per meter squared
psi (pounds per square inch) = kg per square meter

1 liter = 1 kg (of pure water)
1 kilometer = 1000 meters
1 meter = 100 centimeters
1 meter = 1000 millimeters

Gardening Indoors

Glossary

absorb: to draw or take in: Rootlets absorb water and nutrients.

AC (alternating current): an electric current that reverses its direction at regularly occurring intervals: Homes have AC.

acid: a sour substance: An acid or sour soil has a low pH.

active: a hydroponic system that actively moves the nutrient solution

adobe: heavy clay soil that drains slowly: Adobe is not suitable for container gardening.

aeration: to supply soil and roots with air or oxygen

adventitious roots: roots that grow from unusual spots, as on the (stem) pericycle or endodermis of an older root. Auxin level may influence this type of root growth.

aeroponics: growing plants by misting roots suspended in air

aggregate: a substrate that is of nearly uniform size and used for the inert hydroponic medium

agronomically: having to do with the economics of agriculture

alkaline: refers to soil, or any substance, with a pH over 7

alkylation: a process in which an alkyl group is substituted or added to a compound

amendments: can be either organic or mineral based: Amendments change the texture of a growing medium.

ampere (amp): the unit used to measure the strength of an electric current: A 20-ampere circuit is overloaded when drawing more than 16 amps.

annual: a plant that normally completes its entire life cycle in one year or less

arc tube: container for luminous gases; houses the arc in an HID lamp

asexual propagation: reproducing using nonsexual means such as taking cuttings from a parent plant: will produce exact genetic replicas of the parent plant

auxin: classification of plant hormones: Auxins are responsible for foliage and root elongation.

bacteria: very small, one-celled plants that have no chlorophyll

ballast: stabilizing unit that regulates the flow of electricity and starts an HID lamp: A ballast consists of a transformer and a capacitor.

beneficial insect: a good insect that eats bad, plant-munching insects

biodegradable: to decompose through natural bacterial action. Substances made of organic matter can be broken down naturally.

biosynthesis: the production of a chemical compound by a plant

bleach: household laundry bleach is used in a mild water solution to sterilize indoor gardens and as soil fungicide

blood meal: high-nitrogen organic fertilizer made from dried blood: Dogs love blood meal!

bloom: to yield flowers

blossom booster: fertilizer high in phosphorus and potassium that increases flower yield and weight

bonsai: a very short or dwarfed plant

breaker box: electrical circuit box having on/off switches rather than fuses: The main breaker box is also called a "service panel."

breed: to sexually propagate plants under controlled circumstances

bud: a small, undeveloped stem or shoot

bud blight: a withering condition that attacks flower buds

buffer: a substance that reduces the shock and cushions against fluctuations: Many fertilizers contain buffer agents.

bulb: outer glass envelope or jacket that protects the arc tube of an HID lamp

callus: tissue made of undifferentiated cells produced by rooting hormones on plant cuttings

cambium: layer of cells which divides and differentiates into xylem and phloem and is responsible for growth

carbohydrate: neutral compound of carbon, hydrogen, and oxygen, mostly formed by green plants: Sugar, starch, and cellulose are carbohydrates.

carbon dioxide (CO_2): a colorless, odorless, tasteless gas in the air; necessary for plant life

caustic: a substance that destroys, kills, or eats away by chemical activity

cell: the base structural unit of plants: Cells contain a nucleus, membrane, and chloroplasts.

cellulose: a complex carbohydrate that stiffens a plant: Outdoor stems contain more stiff cellulose than plants grown indoors.

centigrade: a scale for measuring temperature where 100 degrees is the boiling point of water, and 0 degrees is the freezing point of water

cfm: cubic feet per minute; measures air velocity. Ventilation or extraction fans are measured in the cfm of air they can move.

Glossary

chelate: combining nutrients in an atomic ring that is easy for plant to absorb

chlorophyll: the green photosynthetic matter of plants: Chlorophyll is found in the chloroplasts of a cell and is necessary to photosynthesis.

chlorosis: the condition of a sick plant with yellowing leaves due to inadequate formation of chlorophyll: Chlorosis is caused by a nutrient deficiency, often iron or imbalanced pH.

chromosomes: microscopically small, dark staining bodies visible in the nucleus of a cell at the time of nuclear cell division; the number in any species is usually constant. Chromosomes contain the genetic material of a species.

circuit: a circular route travelled by electricity from a power source, through an outlet, and back to ground

clay: soil made of very fine organic and mineral particles: Clay drains slowly and is not suitable for container gardening.

climate: the average condition of the weather in an indoor garden or outdoors

cutting: 1. a rooted cutting of a plant 2. asexual propagation

CO$_2$ enrichment: used to augment indoor garden or greenhouse atmosphere to speed growth

cold: for warm-season annual flowers and vegetables, air temperatures below 50ºF (10ºC)

cold frame: an unheated outdoor structure usually clad in glass or clear plastic, used to protect and acclimatize seedlings and plants

color spectrum: the band of colors (measured in nm) emitted by a light source

color tracer: a coloring agent that is added to many commercial fertilizers so the horticulturist knows there is fertilizer in the solution: Peters has a blue color tracer.

compaction: soil condition that results from tightly packed soil which limits aeration and root penetration

companion planting: planting garlic, marigolds, etc., along with garden plants to discourage pests

compost: mixture of decayed organic matter, high in nutrients: Compost must be well-rotted before use. When too young, decomposition uses nitrogen; after sufficient decomposition, compost releases nitrogen.

core: the transformer in the ballast is often referred to as a core

cotyledon: seed leaves, first leaves that appear on a plant

critical daylength: maximum daylength which will bring about flowering in warm-season annuals

cross-pollination: fertilizing a plant with pollen from an unrelated individual of the same species

crystal: fertilizers often come in soluble crystals

cubic foot: volume measurement in feet: width × length × height = cubic feet

cultivar: a contraction of "cultivated variety," a variety of plant that has been intentionally created or selected; not naturally occurring

cure: 1. slow plant-drying process 2. to make a sick plant healthy

cuticle: thin layer of plant wax (cutin) on the surface of the aboveground parts of plants

cutting: 1. growing-tip cut from a parent plant for asexual propagation 2. clone 3. slip

cytokinins: plant hormones that promote cell division and growth and delay the aging of leaves

damping-off: fungus disease that attacks young seedlings and cuttings causing stem to rot at base: Overwatering is the main cause of damping-off.

DC (direct current): a continuous electric current that only flows in one direction

decompose: to rot or decay, etc., through organic chemical change

dehumidify: to remove moisture from air

dehydrate: to remove water from foliage

deplete: to exhaust soil of nutrients, making it infertile: Once a soil is used to grow a container crop, it is depleted.

desiccate: to cause to dry up: Insecticidal soap desiccates its victims.

detergent: liquid soap concentrate used: 1. as a wetting agent for sprays and water 2. pesticide, Note: detergent must be totally organic to be safe for plants.

diapause: a period of plant dormancy during which growth or development is suspended or diminished

disease: plant sickness of any kind

dose: amount of fertilizer, insecticide, etc., given to a plant, usually in a water solution

double potting: a two-pot transplanting technique that minimizes root disturbance

drainage: to empty soil of excess water. Good drainage: water passes through soil, evenly promoting plant growth. Bad drainage: drainage water stands in soil, actually drowning roots.

Gardening Indoors

drip (irrigation) system: efficient watering system that employs a main hose with small water emitters (tiny holes) which meter out water one drop at a time at regular, frequent intervals

drip line: a line around a plant directly under its outermost branch tips: Roots seldom grow beyond the drip line.

dry ice: cold, white, solid substance formed when CO_2 is compressed and cooled: Dry ice changes into CO_2 gas at room temperatures.

dry soil pocket: small portion of soil that remains dry after watering: Dry soil pockets may be remedied by adding a wetting agent (soap) to water and/or waiting 15 minutes between waterings.

dry well: drain hole filled with rocks, to receive drainage water

electrode: a solid electric conductor used to establish electrical arc between contacts at either end of an HID lamp

elongate: to grow in length

embolism: bubble of air in the transpiration stream of a cutting; blocks uptake of water and nutrients

emit: to give off , send out (i.e., light or sound)

embryo: a young plant, developing within the seed

Encarsia formosa: a parasitic wasp that preys on whiteflies

envelope: outer protective bulb or jacket of a lamp

Epsom salts: hydrated magnesium sulfate in the form of white crystalline salt: Epsom salts add magnesium to soil.

equinox: when sun crosses the equator and day and night are each 12 hours long: The equinox happens twice a year.

essential oils: volatile oils that give plants their characteristic odor or flavor; contained in the secreted resins of plants

ethane methyl sulfonate: a mutagenic chemical that causes changes at the DNA level; induces genetic mutations

etiolation: growth of a plant in total darkness to increase the chances of root initiation

F1 hybrid: first filial generation, the offspring of two P1 (parent) plants

F2 hybrid: second filial generation, resulting from a cross between two F1 plants

fan leaves: large, fanlike leaves

female: pistillate, ovule, seed producing

fertilize: 1. to apply fertilizer (nutrients) to roots and foliage 2. to impregnate (unite) male pollen with female plant ovary

fertilizer burn: overfertilization; first, leaf tips burn (turn brown), then leaves curl

flat: a shallow container used to start seedlings or cuttings

flower: blossom, a mass of calyxes on a stem, top, or bud

foliage: the leaves, or more generally, the green part of a plant

foliar feed: misting fertilizer solution, which is absorbed by the foliage

foot-candle (fc): one fc is equal to the amount of light that falls on one square foot of surface located one foot away from one candle

fritted: to fuse or embed nutrients with a glass compound: Fritted Trace Elements (FTE) are long lasting and do not easily leach out of substrate.

fungicide: product that destroys or inhibits fungus

fungistat: product that inhibits fungus

fungus: a lower plant (lacking chlorophyll) that may attack green plants: Mold, rust, mildew, mushrooms, and bacteria are fungi.

fuse: an electrical safety device made of a metal that melts and interrupts the circuit when overloaded

fuse box: electrical circuit box containing circuits controlled by fuses

gene: part of a chromosome that influences the development of a plant: Genes are inherited through sexual propagation

gene pool: collection of possible gene combinations in an available population

genetic makeup: the genes inherited from parent plants: Genetic makeup is the most important factor dictating vigor.

gibberellin: a class of plant growth hormone used to promote stem elongation: Gibberellic acid is a form of gibberellin.

gpm: gallons per minute

green lacewing: insect that preys on aphids, thrips, whiteflies, etc., and their larva and offspring

greenhouse: a heated structure with transparent/translucent walls and ceiling which offer some environmental control to promote plant growth

guano: dung from birds, high in organic nutrients: Seabird guano is noted for being high in nitrogen, and bat guano is high in phosphorus.

halide: binary chemical compound of a halogen(s) with an electropositive element(s)

halogen: any of the non-metallic elements fluorine, chlorine, bromine, iodine, and astatine existing in a free state: Halogens are enclosed within the arc tube of a metal halide lamp.

hardening-off: gradual adaptation of indoor or greenhouse plants to an outside environment

hermaphrodite: an individual having flowers of both sexes on the same plant, more correctly referred to as "intersex"

Hertz (Hz): a unit of a frequency that cycles one time each second: A home with a 60 hertz AC current cycles 60 times per second.

HID: High Intensity Discharge lamp: This is the type of lamp used in many indoor gardens.

honeydew: a sticky honey-like substance secreted onto foliage by aphids, scale, and mealy bugs

hood: the reflective cover of a lamp

HOR: the abbreviation stamped on some HID bulbs meaning they may be burned in a horizontal position

hormone: chemical substance that controls the growth and development of a plant: Root inducing hormones help cuttings root.

horticulture: the science and art of cultivating plants

hose bib: water outlet usually found outdoors that contains an on/off valve

hostile environment: environment that is unfriendly and inhospitable to pests and diseases

humidity, relative: ratio between the amount of moisture in the air and the greatest amount of moisture the air could hold at the same temperature

humus: dark, fertile, partially decomposed plant or animal matter: Humus forms the organic portion of the soil.

hybrid: an offspring from two plants of different breeds, variety, or genetic make-up

hybrid vigor: greater strength and health or faster rate of growth in the offspring resulting from the cross-breeding of two gene pools

hybridizing: *see* cross-pollination

hydrogen: light, colorless, odorless, highly flammable gas: Hydrogen combines with oxygen to form water.

hydroponics: growing plants in nutrient solutions without soil, usually in an inert soilless mix

hygrometer: instrument for measuring relative humidity in the atmosphere: A hygrometer will save time, frustration, and money.

IAA: Indoleacetic acid, a plant hormone that stimulates growth

induce: to effect, cause, or influence via stimulation: A 12-hour photoperiod stimulates flowering.

inductive photoperiod: daylength required to stimulate flowering

inert: a substance that will not chemically react. Inert growing mediums make it easy to control the chemistry of the nutrient solution.

insecticide: a product that kills or inhibits insects

intensity: the amount or strength of light energy per unit or area: Intensity decreases the further away from the source.

jacket: protective outer bulb or envelope of lamp

Kilowatt hour (kWh): measure of electricity used per hour: A 1000-watt HID uses one kilowatt per hour.

landrace: a (wild) plant variety that is not improved by humans

leach: to dissolve or wash out soluble components of soil by heavy watering

leader: *see* meristem

leggy: plant that is abnormally tall, with few leaves: usually caused by lack of light

life cycle: a series of growth stages through which plants must pass in their natural lifetime: The stages are seed, seedling, vegetative, and floral.

light mover: a device that moves a lamp back and forth or in a circular path across the ceiling of an indoor garden to provide more balanced light

limbing: cutting off lower, secondary plant branches to encourage primary growth

lime: calcium compounds such as dolomite or hydrated lime that determine or alter soil pH level

litmus paper: chemically sensitive paper used to indicate pH levels in colorless liquids

loam: organic soil mixture of crumbly clay, silt, and sand

lumen: measurement of light output: One lumen is equal to the amount of light emitted by one candle that falls on one square foot of surface located one foot from one candle.

macronutrient: one or all of the primary nutrients N-P-K (nitrogen, phosphorus, or potassium) or the secondary nutrients Mg (magnesium) and Ca (calcium)

meristem: leader: plant tissue from which new cells are formed; the active growing tip of a root or stem

Gardening Indoors

meristem pruning: cutting away the growth tip to encourage branching and limit height

micron: one-millionth of a meter. The symbol "µ" is used to denote micron.

micronutrients: trace elements necessary for plant health, including S, Fe, Mn, B, Mb, Zn, and Cu

millimeter: 0.04 inch

mist: to manufacture rain with the help of a spray bottle

moisture meter: electronic device that measures the moisture content of a substrate at any given point

monochromatic: producing only one color: LP sodium lamps are monochromatic.

Mother Nature: the vast outdoors and all she holds: The indoor horticulturist assumes the role of Mother Nature.

mother plant: plant held in vegetative state and used for cutting (cloning) stock: A mother may be grown from seed or be a cutting.

mulch: a protective covering for the soil of compost, old leaves, paper, rocks, etc.: Indoors, mulch keeps soil too moist and possible fungus could result. Outdoors, mulch helps soil retain and attract moisture.

mutation: an inheritable change in genetic material

mycelium: the mass of strands that form the root-like part of fungi, often submerged in soil or a host body

nanometer (nm): 0.000000001 meter, one billionth of a meter, nm is used as a scale to measure electromagnetic wavelengths of light: Color and light spectrums are expressed in nanometers.

necrosis/necrotic: localized death of a plant part due to injury or disease

nitrogen (N): essential element to plant growth; one of the three major nutrients N-P-K.

node: a joint: the position on a stem from which leaves, shoots, or flowers grow

N-P-K: nitrogen, phosphorus, and potassium: the three major plant nutrients

nursery: gardening business that grows plants for sale or experimentation: A nursery is a great place to gather information.

nutrient: plant food, essential elements N-P-K as well as secondary and trace elements fundamental to sustaining plant life

Ohms Power Law: a law that expresses the strength of an electric current: Volts × Amperes = Watts.

optimum: 1. the most favorable condition for growth and reproduction 2. peak production.

organic: 1. made of, derived from, or related to living organisms: Organic gardeners use fertilizers and insect control methods of animal or vegetable origin. Unaltered rock powders are also considered organic.

osmosis: the equalizing movement of fluids through a semipermeable membrane, such as in a living cell

overload: load to excess: An electrical circuit that uses more than 80 percent of its potential is overloaded. A 20-amp circuit drawing 17 amps is overloaded.

ovule: egg which contains the female genes and is found within the plant ovary: When fertilized, an ovule will grow into a seed.

oxygen: tasteless, colorless, odorless element: Plants need oxygen in the soil in order to grow.

parasite: organism that lives on or in another host organism without benefiting the host: Fungus is a parasite.

passive: hydroponic system that moves the nutrient solution through absorption or capillary action

pathogen: a disease-causing microorganism, especially bacteria, fungi, and viruses

peat: partially decomposed vegetation (usually moss) with slow decay due to extreme moisture, cold, and acidic conditions

perennial: a plant, such as a tree or shrub, that completes its life cycle over several years

perlite: amendment of sand or volcanic glass expanded by heat, which aerates the soil or growth medium

pH: a scale from 0–14 that measures a growing medium's (or anything's) acid to alkaline balance: a pH of 7 is neutral, lower numbers indicate increasing acidity, and higher numbers increasing alkalinity: Warm-season annuals grow best in a 6.5 to 8 pH range.

pH tester: electronic instrument or chemical used to measure the acid or alkaline balance in soil or water

phloem: the food- and water-conducting tissue of vascular plants

phosphor coating: internal fluorescent bulb coating that diffuses light and affects various color outputs

phosphorus (P): one of the macronutrients that promote root and flower growth

photoperiod: the relationship between the length of light and dark in a 24-hour period; affects the growth and maturity of plants

photosynthesis: the building of chemical compounds (carbohydrates that plants need for growth) from light energy, water, and CO_2

phototropism: the environmental response movement of a plant part toward or away from a light source

phytotron: a completely enclosed indoor area with extensive environmental controls for the experimental growth (and study) of plants

pigment: the substance in paint or anything that absorbs light, producing (reflecting) the same color as the pigment

pod, seed: a dry calyx containing a mature or maturing seed

pollen: fine, yellow, dust-like microspores containing male genes

potbound: root system that is bound, stifled, or inhibited from normal growth by a too small container

potassium (K): one of the macronutrients necessary for plant life

power surge: interruption or change in flow of electricity

predatory insect: beneficial insect or parasite that hunts down and devours harmful insects

propagate: 1. sexual propagation: to produce a seed by breeding male and female plant parts 2. asexual propagation: to produce a plant by taking cuttings.

pruning: trimming branches or parts of plants to strengthen those that remain, or bring shape to the plant

PVC (polyvinyl chloride) pipe: plastic pipe that is easy to work with, readily available, and used to transport liquid and air

pyrethrum: natural insecticide made from the blossoms of various chrysanthemums

RH: relative humidity: *see* humidity, relative

radicle: the part of a plant seedling that develops into a root, the root tip

recovery: hydroponic system that reclaims the nutrient solution and recycles it

root: 1. the underground part of a plant: Roots function to absorb water and nutrients as well as anchor a plant in the ground. 2. to root (start) a cutting or clone

root hormone: root-inducing substance

rootbound: *see* potbound

roguing: to weed out inferior, diseased, or undesirable plants from a crop, field, or population area

salt: crystalline compound that results from improper pH or toxic build-up of fertilizer: Salt will burn plants, preventing them from absorbing nutrients

scion: the shoot (containing buds) that is used for grafting

scuff: to scrape and roughen the surface: Seeds with a hard outer shell germinate faster when scuffed.

secondary nutrients: calcium (Ca) and magnesium (Mg). Ca and Mg are considered to be primary nutrients by some sources.

seed: the mature, fertilized ovule of a pistillate plant, containing a protective shell, embryo, and supply of food: A seed will germinate and grow, given heat and moisture.

senescence: the (declining) growth stage in a plant or plant part from its prime to death

sexual propagation: in plants, the reproduction by means of seed following fertilization

short circuit: condition that results when wires cross and form a circuit. A short circuit will trip breaker switches and blow fuses.

soap: 1. cleaning agent 2. wetting agent 3. insecticide: All soap used in horticulture should be biodegradable.

socket: threaded, wired holder for a lightbulb

soilless mix: a growing medium made up of mineral particles such as vermiculite, perlite, sand, pumice, etc.: Organic moss is often a component of soilless mix.

soluble: dissolvable in liquid, especially water

solution: 1. a mixture of two or more solids, liquids, or gases, often with water 2. answer to a problem

sponge rock: large pieces of perlite, a light, mineral soil amendment

spore: seed-like offspring of certain bacteria, fungi, algae, and some nonflowering plants

sprout: 1. a shoot of a plant, as from a recently germinated seed 2. small, new growth of leaf or stem

square feet (sq. ft.): length × width; a measurement of area

stagnant: motionless air or water: for healthy plant growth, water must drain and not become stagnant

sterilize: to make super clean by removing dirt, germs, and bacteria. Disinfect pruning tools to avoid spreading disease.

Gardening Indoors

stigma: the tip of the flower's pistil, which receives the pollen

stipule: one of a pair of small, leaf-like appendages found at the base of the leafstalk of many plants

stomata: small mouthlike or nose-like openings on leaf underside, responsible for transpiration and many other life functions: The millions of stomata must be kept very clean to function properly.

stress: a physical or chemical factor that causes extra exertion by plants, usually by restricting fluid flow to foliage: A stressed plant will grow poorly.

substrate: the medium on which an organism lives, as soil, soilless mix, rock, etc.

sugar: food product of a plant

sump: a reservoir that receives drainage; a drain or receptacle for hydroponic nutrient solutions used for growing plants

super bloom: a common name for fertilizer high in phosphorus and potassium that promotes flower formation and growth

synthesis: the production of a substance, such as chlorophyll, by uniting light energy, elements, or chemical compounds.

taproot: the main or primary root that grows from the seed: Lateral roots will branch off the taproot.

taxonomy: classification of plants and animals according to their family relationships

Teflon tape: tape that is extremely useful to help seal all kinds of threaded pipe joints. I like Teflon tape better than putty.

tepid water: lukewarm 70–80°F (21–27°C) water: Always use tepid water around plants to facilitate chemical processes and ease shock.

terminal bud: the growth tip of main stem or branch

testa: the hard outer covering of a seed

thermostat: a device for regulating temperature: A thermostat may control a heater, furnace, or vent fan.

timer: an electrical device for regulating photoperiod, fan, etc.: A timer is a must in all indoor gardens.

toxic life: the amount of time a pesticide or fungicide remains active or live

transformer: a device in the ballast that transforms electric current from one voltage to another

transpire: to give off water vapor and by-products via the stomata on leaves

transplant: to uproot a plant and root ball and replant it in new soil

trellis: a frame of small boards (lattice) that trains or supports plants

trellising: method of restricting plant growth or altering its shape and size by tying plant to lattice work or wire screen

tungsten: a heavy, hard metal with a high melting point that conducts electricity well: Tungsten is used for a filament in tungsten halogen lamps.

ultraviolet: light with very short wavelengths, out of the far blue visible spectrum

variety: distinct subspecies, phenotype

vascular: referring to a plant's circulatory system which carries sap throughout the body of the plant

vector: 1. an organism (as an insect) that transmits disease, a pathogen 2. an organism that transmits genes, a pollinator

vegetative: growth stage in which plants rapidly produce new leafy growth and green chlorophyll

vent: an opening such as a window or door that allows the circulation of fresh air

ventilation: circulation of fresh air, fundamental to a healthy indoor garden: An exhaust fan creates ventilation.

vermiculite: mica processed and expanded by heat: Vermiculite is a soil amendment and medium for rooting cuttings.

vitamin B$_1$: vitamin that is absorbed by tender root hairs, easing transplant wilt and shock

wetting agent: a compound that reduces the droplet size and lowers the surface tension of the water, making it wetter: Liquid concentrate dish soap is a good wetting agent if it is biodegradable.

whorl: where three or more leaves or petals arise from the same point and form a circle around it

wick: the part of a passive watering system the nutrient passes up to be absorbed by the medium and roots: A passive hydroponic system uses a wick suspended in the nutrient solution.

wilt: 1. to become limp from lack of water 2. plant disease/disorder.

wire ties: paper-coated wire ties are excellent for tying down or training plants

xylem: vascular tissue that transports water and minerals from the roots throughout the stems and leaves

This greenhouse in the Netherlands is computer-controlled, managing the hydroponic system, atmosphere, and nutrients for the plants. During the day as the light changes inside the greenhouse, the computer moves the giant trays around to get even lighting for all plants.

Another Dutch greenhouse has masses of gorgeous tomatoes growing hydroponically as tall as twenty feet in the air. Harvesting is easy, and there are virtually no pests in this controlled environment.

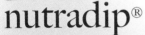

GENERAL HYDROPONICS®

Providing growers world wide with quality products for over 30 years

eurohydro.com

genhydro.com

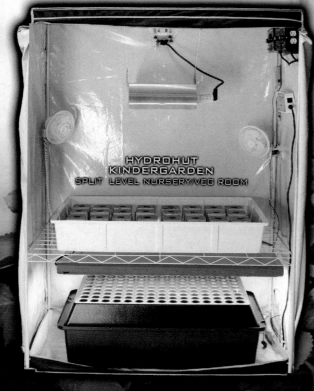

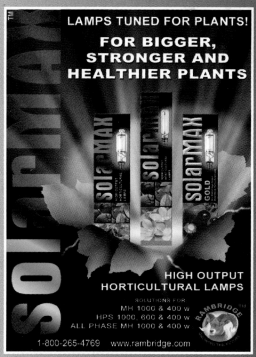

Gardening Indoors with Soil & Hydroponics
by George F. Van Patten

ISBN-13: 978-1-878823-32-8

6 x 8.25-inches (21 x 15 cm), 384 pages, 670 color images, glossary, appendix, index, $24.95

This Fifth Edition of Gardening Indoors with Soil & HYDROPONICS, a Best Seller since 1986, is expanded and completely rewritten with all new information. More than 670 full color photos, drawings, charts and graphs illustrate every detail of this authoritative easy-to-understand book. Numerous simple cultivation solutions make it appealing to novice gardeners. Seasoned gardeners are also able to find answers to all their questions. Discover how to achieve the biggest best yields even with limited space and a small budget. Learn how to grow while taking an exclusive photo tour of some of the most interesting indoor and outdoor gardens and greenhouses in the world.

Hydroponic Basics
by George F. Van Patten

ISBN-13: 978-1-878823-25-0

4 x 5.5 inches (10 x 14 cm), 80 full color pages, 225 full color drawings and photographs, index, appendix, $4.95

This simple little book is packed with information on hydroponic gardening. The graphic color layout and design guide a hydroponic gardener through basic plant science and environment to purchasing a garden and appropriate supplies. Plans for making your own hydroponic garden, nutrient deficiencies, plant problems and growing a garden beginning to end are all included in this invaluable guide.

Gardening Indoors with CO$_2$
George F. Van Patten
and Alyssa F. Bust

ISBN-13: 978-1-878823-19-9

5.5 x 8.5 inches (14 x 21.5 cm), 96 pages, illustrated, index, $12.95

This book is packed with the latest information about CO$_2$ enrichment. Double plant yields with Carbon Dioxide. Learn to get the most out of CO$_2$ generators and emitters. Follow easy-step-by-step instructions on setting up a CO$_2$ system in your garden room and harvest bumper crops!

Gardening Indoors with Cuttings
by George F. Van Patten
and Alyssa F. Bust

ISBN-13: 978-1-878823-20-5

5.5x 8.5 inches (14 x 21.5 cm), 96 pages, illustrated, index, $12.95

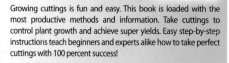

Growing cuttings is fun and easy. This book is loaded with the most productive methods and information. Take cuttings to control plant growth and achieve super yields. Easy step-by-step instructions teach beginners and experts alike how to take perfect cuttings with 100 percent success!

Gardening Indoors with Rockwool
by George F. Van Patten
and Alyssa F. Bust

ISBN-13: 978-1-878823-22-9

5.5 x 8.5 inches (14 x 21.5 cm), 128 pages, illustrated, index, $14.95

This new and updated book was previously called Gardening: The Rockwool Book. It is reformatted and packed with the latest information on growing with rockwool. Increase yields by 20-50 percent by using rockwool. Follow step by step instructions in this book to harvest the best garden possible.

Gardening Indoors with H.I.D Lights
by George F. Van Patten
and Alyssa F. Bust

ISBN-13: 978-1-878823-21-2

5.5 x 8.5 inches (14 x 21.5 cm), 128 pages, illustrated, index, $14.95

This is the definitive book on high intensity discharge (HID) lighting and plant growth. It is loaded with the latest information on high-tech lights. If you grow with HIDs, this easy to read book will help you double the efficiency of your lamps and save you money. Max out your HID lights to get the absolute most light per watt of electricity!

Retail Orders:	Wholesale orders:
Canada	Green Air Products (GAP):
www.amazon.ca	1-800-669-2113
France	Bloomington Wholesale
www.amazon.fr	Garden Supply
Germany	(BWGS)
www.amazon.de	1-800-316-1306
Japan	
www.amazon.jp	Hydrofarm:
United Kingdom	1-800-634-9990
www.amazon.co.uk	National Garden Wholesale
USA	(NGW):
www.amazon.com	1-888-478-6544